PÉTAIN:
HERO OR TRAITOR

PÉTAIN:
HERO OR TRAITOR
THE UNTOLD STORY

HERBERT R. LOTTMAN

William Morrow and Company, Inc.
New York

Copyright © 1985 by Herbert R. Lottman

Library of Congress Catalog Card Number: 84-61255

ISBN: 0-688-03756-9

Printed in the United States of America

First Edition

1 2 3 4 5 6 7 8 9 10

BOOK DESIGN BY JAMES UDELL

FOREWORD

It was somewhat awesome to discover that I would be the first person not a magistrate to examine the totality of the archives of the Vichy government, as well as the personal papers of Pétain himself, for the preparation of a biography. The availability of these heretofore inaccessible materials made it at least conceivable to attempt a total account of his life. For it had been possible in the past to write about Pétain entirely from legend, moving blithely from one popular myth to the next; and these myths dealt with every notable episode of his life. Contradictory sets of legend have made of the Victor of Verdun a saint and a devil, and with rare exceptions efforts to describe his career had begun with one of these sets.

For there have been few neutral witnesses to the significant events of Pétain's career; few private collections of materials were compiled without the intention of proving something. Of course, Philippe Pétain became the subject of memoirs and historical study only after he was acclaimed a hero, which accounts for the epic tone of much of this material. Indeed, in the two decades during which most histories of World War I were published, Pétain was an influential contemporary of those who wrote the books, and often he was able to review the memoirs of fellow officers before they were authorized for publication. As a consequence, many who approached Pétain with the desire to be objective lacked the evidence that would have allowed them to pursue this intention. While the First World War was in progress, military authorities began producing hagiographies which Pétain often accepted even if he had not inspired them, and material from these publications was later incorporated into authorized and unauthorized books about him, particularly during the Vichy era, when, of course, hagiography prevailed.

A room could be filled with the books that have been written about the Vichy regime; this is not another one. In this examination of the ninety-five-year life span of Philippe Pétain, the Vichy era is a vital segment, but not necessarily a culmination. For my subject is Pétain himself; in the Vichy years, and prior to that period, Pétain will answer only for the acts of Pétain.

To keep footnotes within reasonable dimensions, only works containing firsthand reports of Pétain's acts or statements are cited, although, of course, the author has consulted the standard accounts of the two world wars, on the German occupation and on Vichy. When available, the author has utilized original documents and correspondence, although if published versions of the same material are available they are sometimes cited to facilitate verification or further study. When several versions of an event are known, the present work stresses the earliest one, if possible an account contemporary with the event described, for the later versions are more likely to have been colored, intentionally or not, by subsequent developments, or to protect the subject or the writer. In truth, working on this biography has led its author to question the value of oral as well as written memoirs when the subject remains controversial and the source played a role. Such witnesses, even when of good faith, cannot recall the events without also seeking to replay them, nor can they easily avoid confusing their own and their peers' previously published accounts of the same events. It should be remembered that the chief actors in the drama that was Vichy were subject to treason trials. Vichy survivors who wrote memoirs in prison, while awaiting trial

FOREWORD

or after sentencing, often considered it necessary to stress Pétain's involvement in events that led to their own prosecution. Their testimony has been utilized in full knowledge of the perils, and only to give dimension to events that can be confirmed by tamper-proof evidence.

When the author embarked on this adventure he did not know that he would have as much to discover as his readers. What had at first seemed a linear story, the gradual transformation of a hero into a traitor, turned out to be far more complex. One began to see the possibility that the same person might be a resistance fighter with respect to the Axis powers *and* the founder of a dictatorship that borrowed much of its techniques and philosophy from the very Nazi and Fascist regimes he wished to resist.

ACKNOWLEDGMENTS

At the Archives Nationales in Paris, where a considerable quantity of firsthand material on Pétain was found, the author had the privilege of the availability of the director of the Section Contemporaine, Pierre Cézard, during his final years before retirement. At the archives and library of the Service Historique de l'Armée de Terre, at Vincennes, General Jean Delmas and the patient staffs of the military archives and library lightened the author's task. In the Institut d'Histoire du Temps Présent, a newly created research institution when this writer embarked on his study, he found a treasure chest of materials and the friendly suggestions of Claude Lévy, Françoise Mercier, and Lucienne Nouveau. His life was made simpler by access to the library of the Fondation Nationale des Sciences Politiques, to its Documentation Center and archives.

Gratitude is also expressed to the Assemblée Nationale, the Institut de France, and the École Supérieure de Guerre for access to their archives and libraries, to the Collège Saint-Bertin at Saint-Omer, to that city's municipal library for its archives. And to the

ACKNOWLEDGMENTS

Bibliothèque Historique de la Ville de Paris, the Bibliothèque Nationale, the Centre de Documentation Juive Contemporaine, the École de Sorèze, the 33e Division Militaire in Nantes (for access to the Fort de la Pierre Levée on Ile d'Yeu). Outside of France, help was received from the Archivio Storico of the Ministero degli Affari Esteri in Rome, and from the Historical Division of the Department of External Affairs of Canada.

A number of individuals were generous with their time and their personal archives: Henri Amouroux, Odette de Hérain, Jacques Isorni, Gilles de La Rocque, Mme. Bernard Ménétrel. At one time or other I also had the help of Roger Bismut, Pierre Bourget, Elisabeth Bourgois, Pierre Bourgois, Louis-Dominique Girard, Charles Goudard, Colonel Roger Gasser, General René Laure, André Lavagne, Roger Musset, Guy Pedroncini, Jean Pouget, Paul Racine, Marcel Rieunier (for the visit to the Pétain apartment at the Hôtel du Parc in Vichy), Mme. Jacques Rueff, Carin Rueff, Mme. Jean de Séguin, Pierre Véron, Woodruff Wallner.

CONTENTS

CONTENTS

PÉTAIN:
HERO OR TRAITOR

I
YOUNG PHILIPPE

The Pétain legend was forged in the First World War. It was a product of a punishing epoch and its desperate need for heroes, and of the evidence that in Philippe Pétain a hero had been found, with the hero's essential attributes: good looks and bearing, coolness in the face of adversity, understatement and occasional silence. Such taciturn demigods often come of peasant stock, and much was made of this hero's birth on a farm. During the Great War and the years separating it from the fall of France in 1940 this secret man seldom offered his biographers much else to write about, and so the farm boy legend endured. In the Vichy years his impenetrable manner in the presence of allies or enemies reminded onlookers of the peasant's silent watch.

It hardly seemed to matter to the makers of legend that young Philippe, as he grew up, moved quickly from village to city, that his universe was that of the garrison towns before August 1914, and after that of sophisticated Paris, or that he almost never returned to his birthplace. The birthplace stuck. Even today the village of Cauchy-à-la-Tour in the Artois region of northern

France seems a world away; the visitor has little difficulty imagining how it was then. There is the massive facade in soft limestone, windowless, drum-tight as a fortress, the arched gateway into the courtyard—the family dwelling on one side, stables and chicken coop closing the quadrangle. The Pétains were among the oldest families in the area, traceable back to the beginning of the eighteenth century.

This Artois region came to France from Flanders. It was an independent county under Robert I, called the Brave, brother of the King Louis who became a saint. Today's visitor must imagine these unspectacular hills and dull plains as they would have appeared before the advent of the coal mines which transformed the region in the second half of the nineteenth century. And even before the wars of our century trampled this land it was a battlefield, notably during the Hundred Years War, and in the early eighteenth century when the Duke of Marlborough laid siege to northern France.

Local historians quite naturally spread their nets wide for traces of the Pétains. The family name, believed to derive from the Flemish Pithem or Pethem, signifying "house of Piet," was common enough in the borderlands between the Artois and Picardy to the south. It is possible that Etienne-François Pétain came from that region to settle in Floringhem, near Cauchy, some time after 1690.[1] We are told that Jean-Baptiste Pétain, born in 1677, settled in Cauchy in 1705, leaving at his death over forty acres of land scattered through neighboring villages. A grandson of Jean-Baptiste was the grandfather of Omer-Venant Pétain, born in 1816 in Cauchy and a farmer there until his death. And Omer-Venant was the father of Philippe Pétain.[2]

Something else must be said about Philippe's father. He almost didn't stay on the farm. Omer-Venant (both of his names were of local saints), the eldest of three children, went down to Paris to take a job with Louis Jacques Daguerre, then perfecting his prototype of the photograph; Omer-Venant hoped to stay there to open a business of his own in daguerreotype landscapes and portraits, but in the political agitation of 1848 he seems to have abandoned city ambitions to return to the family farm, which then covered twenty-seven acres and employed two horses. He married twenty-seven-year-old Clotilde Legrand, daughter of another Cauchy farmer, Jean-Baptiste Legrand, and of Anne-Constantine, born Lefebvre. This marriage took place in 1851; in rapid succession Clotilde gave birth to Marie-Françoise-Clotilde (1852), Adélaïde (1853), Sara (1854), Philippe (1856), and Josephine (1857)—and then she died, less than a month after this last birth. We know little about Clotilde; no one has yet discovered a portrait of her, although tradition sees her as dark-haired and tall. She had inherited some land and was a farmer in her own right.[3] But what happened after her death concerns us mightily. Omer-Venant remarried on April 7, 1859, just before Philippe's third birthday. His new wife Marie-Reine (born Vincent) gave three children to Philippe's father: Elisabeth (1860), Antoine (1861), Laure (1862). A story told of him—it was sufficiently credible to have been recorded by a local historian—is that after the birth of each child Philippe's father would say at the baptismal fount: "Until next year, Father!"[4]

On his birth certificate Philippe is Henri Philippe Benoni Omer Pétain. Later in his life documents occasionally referred to him as Henri or Henri Philippe, and he took pains to correct them to the preferred form of his name. (He couldn't do anything about the punctilious American press which stubbornly called him Henri Pétain.) Was the Henri of his name the Bourbon pretender, Henri "V" (1820–1883), as has been said? And the Philippe simply his mother's brother, a priest? In any case, Benoni was his grandfather's name, Hebrew for "son of my sorrow"—so Rachel called her newborn infant as she died (Genesis 35:18). It was a popular name at the time, usually referring to the death of the ancient regime.[5] Omer was of course Philippe's father, and a saint. Philippe's birth certificate has him born in the Cauchy farmhouse at ten o'clock in the evening on April 24, 1856.[6]

Concerning Philippe's infancy there is precious little to go by: no written records, no primary school report cards. Thus we learn only through oral tradition that Philippe's stepmother neglected the offspring of her husband's first marriage. Late in life Pétain told a member of his staff that following his mother's death he didn't speak until the age of three,[7] but one can't blame his stepmother for that, for she joined the household only when he reached that age. Tradition also tells us that Clotilde's children were largely raised outside their father's home; Philippe lived with

Grandfather Benoni and Grandmother Hyacinthe (born Cossart), in a house that was apparently only fifty yards from the parental home. The boy went to a local school, took lessons in catechism in the village church, helped out on the farm. At eleven he received confirmation.[8]

The child Philippe seems to have been drawn to two members of his mother's family. First, to Clotilde's maternal uncle, Philippe-Michel Lefebvre (1771–1866); conscripted out of seminary school into the Army of the Revolution, he served Bonaparte in Italy, returned to France a teacher and a priest. Second, to Jean-Baptiste Legrand (1818–1899), Clotilde's brother, pupil and later teacher at the Collège Saint-Bertin at Saint-Omer (where Philippe would study), and at the time of Philippe's birth parish priest of Bomy, a village near Saint-Omer. Father Lefebvre spent the last decade of his life in Bomy, at his nephew Jean-Baptiste Legrand's presbytery. In this presbytery Philippe found his reading matter, if not more.[9]

One writer is convinced that Philippe was excited by the older priest's reminiscences of war, while modeling his character, and even his handwriting, on that of the younger one. And when it was time for the celebration of Father Legrand's half-century of priesthood in 1895, Captain Philippe Pétain, representing the family, paid tribute to the old man's role as counselor and spiritual father of his nephews and great nephews. Legrand replied: "My dear nephew, I wish only one thing, that my family will always possess men who bear the cross or the sword."[10]

In October 1867, Father Legrand saw to Philippe's enrollment at the school where he had been a teacher, and it is possible that Philippe had the benefit of a scholarship established by Father Lefebvre just before his death. (He died at ninety-five, on April 7, 1866, just before Philippe's tenth birthday.)[11]

The Collège Saint-Bertin, in the sober monument of a town called Saint-Omer, is one of the way stations of Philippe Pétain's life that have remained more or less as they appeared in his day. The massive red-brick compound of the school itself reminded at least one old soldier of a barracks. Its teaching staff was composed of diocesan priests.[12] Philippe's school years coincided with acute tensions in church-state relations, for if the Second Empire had begun by encouraging religious schools as a means to maintain order in the realm, by the time Philippe was ready for school Napoleon III was in open conflict with the church, in part a function of his challenge to the papacy on the international scene; the government interpreted the laws on religious institutions strictly.

Students wore a uniform consisting of a tunic with tails, a long row of buttons in front, a metal buckle, a military-style peaked cap.[13] For this school had a clear military vocation. The local newspaper stressed the point (the year was 1873, when France was licking her wounds after the Franco-Prussian War): "The academic program takes five years and prepares pupils for successful passage of the examination for voluntary enlistment. . . ."[14]

What we know of Philippe's years at Saint-Bertin is scanty indeed: records of his piety, for instance (in February 1874 he was received into the Congregation of the Virgin).[15] An anonymous contemporary saw him as "a tall young man with a large frame, an oval face, open and pleasant, crowned with light chestnut hair slightly waved, an intelligent, lively expression and a mouth ready to laugh"—but the description may come from careful examination of a photograph. It was said that Philippe walked from Saint-Omer all the way home to Bomy or to Cauchy—fifteen or twenty miles—at vacation time.

One of the rare personal recollections of the schoolboy, published in a local newspaper after he had become a national hero, consists of a few lines: Philippe spoke little, causing him to be called Pétain-le-Bref, from Pepin-le-Bref, a king known in English as Pepin the Short (in French *bref* can mean either "brief" or "short").[16] We can also find the young man on the lists of prizes and honorable mentions. At the close of the school year in August 1871, Philippe received a second prize for Latin translation, and mentions in religion, Latin poetry, Greek translation, history and geography, and overall achievement. In August 1872, there were mentions in Latin poetry and in geometry; in August 1873, first prizes in geometry and English, a second in Greek translation, mentions in daily schoolwork, Latin poetry; in August 1874, there is a mention for work during school holidays.[17]

An oft-repeated anecdote evokes an incident in the boy's last years at the school: One day the study hall was invaded by a disagreeable odor. The principal of the upper school was summoned, and without hesitating he ordered: "Send me Pétain." The young man arrived, "as serious as Aristotle." "Are you the one who did it?" "Yes, sir." "What did you do?" "I put hydrogen sulphide on the monitor's chair." "Tell that to the Superior." "Yes, sir." So astounded was the headmaster by the cool confession that he took the young man by the arm, walked him around the courtyard a couple of times in silence, then stopped at the door of the study hall to say: "Go inside, the smell is gone."[18]

Most of the recorded anecdotes concern the school's military drill, which is usually described as a game, but sometimes as part of the official curriculum. The simplest expression of it is Pétain's own, in a penciled autobiographical sketch composed for unknown reasons (seized in his Paris apartment in 1945). He points out that Saint-Omer was a garrison town, headquarters of a battalion of light infantry (one day he will command it). He had come to know most of the lieutenants by sight; in some of them he discovered models for his own career. "From that time on my choice was made: I would be a lieutenant in the light infantry." Reports from the battlefields of the Franco-Prussian War stirred the pupils, who spent their recreation periods in military drill. "I made myself a captain with the tacit agreement of my soldiers, and during a period of several months the school's yard echoed the sounds of military orders, while true military operations were saved for our outings, usually taking the form of an attack and defense of a fortress."[19] It is certain that after the shock of France's defeat at the hands of the Prussians, there was a conviction that neglect of national defense was the cause; the Third Republic which inherited the shattered Second Empire undertook a radical reorganization of the army. Apparently a rudimentary form of drill was introduced into junior and senior high schools, and at Saint-Bertin the pupils marched with bats, later with breech-loading rifles.[20]

Virtually all biographies of Pétain tell us, without supporting documents, that he attended the final year (the preparatory year for the national examination—the French *baccalauréat*) at Saint-Omer, took and passed the examination; there is even a photograph, occasionally published, purporting to show this class. But there is better evidence that he did not stay for the final year, that he spent it with private tutors or went directly on to the Collège Albert-le-Grand at Arcueil, on the outskirts of Paris, to prepare for admission to the Saint-Cyr military academy.[21] In the records of Saint-Bertin this better-than-average student is cited for no prize or mention in what would have been his final year. Educational registers with the names of all who passed the *baccalauréat* do not show Pétain in 1875 or any proximate year.[22]

In those times, and in that place—the frontierland of the Artois, the garrison town of Saint-Omer—it was hardly remarkable that a young man with little hope of inheriting property or a father's business, with no pronounced ambitions or particular skills, would think of a military career. And it hardly matters that we have no firm evidence that Philippe's vocation was decided in any other way than the one he later recollected: the sight of junior officers on the streets of Saint-Omer. So he prepared for entrance to the Special Military School at Saint-Cyr, enrolling for that purpose at the Collège Albert-le-Grand in Arcueil, and apparently without having received the high school diploma at all (this was possible under the rules then prevailing).[23] This Collège Albert-le-Grand had been created only a dozen years before young Philippe entered it by the teaching order of the Dominicans. The first director of the school, François-Eugène Captier, had to overcome the opposition of the Ministry of Public Instruction, which was reluctant to see the establishment of a school by an unauthorized congregation, and so close to Paris.[24] During the Franco-Prussian War of 1870–1871 the Dominican fathers raised funds for the war wounded, then during the seige of Paris set up a temporary hospital in their school. The insurrection of the Commune found them there. On May 18, 1871, Captier and several other Dominicans and lay helpers were arrested by Communard revolutionaries, taken to a nearby fort; on May 25 they were moved to Paris. Alarmed at reports of the advance of governmental forces, their captors lined them up on the Avenue de l'Italie and shot them.[25]

When this occurred, Philippe had just turned fifteen and was still attending Saint-Bertin. Surely the news of the massacre of these pious teachers reached his own school quickly, and in a tone of urgency he was unlikely to forget. Albert-le-Grand was soon reopened, with new teachers and new equipment; and the vicar-general of the Dominican teaching order, Laurent Lecuyer, took on the additional responsibility of running the school.[26] In his speech at the first prize distribution following the shooting of his predecessor, Father Lecuyer made it clear that when his students spoke of revenge—everyone's rallying cry after the Prussian victory—they gave it a dual meaning here. "For the generation we are raising," he explained, "the future is revenge: revenge against the foreigner who surprised and defeated us in our ignorance and our softness; revenge also against the revolutionary spirit which surprised us, which our soldiers put down with heroism, but which might be victorious tomorrow."[27]

We have some oral tradition concerning Philippe's year at Arcueil. The students were organized into an informal squadron; Philippe was the sergeant major who commanded it during ceremonies. He was remembered as athletic, enjoying riding and swimming, detesting sloth to the point of pushing a classmate into a pool when he hesitated to dive.[28] Slim pickings. There is a photograph in an authorized biography showing the young man at Arcueil at age nineteen. He is soberly good-looking with a mustache and beard, and a sober dark uniform coat.[29]

II
CAREER SOLDIER

He no longer wears a beard, but the mustache has been allowed to grow; it is a handlebar in the photograph we have of Pétain at the Saint-Cyr military academy. The uniform coat seems over-sized, the epaulets too.[1] On the list of candidates admitted to his class by order of merit, which filled two columns of the *Journal Officiel* on October 13, 1876, Pétain is lowly number 403 of 412. Some days after that he was home, to enlist in the army for a five-year period. The register indicates that he has blond hair, gray eyes, a large forehead, an oval face, and measures five feet, eight and a half inches.[2]

Once again the young man was entering an institution in the process of transformation. The Imperial Special Military School of Saint-Cyr had been established by Napoleon to teach the arts of war. After the defeat of 1871 a reorganization was in store, its chief purpose to increase the number of officer candidates, and so to prepare the "hour of revenge" against the Prussians.[3] Courses were revised to stress military science; more attention was paid to topography, fortifications, artillery, but also accounting and legislation. Military training was transformed from simple exercises such as manipulation of arms into practical fieldwork; students were given firing practice on a true range. The program also offered riding, swordsmanship, physical education, singlestick, boxing. At the time of Pétain's enrollment a new building was inaugurated; the dormitories could now sleep 860.[4]

We are told that on leaves Pétain would return to the Artois, roaming familiar fields with a rifle or carbine;[5] on Sundays he would visit Paris or Versailles (the school was fifteen miles from the former, just three from the latter) accompanied by his new friend Alphonse Guide.[6] It is said that his ranking among the bottom ten on the admissions list earned him entry into a picturesque club with a song of its own, whose members were called on to settle quarrels, and year-round provided some color to daily routine.[7] What we lack—every witness is dead, and none bothered to offer it while living—is information about Pétain's behavior in this school, about his reaction to it. What, for example, did he think about the storm raised when it was learned that the school's commandant had included a chapter on religious practice in his regulations? This was attacked as a "Jesuitical" innovation, a serious charge in that touchy time. The commandant left the school two years after Pétain's graduation, at least in part because of this dispute.[8]

In 1878 the War Ministry once more announced "by order of merit" candidates "recognized as qualified for the grade of second-lieutenant after examination," and Philippe Pétain was number 229 of 386 candidates.[9] Among fellow graduates (higher on the list) who would play a role in his subsequent career: Émile Fayolle, Charles Mangin, fellow generals in the Great War.

Perhaps a new officer's first assignment is the one he remembers with most fondness, and there could not have been a more attractive garrison than Pétain's, in the sun-blessed Mediterranean port of Villefranche-sur-Mer. He was attached to the 24th battalion of Light Infantry. He would always remember this unit; its officers later had a particular place in his affection. The battalion remembered him too. From 1924 until 1939, its flag included a marshal's stick.[10]

Just before settling in his new post, he was sent (on the first of January 1879) to Valbonne, near Lyon, to take a course at the Firing School: theory, practice (the latter won him the notation: "Skillful marksman"). His authorized biographer tells us that it was at Valbonne, at the very inception of his career, that he developed his guiding principle on the primordial importance of firepower.[11]

The new officer joined his infantry battalion just at the time a degree of specialization was being introduced. Certain groups were being trained for mountain warfare, and as an athletic young man Second Lieutenant Pétain was cut out to lead one of them. The rigors of climbing, the close quarters in the shelters found up on the slopes led to close contact between officers and men. "We helped each other up the mountains without distinction of rank," Pétain later recalled. "With several months of this kind of cohabitation each year it was easy . . . to penetrate the thoughts of the men. . . . There was plenty of opportunity to talk to them about their families and to give them advice."[12]

We have a photograph of Lieutenant Pétain, looking a bit too serious for the part, dressed as a jockey for a costume ball in Menton in 1881.[13] An anecdote told later has Pétain in the casino of Monte Carlo, where officers were admitted but not allowed to gamble. He places a bet on the roulette table, watches his 20 francs become 40, then 80, 160, 320. But a general at the same table became curious as to who was winning all that money, so the uniformed junior officer didn't dare pick it up; he abandoned the table without his small fortune. Later, when he wished to gamble, he wore civilian clothes.[14]

Still more stories passed from one generation to the next in the family of his comrade and fellow officer Alphonse Guide, whose home in nearby Antibes often received Pétain in those years (and in later decades); not surprisingly for the handsome bachelor he was, the stories often involved mistresses.[15] Throughout his years as a junior officer Pétain took longer leaves in the north, at Cauchy-à-la-Tour, until the death of his father in 1888, then with his oldest sister Marie a couple of miles away, or at Father Legrand's presbytery in Bomy, later on at Mazinghem—always the Artois.[16]

Lieutenant Pétain was posted in January 1883 to Besançon at the foot of the Jura mountain chain—not a merry prospect after Villefranche, he remembered. "Work was the only thing you could do." The long winters allowed him to prepare for advanced study at the War College in Paris; in this way was Besançon "decisive for my career." [17] He was assigned to instruct recruits, then non-commissioned officers, giving particular attention to tactical discipline and utilization of weapons.[18] What was he thinking during those five years in Besançon? He later recalled that his bedside book was *L'Etude sur le combat antique et moderne,* a study of battlefield tactics by Charles Ardant du Picq, an officer killed in action in 1870.[19] This work was influential in shaping the generation of officers that would command in the First World War. Pétain also read everything he could about the Napoleonic wars, and let it be said that he had studied 500 different strategic and tactical situations.[20] In 1916 he told Henry Bordeaux, then a young information officer, to read a volume of *Les Contemporains* by Jules Lemaitre, in which there was a chapter on the military career of the seventeenth-century Prince of Condé Louis II, known as the Great Condé. It contains a lyrical passage on the grandeur of the man of war: "He makes history not, as the politician, or the writer does in round-about ways; he makes history directly, on the scene. . . ."[21]

An undated information sheet has been published, which may have been filled out at the time of Lieutenant Pétain's enrollment in the War College, which he joined on November 1, 1888, one of forty officers in the infantry section.[22] The sheet noted that Pétain had won promotion to first lieutenant "by seniority," the first of many promotions to be earned that way.[23] At the War College he was exposed to military instructors considered to be the army's best. However, according to his biographer, Émile Laure, the young officer was beginning to keep his distance from official doctrine, already convinced that it neglected the overwhelming importance of firepower.[24] He himself later remembered the vagueness of tactical instruction, the predominance of dogma. "Very few examples to support so-called principles, or the examples went back to Napoleon, which from the tactical point of view seemed archaic to me." It was only when the Germans began publishing their accounts of the war of 1870–1871 that the school's program was adapted to modern times. But Pétain had to wait until he himself was teaching at the war school to have these materials at his disposal.[25]

In May 1889 he took part in a field exercise employing artillery and fortified defenses, receiving 16 out of 20 for his part in it, and the remark: "Distinguished, perhaps a bit cold; has everything it takes to make a very good officer." In June he spent a week with an artillery battery at the Nimes firing range, where the regimental commander noted that he "distinguished himself by his assiduity and the intelligent manner in which he followed the course."

In his second and final year at the École Supérieure de Guerre—which we call War College—one report is worth citing (June 5, 1890): "Cold. Worth getting to know, perhaps not entirely developed, will be a good officer." Later that month he was attached to an artillery battery, whose squadron chief observed: "By his intelligence, his education and his tact, Mr. Pétain has shown himself apt to fill the job of staff officer." The regimental commander added: "Considerable self-control, a clear and firm commanding voice, much skill in sighting." He moved on to the staff of an infantry division. "Distinguished officer, cold in manner but intelligent . . ." In August his class toured a battlefield of the 1814 campaign. His work there was graded 18 out of 20; he was sized up as a "Distinguished and intelligent officer, fine appearance, character cold but agreeable." And he is a captain now. The promotion, which also assigned him to the 13th Battalion of Light Infantry, is dated July 7, 1890.[26]

He was promoted "by consulting the directory," as they said in the officers' messes; he was thirty-four years old. Later, when Pétain became controversial, these slow promotions would be attributed to his political or religious beliefs, or to his dissenting views on tactics. Pétain himself suggested that other considerations played a part. "One succeeded only by intrigue, connections, visits. . . . Commandants of the army corps held committee meetings to draw up promotion tables; it was a matter of bargaining, to buy votes so one's candidates or protégés would be promoted."[27]

We know something about the officer's social successes with the daughters of local elites. It is a repetitive story. Handsome Philippe seems a perfect fiancé: His bearing, his evident seriousness suggest that he will go far. But then the parents of the prospective bride undertake their investigation, find the officer wholly without prospects. The mornings after the ballroom encounters were often bitter.

Thus a biographer describes two young women of Besançon, one the daughter of an engineer, the other of a bank manager, whose parents rebuffed Pétain. Then there was Marie-Louise Regad, blond, slim, beautiful, who fell in love with the officer after a ball in the summer of 1888. When her well-to-do parents discovered that Pétain was without resources they consented to the marriage only if the young man agreed to give up the army and to join the family manufacturing business. We are to believe that Lieutenant Pétain traveled up to Mazinghem to consult his spiritual adviser, Father Legrand; after talk and prayer uncle and nephew agreed that Philippe must remain faithful to his true vocation. Philippe then took an oath, renewing the pledge already made at Saint-Cyr, swearing to be faithful to his "mystical fiancée," the army.[28] Later, in an interview while he was chief of state, he would evoke this "gift of my person": "I was a young officer, and it was a private oath. When I renewed this oath for France I renounced everything."[29]

But what exactly did he renounce? For there were other young ladies then, later, always—until he was in his eighties. Some became "very old spinsters . . . who never married because they kept in their heart the image of this infantry lieutenant . . ."[30]

In any case he never forgot Mazinghem, nor Father Legrand, as his uncle's obituary in a diocesan newspaper attests. "Seeing at his bedside his nephew, a captain of whom he was justly proud, the priest said: 'You'll certainly be decorated soon enough; as for me, here is my Legion of Honor,' and he pointed to his crucifix; then he expressed the desire to talk to his nephew about the religious and political questions which divide our unfortunate country."[31] What questions? The Dreyfus affair was at a turning point, and as we shall see Pétain's assignment in Paris had brought him close to some of its protagonists.

Pétain's next assignment took him still further from home. After War College he was posted to Marseille, as trainee in the general staff of the 15th army corps, "where I spent three years harnessed to a monotonous office routine, carrying out as well as I could the job of staff writer for which, I admit, I had no inclination." (So he chose to say in his autobiographical sketch.)[32] After serving in the headquarters of two infantry regiments he was assigned as orderly officer to the general commanding the 15th corps, who later set down this evaluation: "Silent, cold, calm, hostile to hasty judgments and always working methodically."[33] All we know about Marseille we know from the friends he will make among the first families of the Mediterranean port city; once again this dashing officer (his photographs tell us much) had entry everywhere. The uniform was not so much an equalizer as a stepping stone.[34]

The Marseille assignment concluded with an attack of typhoid fever which kept him in a Nice military hospital for two long months.[35] He was then required to spend part of his time in his captain's rank in an active command; it was to be the 29th battalion of light infantry at Vincennes on the eastern edge of Paris. "I threw myself into my job as instructor, which I loved," he recalled in his autobiographical sketch. "The opportunity to lead maneuvers in the woods of Vincennes and to ride horseback made this post most enjoyable."[36]

From there Captain Pétain moved to the heart of Paris, the seat of the general staff of the Military Governor of Paris on the Place Vendôme; the date of this appointment was July 17, 1895. The military governor was General Félix Saussier, who served at the same time as vice-chairman of the Supreme War Council, in which capacity he would automatically be commander in chief in time of war.[37] On Saussier's retirement he was replaced by Émile Zurlinden. Pétain became Zurlinden's orderly officer, the indispensable right-hand man every senior officer enjoys, who transmits his orders, shares or keeps his secrets.[38]

Then what did the new orderly officer—the aide de camp— think about the Dreyfus case; what part did he play in it? For Pétain's years at the military governor's headquarters coincided with the most violent episodes of this affair which had divided all France into two camps: nationalists supporting the army's charge that Captain Alfred Dreyfus had given military secrets to the Germans, and defenders of the Republic who were discovering the fragility of the case against Dreyfus, and the likelihood that the true culprit was known. When Pétain joined General Saussier's staff Dreyfus was already imprisoned under ghastly

conditions on Devil's Island. Saussier, who was apparently un-
convinced of Dreyfus' guilt, signed the order bringing the true
culprit, Ferdinand Esterhazy, before a court-martial; precisely a
fortnight after that Saussier was retired and replaced by Zurlinden.[39] Zurlinden sought indulgence for Esterhazy and was involved in the attempts by the high command to cover up the affair,
leaving Dreyfus in his tropical hell for the good of the army. Finally Zurlinden was appointed minister of war, resigning after
only a few days when the government allowed arguments to be
heard favoring a new trial for Dreyfus; but then he returned to
the post of military governor.[40]

For right-wing extremists, anti-Semites, the Dreyfus case offered a chance to put down the Republic; for conservative Catholics, a chance to regain lost positions; for defenders of the
Republic, a question of principle as to whether civil power would
prevail over the military; and Émile Zola made it a matter of simple justice.

It would be helpful to know where Pétain stood. An American biography, published during the Second World War, put
words in his mouth: When asked where he stood on Dreyfus, Pétain is alleged to have replied that between him and General
Zurlinden there was "perfect understanding."[41] In fact, this phrase
was not Pétain's reply to a question about Dreyfus, but simply his
biographer Laure's characterization of the general harmony that
prevailed between Zurlinden and his aide de camp.[42] There is no
contemporary record of what in fact Pétain *did* think, and we shall
see that his later remarks on the Dreyfus affair were ambiguous—or contradictory.

Living in Paris allowed Captain Pétain to resume relations with
a family he had first known as a second lieutenant on the Riviera. At their home in Menton, Pétain had chatted with her parents while bouncing four-year-old Eugénie Hardon on his knee.
Then he watched her grow up, on visits to the family at their
country estate not far from Paris and then at their Paris apartment. He would continue to see Eugénie's parents, and Eugénie,
when he returned to Paris to teach at the War College.[43]

Soon after Zurlinden's replacement as military governor by
General Henri Bruyère, Pétain returned to an active command.
He was assigned to the 8th battalion of light infantry at Amiens,

close to the northern frontier and to his birthplace. There he was given a company, and was soon to be rated by his commanding officer, General Guillaume Bonnal (who had already remarked "this big, fair-haired lieutenant, distinguished, slightly bald" among his students at the War College): "Remarkable captain, both as staff officer and line officer. Combines the qualities of energy, character, sizing up, decision and intelligence in the right proportions desirable in a future leader. First class."

On July 12, 1900, the officers' mess toasted Pétain's promotion to battalion chief (the French army's equivalent of major). He had been on the promotion list since 1898. Commenting on his age—forty-four—his ten long years as captain after five as second lieutenant and seven as lieutenant, Émile Laure writes: "banal career, almost inferior to the normal, guaranteeing him against envy and jealousy."[44]

At forty-four he was a mature man, a senior soldier, possessing a mind of his own, having accumulated a body of personal doctrine, lacking only the rank to enforce it. The new battalion chief was assigned to the School of Marksmanship at Châlons-sur-Marne. Later, speaking of this experience, he was to say that he had been sent there "to try to fight against the exaggerations introduced into the teaching of marksmanship by a school of mutual admiration. . . ."[45] So Pétain didn't initiate a challenge to accepted doctrine, but was the instrument for this challenge. Indeed, he worries in a letter that he is not "ripe for carrying out what is expected of me."[46] In essence, the War Ministry was alarmed by the philosophy of the Châlons school, which preached blanket coverage of the battlefield by riflemen, to the sacrifice of precision firing. For the purpose of obtaining this broad but undirected coverage, the school had even found it disadvantageous to train soldiers to aim carefully.

Speaking from conviction as well as on instruction, Pétain argued for individual expertise, skilled marksmanship. Apparently his lectures surprised the school's commander, who then sought to change the orientation of Pétain's teaching. The commander found fresh support in the War Ministry, where the director of infantry responsible for Pétain's assignment was replaced by an officer sympathetic to the school's prevailing philosophy. Six months after his arrival Pétain had to leave the school, but he was given his first choice of a new assignment: Paris again, with the 5th regiment of infantry.[47]

He joined his new regiment in February 1901; that autumn he was teaching at the War College, as associate professor of applied infantry tactics. General Bonnal, his commanding officer in Amiens, had become the school's commandant in February, and it was he who brought Pétain into the teaching body.[48]

The École Supérieure de Guerre had been opened in 1878, housed in the palatial École Militaire on the Champs de Mars, to prepare officers for the general staff. Its students were lieutenants and captains (Pétain had been a lieutenant when he took the two-year course in 1888–1890). Each year eighty young officers were admitted; on successful completion of the program they would receive a staff college certificate and additional seniority of six months.[49]

Pétain arrived at the school—once more—during a period of transition. Teaching was being adapted to lessons drawn from recent experience, the Boer and Manchurian wars. Some understood the lesson to be that battles must be fought as Napoleon had conceived them, with massive charges. Others looked to firepower, convinced that even a large body of troops could not advance against well-directed enemy fire. By 1902 a provisional regulation seemed to have settled the debate by supporting the method of throwing massive forces against enemy lines. But this was countered in 1904 by a regulation recognizing the danger of exposing even small groups of men to enemy fire.[50] It is not known to what extent Battalion Chief Pétain argued his own case, to what extent he served the doctrine spelled out in the 1904 regulation, but all sources agree that he stood firmly against the expense of lives in undirected attacks, stressed the danger of enemy fire, and wished the French side to learn how to direct its own.

He was remembered by one of his students as "an officer with limpid eyes, cold, bald," speaking in "icy tones," although a fellow officer assured the first one that Pétain was a master of deadpan humor.[51]

Perhaps it was at this time that a delicate question arose concerning a promotion. The authorized biography by General Laure places it in 1902–1903 although Pétain himself in his autobiographical sketch recalls it as happening "some years" after he began teaching. He was summoned to the War Ministry to be offered command of the School of Marksmanship at Châlons. It seems that General Alexandre Percin, who was private secretary of War Minister General Louis André, was impressed by Pétain's ideas on the role of the infantry, firepower, battlefield tactics. Pétain replied that Châlons was normally commanded by a lieutenant-colonel, whereas he was of lower rank, and the school already employed others of his rank, and with more seniority. "That doesn't matter," Percin or his inspector general replied; they would promote Pétain immediately.[52]

"This would place me in very advantageous conditions for future promotions," Pétain recalled in his autobiographical sketch, "and yet I refused to accept so as to owe nothing to one of the chief promoters of the Dreyfus affair. In fact I received the rank of Lieutenant Colonel only four years later, thus giving up the possibility of attaining high rank."[53]

This confession was never published during Pétain's lifetime. In the Laure biography, which appeared during the German occupation in 1942, there is no mention of Dreyfus, nor anything else that would have revealed Pétain's feelings about the still incendiary affair. This General Percin and his superior, General André, represented a new state of affairs in the high command. In September 1899, when most of the original evidence against Dreyfus had been exposed as fraudulent, the army nevertheless convicted him a second time on the same charges, and he was saved only by a presidential pardon. National elections in 1902 ushered in the moderates. It was now that General André, war minister under Premier Émile Combes, reopened the Dreyfus file to discuss the forgeries and suppression of evidence, triggering a judicial review that was completed only in 1906 with the definitive rehabilitation of Dreyfus by an appeals court.[54]

The purging of the army of its hardliners, however, was compromised in 1904 by the "index card affair." In that year a member of Parliament, Jean Guyot de Villeneuve, who had resigned from the army as a result of sanctions taken against him because of his anti-Dreyfus position, denounced the practice of compiling lists of officers known to be religious or who expressed anti-democratic tendencies. He described the system of index cards compiled in the office of War Minister André, under Percin's supervision, from information supplied by the Grand Orient Lodge of the Freemasons.[55] It didn't matter that Minister André explained to the same audience that the file was being used to eliminate the intolerance and anti-Republic sentiment that he had discovered in the army;[56] the opposition now had a serious weapon to utilize against the liberal Combes government. Army morale was damaged; officers were divided into two camps.[57] The Freemasons had been a constant target of militant Catholics, blamed for the Revolution of 1789 and for every democratic event ever after, the fall of Napoleon III, France's weakness against the Prussians, parliamentary government, the Third Republic and the defense of Dreyfus—and now there were the index cards.[58]

Had Pétain been a victim of the index cards? During the Vichy years a journalist made the claim that he had been told by a Grand Orient official, Jean Bidegain, whose defection had launched the index card affair, that he actually possessed Pétain's card. "It is very curious and would cause a stir," is all he would say of it.[59] After the Second World War one of those involved in Vichy's purge of the Freemasons, Bernard Faÿ, announced during his trial that Pétain had given him the anti-Mason assignment "because this old soldier still had the index card affair in his heart."[60]

III

BEFORE THE WAR

After Pétain refused to be promoted he was given another active command. This time he was posted to the 104th Infantry Regiment based in Argentan and Paris, serving in it from June 1903 until March 1904, when he was brought back to the War College, still associate professor of applied infantry tactics.[1] Pétain's biographer Laure thinks he sees an allusion to Pétain's attitude to General Percin's offer in the note placed in Pétain's file at this time: "Of a firmness of character and of ideas which keeps him from being the slave of anyone." He was also getting high praise for his teaching. "He defends his views with a force of argument and an enthusiasm which make him a champion," reads an evaluation in his file. "On the question of infantry firepower, notably, this has made him one of the two or three leading authorities in France. Most striking personality."[2]

He taught at the War College for three successive years (1904–1906). A memorandum recommending him for promotion in November 1905 included this enthusiastic endorsement: "Remarkable scholar and even thinker, commandant Pétain has taken the leadership and formulated the main lines of a movement which has now resulted officially in the renovation of the teaching of gunnery." He was largely responsible for progress achieved in this field, and it was "in the interest of the army" that he be promoted. But he was to wait another eighteen months to attain the rank of lieutenant-colonel.

Biographer Laure speaks of the cool, methodic behavior of Associate Professor Pétain. He was becoming known as Précis-le-sec (i.e., the "dry"), apparently evoking a village in the Yonne, Précy-le-Sec, which had served as the target of attack during maneuvers. The essence of his teaching: The foot soldier must become master of the battlefield through firepower; and this required accuracy, perfect coordination.[3]

Pétain was promoted out of the War College, his commanding general at the time believing that he was becoming too famous.[4] He had wanted to serve in eastern France, on the frontier with the traditional enemy, where the best officers were posted and where there was greater opportunity to test his theories. Instead he was sent to "the extreme west," to Quimper in Brittany,[5] to the 118th Infantry Regiment, where he was responsible for training junior officers. He led the regiment in maneuvers and did so well that he received temporary command of it for three months.[6] "The winter here is severe," he wrote a nephew. "By working hard I manage not to be bored." But he would not stay in Brittany forever: "The War College is asking for me again, but I have a bad press at the Ministry and don't know who will win: bets are open!"[7]

General Joseph Maunoury, the new commandant of the War College, brought Pétain back in April 1908, and this time as full professor of applied infantry tactics, replacing Lieutenant Colonel Louis Guillaumat, who had held the job only a year. Now he had the backing of his superior, and for three successive years could preach his doctrine. In his view cannon fire was meant to support the infantry, not to choose targets of its own. He now had the support of General Percin, who in 1907 had become inspector general of artillery instruction. During autumn maneuvers Percin commanded a division and took Pétain along as his chief of staff; following these maneuvers a new artillery regulation was issued that endorsed Pétain's ideas on coordination, making it possible for the infantry to call for artillery support.[8]

At the school Pétain's course consisted essentially of a review of infantry tactics under Napoleon and in the 1870–1871 campaign, showing the evolution of tactics since that time, stressing, according to the course program, "the increasingly deadly power of rifle and cannon fire. . . , the need to assure . . . the superiority of firepower. . . ," and "doing away with massive attacks in favor of a new form of attack by the disposition of reinforcements"—almost a preview of his strategy in the defense of Verdun.[9]

We have the text of the course given by Colonel Pétain—a full colonel since December 31, 1911—given during the 1911 teaching year. It is a rejection of formalism, an invitation to an empirical approach to combat. For it was still necessary at that time to mock the notion that troops could be marched into battle. "One of two things happens," he explains, "either the enemy stands firm and the marching columns are pulverized, or he gives ground, and this march to the sound of trumpets and drums becomes without object. . . ." With modern weapons—machine guns as well as rapid-firing rifles and cannons, "the basis of all tactics must be to obtain movement by fire."[10]

The legend is that the revolutionary professor acquired a formidable adversary in the school's new commander, Ferdinand Foch, whom military historians have always described as the diametrical opposite of Philippe Pétain: audacious and mystical to Pétain's caution and cold reason, a romantic from the south to Pétain's northern sobriety.[11] In fact, if differences of character and of doctrine were to make them notorious rivals during the course of the First World War, they seem to have gotten along well at the War College. Foch's endorsement of Pétain's nomination to the rank of colonel includes this language: "Of a nobility of sentiments, a rectitude of character seldom seen, a clear and precise intelligence, rigorous method, a faultless conscience, a just sense of tactics and deep knowledge of his field, Pétain carries out a program at the school which is first class from every point of view."[12]

Colonel Pétain lived modestly, all his possessions united in two regulation trunks, and stayed in second-class hotels when traveling.[13] But he did like good food; in Paris he was a regular at

Gangloff, a restaurant close to the War College patronized by higher-ranking officers who could afford it.[14] In 1906 this inveterate bachelor drafted a will leaving the totality of his possessions to his sister Sara in Mazinghem.[15]

Correspondence reveals that he maintained a wide range of social contacts before the war. His old friend Alphonse Guide was in Paris, retired from the army for health reasons. Pétain visited the Guides at their home not far from the War College, and soon became acquainted with the Guides' neighbors, the Louis Ménétrels.[16] Ménétrel was a physician; he was to become Pétain's doctor, and a lifelong friend; on his death, Ménétrel's son Bernard replaced him in both roles, as well as becoming one of the men behind the throne in Vichy.

With one of his closest friends of these prewar years the relationship was complicated, or enriched, by the liaison that Pétain was enjoying with the man's wife. In one of her later letters she informed him: "Of all the feminine hearts you have conquered, there is none (am I too bold?) which understood you more than mine did, which devoted more faithful admiration, fervent tenderness. . . ." Although she had now become "wiser," she said, she wished him to know that "You were, you are and you will remain for me, whatever happens, the Only friend."[17] Some later whispered that Pétain was the father of one of her children.

Available correspondence contains allusions to other affairs— brief, or on-and-off; many of the women had husbands.

Eugénie Hardon has already been introduced. The child he bounced on his knee in Menton was a woman in 1901, and he asked her hand in marriage. Her stepmother and grandmother refused his suit because of the great difference in their ages but apparently did not tell their daughter that he had asked. (Had they, she later confessed, she would have married him without their consent; she was in her twenty-fourth year.) He advised her to marry all the same, and she did: the artist François Dehérain, with whom she was to have a son.[18] But it is clear from later correspondence that Pétain's liaison with Eugénie was ardent while it lasted.[19] It is also clear that they were back in each other's arms soon after her separation from her husband, before her divorce in March 1914. In a letter dated November 1, 1913, Pétain wrote Eugénie after a break of several months. They had been seeing each other at a bachelor flat he had taken for these trysts (for he was then stationed in Arras), but she was apparently committed to someone else. And so he resolves to stop seeing her, to forget her; later on they might become just friends. (He tells her that she can pick up a packet of photographs in his flat: "You needn't worry about any unfortunate encounter," he assures her, "for no woman stepped foot in the place since April 17, and that woman was you."[20] In December 1913, Pétain pursues his argument: His love is stronger than hers, and considering his character "so inclined to jealousy," only complete separation would cure him. So this had to be their last contact until she found herself alone.[21]

Then, in hospital while recovering from a fall from his horse (his knee was being operated on that morning), he wrote: "I had given you all my love, all my devotion, all my life. I'll never get over this. And it's because you had all of me that I refuse the friendship you offer . . ." A few days later, out of hospital, he suggested a meeting in a public park or "even at my place." The next letter reveals what happened at that meeting: ". . . With what intoxication my lips took your kisses in total forgetfulness of everything that separates us." But the wound had already re-opened, "more painful than ever." She had reproached him for thinking about physical love too much. "But if I didn't love you physically it would not be love, for love takes over the entire physical and intellectual being."[22] Their encounters were to continue during the war, often as close to the front lines as his headquarters were.

In June 1911, Colonel Pétain had been assigned to Arras in the Pas-de-Calais district of his childhood, to take command of the 33rd Infantry Regiment there. Photographs show him slender at fifty-five, standing straight, with the inevitable mustache, the peaked cap (so that one forgets he is bald). At Arras his superiors lost no time assessing his worth. "He should be put forward for the rank of General immediately," one of them noted.[23]

To hear his authorized biographer tell it, there were real problems to deal with in Arras. Pétain discovered considerable negligence—overstaying of leaves, for instance. He attempted to deal with this abuse by tightening up punishments but then decided to write to the parents of the soldiers, and this worked. A peacetime regiment engaged in regular exercises, including twice-weekly maneuvers; here he had one more opportunity to test his theories.[24]

There was a singular encounter that autumn. A young officer reported to him fresh out of Saint-Cyr: Second Lieutenant Charles de Gaulle. Colonel Pétain greeted his new officers in a brief talk he took the trouble to write out (and to keep): "It's of our first garrison, of our first regiment, that we keep the most lasting impression. We'll do what we can to plant in you the essential seeds, necessary for the development of your careers."[25] "My first colonel, Pétain, showed me the gift and the art of commanding," de Gaulle acknowledged simply, in memoirs written after the Second World War.[26]

It was the beginning of a relationship that would become the single most significant clash of personalities and politics of twentieth-century France. Neither of the protagonists said much else worth recording about those first months, but we do have copies of Pétain's ratings of de Gaulle. For the first six months of 1913: ". . . Shows himself from the start as an officer of true value who offers great hopes. . . ." Second half of that year: "Most intelligent, loves his work with passion. Perfect command during maneuvers. Worthy of all possible praise."[27] Later Pétain was to remember the young officer, and to take him into his inner sanctum. But the opportunity to say something more about their first association in Arras is too tempting and stories were told—apparently even by de Gaulle himself—of a pretty young lady of Arras who loved the junior officer but also appreciated the colonel's experience. "He could still be a formidable rival," de Gaulle is quoted as confiding to a comrade.[28]

In April 1914, Pétain was given command of a brigade, and in Saint-Omer, the town of his high school days. If he was close to home he was also close to the northern frontier; in those days the best officers, the best-trained men manned those outposts. It was a temporary appointment, for a brigade was normally commanded by a general. He found a small house in the nearby countryside, planning to settle there when he retired, for retirement was approaching; he had just turned fifty-eight.[29]

The Saint-Bertin schoolboy was the star of the troop review on Bastille Day, July 14. As the *Marseillaise* was played, Colonel Pétain saluted with his sword local dignitaries seated in the grandstand. "Immediately after that," the town's daily newspaper tells us, "galloping on a superb and well-trained white horse, the colonel, followed by two aides de camp, inspected the admirably aligned troops." It was a rousing ceremony. "Yet there was no shout, no motion; one felt that the spectators were thinking that France's hope was there and that . . . the hour is grave. . . ."[30]

The year before, back in Arras, a survey of the senior officers in the First Army Corps had made the case for Pétain's promotion to general. "The matter is urgent because of his age."[31] Why wasn't this brilliant officer promoted? Obviously the Pétain legend has given birth to a variety of stories. In their simplest expression they range from "my religious convictions" (Pétain was quoted as saying that to friends in Mazinghem)[32] to Paul Reynaud's explanation after the Second World War: Pétain's superiors found him lazy and negative.[33] In truth, Pétain's slow rise was not untypical of the peacetime army. It was when an officer approached the top that personality differences, cabinet maneuvers, general staff lobbying became significant. We know from one of his close aides that Louis Franchet d'Esperey, general in command of the First Army Corps, admired Colonel Pétain and felt that he was being held back for political reasons. He wanted to make Pétain a brigadier general in June 1914 so that he would have time to move up to major general (which would save him from forced retirement; brigadiers were retired at sixty-two). D'Esperey put in a request to the minister of war, Adolphe Messimy, whose private secretary replied crisply: "Pétain will never become a major general." Then d'Esperey, who himself was a staunch churchman, remembered that after Pétain's exile to Quimper he had been recalled to become full professor at the War College, and the officer he replaced was the minister's private secretary who had just said that Pétain would never make major general.[34]

The war minister's private secretary, General Louis Guillaumat, had indeed been displaced by Pétain in his professional chair; he was also apparently an ardent defender of the Republic.[35] Were his motives for blocking Pétain's promotion personal or political, or both?

IV
THE LAST OFFENSIVE

The war on the eastern front began with a full-scale invasion by Kaiser Wilhelm's armies; violating Belgium's neutrality, they moved into France from the north. Franchet d'Esperey's First Corps was now part of the front. The French discovered that their offensive doctrines had to be supplemented by equally firm principles of defense. General Joseph Joffre, commander in chief of French forces, kept them intact in the first weeks of combat by retreating. This is not the place for a history of the Great War: The history exists and fills many volumes. This single volume follows only Pétain's war, and Pétain in the war.

He felt, he later confided to Émile Laure, that the German attack had caught him unready. He had not had time to command his entire brigade; he didn't have it "in hand."[1] The immediate task was to move north and east quickly, to meet the Germans inside Belgium so as to bolster that country's small army. For the first and apparently for the last time Pétain kept a log, written in pencil in a school notebook. (It had the extra feature of describing the women of the homes in which he was billeted,

e.g., "Agreeable physique, despite a scar on the nose . . .") On
August 12 he noted that he was supervising the construction of
a road into Belgium; next day he described the warmth of the
welcome of the local population.[2]

We also have that moment captured by one of his Belgian
hosts. Pétain and his soldiers had reached Olloy-sur-Viroin at eight
that morning, "exhausted by the march, white with dust," to be
cheered by the villagers, who offered them flowers, candy, ci-
gars, even money. Pétain's host, a history teacher, describes the
colonel: "The facial lines are distinguished, the complexion reveals flourishing health. Alert eyes, graying hair, a strong, slightly
hooked nose, a generous mustache . . . a clear gaze, by turn mild
and dreamy, cold and willful, sparkling and ironic, no exuber-
ance or immoderation in his speech, nothing useless, rather the
stamp of ponderation . . ." A long perception for so brief a visit.

At lunch the colonel seemed not to share the history teacher's
optimism concerning the value of France's intervention. And that
evening Pétain made it clear that he didn't even realize he was in
Belgium; he thought he had reached neighboring Luxembourg.
"We left last night in a hurry . . . We didn't even have time to
look at a map." He betrayed his concerns: "They are strong, so
very strong! . . . The avalanche hasn't reached us . . . If only it
can be held back for a few days!" At eight that evening a mes-
senger handed him a note which ordered his departure for one
in the morning. When Pétain described the route he was to take,
his host warned it would be dangerous and suggested a better
one. The teacher's wife asked whether the likelihood of a German invasion of Belgium had been envisaged and planned for in
France. Indeed yes, replied the colonel, but they hadn't really
believed that the Germans would provoke British hostility by violating Belgium's neutrality.[3]

On August 15, Pétain's men held the crossings of the Meuse
river south of Dinant. When they came under fire two days later
he had an opportunity to see what his artillery could do, and to
dig trenches and lay barbed wire under combat conditions.[4] These
defenses were not to hold long against the German advance; the
French risked being trapped, and by August 22 they were retreating. Pétain recorded his feelings about the inadequacies of
the reserve divisions they had been obliged to call in. "Perhaps,"

he told his log, "they are going to blame the army once more for something the government did. A nation has the army it deserves." More bitterness, during the ensuing march south, when his men were covering the retreat of the army corps: "It even looks as if they want to give me command of a division. Are they already obliged to employ such revolutionary measures?"[5]

He now held a temporary appointment as brigadier general. On August 28 he noted that his hosts of a night had offered him the stars of the uniform of a family hero, General Gaston de Sonis, who had fought in 1870 and died a quarter of a century before World War I began.[6] On the next day his brigade attacked, in what was later known as the Battle of Guise, conceived to block the relentless German advance; territory was recovered. Pétain later told Laure that this had been the first really cruel day of war for him. He and his officers had begun to realize their powerlessness in the face of the well-designed German steamroller. Another retreat, the beginning of the withdrawal from Belgium, had begun.[7]

As brigadier general Pétain received temporary command of the 6th infantry division. His official biographer has him reviewing "a strange parade": the troops are "like skeletons," they march "with heavy steps"; passing their new chief they turn their eyes toward him "and seem to implore some respite from their miseries without end." So he would devote himself to taking his troops in hand, giving close attention to behavior, combating "slovenliness, negligence, lazy thinking."[8]

Still, the new division seemed "at the end of its physical and moral possibilities" when the order came in to attack on September 6. Pétain was in the front line, under heavy enemy artillery fire, but at the end of the day his 6th division had opened the way for the 18th corps at Montceau-les-Provins. Laure says that the "Pétain method" could be observed in its entirety that day: the battle delivered according to rule.[9] Pétain's fellow cadet Charles Mangin was more severe in his judgment, and his is probably the first unfavorable assessment of Pétain in battle. "He spares himself, not personally," Mangin wrote his wife in one of his regular reports from the front, "because he knows how to advance under fire, but in the utilization of his men. He has no confidence in them, and says so clearly." Mangin complained that if Pétain was "prudent" and "skillful" in retreat, in the attack that followed "he advanced without haste," leaving Mangin's division alone to confront the enemy. Mangin felt that Pétain had shown himself to be "mediocre" in the organization of his front.[10] This is an early manifestation of the differences in character that would separate "prudent" and "skillful" Pétain from his blood-and-thunder fellow officers: Nivelle after Mangin, and then Foch.

On September 14, Pétain received temporary appointment as major general. The fighting took his 6th division to the Aisne Canal, where the Germans held firm and then counterattacked. Although prevailing doctrine had it that one never gave ground, Pétain didn't hesitate to do that. Instead, he gave his attention to defense in depth, coordination between artillery and troops. Already the war had become what it would be for most of the next four years: holding the line. Citations would be awarded not for capturing terrain but for hanging on to it. On September 27, Pétain's division stood fast under heavy attack, and a citation appraised him: "Has, by his example, his tenacity, his calmness under fire, his incessant foresight, his constant intervention at difficult moments, obtained from his division during fourteen consecutive days of the Battle of Rheims, a magnificent effort, resisting repeated attacks by day and by night and, the fourteenth day, despite losses, victoriously repelling a furious enemy attack."[11]

On October 20, he received command of an army corps, the 33rd, which was defending the province of his childhood and of his last peacetime command. Modern military historians refer to this campaign as the Battle of Artois. And henceforth he had a sharp but judicious critic in one of his division generals, Émile Fayolle (another former classmate). Fayolle kept a confidential diary throughout the war. "I don't think Pétain will push me as his predecessor [General Victor d'Urbal] did," he noted. "And why should he? To gain some hundreds of yards that I'd probably lose again the next day. . . ."[12]

At the general staff of the 33rd, Pétain acquired another diarist and a lifelong friend in Captain Bernard Serrigny, then forty-four, whom he had known fifteen years before at the 8th battalion of light infantry, and later at the War College. "He seems to have quite another conception of his role as chief," Serrigny says of Pétain in his diary (published posthumously). "Almost as soon as he got here he called on his division generals, something d'Urbal had never done." Serrigny knew that the new commander would have a difficult beginning, with the unceasing German attacks and the threat to Arras. "Happily Pétain is unmoved. He is really very plucky. . . ." He listened to everyone's advice before making decisions. "A born foot soldier, he studies all questions in their slightest details. . . ." He even makes certain that good food is served, understanding the importance of physical well-being for the success of operations.[13]

When he took over the army corps, Laure tells us, Pétain also inherited the offensive doctrine then prevailing. Soon, however, he had rejected the tactic of constant attacks which he felt "for worthless results dilapidated troops who will be wanting later for more significant actions." Instead, he stressed centers of resistance inside villages, camouflage; trenches were dug deeper, barbed wire used generously, communication trenches crisscrossing the battlefields. The Germans pressed hard north of Arras. Pétain organized a second line, the line that was to stop and break the German attack when it came.[14] The town was saved. "As soon as the battle had become calmer, I couldn't resist the desire to visit Arras," Pétain later remembered. "With a heavy heart I followed familiar streets. . . . The whole city, with its decapitated belfry, was no longer anything but a heap of ruins. . . ."[15]

On November 3, President Raymond Poincaré visited the headquarters of the army corps. This seems to have been Pétain's first contact with the high and mighty, and with a statesman who was to play a role in his career. Much later Pétain told a story about this visit. When Poincaré asked what he thought of the way things were going, Pétain replied crisply: "Not much!" And he went on to blame "our misfortunes" on the fact that "we are neither commanded nor governed. The invasion and our failures since go back to a system of government which is not equipped to win a war."[16]

Those who had the opportunity of meeting Pétain during this period offer contradictory views. We have Henri Mordacq's judgment: "Quite cold, speaking little, never beginning a conversation, yet having a look in his eyes of great goodness."[17] But also this surprising and never explained diary entry by Fayolle (November 5, 1914): "Doesn't hesitate to demote the mediocre and to shoot cowards." Fayolle quotes Pétain: "I played the part of a butcher." The reference seems to concern the retreat from Belgium, when the need to reinforce discipline may have called for extreme measures.[18] Fayolle's diary was published posthumously, and after Pétain's death as well. During the twenty-one between-the-wars years when most World War I history was written, and when Pétain often had the opportunity to review what was written before publication, no one else made such comments about his first year of combat.

Another regular visitor to headquarters was Colonel Edward Spears, then a British liaison officer, the same Spears was to deal with Pétain again in the weeks preceding the 1940 armistice. Now Spears found only things to admire. Pétain's tactics, notably in the use of firepower, impressed him. The Englishman found that the Frenchman had "a marked sense of humour deeply concealed under his frozen exterior, like *edelweiss* beneath a snow-drift."[19]

On November 30, 1914, General Foch arrived, to outline an offensive whose objective was "to break through the enemy line." Pétain duly went about planning such an attack and then (after it floundered in winter mud) convinced his superiors—Foch included—that it would be better to postpone further action of the kind for a drier season. He won the argument,[20] but henceforth would find himself in constant opposition to the high command about the feasibility of offensive action. Usually it was Pétain against Foch; Foch's orders were "glazed with imperative phrases, irresistible expressions," Pétain later commented. Foch's conception of "the breakthrough" in the winter of 1914–1915 was "that of most leaders of the army, who had not yet realized the necessity of a gigantesque effort. . . ."[21] Pétain's 33rd corps was poorly judged because it did not issue glowing accounts of its victories, so Serrigny offered to write such accounts.[22]

Serrigny also describes Pétain's efforts at morale building: leaves to Amiens, theatrical performances. The general made it a point to visit all front-line units, climbed into trenches; he even verified firing positions. On the war's first Christmas, midnight mass was held in staff headquarters. Next day Pétain confided: "It's curious how in getting older I am moved by religious ceremony. My childhood memories rush to the surface and it would take very little to convert me."[23]

And then we have Fayolle again, reporting (and he is the only one who does, in these posthumous notes) a meeting on January 23, 1915, dealing with an incident in which forty soldiers shot

themselves in the hand so as not to be sent to the front. Pétain
wanted to execute twenty-five of the group, and then changed
his mind. "He gave the order to tie them up and to throw them
over the parapet toward the closest enemy trenches. They would
spend the night there. He didn't say whether he would let them
die of hunger there." Nor does Fayolle tell us what finally happened to them, but he does size up his chief: "Character, energy! Where does character end and where begins ferocity,
savagery! . . ."[24]

That month Pétain informed Fayolle that he was being made
a major general, a permanent appointment that came through
on April 20.[25] It is the last promotion Pétain was to receive, until
his appointment as marshal of France following the armistice.

The long-awaited attack began on May 9, 1915, and it was a
success for the 33rd, the only one of the 10th army's five corps
to achieve a penetration of enemy lines.[26] Pétain was urged by
his superior, d'Urbal, to persevere, but he didn't see it that way.
His flanks weren't covered. But he dutifully attacked on the eleventh and failed as he knew he would.[27] Later he recalled a meeting with Foch in the presence of Joffre: When Pétain informed
them that it would take a month to prepare another attack Joffre
sat down, "put his elbows on the table and began to sob," so sure
had he been of imminent victory.[28] Fayolle saw Pétain "furious"
against d'Urbal and Foch. "They are madmen," Pétain told him.
"Foch tells us to attack, without caring about the state of preparation." The May 9 attack and its follow-up had cost the French
forty to fifty thousand men; the next attack would cost a hundred
thousand, and to gain what?[29]

But General Pétain was moved up again, to take command of
a whole army, the 2nd, replacing Edmond de Castelnau; Pétain's
33rd was taken over by Fayolle.[30] Pétain summed up the lessons
learned so far in a "Note on the operations in the region of Arras": "The present war has taken the form of a war of attrition.
There is no longer a decisive battle as in the past." Success would
go to the side "which will possess the last man." He urged the
building of a strategic reserve to be ready when the Germans were
finally exhausted.[31]

Pessimism, reticence—the man could make Joffre break down
and sob. But Joffre had now given him even greater responsibil-

ity, and in a region—Champagne—no less vital. Of course, the watchword from general headquarters was "attack": Pétain's was "prepare." Joffre was planning a major offensive to be undertaken by two armies, one of them Pétain's (with its thirteen divisions). The hope was that this attack would pave the way for total liberation of French territory, for many strategic centers—industrial areas, sources of raw materials—were now in enemy hands.[32] Pétain argued that conditions had worsened in recent months: the enemy now possessed a second defensive position all along the line, out of range of most French guns. The attack was nevertheless set for September 1, although at Pétain's urging Joffre put it off until the twenty-fifth to allow more time for detailed planning.[33]

As Pétain had feared, the second German line proved impenetrable; still, he ordered his divisions to persist. Several times it was believed that enemy lines had been pierced, but each of the hoped-for breaches proved illusory. On September 27, Pétain ordered a suspension of operations to allow further preparation, but the 4th army reported a breakthrough and Castelnau, now commanding a group of armies, ordered Pétain's 2nd to support it with further attacks. This breakthrough also proved illusory, stopped at the Germans' second position. Joffre ordered further preparations, called in fresh troops, increased ammunition distribution. Both armies attacked again on October 6 but were halted by defenses that had not been damaged sufficiently by French artillery and aviation. Fighting continued until early November: no decision, and perhaps this time the lesson would sink in. "The Battle of Champagne demonstrates," concluded Pétain's report, "the difficulty if not the impossibility, in the present state of armament, of methods of preparation and of the forces opposing us, of taking in a single thrust the successive positions of the enemy." He argued for a two-part solution: wearing out the Germans all along the fronts—British as well as French—and then "the decisive effort."

This was not quite what Joffre, or the nation at large, wished to hear. So Pétain, the man who advocated preparation, was now to be given the opportunity to work at it. On January 5, 1916, he was assigned to command four army corps held in reserve.[34]

V

VERDUN

The interlude was short-lived. A particularly sensitive, exposed salient of the long eastern front had come under enemy pressure. On today's maps Verdun seems a safe distance from the German border, but during the 1914–1918 war, indeed ever since the defeat of 1871 deprived France of Alsace-Lorraine and Rhine River defenses, the town was virtually a frontier post. German advances in the first year of the war exposed Verdun to enemy fire, so that even the railway line that served it was vulnerable to its artillery.[1]

The Germans opened fire at 7:00 A.M. on February 21, 1916, subjecting the entire sector—left and right banks of the Meuse, the town itself—to shelling of an intensity never to be felt again in the Great War. The infantry attack began the same afternoon, a full-scale offensive designed to effect a breakthrough. On the following days the Germans advanced over four miles, capturing the old fort of Douaumont on February 25.

In his memoirs Marshal Joffre gave himself credit for sending Pétain to Verdun.[2] Other versions tell us that Joffre was sleeping when Castelnau arrived at his Chantilly headquarters to protest against a plan to abandon Verdun; Joffre s aides refused to wake the old soldier, but when Castelnau insisted, Joffre opened his eyes to say, "Let him do as he likes," and went back to sleep. Castelnau then returned to his own headquarters at Châlons to summon Pétain.[3] It hadn't actually been planned—nothing was in the Great War—but something remarkable was about to take place on the eastern front all the same. An officer who specialized in defense was to be assigned to defend a crucial sector. Clearly, by instinct or in desperation or for want of a better candidate, the most fitting possible general officer had been chosen. At Verdun successful defense would represent victory. The stopping of the Germans there was soon to be called the Verdun victory, and Pétain the victor.

The Germans were superior both in troop strength and firepower, and possessed the advantage of position for deploying their big guns. They had better communications. Only one road, running from Bar-le-Duc to Verdun, supplied the French salient, with a narrow-track rail line. Nor was there hope of relieving the pressure on Verdun with an attack elsewhere, for the combined French-British offensive on the Somme was not expected to be ready until July. To improve communications, Pétain called in airplanes, balloons; ordered construction of a standard-gauge rail line and improvements in the existing line, as well as maintenance of the road link.[4]

The road: Its story is the story of the defense of Verdun. The narrow dirt road running from Bar-le-Duc eighty-four miles north and east toward Verdun, passing before the stone steps of Pétain's headquarters at the Souilly town hall on the way, was soon to be known as the Sacred Way. Prodigious ingenuity was applied to keeping it open. Reserve troops—the older draftees known as territorials—were stationed along the shoulders with shovels to scatter limestone gravel found just below the surface of surrounding fields; there were no rollers to flatten the gravel, so the passing vehicles did that job.[5] Soon 1,700 trucks were moving in each direction daily; from February 27 to March 6, 190,000 men were transported over the road, with 23,000 tons of ammunition, 2,500 tons of supplies.[6] There was a clockwork exchange of troop units, the exhausted defenders moving south toward rest zones around Bar-le-Duc, fresh troops moving up.[7]

* * *

When the Germans attacked the left bank of the Meuse on March 5, they advanced further than expected. There was pressure from headquarters, and from public opinion, for an offensive, but Pétain resisted, convinced that his first task was to make his defenses impenetrable.[8] Perhaps his chief contribution to military tactics—the innovation that made the defense of Verdun exemplary—was his constant renewal of troop units, made possible by his persistent calls for fresh reserves, and by the rotation of men already engaged in battle, this in turn made possible by the transportation network that had been established in the first days of his command. It reached the point, Laure says, of Joffre's staff feeling that the whole French army was being asked for as a reservoir for Verdun. Joffre saw Verdun as only one battle in a long front and worried that Pétain did not see it that way. He thought that he might change Pétain's view by giving him a larger front to deal with: hence Pétain's being moved up to command the Group of Armies of the Center, leaving the operations at Verdun to Nivelle.[9] Joffre admired Nivelle's offensive spirit, and, in fact, so-called young Turks all along the line were impatient with Pétain's tactics.[10]

But whatever the mood at General Headquarters, Pétain was a popular hero now. He had stood fast at Verdun; the Germans had not gotten through. With fame came myth. Thus a Paris daily, *Le Petit Journal*, noted that he skipped rope each morning before shaving, selected his staff officers from the ranks of bicycle racers and track champions. Visitors flocked to his table: senators and deputies, authors and journalists. The Prince of Wales dropped in, as did Lord Northcliffe (Alfred Harmsworth), publisher of the *Times* of London.[11] Maurice Barrès, already a famous author, patriot, and polemicist, described a visit to Souilly on April 13 in *L'Echo de Paris:* "A half dozen officers and noncommissioned officers in the corridor and on the stairs, then on the upper floor a town hall council room with white plaster walls, straw chairs, a grimy wood table." And then he saw Pétain, "tall, completely bald, a certain natural majesty, a glacial facade behind which one perceives a warm human being." All his life, exclaimed Barrès, only the army counted for this general, and in the present situation he was more absorbed than ever by his tasks, refusing "vain influences."[12]

On April 4, Pétain wrote his brother Antoine: "I am horrified by the publicity I am getting and furious at the stories that have been written about me. I have in front of me an article from a local paper reproducing my birth certificate. What right did the town hall clerk have to give this to a stranger?" He begged Antoine to help him maintain "perfect tranquillity."[13] He wrote Antoine again on June 2 after a reporter for *Le Matin* visited Cauchy: "I am angered by the cheek of these reporters . . . I was warned in time and was able to stop the article." After requesting that Antoine not let himself be interviewed, Philippe concluded: "You have to escort these reporters to the door and make them understand that I don't want the press to speak about me, except to report military events."[14]

April began with a French attack to ease the pressure on the sector between Forts Vaux and Douaumont, followed by a German attack all along the line. Next day Pétain issued an often quoted order of the day to congratulate the 2nd Army, concluding: "The Germans will undoubtedly attack again. Let everyone work and remain vigilant to repeat yesterday's success. Keep a good heart. We'll beat them." Serrigny takes credit for drafting this statement, Pétain's contribution limited to the correction of a "perhaps" to the "undoubtedly" of the final version; Pétain is also said to have objected to the "We'll beat them," which in French is perhaps inelegant but powerful: *"On les aura."* The order of the day was widely reprinted; Pétain was amused that writers sought to define his character through this phrase he hadn't himself composed.[15]

Still, Paris was not convinced that Pétain was winning, despite assurances by Poincaré, and Joffre, that Pétain knew what he was doing. Pétain himself told Poincaré, when the president visited Souilly on April 19, that French losses since the beginning of the attack until April 5 were 12,163 dead, 68,835 wounded, 16,043 missing, with another 10,000–11,000 casualties to April 15.[16] "They say I'm a great devourer of men," Pétain commented to information officer Henry Bordeaux after a day of intense fighting (April 14). "Yet I spare them as much as I can."

Bordeaux was present to celebrate the general's sixtieth birthday on April 24. "He bears his age well," he told his journal,

"but he seems above the question of age; his old age will yield to
the extraordinary calm and nerveless strength that one perceives
in him." Still, even Bordeaux was severe in his judgment of Pétain's lack of initiative. "Couldn't he, with all the troops at his disposal, have tried a general offensive before the Germans had time
to build extensive defenses?" Bordeaux summed up: "He isn't sure
of himself and he doesn't have genius. He's a man of character
and authority, and he saved Verdun, but he doesn't hold victory
in his hands."[17]

Was Pétain himself bitter about Verdun? It would seem so.
When Paul Painlevé, then a cabinet minister concerned with in-
ventions of use to the war effort, soon to be war minister and
premier, visited Pétain in the middle of May, the general greeted
him with, "You see in me a general who has just been relieved
of his command."[18] In fact, he continued to fight the battle of
Verdun from his new command, in the way he fought best:
keeping up the pressure for fresh troops, more artillery, munitions. Poincaré was sure that General Headquarters was holding
back new guns to use in the planned offensive in the north and
gave instructions that Pétain was to get what he needed.[19]

Foch attacked on the Somme July 1, pursuing his offensive
all summer and until winter prevented further movement, with
a net gain of territory. In October, Nivelle recaptured both
Douaumont and Vaux, and kept the offensive rolling along his
front until December. Writing nearly half a century after these
events, a British historian concluded: "In the position to which
Joffre had cunningly elevated him, Pétain found himself caught
in a monstrous nutcracker between Nivelle and Joffre," Nivelle
on one side wasting manpower with futile counterattacks, Joffre
on the other refusing fresh troops and even withdrawing heavy
guns for the Somme.[20]

Joffre's memoirs, published after his death, contain some
harsh criticism of Pétain, often quoted to prove that he was a
defeatist. Thus Joffre complains of Pétain's constant demand
for fresh troops "without ever alluding to plans for a counter-
offensive. . . ." When Joffre toured command posts with Pétain
in early July 1916, writes Joffre, "his pessimism struck me." Nivelle was more to Joffre's taste: "If history recognizes my right
to judge the generals who operated under my orders, I wish to

state that the real savior of Verdun was Nivelle, happily assisted by Mangin."[21]

"I am good," Pétain told a writer visiting his headquarters. "I know it and I try to be careful. Fortunately I have a chilling mask."[22] It was a highly efficient mask: it allowed its owner to appear to be a sphinx calling for interpretation, while not preventing him from having a private life. Yet this "chilling" aspect kept him from enjoying genuine popularity, as a contemporary observer noted: Nivelle with his ardor represented "the national mood" while Pétain "doesn't please the masses. He is too disciplined, too self-contained. . . ."[23] Such a personality was vulnerable to legend. Pétain's contempt for politicians gave birth to rumors of his outright dissidence. He was said to have remarked to fellow general Castelnau that after the war they'd "drop over to the Palais-Bourbon"—seat of the Chamber of Deputies; in other words, they would overthrow the Republic.[24] One of his more puritanical peers confided to his diary: "The bad taste of Pétain, who spoils his good qualities by the flightiness of his conversation and in letting everyone see how much he thinks of himself. He is better than he seems to be. . . ."[25]

Something else can be said about Pétain's summons to Joffre's headquarters back in February to receive his assignment to Verdun. When Joffre's telegram arrived at eleven on the night of the twenty-fourth Pétain could not be reached, for he had gone to Paris. So his faithful aide Serrigny packed his own and Pétain's trunks and took Pétain's automobile along with his own to Paris at top speed. Acting on a hunch, or so he later said, he knocked at the street door of a hotel near the North Station to wake up the owner at three in the morning, and to ask point-blank if Pétain was staying there. She denied it energetically until Serrigny had made it clear that the welfare of the nation was at stake. She then took him up to a door before which Pétain's yellow boots stood alongside some unambiguously feminine shoes. Serrigny knocked, to confront his general in "lightest attire." The aide took a room for himself to finish the night, then drove off with Pétain for Joffre's Chantilly headquarters. Later Pétain said that when he told the woman who shared his hotel room the nature of the task that confronted him she broke into tears, then demonstrated an ardor that made the night unforgettable.[26]

The woman was Eugénie Hardon Dehérain, who was certainly the most important of Pétain's feminine companions of the time. Their dormant affair was revived in 1916: She received no fewer than eighty-one letters from her general that year (this many have been saved). Shortly before their night in the station hotel, he had faced up to the matter that she was still seeing the man whose mistress she had been. Pétain refused to share her but was prepared to forgive. In early February they began meeting regularly in Paris (in a letter of February 3 he warned her not to greet him at the station if he arrived with others, but to join him at the hotel immediately afterward). His letters evoke their "delicious hours." From Souilly (in March) he pleaded: "You must avoid causing me even the shadow of suffering so that I can devote myself to my task. . . ." As his preoccupations grew and their separation was prolonged, his needs became more explicit: "You cannot imagine the thrill I felt in finding myself in your arms again. Yes, I confess it, I love your body also. The memory of your caresses makes me weak." After an evocative passage in another letter he wrote: "It's crazy to write this way, but I adore you, this is my excuse."

Soon she was to be able to approach his headquarters. In May, when he moved to Bar-le-Duc, they met in Châlons. The meeting place was a hotel room, for they had to avoid dining in public. "Come Monday at the usual hour," a note dated June 17 reads. "It is possible that I can't have dinner with you, but if my work goes well I'll come to wake you during the night. . . ." She wished to stay even closer to him, but he warned: "All my acts and moves are remarked with a disconcerting precision." By mid-September he had sent her a formal authorization to settle in Châlons, to work there as a nurse.

Often he had to reassure her, for Eugénie had heard reports of his flirtations, even rumors of his engagements, or marriage, to other women. "For you I abandon all relationships contracted in the past three years," he promised.[27] A particularly cumbersome relationship was that with Yolande de Baye, an intense young nurse who was running a hospital at Verdun, exposing herself to enemy fire. Serrigny warned his chief that Miss de Baye's open flirtation was causing tongues to wag, "that his reputation would suffer and that he would make himself ridiculous if he married a young girl at his age. . . ." Pétain assured Eugénie, who had heard all about Yolande, that the nurse was herself spreading the story that she had married Pétain. In fact, so he told Eugénie, he was receiving offers of marriage from all over the world, even from the United States.[28] We have evidence that Serrigny served more than once as marriage broker: The example he himself offers is a certain Jeanne d'Hincourt, whom they called in jest "Madame la Maréchale"; she was "stunning."[29]

The autumn of 1916 found General Pétain, in his somewhat lofty position as commander of the Group of Armies of the Center, watching Nivelle's developing offensives in the Verdun sector, encouraging them, fighting headquarters for more support for them. But it was really Nivelle's show now, Nivelle's and that other pugnacious general's, Mangin's. Mangin's letters to his wife made the contrast even more striking. "With this clear, cold weather we could have staged a beautiful attack," he wrote her on September 16. "But Pétain is very defensive; he thinks that we are economizing our forces." And on November 29: "Pétain is really too defensive . . . Nivelle feels this and Joffre seems to agree. In any case, he would never use Pétain again for a serious attack. . . ."[30]

From September to the end of 1916 the Nivelle-Mangin steamroller pushed the Germans back all along the Verdun front. This was enough for the government: With Joffre's semiretirement on December 12, Nivelle was appointed general in chief of the eastern front. It was a way of announcing that the government judged Pétain incapable of exploiting the successes of what Painlevé called "the young school of Verdun."[31] Mangin proclaimed to his men: "We have the method and we have the Chief. Success is certain!"[32]

VI
THE GENERAL IN CHIEF

The first months of 1917 were a purgatory. The victor of Verdun was not quite in disgrace, but he was in reserve; unable to conform to prevailing doctrine, he declined to pretend to conform. Thus in January, when the new general in chief, Nivelle, began mapping out his spring offensive, he saw an attack on the sector between Rheims and Soissons as the principal element in it, and even considered putting Pétain in charge of the special group of armies assembled for this attack. But Pétain did not approve a direct assault in this area (which was later to become notorious as the Chemin des Dames) and said so.[1]

His resistance to a futile offensive was becoming known, and winning supporters in the press as well as among officers.[2] "Pétain insists that I look at Verdun with him," General Fayolle recorded in his diary in early January. "Pétain is hypnotized by Verdun." So Fayolle went along with Pétain but saw nothing terribly interesting. That night at dinner Clemenceau joined the two generals. Fayolle notes: "Pétain thinks himself a great man; he tells us seriously that the Republic is afraid of him. Clemenceau must be plotting with him."[3] This is a striking perception of Pétain's mental state at that instant, of his frustration and scarcely suppressed anger.

On March 19 the Alexandre Ribot cabinet was formed, with Paul Painlevé as war minister. Painlevé, who before entering government had been a noted mathematician, tended to favor the "Pétain manner"—prudent and methodical—rather than Nivelle's.[4] In Paris, Pétain dined with Painlevé, new Premier Ribot, and Franchet d'Esperey. Pétain told the assembled guests—who included Nivelle—that he doubted the efficacy of a wide-scale offensive. For him there was only one tactic: to wear out the enemy by repeated attacks, by short punches that make him groggy, that weaken him little by little.[5] In a subsequent meeting, Armament Minister Albert Thomas, after hearing Pétain's objections to an attack that would "put all their eggs in one basket," protested: "But then we're not going to finish the war?" Petain: "No, we're not going to finish the war, but isn't that better than to finish it with a defeat?"[6]

The cautious Painlevé was seriously worried now. He took Pétain and Franchet d'Esperey to dinner with President Poincaré. It was now April 3. D'Esperey said nothing, and once more Pétain delivered an argument against Nivelle's plan, which he felt would expend all of France's reserves in a single battle (those were the eggs in one basket), and with no hope of accomplishing anything.[7] Painlevé assembled a war council at Compiègne, the new General Headquarters, on April 6; President Poincaré presided. All the army group commanders opposed the Nivelle offensive, Serrigny tells us, but they could not agree on an alternative, so it was decided to go ahead, with Nivelle promising to stop the attack if it did not succeed in the first three or four days.[8]

The main attack was launched on April 16 along the Chemin des Dames, a road running along a crest above the Aisne River. Two armies were thrown at the Germans in an attempt to pierce the lines and open the way for a third, waiting in reserve. The French took heavy punishment, gained some ground at an enormous sacrifice—20,000 dead, 91,000 wounded, 3,000 taken prisoner—but they did not get through. Now there was a new tone in the dissatisfaction with Nivelle: "Should Nivelle be replaced by Pétain?" Premier Ribot asked his private diary. Already there was public support for such a solution, particularly, he notes, in the right-wing press.[9]

Could Pétain fill the job? The premier sounded out Douglas Haig, commander in chief of British forces in France. Haig liked Pétain but worried about a change in the middle of an operation. He also feared that Pétain would throw out all the offensive plans if he took over at Compiègne. At a war committee meeting on April 26 everyone except Painlevé opposed dismissing Nivelle, and Louis Malvy, interior minister, declared that the appointment of Pétain would be "dangerous."[10]

Was a compromise possible, like naming Pétain deputy to the chief? No, since Pétain was not subordinate but clearly Nivelle's successor. So Nivelle kept his job for the moment, while Pétain was appointed chief of the General Staff, attached not to Nivelle's headquarters but to the War Ministry; and he moved into an office at 4b, Boulevard des Invalides, once occupied by Joffre.[11] He became an adviser to Painlevé, who now had direct responsibility for making war policy.

The compromise lasted until May 15, when Pétain replaced Nivelle as general in chief, commander of the entire eastern front, at the same time that officer of quite another temperament, Ferdinand Foch, moved in as chief of the General Staff.[12] Speaking to an agitated Parliament in July, admitting that grave errors had been committed in the April offensive and pointing out that the responsible officers had been relieved of their commands, War Minister Painlevé reminded the deputies that Pétain was now in charge. "He is a far-seeing, determined and wise chief, who has the full confidence of his officers and men, as well as of our allies." Painlevé was "heavily and unanimously applauded," a newspaper reported.[13]

When Pétain joined Compiègne headquarters there were 3.2 million Allied soldiers on the eastern front, in 109 French divisions, 62 British, 6 Belgian, with smaller Portuguese, Russian, and Polish contingents; they faced 2.8 million enemy troops in 155 divisions. Émile Laure sums up Pétain's guiding principle of the time as, "We have to wait for the Americans." For the United States had entered the war on April 6, and was now beginning to draft and equip and train hundreds of thousands of soldiers, soldiers who were needed to break the deadlock. The waiting period was to be employed in building up French and other Allied forces: improving training, augmenting their equipment with new arms such as tanks and aircraft.[14]

But very quickly there was something else to do. Outbreaks of mutiny were being reported from various sectors of the French front, in the zones that had borne the brunt of the April offensive, particularly in parts of the front where fighting was still going on. On April 29, between two and three hundred men from a regiment that had been ordered to return to lines it had already occupied at Monts de Champagne failed to appear at roll call, then announced that they would not move. The word got out, and similar acts of resistance took place elsewhere. On May 4, troops in the Chemin des Dames sector deserted; stickers bearing slogans such as "Down with war" and "Death to those responsible" were making the rounds. Later in May, there were noisy demonstrations, collective and individual acts of revolt, an organized protest with the election of delegates; on May 21 and 22, soldiers attacked officers while singing *L'Internationale*. Official reports described 151 incidents in all, 110 of them representing serious collective protests; 112 of these incidents occurred in the Chemin des Dames sector. The 54 divisions affected represented over half the divisions in the French army as then constituted.[15]

Pétain's response—his effective putting down of the mutinies with a minimum of shed blood, the steps he took to deal with the causes of the mutinies—is often considered his most important achievement as commander in chief. Certainly, it represented an essential condition for France's further pursuit of the war.[16] It has been said that if the Germans had known what was happening (and apparently they did not until late in June), they could have marched to Paris.[17]

In Pétain's postwar autopsy of the mutinies, he placed the blame squarely on France's civil and military leaders for having planned the spring offensive without considering the moral state of the nation as well as of its army. He also blamed the press for aggravating the crisis by discussing military operations, reporting parliamentary complaints about their conduct, and revealing plans discussed at secret conferences. Within the armed forces, he said, insufficient attention had been paid to rest leaves, their regularity, even the transportation of soldiers to leave stations. Food was inadequate at the front, and during combat men were asked to make needless sacrifices, such as charging into buried machine-gun emplacements and barbed wire in vain hope of a breakthrough. Most blame went to the ill-conceived Nivelle offensive.[18]

Indeed, for the new general in chief, who took possession of his quarters at Compiègne on May 16, 1917, dealing with the mutinies and with the offensives of his predecessor were one and the same thing. Among the emergency measures were rules of behavior for officers faced with dissent in the ranks, reinforced military justice. The chief mutineers were to be punished speedily, the army to be defended against "contagion" from the home front. A "Note Concerning the Attitude of the Command" made the case for better understanding between officers and men. Pétain himself undertook daily visits to front-line units, talked to officers and noncommissioned officers, sometimes to ordinary soldiers, stressing their certain victory and, Laure tells us, "showing at the horizon the American fleet growing larger, ready to overflow on to the coasts of France."

But the punishment would also have to be exemplary. A telegram of June 8 to army commanders warned that failure to put down mutinies were equivalent to complicity.[19] Because the mutinies were kept secret at the time, and spoken of only in whispers thereafter, accounts of the repression have been exaggerated. But it is certain that justice was expeditious in those dangerous weeks. A considerable number of death sentences were handed down, but because of pardons and commutations of sentence, only seven were carried out by order of the general in chief, and forty-eight more after presidential review.[20]

As soon as it could, Pétain's staff began planning for the longer term. A system of rewards for good behavior was devised, including new medals and guaranteed leaves. Improved food was accompanied by severe restrictions on alcoholic beverages, the belief being that drunkenness had helped the rebellion spread. Soldiers were encouraged to bank their money rather than spend it immediately. But something else worried the high command. Pétain was convinced that home-front pacifism and left-wing agitation had influenced men in uniform. His headquarters called attention to subversive propaganda found in camps and asked

Paris to keep it informed of "movements of opinion" in the country. Pétain put all the pressure he could on the interior minister and was never quite satisfied with the quality or the quantity of intelligence obtained. On the positive side he set up press visits, escorting reporters to front-line units. "Then," as he later explained it, "the stories would go through the censorship office in Paris, which had been reorganized to follow the wishes of the high command." The big dailies did not like what was being asked of them, which didn't stop the general in chief from telling his war minister: "The reading of newspapers must not be a source of skepticism or bitterness for the men, but rather one of perseverance and of enthusiasm. . . ."[21]

The Pétain method worked. In any case, the number of incidents of mutiny diminished steadily. By September 1917 confidence seemed to have been reestablished, enough to make new military operations (of the Pétain kind) possible.[22]

It was Pétain's personal engagement—the expense of himself—that most impressed those who watched him handle the "moral crisis." Thus liaison officer Edward Spears admired this "indomitability of purpose which would have been impossible had [Pétain] the slightest doubt of the soundness of the remedies he proposed to apply. . . ."[23] Reminiscing after the war with fellow commander in chief Douglas Haig, Pétain expressed pride in the way he dealt with the mutinies: that and Verdun were his two contributions to the war, he said. He also told Haig that when he had informed him about the mutinies during the summer of 1917 "the state of the French Army was much worse than he had dared tell [the British commander] at the time."[24]

We also have the testimony of the American commander in chief, General John J. Pershing, who received a briefing on problems of morale from Pétain on June 22, 1917. Pétain had wished him to know why it was so important that the Americans send at least a token contingent to France right away. Confidentially, Pétain even asked Pershing whether he could have President Woodrow Wilson use his influence to convince certain members of the French government to show themselves more resolute. If the French government and French people failed to come to the defense of their army, failed to restore the country's confidence in itself, instead of undermining morale, Pétain feared that the situation could become revolutionary, allowing the Germans to dictate the peace terms.[25]

Pétain's headquarters were in the Compiègne castle built by the last French kings and restored by Napoleon. He actually occupied an apartment decorated for Marie-Antoinette just before the Revolution. Nearly everything of artistic value had been removed for safekeeping, but Serrigny found a bust of the Empress Eugénie which he wanted for his room. Pétain asked for it too, but Serrigny told him that too many women turned around him as it was, and this one at least wouldn't distract him from his work. Concerning these women, Serrigny is explicit: "A number of these women, I fear, received unequivocal tokens of the admiration of the Chief." Serrigny also informs us that the French had decoded a telegram sent by the German ambassador in Madrid to his government to announce that a mistress had been found for Pétain. When Serrigny asked Pétain if he suspected the identity of the woman spy, he replied "after some hesitation" that he did.[26]

He was certainly at the height of his power now, and knew it. Jean de Pierrefeu, information officer at General Headquarters, who had his first glimpse of the general in chief shortly after his arrival in Compiègne, remembered: "I had the impression of a marble statue: a Roman senator in a museum. Tall, energetic, with an impassive regard, a complexion white as marble, a steady, thoughtful gaze, in his blue uniform he was of incomparable majesty."[27] Not very different from descriptions of Philippe Pétain as junior officer, not really different from accounts by visitors to the chief of state of Vichy a quarter of a century later. Pétain and his legend were well served at Compiègne by a team of public relations specialists guided by Serrigny. Two of them were to become members of the French Academy: the novelist Henry Bordeaux and historian Louis Madelin. Serrigny reached public opinion through the French press, and he says that he had particular success with American correspondents, who were extremely pro-French and sent stories inspired by Serrigny to their papers in the United States, which stories would then be picked up in the *French* press.[28]

The war was at a standoff when Pétain moved into Marie-Antoinette's chamber. Neither side was strong enough to penetrate the other's positions. But the Germans were soon able to mobilize more troops for their attacks, as the Russian war effort collapsed. It seemed as if infantry soldiers, unassisted, would never again be able to carry out an effective breakthrough, and the slow buildup of France's arsenal of tanks was under way. "We must have mastery of the air," Pétain also told Painlevé. He spoke of "the industrialization of the war."[29]

Gone forever were the heroic gestures of Joffre, the spectacular schemes of Nivelle. The war was not going to be won in a single, all-out battle. Pétain's directive number one of May 19 put an official stamp on the new tactical approach: "The balance of opposing forces . . . doesn't allow us to envisage, for the moment, a rupture of the front followed up by its strategic exploitation. We must therefore wear out the adversary with a minimum of losses." Instead of "deep attacks" there was to be an emphasis on "attacks with limited objectives launched suddenly. . . ."[30] On June 20 directive number two set forth a system of training of large units that emphasized artillery preparation before each attack, limiting the objectives of infantry advances to the range of artillery support.[31] Large units were transferred, one after the other, to training camps, where they received the new doctrine. Complaints were heard that Pétain was sending everybody to school, as if peace had arrived.[32] There was time for this, in Pétain's view, for he was telling his intimates that the war would end neither this year nor next, but in 1919, when the American army would be present in strength.[33]

Also in June, Pétain called his top staff together and asked for suggestions for offensives with strictly limited objectives. So plans were drawn up for attacks at La Malmaison (in the Chemin des Dames sector), the forest of Houthulst in Belgium, and at Verdun, this last to restore the lines to their situation prior to the German offensive of February 1916. The three operations were launched as planned, and succeeded within the limits the general in chief had set for them.[34]

But not only tactics received Pétain's personal mark. He had a strategic goal: to maintain France's place in the first rank of the Allied coalition and to direct his efforts toward a victory that would be of most significance to France. Hence a concentration on the vital center: Alsace-Lorraine, to be certain that the French would be present in at least part of these lost provinces in the event the war ended in compromise. In this view Flanders was a British concern. Pétain's strategic planning took into account the likelihood of the disappearance of the Russians, whose country was in the throes of revolution, and the slow but sure buildup of aid from the United States: supplies, funds, aircraft, and, one day, a large and fresh army to fight alongside the French.[35]

VII

WAITING FOR THE AMERICANS

The British were an old story. They had been friends or enemies, as often the one as the other, throughout modern history. The Americans were something else: They were so far away, so unconcerned with French and continental history that they tended to be idealized. Their entry into the war was not quite an unexpected gift from heaven, but almost. Philippe Pétain would always manifest a certain tenderness for American soldiers, for Americans and America; the love affair began right then in 1917.

Soon after his installation at Compiègne, Pétain traveled to Amiens to meet Marshal Haig; Marshal Sir Henry Wilson, the chief liaison officer with the French; and General Sir John Davidson of Haig's staff. The meeting went well enough on the surface, Pétain promising troops for Haig's offensive, promising also to time his own attacks so as to provide maximum support to the British.[1] Haig felt that Pétain seemed to be going out of his way to be courteous, found him clearheaded and easy to talk to. Moreover, Pétain was "businesslike, knowledgeable, and brief of speech. The latter is, I find, a rare quality with Frenchmen!"[2]

Pétain and his staff also began planning for the arrival of the Americans. Their commander in chief, John J. Pershing, landed in France in June 1917 and visited Compiègne soon after that. "He has a kindly expression, is most agreeable," he noted of the Frenchman in his memoirs, "but not especially talkative." Their friendship, says Pershing, began on that day (June 16).[3] Serrigny places their first meeting in July, telling us that Pershing arrived ignorant of France and the French, filled with preconceptions, unable to comprehend much of what Pétain told him about the organization of the French army. But he concurs that "a lively current of sympathy" was established.[4] On July 3, Pétain issued a general order to mark America's Independence Day, to be celebrated the following day in Paris with a parade of newly landed American soldiers. "The United States intends to place at our disposal, without stinting, its soldiers, its gold, its factories, its ships, its entire country," the order read. "Let a single shout be heard, on this fourth of July, from all parts of the front: Honor to the great sister republic!"[5]

Before the American entry into the war there was not a single organized unit even approximating a division in the U.S. army, but Pershing drew up a plan for one million soldiers to be ready to fight in 1918, and for an eventual strength of three times that number. Training was a priority. Pershing felt that the French and British had been in the trenches for so long that they had given up training for offensive combat, while this was the very type of preparation the Americans needed.[6] Pétain brought Pershing into the picture at once and took him along to inspect the front. In one village where American troops were billeted in haylofts the American commander happened to be inside one of the barns when Pétain arrived. Taking Pershing for a platoon sergeant, Pétain asked him how he liked the billets and posed other questions about the life of the Americans in France. Pershing replied respectfully, playing the part as well as he could. Pétain learned the truth later from amused members of his staff.[7]

All smiles for the public, privately Pétain was less serene. He had hoped to integrate fresh American infantrymen into his own army, but his new ally insisted on remaining autonomous. Pétain told his government in early September 1917 that the American commander was "inexperienced and difficult to handle."[8] By

October he was saying that Pershing had "a time bomb in his brain: it took time for him to understand."[9] Clearly, an ocean still separated the Frenchman with his three years of war from the new boy. Meanwhile, Pershing was reporting home to his secretary of war that he had insisted on total preparation for his men before they were ordered into combat; they would benefit from French artillery support and remain in close contact with French troops: It was important that their first engagement be a victorious one.[10] In December the French and British went over Pershing's head to President Wilson to force acceptance of a merger of American forces on the regimental and company levels, so as to strengthen Allied forces. Pershing complained to Washington about the lack of frankness on the part of the French and told Clemenceau bluntly that such questions should be worked out on a friendly basis between Pétain and himself; for his part, he was determined to keep his divisions intact and to complete their training, with "our own Army under our own flag," as he later put it. He told Pétain that each people had its own way of fighting. The Frenchman disagreed: You fight to win, he said, and so you adapt your tactics to the enemy's way of fighting.[11]

And then, when Pershing discovered that Pétain had criticized the nature of American troop training, and Munitions Minister Louis Loucheur complained about rising prices caused by American purchases, Pershing decided to have it out with the French commander. He also expressed regret that Pétain had revealed plans for the first American offensive, the attack on the Saint-Mihiel salient, to an American visitor (Colonel Edward M. House); Pétain promised that it would not happen again. Privately Pershing decided that the complaints had really been efforts to measure the extent of his powers.[12]

Between the British and the French the outstanding difference concerned Marshal Haig's conviction that Pétain was dragging his feet, not providing the offensives that would have relieved his forces,[13] and Pétain's that the British could ease the situation of the French by sending troops to relieve them. It was only at the end of December 1917 that the two commanders in chief came to an agreement on an extension of the British front.[14] Before that happened, however, Pétain sailed across the channel with Painlevé on a destroyer for talks with the British. (Pétain having expressed the wish to meet the three most beautiful women in London, a selection of them was invited to tea. Serrigny, who records these details, remembered that the most beautiful of all was the Duchess of Sutherland.)[15]

Back in Paris, Pétain was seeing Eugénie. One of their meeting places was an apartment he had taken at 8, Square Latour-Maubourg, a dead-end street off the Rue de Grenelle a few minutes' walk from military headquarters in the Hôtel des Invalides. This would be his Paris residence henceforth, until confiscation by the liberation government at the end of the Second World War. For the year 1917, sixty-four letters from Philippe to Eugénie have survived, and they betray the same ardor and impatience: letters of love and war.[16] But one can also read letters from many other female friends; some evoke the recent past, some the present. This, from a "passing girl friend," as she signs herself: "I must tell you that even if I never see you again as you were, you will remain for me a living emotion augmented with much pride." The nature of their relationship is clear from another line in the same letter: "You have a terrible power over willpower."[17]

Another correspondent wrote Pétain that she heard he was seeking a "war godmother." "Who I am from the worldly point of view you will discover, General, if you deign to reply." He jumped at the bait, on April 21, 1917 (it was when the consequences of Nivelle's failure at the Chemin des Dames were becoming known in all their horror): "To correspond with a woman of wit tempts me a great deal, but you will understand, I hope, that it is impossible for me to write to an anonymous person; you would be the first to criticize me for frivolity." So she gave him her name, confident "in your discretion as a gentleman"; she turned out, "from the worldly point of view," to be a countess.[18]

There was also Henriette. "If you want to be temperamental," she reproached him in October 1917, "why did you give me those kisses . . . ?"[19] And Serrigny tells us that during a moment of quiet on the eastern front, Pétain went up to Belgium to meet the king and found himself in private conversation with the queen, "deliciously blond." The general in chief seemed shy at lunch but at last found his voice, and began to flirt with her as if she had been another of his camp followers.[20]

* * *

The final months of 1917 were taken up with planning for the following year. On October 31 an "Instruction on the Offensive Action of Large Units" was issued, once again calling for "attacks for precise and limited objectives," although making it clear that these attacks would be frequent and far-ranging, "to the point of provoking the breaking up of enemy defenses." Airpower, mastery of the skies, was indispensable from the beginning of the battle to the end.[21] Alsace was earmarked for a major offensive in 1918, to break through the German front and reach the Rhine River.

Meanwhile, as Pétain reported to the War Committee in November, the situation required "waiting tactics." Pending the arrival of the Americans in strength, and taking account of the collapse of the Russian war effort, the Allied armies simply had to hold on.[22] Pétain defended this essentially passive position in a stormy session of the War Committee on December 12. "I should like to say that if you believe that another method is better than mine, I am ready to stand aside, and to return quietly to the ranks." Clemenceau came to Pétain's defense now, and so did Poincaré: "General Pétain's demonstration is such that discussion no longer seems possible."[23]

The Pétain doctrine was explained in controversial directive number four on December 22. It called for breaking enemy attacks on the first line, stopping them on the second. Because it allowed for—even called for—conceding terrain to the attackers, it was considered defeatist.[24]

Now the clash of doctrines, and of wills, between Pétain and Foch was to become sharper. "Be patient, be obstinate," Pétain told his armies in an order of the day on January 1, 1918.[25] On that same day Foch made it clear that he did not agree that the Allies had to wait until they were stronger before taking the offensive. Receiving a copy of Foch's message from Clemenceau, Pétain held firm: "The battle of 1918 will be defensive on the Franco-British side not by the obstinate will of the High Command, but through the necessity of the situation."[26] Pétain had another adversary, although a more benign one, in Premier Georges Clemenceau, Clemenceau who was quicker than Foch to recognize the merits of Pétain's case. In the politician's view preparations were important, and so were second lines, but it was time to move ahead all the same.[27] On January 24, 1918, at

Compiègne headquarters, where Foch joined the Allied commanders (Pétain, Haig, Pershing) in an attempt to improve coordination, Pétain was true to form. Lacking troop strength, he argued, the Allies simply had to remain on the defensive. Prudence was the watchword. And Haig agreed.[28] But, countered Foch, wasn't the best way to stop an enemy attack to launch one's own powerful offensive?[29] When Pershing described the material difficulties he was encountering in getting his army ready to fight in France, and Foch replied that this information had not been brought to his attention, Pétain pointed out that one didn't wait until one's attention was drawn to things like that; one looked around for oneself.[30]

The Supreme War Council of the Allies, which met in Versailles from January 30 to February 2, decided that Foch would henceforth be chairman of its executive committee. "To some extent it makes Foch a 'Generalissimo,' " Haig told his private diary. (And soon enough he was going to be called that.)[31] "All the commanding generals . . . seek to replace Pétain," Deputy Abel Ferry noted in his own private diary. "Pétain bothers them more than the Boche."[32] Pétain told Poincaré that he saw hope only in the rapid buildup of American troop strength, with the merger of the Americans into the French army. He promised that if the Germans did not attack in 1918 he would carry out a limited offensive of the Malmaison kind every two months, but nothing more than that. After this meeting Poincaré noted: "All that is somber. Pétain is worn out by flu. I recognize the responsibility of his somewhat pessimistic character, but illness has been added to that."[33]

On March 21, 1918, the Germans attacked along a front extending fifty miles, throwing two hundred divisions into the battle. The main thrust was in the north, against the British and Arras; a second attack aimed at the Somme valley farther south. In the north the Germans faced forty British divisions and rapidly overran their lines. The following punishing days were to test both British and French defense tactics, above all their coordination. Depending on who did the judging, the outcome was seen either as an indictment of Pétain or a vindication. But when the smoke cleared, Foch was indeed the generalissimo.[34]

The burden of the grief against Pétain was that he had not

provided immediate and sufficient support to the hard-pressed British ally. In its most extreme form, the accusation had it that Pétain accepted the possibility that the British and French armies would be separated by the enemy thrust.[35] When Pétain advised Fayolle, on March 24, to get his group of reserve armies in contact with the rest of the French forces as a first priority, and "then, if possible, conserve the liaison with British forces," was he compromising in advance the likelihood of that vital liaison?[36]

We have contemporary evidence of Pétain's state of mind during the crucial hours of the battle. According to Haig's diary, Pétain met the British commander on March 23, promised all possible support and to "do his utmost to keep the two Armies in touch." But Pétain also indicated his concern that the Germans were about to attack him in Champagne. Next day Pétain came to see Haig at his castle in Dury, near Amiens. "Pétain struck me as very much upset, almost unbalanced and most anxious," Haig recorded. The Frenchman repeated his fears about Champagne, for "he did not believe that the main German blow had yet been delivered." If Pétain promised that Fayolle was receiving all available troops to keep contact with the British, he also disclosed that he had ordered Fayolle, should the German advance continue, to fall back in order to cover Paris. Haig felt that this would allow the Germans to drive a wedge between French and British armies, to abandon the British right flank. Pétain agreed that this was likely and added that "it is the only thing possible, if the enemy compelled the Allies to fall back still further." Yet in Haig's opinion the existence of his army depended on contact with the French.

So it was a seriously perturbed Douglas Haig who cabled London that night to urge a Franco-British meeting at cabinet level, "in order to arrange that General Foch or some other determined general who would fight, should be given supreme control of the operations in France."[37] Meanwhile, Pétain was seeing Clemenceau, who was himself upset by the general's "exaggerated pessimism," as he reported to Raymond Poincaré the next day. "Imagine," Clemenceau told his president, "that he told me that if we are beaten we would owe it to the British."[38]

In response to Haig's desperate call, Henry Wilson, chief of the Imperial General Staff, crossed the channel the next morn-

ing (March 25) to meet Haig at Abbeville. That same afternoon
Lord Milner, representing British Prime Minister David Lloyd
George, traveled up to Compiègne with Poincaré, Clemenceau,
and Foch, to see Pétain. Once more the prudent—or (in Milner's
description) pessimistic—Pétain clashed with Foch. Foch wanted
more men, and faster, to save the British front and the Franco-
British link-up, even if it meant taking risks elsewhere. Poincaré
and Clemenceau concurred. It was decided to meet again the next
day in the presence of Haig and Wilson. They, at Abbeville, had
already agreed that Foch should become Allied commander in
chief.[39]

The fateful March 26 meeting was held in the auditorium of
the town hall of Doullens, a small town between Amiens and Arras, and this time everybody was there. While the French waited
for their British colleagues Pétain complained that the British were
not pulling their weight, not doing all they could to maintain
contact with his forces.[40] Meanwhile, Clemenceau was confiding
to Poincaré that Pétain envisaged a French retreat toward the
south while the British withdrew north; Foch put in that he opposed such a retreat. Clemenceau took Poincaré aside to say:
"Pétain is irritating with his pessimism. Imagine that he said
something to me I shouldn't like to tell anyone besides yourself.
He said, 'The Germans will beat the English hands down, and
then they'll beat us.' " Poincaré noted this in his journal and also
noted that Louis Loucheur heard Pétain say that they should begin peace negotiations.[41]

Inside the Doullens town hall, the British and French delegates listened as the commanders described the military situation. Pétain assured the British that he was sending them all the
men he could and asked them to do as much; Haig said there
simply were no more British soldiers to draw upon. Foch asked
for more energy. There was a moment of hesitation. Then Clemenceau led Lord Milner away from the table: "We've got to finish. What do you suggest?" Milner was ready with his suggestion,
which by that time was nearly everyone's solution, but Clemenceau wanted it to come from the British. So Milner said that Foch
should be put in charge of both armies. Clemenceau called Pétain aside to tell him what Milner had proposed. "Quite nobly,"
in Henri Mordacq's account, Pétain replied that he would accept

whatever was decided in the interest of France and of her allies.[42] The British were not quite prepared for a united command; instead, Foch was given responsibility for "coordinating the action of the Allied armies," working through the two generals in chief; it was only at the Beauvais conference a week later that the British, the French, and the Americans agreed to give Foch "the strategic command of military operations."[43] "Foch seemed sound and sensible but Pétain had a terrible look," Haig confided to his diary. "He had the appearance of a Commander who was in a funk and has lost his nerve." A couple of days later Haig reported being told by Clemenceau that "Pétain is a very nervous man and sometimes may not carry out all he has promised." Haig commented to his diary: "Personally, I have found Pétain anxious to help and straightforward, but in the present operations he has been slow to decide and slower still in acting. At times his nerve seems to have gone, and he imagines that he is to be attacked in force. . . ."[44]

VIII
VICTORY

Was Pétain pleased to be relieved of the double responsibility of his own and the British army? This is what a military historian not considered favorable to him later insisted.[1] In any event, he now ordered his reserve group to cover both Amiens and Paris,[2] which the group's commander considered "impossible."[3] And Pétain seems to have focused his resentment on the British rather than on Foch. "As if personalities mattered at this moment," he said to Henry Bordeaux. "The important thing is to have a single chief." How far Pétain had fallen is suggested in an incident observed by Bordeaux. When the army historian walked in to see the general in chief on April 6, Pétain told him he could not invite him to lunch because Clemenceau was coming to see Foch, and Pétain expected to be asked to join them. But a little later he informed Bordeaux, "Well, I wasn't invited. So I have lunch with you."[4]

There was indeed little warmth in the relationship between Pétain and Foch. Foch told Poincaré that his relationship with Pétain was good, for as an executor of orders "Pétain is perfect," but he felt that "he backs away from responsibility and cannot be the top commander." Soon Clemenceau was agreeing that "Pétain is better in the second rank than the first."[5]

This new division of responsibilities, established at Beauvais on April 3—Foch for overall strategy; Pétain, Haig, and Pershing for the tactics of their own armies[6]—was not always easy to grasp, even for the high command.[7] To Pétain's distress, Foch, who on May 2 became commander in chief of Allied armies in France at the conclusion of an interallied Supreme War Council session at Abbeville, flatly opposed the tactic of second lines of defense set forth in Pétain's directive number four, telling army commanders that contact must be made at the front, and that any retreat served the enemy.[8]

Fayolle summed up the dilemma: "Pétain exaggerates the power of the Boche, Foch doesn't appreciate it sufficiently. They are both right and they are both wrong. They should be combined to make a single man, a complete chief."[9] Pétain himself took it out on Napoleon. "He denigrates him systematically," noted Bordeaux, dinner guest with Louis Madelin at Pétain's villa in the woods outside Chantilly. "One imagines that in attacking the Emperor he is thinking of all those who make oversized plans."[10]

The standoff continued: Foch arguing for renewed attacks, Pétain warning of their dangers, until the Germans began to move again, this time in the sensitive Chemin des Dames sector, and they broke through, to the Aisne and then the Marne River, closer than ever to Paris, leaving 92,000 dead or missing on the French side.[11] The results were sufficiently grave to create an uproar in Parliament, but Clemenceau managed to get the deputies to applaud Foch and Pétain both. "Do you think it possible," he shouted at the critics, "to wage a war in which one never retreats?"[12] "I know they want my head in Paris," Pétain told Clemenceau's aide Henri Mordacq. "Let them take it . . . Let them give me command of an army corps. . . ."[13] What is certain is that Pétain not only survived the German breakthrough of May 1918, his position was eventually reinforced by it. Between March 21 and July 17 the Germans launched five offensives, three of them against French lines. Pétain was instrumental in containing them, and this kept his armies intact until it was time for the Allies to move forward in their final offensive.[14]

Receiving the president at his Chantilly headquarters on June 7, Pétain expressed a measure of optimism. He had been concerned for the Flemish front, but he felt better with five American divisions at his disposal. He was sure that the French could hold before Paris.[15] Yet on June 9 the Germans were to test the French once again, this time on the Matz River just north of Compiègne. General Mangin stopped them; Pétain's stock seems to have fallen lower than ever. "Pétain is heart-breaking in his lack of confidence," Fayolle noted. "And so we live from day to day more or less submitted to the will of the enemy."[16] On June 20, Poincaré found Clemenceau "very harsh" concerning Pétain's behavior during the German Aisne offensive the previous month. "Grave errors have been committed," said Clemenceau, "and I even think that Pétain's personal responsibility is engaged."[17] At a meeting of the War Committee on June 26 it was agreed that Foch should be given Pétain's general staff, and that Pétain obey Foch without the right of appeal to his government, which the other Allied commanders had been accorded by the Beauvais agreement.[18] "It's possible that in a little while they won't be needing me any more," Pétain broke the news to Eugénie Dehérain in a letter dated June 28, "because I'm not ready to swallow all the blame."[19]

There was a month's respite, utilized on the French side to thrash out Pétain-Foch differences on the positioning of reserves, a fight won by Pétain.[20] All this against a growing climate of opinion that the French had done enough, that it was time for the Americans to do some of the fighting.[21] But the Germans were readying themselves for still another attack; the French expected it and began preparations for a counterattack. Foch, with Pétain's approval, planned to launch it on July 18 "whatever happens."[22]

The Germans attacked on July 15, massively, along the Champagne front. Even partisans of Foch realized that it was Pétain's defense in depth—directive number four—which stopped them.[23] But once more Pétain made trouble for himself, stepping in to suspend preparations for the counteroffensive to be led by his old nemesis Mangin, on the grounds that it was more important to hold in reserve the forces Mangin would have to draw upon in case of difficulty. "There cannot be any question of slowing down and even less of stopping the Mangin preparations," Foch replied, in a telephoned order, as soon as he heard what Pétain had done.[24] And so on July 18 the French counter-offensive got under way. In a vignette of that moment—hostile to Pétain—he is seen telling Mangin, at 3:00 P.M. on the first day of the French advance, that he had no more reserves to give him. "You must stop. Be happy with the great success already obtained." Mangin replied that they couldn't call a halt to an attack just when it seemed as if it would produce decisive results. Pétain told him that he must first think about enemy advances elsewhere (south of the Marne). After Pétain's departure Mangin issued the order: "The attack will resume tomorrow." And informed Foch of what had occurred.[25] On July 24, Foch called a meeting at his headquarters at Bombon in the Seine et Marne district and asked his chief of staff Maxime Weygand to read aloud his memorandum to the assembled Allied commanders: Pétain, Haig, and Pershing. "The moment has come to shed the general defensive attitude imposed on us until now by numerical inferiority," Foch's paper declared, "and to move to the offensive."[26] Haig took the floor to say that his army had hardly recovered from the spring offensives, Pétain to add that the French were exhausted, Pershing to inform the group that the Americans were anxious to begin fighting but were not yet fully trained. Pétain followed up with a written reply suggesting that they limit the effort to two operations, for these alone would probably exhaust French resources for the year 1918.[27]

One of the rare descriptions of Pétain during that decisive summer comes from Jean de Pierrefeu, who called on him in July in the comfortable villa he then occupied on spacious grounds overlooking a pond outside the town of Provins. Pétain rose each day at seven to inspect his vegetable garden (commenting that on retirement he planned to become a farmer and would buy a farm with a view). He went to bed at midnight, often reading until two. During long evening talks with his aides he showed himself to be more of a philosopher than the pragmatic officers to whom Pierrefeu was accustomed; his philosophy was fatalistic. Pierrefeu evokes the stoic philosophy of equanimity of Marcus Aurelius: belief in human will and effort, but only if they are exercised in the direction of events that cannot be resisted. Pétain did not believe in genius, unless this meant keen intelligence, good sense. In politics he took the long view. Thus he disagreed with the plan to dismantle the Austrian empire, feeling that it alone was capable of maintaining unity and order among "naturally hostile races which, delivered to themselves, would never stop squabbling and would compromise peace in Europe." France needed a friend in the east; since it could not be Russia for a long time to come, he saw Austria and Britain as allies, and a counterweight to Germany.[28]

From now on it is Foch's war: the summer campaign, and the decision to maintain the initiative from then until final victory. This is the way it was seen in the field, notably by Fayolle, who at the end of August 1918 observed: "At bottom, it is certain that if Pétain had been alone, we should not have attacked. We owe it all to Foch. It's not that he organized this series of victories, but he gave the order to fight. . . . Pétain furnished the means, from an eye-dropper actually, and I put them to use."[29]

The first engagement of the final round was British: an attack north of Amiens. Soon Pétain's armies were engaged, and then came the Americans, their task to reduce the Saint-Mihiel salient. The success of Pershing's troops in their first major operation told the Germans that the Americans were ready (there were half a million men in the American First Army, although 70,000 of them were French). From then on the Americans participated with the French on a wider front: Between September 26 and the armistice, 22 American and 4 French divisions on a front extending from Verdun to the Argonne forest engaged and defeated 47 different German divisions representing 25 percent of German strength on the French front; the 1st Army suffered 117,000 killed and wounded. This combined effort became possible only when the Allies had come to terms with their realities, Pétain attributing American failures to Pershing's inexperience and seeking in vain to effect some form of fusion between the untried Americans and the experienced French; he was joined in this uphill struggle by Foch and by Clemenceau, who blamed Pershing's "invincible obstinacy" for the inability of the Allies to make maximum use of "these fine troops."[30]

In August, Foch received his promotion to marshal, and Pétain received the Military Medal, a small gold and silver decoration given only to soldiers and noncommissioned officers on one hand, and to generals who already possessed the highest rank in the Legion of Honor. "Has acquired the imperishable right to national recognition by blocking the German thrust and throwing it back victoriously," read the decree that accompanied Pétain's medal.[31] Soon after that Henry Bordeaux came to see Pétain, "younger than ever, still of fair complexion, although well fleshed out and even a bit heavier," he noted. And Bordeaux got an earful: Poincaré in handing Foch his marshal's stick had referred to Foch's role in coming to the defense of the British in March. "That was my doing," objected Pétain, "mine alone." And on the July 18 offensive: "I was the one who had the idea."[32]

Even now, with the Allied steamroller well under way, Pétain remained a dissident. He worried that poor planning was exposing salients to an unnecessary degree. On September 25, Foch warned him not to set limits to the offensive, for "we must develop the striking power of the Allied armies first of all." Once more it was Foch's impetus against Pétain's prudence.[33] But another witness heard Pétain praise Foch's energy. "I couldn't encourage him enough to push the offensive to the limit," Pierrefeu quotes him following one of their evening discussions. "It's the final rush, and we mustn't give the enemy time to catch his breath, nor to concentrate." Pétain said he was doing all he could to keep sufficient men and matériel in the front lines. "Right now I'm improvising every day . . . ; my army is dismembered but it's moving forward. . . ."[34]

In October, Franco-American differences came to a head. Because it was clear that Pershing would not take orders from Pétain, invoking his status as commander in chief of an army of his own, Pétain suggested to Clemenceau that the American commander be placed directly under Foch, and this was done.[35]

There was another portentous meeting in October. On the twenty-fifth, in Senlis, the Allied commanders met at Foch's headquarters to hear a draft of armistice terms prepared by Foch with the help of Pétain and the War Ministry. Haig spoke first, agreed that the return of Alsace-Lorraine was paramount, but expressed the fear that the terms were too harsh and might incite the Germans to pursue the war. Pétain suggested setting up depots in which the Germans would be required to leave their arms and munitions, the enemy retreat to be followed at a day's march by the Allies so that the armistice would be signed on enemy territory. Pershing, who had asked to speak after Pétain, said that he agreed with him entirely.[36] A fortnight later, thinking that the time was ripe, General Mordacq reminded Clemenceau of what he had recently said when Pétain had accepted Pershing's subordination to Foch with good grace: "Another general who we must make a marshal without delay." Clemenceau now smiled and agreed that the time had come but suggested that they wait until the Germans had officially requested an armistice. That very night the German telegram arrived.[37]

But wasn't it too early to accept a German surrender? Pétain seems to have felt so. He had wished to pursue the offensive so that France would be in the strongest possible position before the cease-fire.[38] Twenty-one years later Pétain revealed to a journalist that when he learned on the morning of November 9 that Foch and Weygand were drafting an armistice, he rushed to their headquarters to attempt to convince Foch of "the immense difference between a war terminated on present positions by mutual agreement, and a clear French victory on German soil." As Pétain then recalled it, Foch "seemed troubled" but replied that he could not allow more French soldiers to die if the armistice was going to give them what they demanded. Pétain: "We have to think not of the soldiers who might fall in our final offensive, but of the million and a half who have already fallen and who have a right to the peace appropriate to their sacrifice." He asked for authorization to speak directly to Clemenceau. Foch: "I'm sorry for you, but you'll have to forget about your offensive." Pétain remembered that for the first time in his life as a soldier "I broke down and cried in front of my superior." Foch: "You can't say that I'm not an attacker and that I prefer easy solutions, but this time I've given my word."[39]

What independent evidence do we have of Pétain's feelings (and of their expression) in the days preceding the signing of the armistice? We know that he did see Clemenceau, at the latter's request, on November 9.[40] But neither Clemenceau nor his faithful aide Mordacq, nor indeed anyone else, recorded Pétain's protest.[41] There is certainly ample evidence of Pétain's later expressions of regret. "The armistice . . . spared the proud German army a humiliating disaster. . . ." was the way he put it in his speech on Foch at the French Academy in 1931.[42] Still later, he was to assure intimates that "the British had begun to betray us in August 1918 so that we would not have the left bank of the Rhine . . . On the night of the armistice I cried!"[43]

According to Émile Laure, recalling the atmosphere at their headquarters on the evening of November 10, Pétain's men felt both joy and regrets. "I do think that joy predominated." And what of the evidence from Pétain himself? The well-known victory statement signed in Pétain's hand carried his penned postscript: "Closed because of Victory."[44] Still more intimate evidence is the letter to "My loved one," Eugénie Dehérain, dated November 11 and beginning, "My first thought this morning, on learning of the signing of the armistice, was for you. I should have liked you to be here to kiss you and show my happiness." Not a word here of dissent or regret, and yet in the past Pétain had allowed himself to say what he really thought in these letters.[45]

It is even possible to recapture the atmosphere of that moment from the memoirs of a man who knew Pétain well, for Colonel Émile Herbillon was his liaison with the government. He paints a picture that leaves no room for anger, regret, tears. "Lunch was quite merry at General Pétain's table today," he notes on November 10; Pétain even autographed his menu as a souvenir. Just then the telephone rings; it is Foch, inviting Pétain to Rethondes; Pétain asks Herbillon to accompany him. After a private meeting between Foch and Pétain, Foch makes a triumphant statement to Herbillon: no sign of strain on his side either.[46] It is reasonable to conclude from available evidence that joy and relief predominated in those heady November days, regret, it would seem, was more latent than apparent.

"A little patience, my darling," the victorious general in chief wrote to his Eugénie, "my task is coming to an end." The date is November 17, 1918. "The day isn't far off when I shall at last be able to spend more time with you, when we shall be able to join our two solitudes."[47] But that day had not come. First there had to be the ceremonies, the decorating of heroes. Clemenceau lost no time in drawing up the promised decree appointing Pétain

marshal of France. The premier sent his private secretary to inform Foch; as Mordacq recalled it, Foch told him: "It's not in a
week or a fortnight that you should make the appointment, but
right away. He must have his marshal's stick in hand when he
marches the French army into Alsace-Lorraine. . . ."[48]

On November 19, armed with the knowledge that he was about
to join Joffre and Foch in the rare and exalted dignity of marshal, Pétain led the triumphal march of the French into Metz. A
reporter for *L'Illustration* was present: "Cannons thunder in the
distance. Soon the shouts of the crowd, rolling like a sea swell,
announce the arrival of the troops. Here they are: the squadron
of escort cavalry, then, on a white horse, General—no Marshal
Pétain (because the news had begun to spread). . . ." Pétain wore
his field uniform without visible decoration, a regulation blue
overcoat. "In this sober dress," the reporter went on, "the face,
grave and strained by emotion, is handsome, of a profound
beauty." And the crowd cheered.[49]

Now that the essential things were done, the new marshal was
able to inform Eugénie that he would soon be in Paris, on November 28. He would have to dine at the presidential palace, the
Elysée, with Poincaré, but would join her right after that in their
railroad-station hotel. "And then we shall love each other as you
desire to be loved."[50]

But soon he was back in Metz. It was in the reconquered Lorraine province that Poincaré made the ceremonial presentation
of his marshal's stick on December 8.[51] Henry Bordeaux caught
up with him there. Pétain told him that it had been suggested
that he accept election as a senator, but that he did not want to
join a party, that he could only be "an arbiter of divided parties."
He wished to speed up the demobilization, while holding on
to a standing army, well paid, for the occupation of enemy
territory.[52]

IX
COMMANDER IN PEACETIME

Celebrity: It meant escorting visiting royalty, the kings of Spain, of Greece, of Denmark, the Shah of Persia, to the tortured battlefields of Verdun where there had been 362,000 French killed and wounded in eleven months of struggle, and 336,000 German killed and wounded.[1] It meant a return as a local hero to Saint-Omer, the town of his schooldays and his last peacetime garrison, to cries of "Long live the Marshal!" There he paraded on familiar streets and, of course, called at his old Collège Saint-Bertin, throwing himself into the arms of a former teacher, listening to the school's superior tell a banquet audience: "This is where he grew up. . . . It is in this very chapel, where he got down on his knees today, that he used to pray." And the superior evoked what he said had been the young man's pledge, after the defeat of 1871: "One day I shall be a chief, and I shall try to reconquer our dear lost provinces to render them to our country."[2]

Celebrity also meant receiving a telegram, in February 1919, from a New York impresario: "Will give you forty thousand dollars to deliver twenty lectures United States in April or May cable answer." There is no record of his reply, but the copy of the telegram he kept among his personal papers bears the notation: "40,000 dollars = one million [francs]."[3]

On July 14, 1919, Bastille Day, "France celebrated the end of all war," or so they then thought.[4] Starting on the previous evening eight million Frenchmen and women camped along the parade route in Paris, and next day all the armies, French and allied, marched, and all their bands played. Astride a white horse Pétain led the French contingent, and he was showered with flowers as he rode through the streets.[5]

We are told, and by the lady herself, that as he trotted along the Rue Royale, Pétain turned his horse to the side, to bow beneath the window of a singer with whom he was flirting. She was Germaine Lubin, then twenty-nine and already famous; they had met when she sang for the troops and sat at his right hand at dinner; she was to be his "war godmother" (another one), and he also asked—although she was married—that she become his companion. But she was unwilling to betray her husband. They continued to see each other, and to write to each other, and she had told him at which window she would be watching the July 14 parade.[6]

Even as he was attempting to seduce Germaine Lubin, the marshal was carrying on his affair—one hesitates to say courtship—with Eugénie. (She saved fifty-two letters from him that year, indicating how often duty continued to keep them apart in 1919.) "No matter how much I think about it, I come to the conclusion that I love you deeply, that to leave you would mean the renewal of great unhappiness, but that despite all my efforts, the past continues to hurt," he wrote her on February 19, 1919. He even wondered if it was not precisely their independence of one another that made their reunions so marvelous. There is a remarkable letter dated February 25 in which he writes: "Enthusiastic little woman, you criticize me for lacking drive . . . and this because I never utilize more energy than necessary to overcome obstacles . . . and I overcome them." He explained further: "It's because I made precise calculations, never tried anything requiring more means than I disposed of, because I had a precise idea of realities and possibilities, and a clear appreciation of what I was up against . . . that I achieved some successes in recent years."[7]

Soon they were talking about the purchase of his dream house in southern France. With the help of friends he had found the house, with ample grounds and vineyards and a sweeping view of the Mediterranean Sea. On September 1, 1919, he wrote Eugénie: "I never stop thinking of you, of the house in Villeneuve-Loubet, of the happiness we shall have in being there together."[8]

When in January 1920 the government decided that Pétain, and not Foch, was to become vice-chairman of the Supreme War Council, automatically making him general in chief in time of war, it was in effect giving him control of the French army. And then in February 1922 a second title was added to the first one: inspector general. Pétain kept both jobs throughout the 1920s decade, so that he was responsible for every aspect of war preparedness and defense.[9] During the eleven years of his tenure, until Maxime Weygand replaced him in 1931, he enjoyed both the responsibility and (thanks to rank and reputation) the authority to define and carry out a program of defense, as well as to build up French forces to face any future enemy. Pétain's official biographer took pride in his eminence;[10] later, when the question of blame for France's defeat in 1940 was at the top of the agenda, Pétain's critics were to remind his defenders of his uncontested leadership in the between-the-wars years.

The marshal argued for a more orderly, more gradual demobilization of the wartime army than public opinion was prepared to accept. Instead, the very first question that he and his staff had to deal with was the demand for reduction in the duration of compulsory military service. They were able to hold it to two years until April 1923, when Parliament reduced it to eighteen months (and without the compensations that had been asked for, such as a regular army of a hundred thousand men). In 1924 the military establishment received another jolt with the coming to power of a coalition of Radicals and Socialists headed by Edouard Herriot, pledged to reduce military service to one year.[11]

The Supreme War Council met regularly. The minutes of its secret sessions are now open and can be followed from the very first meeting on January 31, 1920, at which President Poincaré explained why it was felt to be urgent to revive the council. With France victorious and the peace treaty ratified, the government needed the advice of its experts to provide a new defense plan conforming to necessities but also to a reduced budget. This first session brought together the premier, the ministers of war and the navy, Marshals Joffre and Foch as well as Pétain. In subsequent meetings Pétain showed his preoccupation with the next war. He had begun to conceive the need for a line of defense along France's frontier with Germany.[12] In a note on territorial defense he spelled out a system of "battle fields" along an uninterrupted defense line, but some council members offered a countersuggestion: fortified areas separated by intervals. To resolve the conflict a committee was set up to study the matter, and in 1925 the government chose Pétain's "wall of France." But it also chose to reduce compulsory military service, and this preoccupation with cutting budgets made it necessary to return to the fortification scheme, which could be achieved faster and with less money.

So a new Commission of Frontier Defense was established, and it brought in a recommendation for the development of three fortified regions, at Metz, north Alsace, and Belfort; even though the result would be a discontinuous defense line, Pétain accepted it in the hope that a linkage would come at a later stage.[13] He suggested a system of German-style blockhouses, for why spend money for more ambitious fortifications likely to become obsolete in ten or twenty years? And "whatever happens, we'll enter Belgium to find a battlefield."[14]

In the summer of 1927 Pétain toured the eastern front, after which he drew up a plan for a line of forts, one every six or seven miles, connected by underground passages. These works were to be less visible, therefore less exposed to enemy action, than traditional forts. There would be emplacements for artillery, shelters for personnel and for infantrymen, protected barracks. When completed, the defense line would be known as the Maginot Line, in honor of the war minister (André Maginot) who pushed it through Parliament. This Maginot Line provided for protection of the frontier with Germany to the east—but not of the northern frontier with Belgium.[15]

*   *   *

When he took over his new responsibilities in 1920, the marshal was sixty-four years old. "We are all getting old," he wrote his nephew Paul Pomart. "We frequent death every day. This thought is salutary and prevents us from giving events more importance than they deserve." And to what other honors could he attain? "Paris doesn't interest me any more. Being famous disturbs me. . . . I look forward to retirement, to being forgotten by my contemporaries." But this same letter of January 14, 1920, makes it clear that his wish would not be fulfilled right away. "When one is in gear one has to carry on until the finish. . . ."[16]

This man on the eve of retirement and withdrawal was about to marry. Marriage and retirement, to the dream house in Villeneuve-Loubet, went together. In a letter of April 12, 1920, he informed Eugénie that he was "launching the order to buy" the house known as the Ermitage that very day.[17] But the correspondence also shows him hesitating about his marriage, and almost to the last moment. "Believe me when I say that the day I can be sure that I would no longer hurt you, that I can make you happy, I'll be the first to demand that we join our lives" (July 20).[18] "Every night before sleeping I walk into your room to tell you good night and kiss you in my thoughts," he wrote her on August 13, for apparently she has "her" room in his Square de Latour-Maubourg apartment now. "Despite occasional clashes, I do believe that we shall be happy together. But I'd like to go away for a while and live with you at the Ermitage, which I always imagine to be the most delicious place in the world."[19]

The marriage took place on September 14, 1920, at the town hall of Paris' VIIth district; Marshal Fayolle was the groom's witness. The bride's name was given as Alphonsine Berthe Eugénie Hardon, born in Corquetaine (in the nearby Seine et Marne district) on October 5, 1877, divorced from François Dehérain on March 5, 1914.[20] The sober wedding party went from the official ceremony to lunch at the Café de Paris, then a fashionable restaurant on the Avenue de l'Opéra.[21]

Was it a shotgun wedding? Enemies of Eugénie Pétain—and she was to make many—were prepared to say so. Thus Louis-Dominique Girard, an aide to Pétain in Vichy before marrying the daughter of his great-niece, tells us that in June 1920 Pétain met his old love from Besançon garrison days, Marie-Louise Regad, now a widow, and she proposed that they forget the past and marry. For his part, the marshal had fulfilled the pledge that wedded him exclusively to military life, so he could accept. But he had to warn Marie-Louise that another woman was pursuing him. He promised to ask Eugénie for his freedom. The story has it that when he did, Eugénie took a revolver out of a desk drawer and pointed it at him: "It will be me or I'll shoot you!" He realized what a scandal it would be if the front pages headlined: "Marshal Pétain shot down by his mistress." In biographer Girard's words, Pétain then "gave up his only love to fall into the clutches of the woman who had been torturing him morally for 19 years." But he is also said to have renewed his renunciation of physical love, so as to remain "mystically attached" to Marie-Louise and "pledged to the service of France."[22]

This story was, of course, contested by Madame Pétain's descendants and friends. Certainly the correspondence in his own hand attests to the physical aspect of his relations with Eugénie, and there is no corresponding evidence of a passion for Marie-Louise. (On the contrary, extant letters suggest that their reunion during the First World War was somewhat less than momentous.) But it was certainly true that Pétain experienced difficulties in presenting his marriage to a divorcée to close friends and family. If the bridegroom received hearty congratulations from some relatives, the reaction from sister Sara, the sister to whom he felt closest, was cool. "I don't know how to speak to you of your companion," she wrote Philippe in November 1920. "I don't know anything about her not even her name." Her letters in the following years don't mention Eugénie at all, not even in salutations.[23]

He sought to break the news gently to those he knew as devout Catholics. One of them replied, "I don't know Madame Hardon; since you have chosen her I automatically give her all the right qualities."[24] But another friend wrote on September 16, two days after the wedding, to break off their friendship and to offer condolences. The ex-friend explained that he disapproved of Eugénie too much to be able to meet her now, although if by chance he encountered the victor of Verdun he would talk to *him*. Eugénie was a "blemished woman," who had already cheated on Pétain and would do it again; their marriage proved that those who felt that "you are more the slave of your flesh than of your duty" were right. "It is very sad for your true friends, who would have been so happy to see you establish an honorable household, to be obliged to recognize that you didn't have the energy to rid yourself a second time and irrevocably of a heavy chain both rusty and inopportune," the ex-friend went on, concluding: "And what will be the fate of the poor women whom you gulled and fooled until the last possible moment!"[25]

"Love at first sight," he had written to Alphonse Guide on September 12, announcing his marriage and a honeymoon voyage to the Riviera. The Pétains were to board a train on the evening of their wedding day for Antibes, staying there at a secluded seaside hotel. "The arrival at Antibes will coincide with the beginning of a rest which I'm beginning to need badly. I'm delighted to be settling down at last."[26]

The point, of course, was to be close to his beloved Ermitage. He had acquired the property, with Guide serving as his proxy, in February 1920. The price was 130,000 francs (some 260,000 of today's francs), for which he acquired a little over ten acres of land, with a two-story house, stable, barn, a small house for a farmer, a pigsty; on the same day he acquired two contiguous pieces of land totaling 4,200 square yards for another 11,000 of today's francs (from two other owners), and some 2,160 square yards of ground from still another owner for some 6,000 present-day francs.[27] It didn't hurt that the new owner was Marshal Pétain, as letters from his notary make clear. Neighbors sold their land readily to help him round out his estate. Another neighbor was happy to give up a right of passage; a gardener donated plants.[28]

"The small estate he owns is . . . not very significant and was furnished very simply if one examines how much was spent on it," the certified accountant who audited Pétain's fortune for the High Court in 1945 attested, noting that in the between-the-wars years Pétain "led the very modest existence of a general without a private fortune," living entirely on his marshal's pay, which rose over the years from 150,000 to 300,000 francs annually.[29] Much later, when Paul Pomart's daughter came to see him at the Ermitage, Pétain wrote his nephew: "I think that she expected to find a Marshal's castle and was very surprised to see a comfortable, but small house of a middle-class homeowner."[30]

It was not a castle, but it was certainly the dream house of this farm boy turned marshal, with its millionaire's view of the Bay of Angels, halfway between Nice and Antibes on the road rising to Vence. "It will soon be habitable," he wrote Antoine Pétain's son Omer in 1921, "but there is a lot to do to make the farm produce." He described his holdings: "I have five acres of vineyard but the vines are old; olive trees; a large vegetable garden in terraces, and a piece of land further down the hill which will be grazing land, plus some wheat for my hens, for I want to have two cows and a large chicken coop." He explained his hopes: "I don't expect to get rich on the products of the farm but I'd like to be able to live on them during the periods of time when I'm staying there."[31]

Pétain went down to Villeneuve-Loubet every time he could get away from his duties in that first postwar decade. "If they want to keep me," he wrote Eugénie in 1924, "they will have to loosen the chains and allow me to have longer periods of time for myself in south France."[32] But next year he was complaining, in a letter to nephew Omer: "As I am rarely on my estate and for short periods, because the government still refuses to free me," he had been obliged to turn over management of the farm to a caretaker: "it's his fortune, but the owner's ruin."[33]

A gardener hired in 1929 later recalled that his boss spent a maximum of two months each year at the Ermitage, at Easter and during the September grape harvest. Pétain would rise at eight, tour his garden, give instructions, visit local farmers, and receive distinguished visitors (who might include the Bishop of Nice and the prefects of nearby districts). He employed a cook, a housemaid, and a chauffeur.[34]

In Villeneuve-Loubet a farmer, in Paris a chief, "the living symbol of victory and military honor," remembered Paul Reynaud, who speaks of Pétain's "divinization" between the wars.[35] Streets were named for him all over France. The press, notably the widely read weekly *L'Illustration*, reproduced his photograph at ceremonial occasions, and often enough the occasions were funerals. Thus in a single six-month period in 1928 he was in London for the funeral of Lord Haig (Marshal Douglas Haig), in Rome to accompany Benito Mussolini in a funeral procession for

Marshal Armando Diaz, who had replaced Luigi Cadorna as commander of the Italian army after the defeat at Caporetto, in Monaco to inaugurate a war monument, in Rouen for the unveiling of a statue of Joan of Arc. He also sat for an equestrian statue by François Cogné, which was to be erected at Verdun.[36] And wherever he went, he was expected to talk about Verdun.[37]

He was a prized guest at the best dinners. It would be easy to fill a page with the names of distinguished hosts and hostesses, and the guests included many of the leading statesmen, authors and artists, scholars and journalists of the time. Castles, and the counts or the dukes who owned them, became familiar terrain. He seemed to enjoy the privileges that accompanied his exalted position, but he also enjoyed telling stories about the fragility of fame. Shortly after the war, he would say, he had gone to the French Alps to recover from laryngitis. A local doctor who examined him told him that he was in perfect shape. "You don't seem to have overworked during the war." Another time, in Sospel, a village above Cannes where he had served in the light infantry, he met a woman who had run a small restaurant where he had often dined. After some prodding she remembered her old customer. "But tell me," she finally said, "in all that time, and with the war, you must have gotten promoted. You're perhaps a colonel now?"[38]

A perquisite which both honored and solaced this unrich marshal was his election by the Institut de France, in 1925, as a curator of the Condé Museum in the castle of Chantilly. His functions were largely symbolic, but he received an apartment on the grounds of the castle where he and his family and friends could reside at any time of year, and he often took advantage of the privilege, walked or went riding in the surrounding woods.

Among intimate friends were the Marquis and Marquise Louis de Chasseloup-Laubat. They received the Pétains at their castle and at their Paris home, and the marshal was a witness at the marriage of their daughter.[39] The marquise was Jewish; Pétain had a number of Jewish friends of equivalent social rank: the automobile Citroëns, for example. He kept up his relations with foreign royalty, later apparently joking about the women he had met through Spain's Alphonse XIII, and of his heavy flirting with the wife and then widow of Albert of Belgium.[40] There is evi-

dence of close friendship with the wives of distinguished Frenchmen as well, and unproved allegations that he fathered the
distinguished son of at least one of these distinguished Frenchmen, but it is difficult to commit this evidence to cold print.[41] After
his death, Pétain's widow opened one of his military trunks to
discover hundreds of letters written to him by women, some still
bearing the odor of perfume; she and her secretary burned
them.[42]

One cannot always be sure that the love was consummated.
There was Jacqueline de Castex, born de Coniac, the widow of a
commander of the 24th light infantry battalion (in which Second
Lieutenant Pétain had begun his army career). Major Maurice
Hubert de Castex was cited several times for heroic conduct before dying in combat in October 1917 (in that battle of La Malmaison which Pétain had conceived as a limited offensive). General
Serrigny, a family friend, had arranged for the major's wife Jacqueline to visit her critically wounded husband near the front,
and then to mourn him. Shortly after the war Serrigny introduced Jacqueline to Pétain; he took an instant liking to the widow
and to her young daughters.[43]

Soon the marshal was sufficiently interested in Jacqueline to
propose marriage. She rejected him, for she was unready for new
marriage and wasn't sure of the effect it could have on her children. So Philippe married Eugénie. A few months after that, his
affair with Jacqueline took on serious dimensions. As she put it
then, it was a "whirlwind which drives us together, without my
being able to prevent it although I'm known as 'serious.' " Indeed, she wished to be forgotten, "for I don't have the right to
create difficulties . . . in your life." He was becoming a kind of
godfather to her daughters Hélène and Renée, and had even en-
tertained them when their mother wasn't present. But, she wondered, "What pleasure will we get out of it if we can only see each
other officially. . . . Love me a little, and tell me that you do."
She needed his help, for she was being pursued by a man she
didn't want.

They met regularly, "I'll walk down from Trocadéro square
and shall wait for you near the Iena bridge," she tells him in one
note.[44] "I can't resist the pleasure of coming in to say hello," she
scribbled on a note left in his office in March 1922, "and to thank

you for the exquisite hour you gave me yesterday, for your kind-
nessses, your flowers, for everything. . . ." "I love you more each
day, don't let it frighten you." "This morning I was thinking of
you at Mass. I prayed for you and for me." In June: "You drove
me crazy over you yesterday. . . . I'd like to be in your arms to
kiss you, as I feel like doing right now." In July, from the family
castle of Caumont, on the Seine river above Rouen, "So I must
give up the sweet dream of being with you in your arms. To listen to you, talk to you, kiss you, to do everything that is morally
and physically good to do, when it's done with you." After his
visit to her at Caumont that summer she wrote: "I remember with
delight the little nighttime visit I made to you, and remember it
with infinite happiness. When shall I be able to repeat those happy
moments. . . . But I prefer to have only these brief periods, and
to remain with you."

After this visit a Rouen newspaper reported: "During a visit
to Rouen Marshal Pétain lunched at the Hôtel de la Poste with
his family." "That made me so happy," Jacqueline wrote him. "It's
true that we look like a family and I don't give the impression of
an adventure. My darling, I should so much like to have you like
that! always together." In her next letter—it is now September
1922—she tells him of the confidence her children manifest
toward him. "It took me two years to realize this. Enough time
to allow the impassable barrier to be erected." Clearly she refers
to her rejection of Pétain during the summer of 1920, only weeks
before his marriage to Eugénie.[45]

Henceforth, during that decade and the next one, Pétain was
a regular visitor to the Castex family, in Caumont, at summer re-
sorts, or he would simply join what Jacqueline called the "trio,"
herself and her daughters, on a journey. Jacqueline, her daughters remembered, was devout and did not wish to see Pétain's wife,
a divorcée, which is why she met Pétain in secret; and they also
knew that Madame la Maréchale was a jealous woman.[46]

X

WAR IN THE RIF

In the middle of 1925, Pétain was once again in command of French armies engaged in the field, but this time it was in the French protectorate of Morocco, where a rebel chieftain, Abd el Krim, after standing off Spanish colonial forces in their Moroccan territories, had moved out of his Rif mountain stronghold to threaten the heart of French Morocco.

Two years Pétain's senior, Marshal Hubert Lyautey was France's proconsul in Morocco; he was very much what the French call a *grand seigneur*—a lord. He had been responsible for Morocco since 1912, including the four years of World War I; his was a political as much as a military leadership, for he was convinced that the former could not take second place to the latter in this almost-but-not-quite colony, where an indigenous culture and even a nominal ruler, the sultan, coexisted with his French protectors. Lyautey's pacification of Morocco's varied and dispersed tribes had been considered successful until then, but now the irresistible advance of Abd el Krim seemed to threaten all of the aging marshal's achievements. On June 6, 1925, he warned

Paris that Abd el Krim was preparing "a massive general offensive."[1] The next day in a "personal and confidential" message to the premier and minister of war—Painlevé held both posts—Lyautey expressed the fear that his own strength might "go suddenly," for he was over seventy and had recently been operated on.[2]

Faced with a colonial crisis which was also a French and an international crisis, the government could do nothing less than to send its commander in chief in time of war to the scene, if only to find out what more had to be done. The trouble was, if Lyautey was a lord, Pétain was another, and much legend has come out of the Rif campaign, a considerable amount of it having to do with the epic conflict between the two marshals. The legend has even engendered legend. It has been said that a year before the Abd el Krim offensive, when the left-of-center "cartel" came to power in France, Lyautey became alarmed at the peril these parties represented to traditional French values and considered sponsoring a coup d'état. He contacted Marshal Foch, who offered his support; his second visit was to Marshal Franchet d'Esperey, who also agreed to participate. Marshal Fayolle did the same. And then—fourth and last visit—he called on Pétain. Despite his arguments and his fervor, Lyautey's appeal was met with silence, that "marmoreal" silence. "You disapprove of me," Lyautey supposedly said, to which Pétain replied: "Quite." "If tomorrow I try to overthrow the government with the support of the army, and Herriot appeals to you, what will you do?" "I'll support Herriot as representative of the legal government," replied Pétain.[3]

Whatever happened in 1924, it was clear that the two marshals lived in different worlds. One of the marshals represented what has been called the poetry of colonialism, the other the efficiency of a modern military machine. Even before his departure for Morocco, Pétain privately observed that "the leadership down there leaves much to be desired."[4] On Lyautey's side, at least on the part of his officers, there was the feeling that to send the victor of Verdun to deal with a native rebel was clearly a case (although the expression wasn't used then) of overkill. After having neglected Morocco, Paris suddenly wanted to do too much.[5]

Pétain protested that he had never led a colonial expedition before, while his age (he was sixty-nine) allowed him to reserve his decision. But Painlevé insisted.[6] Leaving the premier's office, Pétain told Georges Bonnet, then an undersecretary of state attached to Painlevé, that he could issue a statement announcing that he accepted. "I know very well that I can only take a beating in this engagement," Bonnet remembered him saying. "Lyautey won't be happy. To defeat Abd el Krim won't add anything to the glory of the victor of Verdun. On the other hand, if I fail, my past will be forgotten quickly."[7]

On July 17 he boarded a small two-wing plane with an open cockpit in Toulouse; photographs show him in pilot's attire: goggles and leather helmet.[8] He wrote Eugénie—and usually he told her the truth about such matters—that he had been "received quite nicely" at the residence of Marshal Lyautey.[9] Once more, the meeting of the two marshals has been accorded epic dimensions. As Georges Bonnet tells it, Pétain reported to Painlevé that he had encountered "a cold—an icy welcome." Lyautey had opened the round: "Well, monsieur le Maréchal, you have come to replace me?" "Not at all. I've come only to deal with military operations."[10]

Both men knew what the stakes were. But the humanist in Morocco saw the war against the rebel chieftain as a political as well as a military engagement: Abd el Krim would be defeated when the tribes in his orbit were won over. Pétain believed that with the powerful means at their disposal the aim should be a decisive victory.[11] Yet after visiting the northern front he noted that the danger was coming not only from the enemy in the Rif mountains, but from growing dissidence among local tribes. "The troops in the field are no longer secure behind their lines. . . . In a region which we abandon, even after a success, everything has to begin again the next day." He recommended, in addition to greater troop strength, bringing in two squadrons of bombers, increasing the proportion of white soldiers so that the North Africans did not feel they were carrying all of the burden.[12]

"I think that my presence has been useful," he wrote Eugénie on July 25.[13] Next day he informed Painlevé that he would return to Paris after a stopover in Spanish Morocco. "I request that no important decision concerning Morocco be taken before my return."[14] What he had in mind was an ambitious operation directed to the vital center of the rebellion. This required a concerted effort with the Spanish colonial army—hence the stop in Spanish Morocco, where he met Miguel Primo de Rivera, who was both dictator in Madrid and high commissioner for Spain's North African possessions.[15]

On August 1, Pétain was in Painlevé's office. He endorsed the previous calls for reinforcements, up to a total of one hundred battalions, and agreed to take over the military effort while leaving political and administrative affairs to Lyautey. In a subsequent meeting he described a three-step program: immediate summer operations coordinated with the Spanish army to compromise Abd el Krim's prestige and tighten the noose around the Rif before the autumn rains; during the winter, political action among tribes in the battle zone; in spring 1926, decisive action, with the Spanish ally, against the heart of the Rif.[16]

On a night train to Spain on August 16, Pétain opened copies of messages just received by Painlevé from Lyautey, and discovered that they offered solutions in contradiction with his own plan. Lyautey was pessimistic about a major military effort before the rainy season.[17] In Algeciras, on the southern tip of Spain and a short sail from Ceuta in Spanish Morocco, Pétain met Primo de Rivera again, this time on board the French ship *Maréchal Lyautey*. They put the final touches on the plan for Franco-Spanish military cooperation against the rebels and toasted it with champagne. On August 22 the *Maréchal Lyautey* sailed into Casablanca harbor, where Lyautey was waiting at 7:00 A.M. to greet Pétain. Pétain informed Painlevé that he had said to Lyautey: "The government wishes me to take charge of operations." Lyautey: "Then I shall leave." Pétain: "You will think about it."[18]

Surely Lyautey was aware that Morocco was no longer big enough for two marshals. He told Pétain that he had waited for him to return, and now that he was there he himself would go to France and remain there until mid-September, when he might return to help deal with the reconquered tribes, unless Painlevé wished him to remain in France. Lyautey was prepared to stay on as Pétain's political adviser, asking only that he be allowed to retain "the facade of commander in chief." In reporting this to Paris, Pétain commented that he saw no reason why Lyautey could not return to Rabat when he desired; he wouldn't be in the way, for Pétain was transferring his own headquarters to Meknès. Lyautey's advice on the tribes might indeed prove useful, and the old resident general was after all only asking for respect.[19]

Pétain moved to Meknès on August 28; Lyautey left for France the same day. The Spaniards under Primo de Rivera attacked the rebels from the sea, the French overland, and both allies made progress. On September 18, Pétain returned to Rabat to meet Lyautey, who was just back from France; the older man was visibly displeased with the reception he had received in Paris; he was reserved and reticent, clearly having lost confidence in Pétain.[20] Soon after that he resigned. "When one has labored for 13 years to achieve something," he wrote his friend François Pietri, "and one sees in less than two months all this effort sabotaged, smashed, and irremediably compromised for the future, one cannot hold on to an ounce of responsibility." He put all the blame on "the military high command" which had sought to establish a World War battlefront. "The whole native policy—mine—has been sabotaged in the operation zone."[21] He felt that he had been tricked, that contrary to what Pétain had led him to believe, Pétain had not supported him in talking to Painlevé.[22]

Henceforth, alongside the Foch-Pétain feud, the French army had a Lyautey-Pétain feud, with the Foch and Lyautey clans seemingly allied. A member of the Foch clan wrote to Lyautey that Pétain's mission to Morocco was obviously a government maneuver. He compared the Pétain plan to win the war in the Rif to using a hammer to kill a fly, although (at the time this letter was written) the fly hadn't even been killed.[23]

Pétain, in any case, promised victory for the following year, 1926, either through French-Spanish cooperation or French action alone, a victory that would be facilitated if "agitation in the Rif no longer received the external support which until now has enhanced its authority."[24] He returned to France via Algeria and a sea journey; back in Paris in early November he declared: "Morocco is now quiet. We no longer need to fear Abd el Krim. My military assignment has been accomplished; it is now a political affair."[25] In January 1926 he wrote nephew Paul Pomart: "I have a great desire to take a rest starting at the end of April, although the government doesn't seem to agree with me entirely." He saw his life henceforth as divided between the Ermitage in winter, the apartment in the Chantilly castle in summer.[26] At the beginning of February he returned to Spain, visiting Toledo with King Alfonso XIII, to be awarded the Spanish Military Cross in a ceremony in the Alcazar. In the business part of the visit an agreement was signed: In separate but concerted French and Spanish operations, Abd el Krim's redoubt was to be captured in the spring campaign.[27]

And by the second week of May the combined offensive was under way. On May 25, Abd el Krim handed his surrender to three French intelligence officers and was brought back to French lines on the twenty-seventh.[28] In June, Pétain took part in a conference with the Spaniards in Paris at which it was agreed that the rebel leader would be exiled to Réunion in the Indian Ocean, while French and Spanish zones of influence in Morocco remained as before.[29]

In October of that year, Lyautey wrote a friend who had invited him to attend a ceremony that he had taken a long leave so as not to have to meet fellow officers. "There are three men that I have resolved not to meet," he said: They were Painlevé, Pétain, and General Marie Debeney (chief of staff). "I don't want to shake their hands at any price and I have decided to turn my back to them if by chance I find myself in their presence. . . ."[30]

XI
AMONG SOLDIERS

Bernard Serrigny, drafting instructions and orders of the day for his chief's signature, was not an exceptional case. The higher-ranking general officers all possessed staff workers who breathed as one with their superiors. This system allowed a prodigious amount of paperwork, and even some memoirs, to go out over the signature of the head men. Pétain made at least as much use of the team system as anyone else, from his first important commands in the Great War through the Vichy years, and some would say more. His subordinates, as he told them, had to be his memory and his imagination. His closest collaborators were often better-than-average writers, and some seem to have been chosen precisely because of this skill. Pétain did a certain amount of public speaking in the 1920s, more in the 1930s, and signed a considerable number of prefaces, brief ones for souvenir albums on military life, longer introductions to the work of authorities on war and defense.[1]

The Pétain team had some devoted nonwriters too, such as the hard-working, easygoing aide de camp Léon Amable Marie

Bonhomme. Born in August 1891 and a bachelor all his life, he had been cited in the Great War: "Excellent non-commissioned officer giving his platoon the example of great sang froid. On March 25, 1918, during violent shelling he brought back through the lines a wounded cavalryman"—a perfect symbol for this man whose life was to be devoted to helping. Omnipresent, the aptly named Bonhomme was virtually Pétain's arms and legs in the 1930s and at Vichy (where he died).[2]

If Bonhomme was not a writer, Auguste Marie Émile Laure was, and when he was not writing for Pétain he was writing for himself (he published two books on the First World War under a pen name). He was born in June 1881; as a young officer at the War College he had Pétain as a teacher; at Compiègne head-quarters during Pétain's reign he served in operations; in July 1924, as a lieutenant colonel, he joined Marshal Pétain's staff; as a brigadier general he was private secretary to Minister of War Pétain in 1934.[3]

At least once the Pétain-Laure collaboration proved lucrative. Pétain had been asked to write a series of articles on Verdun for the American press (the articles were also published in France in *L'Illustration*, and in book form as *La Bataille de Verdun*). The work was bland and sounded more like an official report than a personal account. Indeed, because of the use of collaborators, and perhaps because of their prudence, thanks also to the positions of authority Pétain continued to hold, the gap is substantial between his acerbic conversation recorded in the memoirs of contemporaries and the evenhanded tone of most published articles and speeches. As for the text on Verdun, its readers in *L'Illustration* appreciated it, so Pétain informed Laure, for "the simplicity of the presentation, the role given to the fighters, and the 'modesty' . . . of the author." Of course, ghostwriter Laure shared in the fees received both from the United States and from France.[4]

If he was not much of a writer himself, Pétain did seem to possess a keen eye and an acute ear for the talent of others. In his search for ghostwriters of quality he made one remarkable discovery: He recognized, and hired, one of the army's most original personalities, Captain Charles de Gaulle.

Colonel Pétain first encountered the newly arrived second lieutenant at Arras. They were not to be associated that intimately again for over a decade, although their paths crossed. It was Pétain who put his signature on a citation for Captain de Gaulle, wounded and taken prisoner on the Verdun front in 1916.[5] After the war Pétain kept a paternal eye on the younger officer. There were stories (and it is alleged that de Gaulle encouraged their telling) that Pétain was the godfather of de Gaulle's son, born in December 1921, although apparently it was not true.[6] We are told that Pétain intervened, at the War College, in an attempt to improve de Gaulle's rating in the graduation class. De Gaulle, who wrote his first book (*La Discorde chez l'ennemi*) while a prisoner of war, was taken into Pétain's cabinet in 1925 to work on the reports and speeches that Pétain signed. Pétain also sponsored a series of lectures that de Gaulle gave at the War College, and the story is that the marshal had to force his protégé on the school because his graduation ranking did not entitle him to address his peers.[7]

De Gaulle joined Pétain's staff on July 1, 1925, but he seems to have begun work on a book for the marshal, a historical essay on the French army from prerevolutionary years through the Great War to be called *The Soldier,* at the beginning of that year while still assigned to the general staff of the Rhine army at Mainz. For we have a letter from Pétain dated March 20, 1925, approving a draft chapter entitled "Principles": "There is hardly anything for me to change in the form," the marshal wrote the captain. "The substance is impeccable and of proper doctrine. . . . Keep up the good work." The fact that de Gaulle was moonlighting is suggested by the postscript: "It is understood that you will show this work to no one; it's a matter between the two of us."[8]

What de Gaulle's drafts reveal, above all, is a personal style, in striking contrast to the official tone of most of what was published above Pétain's signature; of course, in his editing of de Gaulle, Pétain tended to blunt the sharp edges. "This description is catastrophic from start to finish," Pétain objects in one place. "It deals with the horrors of modern warfare but insufficiently with that marvelous attitude of the French soldier of 1914 in dealing with them."[9]

With a first draft behind him, de Gaulle received a line command. Promoted to major, he was sent to Trier in the occupied Rhineland to take charge of an infantry battalion. He wrote a friend: *"The Soldier* by Marshal Pétain and your obedient servant is finished, you're a witness to that, but the decision [to publish it] hasn't been made." With this foreboding note: "It will nevertheless be published one day, if I have to do it alone." [10]

What had apparently happened was that Pétain did not consider the job as finished at all. He gave it to another officer on his staff, Colonel Sylvestre Audet, telling him that the first section was fine but that more work had to be done on the Great War; "out of friendship" Audet advised de Gaulle of his assignment.[11] De Gaulle lost no time in replying to his informant: "You know my opinion in advance. A book is a man. This man, until this moment, was me." Even if a Montesquieu had been assigned to revise de Gaulle's draft, "either he would write a different book, or he would demolish mine." He had no objection to Pétain's having assigned someone to write another book; in that case he'd simply take his own back. "But if it's to make mincemeat of my ideas, my philosophy, and my style, I object and I shall say so to the Marshal." He ended sharply: "The Marshal has never been willing to recognize the difference between a book and a general staff report. This is why I have often thought that this whole business would end badly." [12] In a separate letter he warned Pétain that even if he decided to keep de Gaulle's name off the title page, "the future will inevitably put things to rights." [13]

This letter created shock at 4b, Boulevard des Invalides. Laure begged de Gaulle to withdraw it: "Don't pose conditions," he pleaded. "Be a loyal servitor." Then the boss himself followed up with a letter to de Gaulle (on February 1, 1928): "With respect to your participation in this work, it will be acknowledged, as I previously told you, in the preface that we shall draft together when the time comes." [14]

The time never came. At some point, presumably in the following weeks, Pétain put an end to the incipient rebellion by dropping the project entirely and locking up the manuscript. The rebellion broke out all the same, but ten years later, when de Gaulle felt strong enough to renew his challenge.

But because the real reasons for the conflict between the marshal and his protégé were not widely known, their epic clash has given rise to many stories, some partly true, some unlikely to contain any truth at all. They describe card games and bad debts, sexual rivalry. One of the more credible stories has de Gaulle in trouble in Trier, for he had put a soldier in jail for requesting a new assignment, and this after orders for the reassignment had come through. A member of Parliament took the case to the war minister; de Gaulle risked punishment. He went to Paris to call on "the boss," who arranged it all with Painlevé. "I removed quite a thorn from his foot," Pétain is quoted.[15]

Pétain seldom spoke out on politics in the decade following the war and seemed less hostile to the republican form of government than some of his peers; in the late 1930s, a Socialist such as Léon Blum could continue to admire him. Certainly there is a consistency in thought between the general in chief who in Compiègne in 1917 believed it necessary to counter unpatriotic feelings on the home front and the Marshal Pétain who in 1927 spoke at the inauguration of the Ossuary of Douaumont, then being constructed to shelter the remains of the Verdun dead. In this speech he gave credit to "the respect for authority, the will for order, the cult of the fatherland" for the November 1918 victory. "There is no doubt that these basic virtues, which belong to our race, subsist in us. . . . But they do have to be encouraged by our educational system."[16] It was an early version of a theme that was to become central to his thinking: the paramount importance of reviving a sense of patriotism in the public school system.

Much of his professional activity in the second half of the 1920s decade concerned frontier defense, and he followed construction of the Maginot Line from day to day, often on the site.[17] In fact, the structural deficiencies, the strategic errors, of this fortified system, which General Maurice Gamelin was to call "blind monsters," have been blamed on Marshal Pétain.[18] What is certain, and it has often been invoked against Pétain in the light of the 1940 breakthrough by the Germans, is that even after his resignation as vice-chairman of the Supreme War Council and general in chief in time of war, he persisted in his opposition to extension of the Maginot Line north to France's common border with Belgium, arguing that the essential thing was to facilitate the advance of French troops *into* Belgium (to meet the Germans halfway). In a letter he signed, which was read to a session of the

War Council on May 28, 1932, he proposed that the 250 million francs earmarked for this northern defense line be spent instead to build up an air force.[19]

For when Pétain stepped down at last from his exalted position as commander in chief, to be replaced by Maxime Weygand, he accepted another apointment as inspector general of air defense. The decree appointing him to the new job was signed by President Gaston Doumergue on February 9, 1931; Pétain was only two months away from his seventy-fifth birthday.[20] When he turned over the vice-chairmanship of the War Council to Weygand he also surrendered his office, moving a few doors down to Foch's old headquarters at 8, Boulevard des Invalides, which was to be a second home to him for most of the decade. "A vast and simple white room," a visitor recalled, "without decoration. . . . Four large windows on the Avenue de Tourville keep it very bright. The furniture is in Empire style, except the Marshal's armchair, which is genuine Louis XV. . . ."[21] Laure speaks of the surprise, almost indignation, of the public when it was learned that the marshal had been shifted to a secondary role after having occupied "the supreme function" for so many years. Pétain ignored the clamor and set to work, taking a new member into his office, Lieutenant Colonel Paul Vauthier, author of a recent ground-breaking book on the perils of air war.[22]

Now, of course, Marshal Pétain was going to be a more ardent advocate of air power than most of his fellow officers, old or young. The paradox is that this ancient soldier, often accused of wishing to fight the next war with the strategy and tactics of the last one, was actually moving ahead of many progressive military thinkers, whose own forecasts saw only as far as ground combat with tanks. In his very first report to the premier, then Pierre Laval, on June 22, 1931, the new inspector general of air defense argued for the upgrading of the air arm, demanded priority in expenditures for the building of a bomber force and pursuit planes as defense against air attack.[23] He warned that in the next war Germany and Italy as a bloc would launch "powerful chemical air attacks to affect our morale, our political, military and industrial structures, our mobilization and concentration of troops." These early attacks could well be decisive: "At the beginning of a future war, air activity will take on an importance for which the past gives us no precedent." He advocated an independent air command disposing of its own fighters and bombers.[24]

By now he was also asking for a Ministry of National Defense to coordinate the war, navy, and air ministries. ("It is striking that he hadn't noticed this necessity during the previous 14 years, when he was commander in chief of ground forces," Paul Reynaud will later remark with irony.[25]) This ministry was created, although Pétain did not find it sufficiently responsive to the need.[26] There is also evidence that younger government and military people found that they no longer needed the marshal. A memoir drawn up by Gamelin, then Weygand's deputy as chief of the general staff, recommended that he not be a member of a new coordinating group that was to oversee the three war ministries.[27]

But being kept out of this high military committee didn't discourage Pétain. In a memorandum addressed to the minister of national defense on April 18, 1932, he called for a general aviation reserve, and a chief of staff of national defense to be responsible for ground, sea, and air forces as well as of this reserve. In successive memorandums to the government, to Weygand, to the Supreme War Council, Pétain stressed the primordial role of air power. For a session of the council on May 28, 1932, he submitted a note on the defense of the northern frontier which dealt with considerably more than frontier defense: Protesting the plan to set up permanent installations on that frontier, which was a reversal of a previous decision, he said that this would not only be a more expensive solution than the plan for a mobile defense, it would represent abandoning Belgium at the outbreak of a new war. Further, the growing importance of air power made the earlier choice of a light defense even more valid. The next war, he warned, "will begin with powerful air incursions which, in the present state of our aviation, we are unable to prevent."[28] In another note in October of that year he described the next war as a battle between France and its Allies against Germany and others in its orbit, such as Italy, Austria, Hungary, and the U.S.S.R. "Not only will the air factor be common to all the theaters of war where ground and sea forces will be engaged as in the past," he went on, "but it will give birth to new theaters. . . ." He appealed for creation of a high command associating civil and military power to prepare for what he called "tomorrow's 'total' war." Much about his note was revolutionary, to judge from the question marks that can be found on the copies read by members of the high command.[29]

In the face of later criticism of Pétain as having been too old to comprehend modern warfare, it is interesting to see how far in advance Pétain, Laure, and Vauthier really were. In effect they were the French counterparts of Italian general Giulio Douhet and other early proponents of air power, such as the American general Billy Mitchell. When he prefaced a French translation of a work on air defense by a former commander of the antiaircraft defense of London, in April 1933, the old marshal showed himself to be a more fervent advocate of the use of airplanes in new ways than the British author. "The efficacity of air bombing and the dimensions of the danger seem to be systematically underestimated," Pétain wrote—surely his aide Paul Vauthier was the real author of this preface—pointing out that the author's confidence was based on lessons of the past no longer valid. "Next time," warned Pétain, "the air peril will be launched at once in all its power. . . ." The best defense would be attack: bombing enemy bases. Machine guns and barbed wire had transformed ground operations at the beginning of the century, but that was nothing compared to what airplanes would do.[30]

Pétain and his men, Weygand and his, faced a still more formidable obstacle to military preparedness than the inertia of structures. The elections of May 1932 created a new parliamentary majority that was preponderantly left of center. The victorious Radical Socialists of Premier Edouard Herriot, divided on the question of disarmament, needed the Socialists to form a cabinet, and that party favored severe cuts in military expenditures. By that time France was taking part in an international conference on arms limitation in Geneva. And so the growing threat from Germany was met not by resolute action on the part of France, Britain, and the United States, but by the desire of all three to organize a system of collective security that integrated Germany into an international police force. In the battle between the government and the General Staff, Weygand as general in chief in time of war bore the brunt.[31] There is evidence that Pé-

tain was more flexible; e.g., he seems to have endorsed the opinion of Herriot that "To refuse to disarm is to give Germany the
right to rearm, and to isolate France in the event of future war."[32]
Yet in a governmental discussion of disarmament he warned that
"for the moment" France possessed no real guarantee of its security and remained vulnerable to attack by Germany with Italian complicity; Germany's signature on a nonaggression pact could
not be relied upon.[33] In February 1933, shortly after Hitler's
coming to power, he predicted that Germany, with the support
of the Soviet Union, would attack Poland, counting on the non-
intervention of Britain and France. He had his staff draw up a
comparative chart of German and French war potential, opposing the French philosophy of universal peace to German belli-
gerence, France's declining birth rate to German racial vitality,
French individuality and love of humanity to Germany's education for nationalism.[34]

No doubt about it, in the early 1930s the army of Pétain, and
of Weygand, suffered mightily from the budget reductions rendered inevitable by France's and the world's economic crisis, and
by the climate favoring disarmament. In 1934, Weygand reported to Pétain: "Our army has descended to the lowest level
that French security allows. . . ."[35] But by then Pétain himself
was minister of war.

XII
THE DIGNITARY

One way that France honors its great is to receive them into the ranks of the French Academy, limited to forty members at any one time. Marshal Pétain was tapped to take the seat of Marshal Foch on the latter's death in 1929, an irony, for Academy ceremony demands of the new member that in his acceptance speech he render homage to the deceased academician whose seat he has taken. In a note to Émile Laure soon after his election to the Academy in June 1929, Pétain outlined the procedure he would follow in writing this speech. He had asked the army's historical service to undertake a study of Foch's campaigns. But it was going to be difficult in a speech supposedly of praise to correct prevailing evaluations of Foch. "Massive doses of flowers, that's what is wanted," he explained. "In any case it's a task I don't appreciate."[1]

Another tradition called for a welcoming speech by a member of the Academy. The responsibility fell to Paul Valéry, who accepted Pétain's invitation to visit him at Villeneuve-Loubet and then told a friend: "He's at once majestic and given to teasing, a kind of peasant lord, rather ferociously independent."[2] Pétain's admission was scheduled for January 22, 1931. There were a number of witnesses to the event, first in the antechamber where the academicians assembled before the ceremony, the new recruit standing out in the group of green-uniformed members in his "regulation blue tunic . . . his martial bearing which age ennobles without weighting it down . . . especially by the limpid eyes of this face with its harmonious regularity, of a marmoreal lightness. . . ."[3] When Pétain entered the auditorium "a churchlike silence invaded the room crowded as in its best hours," wrote Louis Gillet, himself a future academician.[4]

In his lengthy exposition—Pétain spoke for an hour and a quarter—the unsuspecting might have missed the subtle dissent expressed in the guise of a straightforward history of Foch's war. But Léon Blum detected it and evoked for readers of Le Populaire "the tranquil testimony that [Pétain] offers against the mad illusions of the General Staff and of Marshal Foch himself." Blum's praise of Pétain shows how broadly he was accepted at the beginning of the 1930s. "If I said that of all the great war chiefs he is the one whose modesty, gravity and reflective and sensible scruples call for sympathy," wrote the Socialist leader, ". . . I can only embarrass him by my compliment."[5]

Later the same year Pétain's tolerance of ceremony was to be put to an even more rugged test, when he was called on to represent France as special ambassador at the 150th anniversary celebration of the American war of independence. He sailed for the New World on September 12 for a grueling fortnight of banquets, receptions, inaugurations, each requiring its speech, escorted by his wartime comrade General John J. Pershing. The high point of the visit was the commemoration at Yorktown, Virginia, on the site of the Franco-American victory over the English. Pétain also visited the nation's capital, George Washington's home at Mount Vernon, Manhattan Island, and West Point Military Academy on the Hudson River.[6]

In a biographical résumé of thirteen mimeographed pages, an anonymous publicist described him for Americans as "Tall, robust, white—of a whiteness of a former blond—,cold, speaking little and without gestures. . . ." The writer also pointed out that "he represents a type of Frenchman quite different from the standard type, speechifying and agitated, that with a taste for conformity Americans have forged of our race. . . . ."[7] A reporter for the Associated Press called on "Marshall Henry Pétain" in his "secluded office in the Invalides" to find "a stocky, 75-year-old warrior in civilian clothes." Pétain told the reporter that what interested him was "the American spirit. . . . It's one of the most wonderful in the world," Pétain was quoted, "even more enthusiastic than the French." He said that he was less enthusiastic about those "gigantic things," such as skyscrapers and Niagara Falls.[8]

The *New York Times*, which reported that the French government had authorized a budget of $48,000 for Pétain's voyage,[9] gave generous coverage to the tour, from the departure from Toulon, where Pétain's delegation filled two French cruisers, the *Duquesne* and the *Suffren*. Concurrently the *Times* followed the visit of another important Frenchman, Premier Pierre Laval, who sailed to New York on the *Ile de France*. His task was to discuss economic and security matters with President Herbert Hoover. The presence of the two Frenchmen in the United States at the same time "is not without significance," reported *L'Illustration;* the implication was that Pétain's goodwill mission could be of use to Laval's diplomatic one.[10]

The arrival of Pétain in Yorktown was a two-column story for the *Times,* accompanied by a photograph of General Pershing greeting him at Old Point Comfort.[11] Next day the newspaper reported the festivities at the top of the front page: "With pomp and pageantry of long ago, this hamlet on the bluffs of the York began today the four-day celebration of a battle that 150 years ago meant the end of a war and the birth of a nation." Threatening weather limited attendance, but some 15,000 persons were on hand. And a seventeen-gun salute greeted the marshal's appearance.[12] On the following day, on the *Times* front page announcing the death of Thomas Alva Edison, the conviction of Al Capone for income-tax evasion, and pressure from Paris for reduction of its debt to the United States, a headline read:

PÉTAIN DECLARES
YORKTOWN DEBT PAID

Wearing a horizon-blue uniform, Pétain had spoken at a morning ceremony on October 17 to say (in French) that "America had magnificently wiped out the debt of gratitude which had been contracted at Yorktown. Better still . . . by her disinterested and generous intervention she had inaugurated a new moral and international theory according to which it should no longer be the selfish interests of one country but a higher ideal of justice and mutual respect which should prevail among civilized nations."[13]

Pétain's friend General Adalbert de Chambrun, a descendant of Lafayette, remembered hearing one American participant tell the audience: "If there are any future mothers in the audience I ask them, in honor of Marshal Pétain, to give their child the name of Henry if it's a boy, or Henriette if a girl." (Pétain was fighting a losing battle to make clear that he preferred Philippe as his first name, for the press was aware of what his birth certificate said.)[14]

On October 18, Pétain spoke in Williamsburg, Virginia, at a ceremony during which he received an honorary degree from the College of William and Mary; he was in Richmond, Virginia, on the twentieth, in Washington, D.C., on the twenty-first.[15] The *New York Times* on October 23 employed a three-column headline on the front page, and two full inside pages, to report Laval's reception by Hoover, and there was a photograph showing Pétain and Laval together. Laval was still receiving front-page coverage when Pétain arrived in New York on October 24, where he stayed at the Waldorf-Astoria Hotel as a guest of General Pershing, speaking there at a banquet sponsored by Franco-American organizations and in the presence of New York's governor Franklin Delano Roosevelt; it was their only meeting. In his speech Pétain warned that it was more difficult for France and the United States to preserve their friendship in peace than in war, and defended France against the charge of militarism.[16] On Sunday, October 25, he was host at a reception on board the *Suffren* and the *Duquesne*, docked side by side at Pier 57 on the North River; there was champagne and dancing.[17] And, of course, there had to be the ticker-tape parade from the Battery, along lower Broadway to City Hall, where Mayor James J. Walker received him. "His obvious delight with some details of the reception," the *Times* reported, "dispelled a somewhat stilted air of formality which even Mayor Walker's amiable personality had left intact."[18]

The press reported his departure on October 28. "I leave assuring you that I carry in my heart the deepest affection for this country," he declared, as the two warships weighed anchor.[19] But as soon as they had sailed out of New York Harbor, the *Suffren* cut its motors and by prearrangement waited off Long Island for a motorboat to come out to pick up Pétain and General de Chambrun. For Pétain was now to return to New York incognito. According to Chambrun's later recollection, Pétain had planned the escapade only the previous evening, at a dinner with the general and his son René. "I haven't seen anything of New York and I don't know anything about American life," he complained to his friends. His table companions at formal dinner parties had all been "daughters of the revolution"; now he wished to meet some granddaughters of the revolution and, why not, some great-granddaughters, "on condition that they're pretty, of course."

They visited Harlem, the Stock Exchange; watched a baseball game; ate hot dogs and ice cream; dined with lovely women at La Côte Basque, an elegant French restaurant; and finished the evening at the Central Park Casino nightclub. The Chambruns tell us that colorful Mayor Walker strode into the casino with a woman on each arm and was struck dumb to discover that the marshal hadn't sailed back to France after all. Pétain waved to him, and he burst out laughing, then joined their table.[20] Another source says that the U.S. State Department sponsored Pétain's private visit, putting him up at the Waldorf, taking him to see the *Scandals;* he also enjoyed the Waldorf's kitchen, whose records show that he ordered Sterling Point oysters three times, Philadelphia pepper pot twice, and stuffed striped bass once.[21]

And this time he was really leaving, on the French liner *Lafayette;* Pershing saw him to the pier. "We are real brothers," Pétain said of the American general. And he added that he had an "excellent" impression of America.[22]

Pétain maintained a ledger (or his staff did) listing the organizations to which he belonged, and there were dozens. A separate ledger listed donations to worthy causes, which seem to have totaled 131,328 francs by 1937.[23] He belonged to two social circles, the Bixio dinners and the Paul Hervieu lunches, each composed of personalities in the arts and letters, law, politics, the army. And Redressement Français (literally, French Recovery). At least one aspect of his association with this loose grouping of like-minded technocrats remains a mystery. For Pétain was an occasional participant in the activity of the organization in the early 1930s, when a more active participant was Raphaël Alibert, later to become his political adviser and one of the most controversial personalities in his Vichy cabinet. Yet Alibert was to claim that he first met Pétain much later.

Redressement Français was founded in 1925 by a public-spirited business leader, Ernest Mercier, who had organized France's electrical distribution on an industrial scale. He believed that enlightened managers should join forces to reform and then lead the nation.[24] The program of his movement was drawn up at a Paris meeting in 1927 under the chairmanship of Marshal Foch, and it quickly attracted leaders of the business community, senior military officers, and educators concerned with their nation's domestic and foreign problems. A number of Pétain's associates in Vichy, such as Lucien Romier, Jérôme Carcopino, René Gillouin, Bernard Faÿ, and of course Alibert, took part in its conferences.[25] And as a report on one of its meetings indicates, "certain important personalities, whose position doesn't permit overt collaboration, nevertheless took an active part in our gatherings."[26]

Mercier's concern with efficient solutions led him at least once to an extreme conclusion. When the daily *Le Petit Journal* solicited opinions on the desirability of dictatorship, Mercier declared—the date was March 25, 1933, just after Hitler had won dictatorial powers—"France is tired of attitudes, drunk with words; it seeks a will; we're so unused to it that to express this need we have only one word: dictatorship."[27]

Pétain was present, with Marshal Franchet d'Esperey, at meetings at Redressement Français headquarters in January 1932 where foreign policy was discussed. Among other reports, he heard those of the Commission of Franco-German Questions, delivered by Raphaël Alibert, who began his speech: *"Messieurs les Maréchaux. . . ."* And then, the minutes tell us, Pétain took the floor to support Alibert's conclusions. (The reports described the growth of Germany's economic and military strength, and warned of the threat represented by Pan-Germanism.)[28]

In January 1934, Pétain chaired a Redressement Français

meeting concerned with civil defense. "Gentlemen, you know how interested I am in Redressement Français; I've given you proof of that," he began. "Every time I can attend your meetings—unfortunately my activities don't always allow it—I do it willingly." He then introduced General Laure, who provided a more detailed exposition of the problems of air war. Ernest Mercier thanked Pétain and Laure for speaking so frankly. "In consequence, in the action that we must pursue," he added, "I don't need to tell you that in no circumstances will we refer to what was said here." But he promised that his group would try to get something done about building air power. "We don't think that this effort is compatible with present-day political mores . . . with what I could call 'Staviskyisme.'" So Redressement Français would also devote itself to "the destruction of this political mentality."[29]

Pétain's association with Mercier's group lasted as long as the group did, and when it was disbanded in November 1935 he praised it as "of high national interest."[30] The question remains, was Pétain also associated with Alibert during those years, Alibert who had been on the board of directors of the movement from its founding?[31] Henri Albert François Joseph Raphaël Alibert, born in 1887 in southwest France, trained in law, had been professor at Paris' School of Political Science from 1924 to 1933, after which he became a director of or legal adviser to electrical companies.[32] On the fall of France in 1940 he was to take a leading role in transforming the defeated nation into the French State, and Pétain's entourage readily gave him credit for drafting the laws that brought Vichy France closer to Nazi Germany. Alibert later acknowledged that he had seen Pétain at Redressement Français meetings but claimed that they had never spoken.[33] He had met Pétain "for the first time in my life" on October 9, 1937, at a meeting at the home of mutual friends, at which time their conversation dealt with economic, financial, and social matters; after hearing Alibert's opinions Pétain asked if he would call on him regularly for further discussions, and Alibert did so. He claimed that they met, either at Pétain's apartment or office, seven or eight times between October 1937 and March 1939, when Pétain went to Spain.[34]

Henry Lémery, former minister and deputy, was later to say that he was the one who introduced Alibert to Pétain, in 1936

during one of the lunches at which Pétain presided; Pétain, said
Lémery, was captivated by Alibert's expertise, the clarity of his
exposition and reasoning, and got into the habit of consulting
him.[35] Pétain himself later recalled that he met Alibert through
another of his political advisers, General Charles Brécard, who
denied it to High Court investigators, adding that he and Pétain
had both known Alibert for a long time but that he didn't know
how Pétain had first met him.[36]

XIII

THE MINISTER

When Pétain entered the 1930s he was also entering his seventy-fourth year. All accounts tell of his exceptional physical condition. There is a minority view—it must be heard out—that age had affected his mental capacity. De Gaulle, we are told, was describing him as senile; he and other officers with access to Pétain but not of his circle of admirers also supposedly complained of the old man's hard heart. "He no longer has any generosity, he has no firmness." He had frequent absences, seeming to lack interest in the world around him.[1]

Until his death in 1936 as has been noted, his friend Louis Ménétrel was his doctor. Ménétrel had built up a clientele in his specialties, the treatment of gout and other manifestations of arthritis, neuralgia, and rheumatism by hot air, utilizing a device he had invented. Indeed, the doctor had published a pamphlet to describe his method: The principle was to subject parts of the body to air of varying temperatures; with his apparatus, consisting of two copper cylinders, one encased in the other, an alcohol burner could raise the interior temperature to 200 degrees centigrade.[2] After his death, Louis' son Bernard, then twenty-nine, succeeded him, taking over his clientele, Marshal Pétain included. Bernard was a general practitioner like his father, specializing in rheumatic disease and cardiology; at his patients' demand he made regular use of his father's hot-air treatment. He was also interested in medical applications of electricity and employed diathermy (electrodes) to treat rheumatism and similar complaints. As a tonic he injected oxygen into his illustrious patient and also resorted to the ancient remedy of bleeding.[3]

Bernard was Philippe's doctor, and more. When he married and had children, his family virtually merged into Pétain's. During the 1930s the young man was often in Pétain's company; they would be invited to social events together.[4] The story made the rounds that Ménétrel was Pétain's natural son.[5] By the beginning of the 1940s Bernard would be called more than a natural son; he would be described often enough at Vichy as his *eminence grise.*

In Paris, the Pétains employed two servants. The marshal paid rent on two apartments, one for himself, one for Eugénie; hers was next door at 6, Square de Latour-Maubourg, until he was able to rent one on the same landing as his at number 8. His own apartment contained two bedrooms, an office, and a drawing room, with three other rooms serving to store old furniture, crates, and trunks; military equipment; souvenirs.[6] Approaching his eightieth year, he remained as much of a bon vivant as ever. If he avoided drinking and smoking—and didn't like to be smoked at—he did enjoy his meals.[7] He liked them especially in good company and was delighted by the attentions of the rich and titled, as a letter he wrote to Eugénie suggests. "The Marquis welcomed me as you can guess," he wrote her from Cannes in November 1937. "He waited for me at the station with a sumptuous automobile which will be at my disposal during the length of my stay. . . . When I have told you that I am installed royally at the Grand Hotel and that the food here is perfect, my report will be complete."[8]

In Villeneuve-Loubet, the dream house was now equipped for comfortable retirement, with its morris chairs, ceiling-high bookcases whose contents were bound in leather, photographs of the marshal at significant moments of his career decorating the walls, and even an exotic den called the Moroccan room. With its summer furniture and its curios, the house was a combination resort home and manor.[9] Pétain spent as much time as he could at the Ermitage, especially in autumn, for he liked to harvest his own grapes and supervise the making of wine. And then, usually by correspondence, he followed the aging of the wine in casks, its distillation into brandy. There were olives too, and olive oil.[10]

Pétain's correspondence with his wife in the 1930s betrays a constant preoccupation with income and outgo. He made a budget and stuck to it, particularly for their visits to Villeneuve-Loubet. They had enough money for the time they would spend at the Ermitage, he assured Eugénie in one letter in 1938, but he thought that it would be wise to avoid inviting "Maharajahs"—presumably a reference to wealthier friends. "It is wise from time to time to recognize one's possibilities."[11]

He remained in touch with his family up north, chiefly by letter. His sisters and his brother, nephews and nieces, reported all the local marriages, births, and deaths, the acquiring or disposing of small houses, parcels of land, other investments. He was closest to his sister Sara, and when she entered an old-age home (with her retarded nephew Raphael) he paid the board. When Sara died her funeral was carried out according to his instructions (by then he was in Madrid as ambassador to Spain).[12] His relationship with Eugénie was a subject of curiosity. They lived together and they did not; there were places to which they were invited together and others where Pétain went alone, or with his mistress.[13]

But once more retirement was going to be postponed, the dream house in Villeneuve-Loubet to remain a vacation house. To follow Pétain's career now we must understand what happened before, during, and right after February 6, 1934. The right-wing extremists, organized into veterans' and youth groups, had found a rallying cry in financial scandals, and in the real or imagined collusion of members of Parliament and government with the swindlers; the arch villain was Alexandre Stavisky, who had been accused of fraud on a vast scale. The report of his suicide when facing arrest led to allegations by extremists that those in power had disposed of him to conceal their own complicity. At the end of January 1934 the cabinet headed by Camille Chautemps fell, a scapegoat of the scandals. Extremists called for demonstrations on February 6 against an Edouard Daladier cabinet in the process of formation, the pretext being a protest against Daladier's dismissal of the prefect of police, Jean Chiappe, whom the demonstrators saw as sympathetic to their cause. A clash at the Concorde bridge leading to Parliament was bloody; the demonstrators spoke of throwing the deputies into the Seine River, but what they achieved instead was Daladier's withdrawal. A politician nearly everyone respected, former President Gaston Doumergue, was summoned from retirement to put together a government that all sides could accept.

No one could have provided more reassurance than Marshal Pétain; Doumergue made it known that he needed him in his cabinet. Pétain agreed to take the War Ministry on the understanding that nothing would be done to reduce military strength, the present level being the strict minimum needed for the defense of the nation. He told the press: "The President [Doumergue] told me that the country needs me. I didn't try to run away, but I've never engaged in politics and I don't want to now."[14] Putting the former commander in chief in charge of the army appeared to be a technical decision, and there was that in it. But in that crisis year it had to be a political event too. There is evidence that Doumergue asked Pétain "to be at my side like a flag."[15] The new cabinet was announced as a "government of union of parties and of public safety"; it contained other reassuring personalities—some reassuring to the right, some to the left, such as Edouard Herriot, Louis Barthou, Pierre-Etienne Flandin, and Pierre Laval.[16]

The uncompromising Marshal Lyautey saw the value of the symbol. Lyautey, now living in mainland France, was sympathetic to the right-wing movements that had marched on February 6, and by his own confession he had prepared for the worst. Alarmed at what he considered the "Masonic" conspiracy, which he thought to have been behind Daladier's dismissal of Prefect Chiappe, Lyautey had called on Weygand and, with his agreement, went on to see Pétain, on the eve of February 6, "to agree on the proper move if the event takes place," he told a friend. Were they conspiring, or taking measures to counter a conspiracy? In any case Lyautey wrote a confidant after Pétain's appointment as war minister: "I want you to know that I approve the choice of Pétain entirely. One can't have a better guarantee with respect to the veterans, the Croix de Feu movement, and the army. He remains for them the victor. . . ."[17]

Whatever was happening, it was enough to arouse suspicion on the other side. In the Socialist Party's comment on the appointment of Pétain, *Le Populaire* observed that unlike General Gaston Gallifet, who had put down the 1871 Commune with exceptional energy, Pétain "has until now the disadvantage of not having been an 'assassin' of the working class, but . . . he risks, and perhaps aspires to being one."[18]

Only a few months before Pétain entered the government, the traditional enemy had become more dangerous than ever. Chancellor Adolf Hitler, in office since January of the previous year, had moved Germany out of the League of Nations and the disarmament conference, while making overtures for a new disarmament agreement. The Doumergue government was to reject the prospect of endorsing Germany's rearming under the guise of reducing armament and henceforth resolved to assure its own security by its own means, an ambitious project in this decade of economic crisis. And these were the years of a scarcity of young men, corresponding to the devastation of a generation of fathers by the Great War. Starting in 1936, there was a drop of 50 percent in the draft-age population. In a word, Pétain could not have gotten the army France needed no matter how hard he tried. Did he try as hard as he could; did he ask for the right things? The answers to these questions are all but drowned in the controversy that enveloped his career beginning in 1940.

Thus Weygand, Gamelin, and the Supreme War Council considered it urgent to build up troop strength even if this meant returning to a two-year term of compulsory service. Pétain agreed with the military establishment. But to avoid a fight between the Doumergue cabinet and Parliament—Doumergue wishing to save his reservoir of goodwill for what he considered the essential issue of constitutional reform—Pétain would have to live with the twelve-month limit on compulsory service. The best he could hope to do was to make sure that the twelve months were actually being served.[19]

In a series of urgent appeals, Weygand warned Minister Pétain of the dangerous weakness of the army and asked him to summon a meeting of the Supreme War Council to discuss the question. Pétain refused. Weygand later attributed this refusal to Pétain's feeling that he had been in command of the army long enough to know what to do without the advice of a committee.[20]

Early in the reign of the new minister he appeared before the senate's committee on the army. A complete transcript has survived, and Pétain's critics have not failed to make use of it. For here he spoke as a cabinet officer defending his government's decision to leave compulsory service at twelve months and opposed the creation of a *commandement unique* in peacetime. On the other hand, he did insist on the need for an air force "capable of exercising reprisals or of bringing to bear a crushing attack on the enemy."[21]

On the matter of the northern frontier, he took another strong position that was to be remembered. He objected to extending the permanent defense system of the Maginot Line to France's common border with Belgium. He was talking about the frontier that would be crossed by Hitler's invading army in 1940, and what he said was: "From Montmédy on, there is the Ardennes forest. It is inpenetrable if special dispositions are taken." But if the invader ventured to come that way all the same, "we'll nip him coming out of the forest," he explained. "So this sector is not dangerous."[22]

Then and later, the charge was made that as minister of war Pétain ignored the urgency of constructing modern weapons for modern warfare, and often de Gaulle's progressive views are contrasted to Pétain's. The evidence suggests that Pétain had not forgotten what he had learned while dealing with air defense. "The struggle will begin with powerful aerial operations launched by surprise," he began one memorandum.[23] In this same year de Gaulle published *Vers l'Armée de métier*, in which, after dismissing the value of fixed fortifications and an army dependent on drafted troops, he advocated a skilled standing army of 100,000 men to be assisted by heavy tanks, heavy artillery, a regiment of reconnaissance planes and another of fighter planes. In de Gaulle's offensive strategy, air power existed for observation and camouflage (laying smoke screens) but could accomplish nothing by itself: "Aviation knows how to destory but cannot coerce, or conquer, or occupy territory."[24] (After the Second World War, de Gaulle inserted an acknowledgment of the importance of air war.)[25]

As a member of the cabinet, Pétain was acutely aware of the economic priority. In a memorandum dated March 16, 1934, outlining the conditions under which the budget for 1935 was to be prepared, he called attention to a Finance Ministry directive which warned that not only must all new expenses be rejected without examination, but "we must examine every category for every possible reduction."[26] Finally the government introduced a system of "special accounts" to allow extraordinary defense expenditures to be met outside the regular budget. In this way 1,275 million francs were found for frontier defense.[27]

A remarkable document can be read in the archives of the Army's Historical Service in Vincennes: It is a memorandum drafted by Pétain for General Gamelin outlining his philosophy, "the guiding lines which must inspire the organization of national defense." France had to be strong, had to be ready for war: that was one thing. But in Pétain's view the "formation of the race" had been neglected. France needed better premilitary preparation and a system of grade school education that assured children of healthy bodies and minds. "We must, on both points, take lessons from what is happening in Germany and in Italy."[28] In a letter to the minister of education often quoted, he warned against contamination of the reserve officers corps, in which teachers were particularly numerous;[29] in another letter to the education minister, he observed, "Some primary school teachers represent an evil influence on their pupils, discouraging them from pursuing military preparation." He reminded the minister, Aimé Berthod, that they had agreed to work together for a "moral recovery" which would require "authority and determination."[30]

Pétain wrote a preface for a book by his aide Paul Vauthier which presented Giulio Douhet's arguments for the use of aircraft offensively (it is dated June 7, 1934). In it Pétain made clear that he knew that the Italian general's views were considered heretical, representing a total reversal of values, requiring a reorganization of the high command. "War today involves not only standing armies"—possibly Pétain alluded here to de Gaulle's new book—"but entire populations." He described a modern air force which "leaps over all obstacles, acts as it wishes," and "strikes the entire territory of the enemy, its resources and its faith."[31]

In July, in a closed session of the Army Commission of the Chamber of Deputies, Pétain announced that "unless events require exceptional security measures, an extension of the duration of military service will not be envisaged," and this despite the advent of those "barren years"—corresponding to the depletion of fathers of families in the First World War—which were to span the 1936–1940 period.[32]

XIV
POLITICS ALL THE SAME

If we are to understand the political mind of the marshal in the years immediately preceding Vichy, we shall have to read between the lines and make our way through a large pile of hagiographic writings that tend to suggest he was a political eunuch. Actually, the evidence of those years is that he was as outspoken then as he had ever been.

On October 9, 1934—Doumergue was still premier and Pétain his war minister—King Alexander I of Yugoslavia, on a state visit to France, was shot and killed in Marseille by a Croatian terrorist; Foreign Minister Louis Barthou also died in the attack. The cabinet met on October 13 to replace Barthou, naming Laval in his place, while Interior Minister Albert Sarraut, recognizing the failure of his police to protect the royal visitor, resigned. The reorganization of the cabinet seemed terminated when Pétain spoke out. "We still have a dead weight on our team." To "general astonishment" he went on to say that public opinion could not accept the "dead weight" of unfinished prosecutions—the twin scandals of swindler Stavisky and Albert Prince, a court official

(and a Freemason) accused of negligence in prosecuting Stavisky. Justice Minister Henry Chéron had to go; he promptly resigned.[1] Léon Blum, summing up the lessons of the cabinet
revamping, reminded readers of the Socialist Party's daily organ
that Le Populaire had not been particularly kind to Sarraut or to
Chéron, but he saw them as victims of "the Fascists, their movements and their press."[2]

Just before the Chéron incident, Pétain had joined the official French delegation sent to Belgrade for the funeral of King
Alexander. A photograph in L'Illustration shows him standing
alongside German field marshal Hermann Göring, the latter
bending toward him as if in deep conversation.[3] The meeting of
the two marshals was remembered by at least one of them. In a
speech shortly after this encounter, a speech in which Göring
claimed Germany's right to be strong, he remarked: "Some weeks
ago I had an opportunity to talk to old Marshal Pétain. He's a
soldier and in consequence a man of honor, and he holds the
Germans in esteem. We can get along with men like that."[4] We
next hear of that meeting during a talk between the two men in
occupied France. Göring reminded Pétain of their Belgrade conversation and supposedly added: "You were already very anti-
Semitic then; you pointed to the Greek minister and told me: 'That
one's a Jew!' "[5]

The Doumergue government survived its reshuffling, but not
for long. Pétain continued to carry out his work as war minister
and now even felt emboldened, in an appearance before the
Chamber's Finance Commission on October 29, to call for abandonment of the policy of reduction of forces.[6] But Doumergue's
chief preoccupation now was structural. He presented a scheme
for constitutional reform, which he hoped would reinforce executive power. His reform would allow the cabinet, with the con-
currence of the president, to dissolve the Chamber of Deputies
and call for new elections whenever the situation became unten-
able. He also wanted the government to be able to spend funds
at the level of the previous year's budget when a hostile Parliament failed to vote the budget for the following year. Rumors
spread of further cabinet changes, even the formation of a new
government. Le Populaire reported speculation that the next cab-

inet would be a "union of the dissatisfied" led by Pétain, "an 'active' government which under the marshal's stick . . . will go so far as to ban extreme-right movements. . . ."[7]

On November 3, when the Radical Socialist ministers walked out of the cabinet—Doumergue had made his proposal for constitutional reform, comprising not only dissolution of the Chamber and restrictions on parliamentary budget initiatives, but banning strikes by government employees—Henry Lémery (who had replaced Henry Chéron as justice minister) suggested that Doumergue replace the defecting ministers and go before Parliament with a new cabinet. At this point Pétain is said to have made the comment, widely repeated later, "We can do without the Radicals. I'll be happy to take on the Education Ministry as well as War. I'll handle those Communist schoolteachers!"[8]

Perhaps it is now that Pétain drafted a letter of resignation—it is undated—pointing out that he had agreed to join the "national truce cabinet" in the hope of doing his work "apart from all political interference." The truce had been broken now, and he wished to follow Doumergue in his withdrawal.[9] But the letter would not be necessary: Doumergue took the collective resignation of his cabinet to President Lebrun. In a statement to the press on November 8, Doumergue blamed his government's downfall on "the men responsible for the policies which led to the mutinies of February and the death of war veterans."[10]

The new premier, Flandin, asked Pétain to stay on as war minister, but he refused. He had agreed to serve Doumergue, and he would leave with Doumergue. "Besides, seen up close, I didn't find politics very pretty," he confided to Gamelin.[11]

Had he been the ideal minister of war one hoped for in a former commander in chief? Opinions vary, and they are influenced by the marshal's subsequent career. It goes without saying that those later accused of failing to prepare France for war, such as Edouard Daladier and Pierre Cot, subsequently made public their evaluations of Pétain's ministry. In their view the lack of preparation began with the budget reductions carried out during his tenure, and with his unwillingness to extend the Maginot Line to the vulnerable northern frontier.[12]

Whatever the conclusions of the experts, the nation at large remained impressed. Soon after the fall of Doumergue, a Paris daily, *Le Petit Journal,* published an opinion poll entitled: "A Dictator? But Which One?", making it clear that it did not really wish to find a dictator but "only to probe the national conscience, to diagnose our fears, and above all to draw up a list of our hopes."[13] The paper announced that it had received 194,785 ballots and listed the top four winners as Pétain (38,561), Laval (31,403), Doumergue (23,864), and "Marianne," symbol of the Republic (20,102).[14] "I am very flattered by the confidence the French people place in me," Pétain told an interviewer for the paper. "I do wish to say nevertheless that I won't take advantage of it."[15] When Gustave Hervé, a pacificist-turned-Fascist, campaigned for a Pétain dictatorship in the pages of his newspaper *La Victoire* and in a tract that was prefaced with an endorsement of the dictatorships of Hitler and Mussolini, Pétain requested through third parties that Hervé put a stop to this campaign.[16]

Perhaps even more indicative of the effervescence of that time is a special issue of a left-oriented pictorial magazine called *Vu,* devoted to the likelihood of a clash between left and right in France. "What will the army do?" was the title of the contribution by Pierre Cot, a Radical Socialist who was to join Léon Blum's Popular Front government. In the event of an attempt by the Fascists to overthrow the government, or of agitation by groups such as the nationalist veterans movement called Croix de Feu, declared Cot, the army would obey the government. Should public order be troubled, President Albert Lebrun could appoint someone from outside the political arena to direct affairs of state. Which person? "His courage, his intellectual integrity, his honesty must be unquestionable"; he must be a person who would not take advantage of the situation. "The man exists," wrote Cot. "He is Marshal Pétain." For Pétain is "the true moral chief of the army," not only because he had been a great leader in war but because he was "the most humane and the closest to our misery." There is nothing to fear from him. But was this too much to ask of Pétain? Cot didn't think so, for it wasn't a matter of asking him to run the country. "He only has to keep order for a few hours." But wasn't the idea dangerous all the same? "I think my proposal will be approved," concluded Cot, "by all those who have seen that astonishing thing: Marshal Pétain's gaze."[17]

It reached the point, in the first months of 1936, that a newspaper as responsible as *Le Figaro,* in an appeal at the top of its front page over the signature of the diplomat and writer Wladimir d'Ormesson, called on the premier of the moment, Albert Sarraut, to bow out so that President Lebrun could appoint Pétain, who "incarnates, in the eyes of the entire world, the strong, calm, and humane virtues of eternal France." D'Ormesson did not mention Pétain by name, although the immediate reaction showed that readers knew he was referring to Pétain.[18]

But the French were going to try a different solution. The spring elections brought the Popular Front to power with Blum. The year produced events that made certain elements of the right even more convinced that an extra-parliamentary solution was necessary, and Pétain remained their favorite. We have evidence of Pétain's state of mind during those agitated weeks, and from an unimpeachable source: the notes made by a friendly witness, young Dr. Bernard Ménétrel, immediately after a talk with Pétain. It was during an evening spent in Metz, on June 20, 1936; Ménétrel made his notes on the stationery of their hotel; it is as if a tape recorder had been available then, and we possessed the tape.

Pétain believed, noted Ménétrel, that the French had not yet suffered enough; they hadn't fallen "low enough"; they would have to be frightened. France needed a flag-bearer, but it would not be he. "And yet he is thinking about it," Ménétrel adds immediately, for he hears Pétain suggest the examples of Mussolini, with a king to back him; of Primo de Rivera, with his king; of Hitler, with Hindenburg to back him "morally." In France there was Jacques Doriot; Pétain could help him. (Doriot, formerly a left-winger, was about to announce the founding of a "national" and "social" Parti Populaire Français). There would be some socialism in Pétain's ideal system, but with "clean people." In fact, he expressed admiration for Léon Blum, whose platform was inadvisable perhaps, but he had "a fist."

That night, from eleven to midnight, Ménétrel worked with Pétain on a speech the marshal was to deliver the next day to mark the twentieth anniversary of the decisive battle at Verdun. And then the older man settled down to tell the younger man what had to be done. "To take over the government with five men free of ambition," Pétain said—adding that he hadn't yet found such men. A young leader, with Pétain behind him; at this point Ménétrel offered a candidate: Colonel François de La Rocque of the Croix de Feu movement. Error! replied Pétain: La Rocque would be "pulverized." One had to know how to wait. Would President Lebrun accept Pétain's plan? They didn't need the president, or the constitution, said Pétain. The real problem was his age. Yes, suggested Ménétrel, but you can give orders from your armchair. "No, you have to be at the front." Ménétrel protested: Pétain hadn't, after all, done the actual firing during the war. This led the older man to reflect: He admitted that he could still be the leader behind the lines. Another objection came to him: It would take ten years to restore France; he wouldn't live long enough.

Pétain's conclusion, as Ménétrel heard it that night in Metz: "to find a handful of men who will march under his orders." They would have to be men without blemishes, physical or moral; they would have to be psychologists, technicians, without personal ambition, and they would have to know how to lead men. Ménétrel had the feeling that if such men could be found for Pétain—men already known to Pétain—he would accept, would try to raise France to her feet. Pétain would found his politics on the family, the schools, the army; his social program would permit a reduction in working hours without reductions in pay, the leisure time gained to be devoted to agriculture. He would take advantage of the Blum experiment then under way: Pétain's France would have the advantage of the firm discipline now being imposed by Blum. "Blum would thus pave the way," noted Ménétrel, "without wishing to, for a takeover by men who are both frank and French."[19]

Someone else recognized Pétain's potential, not only for France but for himself. Apparently as early as 1936 Pierre Laval was calling Pétain a symbol, a heaven-sent man around whom patriots could rally. When a visitor expressed doubt that the old marshal's physical condition would allow him to carry out such a task, Laval reportedly replied: "Who's talking about work? We need a flag. A flag doesn't work. You stand in its shade."[20]

Laval was a man of plots, and our information about them comes from many sources. Thus, among German government documents seized after World War II, one can find a dispatch of

Germany's ambassador to Spain in April 1937, transmitting a report of a secret meeting between Laval—at his request—and an emissary of Francisco Franco. Laval expressed sympathy with the Nationalist cause in Spain and went on to talk about the serious internal situation in France. He said that he was in touch with Jacques Doriot, François de La Rocque, and Pétain, and felt that France's salvation lay in a Pétain government; he added that the marshal was prepared to assume this responsibility.[21]

One of Laval's biographers describes his thought processes: France's only hope was a Latin bloc, an alliance with Franco and Mussolini. Laval, who kept in touch with right-wing movements in France, had become increasingly disillusioned with the efficiency of parliamentary government. Hence his dream of a stronger system, in which he would be the moving spirit behind Pétain.[22] The two men had met in 1931 during their respective American missions and had served together in Doumergue's cabinet. Laval wanted Pétain to join the government he himself formed in June 1935, but the old man declined. In August of that year Laval's daughter Josée married René de Chambrun, the son of Pétain's friend and helper General Adalbert de Chambrun. Pétain had watched René—"Bunny"—grow up. In "Bunny" Laval had what he thought was the perfect intermediary.[23]

XV

FRIENDS

When the fall of the Doumergue cabinet in November 1934 left him without a job, Pétain was well past his seventy-eighth birthday. But marshals don't retire, and this particular one seemed to relish responsibility. He still maintained a large enough staff to allow him to handle whatever assignment came his way. The premier who took over from Doumergue, Pierre-Etienne Flandin, had reestablished a High Military Committee to coordinate defense requirements; besides Flandin, it was composed of the three war ministers, top-echelon military officers, and Pétain by name. In another decree, the marshal was made a member of the Supreme Council of National Defense, with the right to vote.[1] He returned to his customary office on the Boulevard des Invalides. Among regular visitors was General Charles Brécard. A former inspector of cavalry, he seems to have had some responsibility for Pétain's political education in the years immediately preceding the fall of France. According to Colonel Alfred Conquet, who replaced Émile Laure as Pétain's private secretary now, Brécard brought the marshal into a dinner circle known as Les Affinités

Françaises, around which he organized lectures and study groups. Here, we are told, Pétain was to meet his future private secretary of Vichy's early days, Henri Du Moulin de Labarthète, and perhaps—as has already been suggested—Raphaël Alibert.[2]

In May 1935, Pétain was a minister again—or almost. The Flandin government was defeated in the Chamber on its request for full powers to deal with the economic situation, and once more there was a call for "a government of union." The choice to head it fell to the president of the Chamber, Fernand Bouisson, an independent who had resigned from the Socialist Party a year earlier to support Doumergue's program for national union. Bouisson drew up a list of cabinet members representing all the parties except the Communists, and Pétain was drafted once again.[3] "The best thing about the Bouisson cabinet, as earlier in the Doumergue cabinet," wrote Léon Daudet on the front page of daily *Action Française,* "is Marshal Pétain."[4] Bouisson won a vote of confidence but lost on a request for a delegation of powers to deal with the economic situation; the experiment was over.[5]

Minister or not, retired or not, year-round the marshal ran a busy office. Colonel Conquet has passed on lively descriptions of the daily grind on the Boulevard des Invalides. The next witness after him was Georges Loustaunau-Lacau, who joined Pétain's staff in March 1935. Pétain explained that he needed someone to write his speeches and articles. "I hasten to tell you that, since I usually don't do my own writing, I'm difficult and even a crank about the drafts that are written for me." He added that he favored "a central theme which sustains the text from start to finish," a minimum of paragraphs, sentences that contained subject, verb, object, but no adjectives.

Loustaunau-Lacau discovered Pétain's acid humor, and the old man warned the new recruit: "Don't forget, irony functions here only from top to bottom." In aide de camp Bonhomme, Pétain had an ideal number two; in Loustaunau's observation, Bonhomme played the role of the wife Pétain never really had. Bonhomme took care of all details, never left Pétain's side. He had good sense and a sense of humor; he was Pétain's only intimate, for Laure was too lofty, Bernard Ménétrel "too much a kid." "I want Bonhomme to be the one who closes my eyes," the marshal would say (the opposite came to pass at Vichy).[6]

In the spring of 1936, Pétain delivered himself of a rare public endorsement of a political movement, and of a political philosophy. The stakes were high, for France was voting. On April 26 the first round of national legislative elections had pointed to a victory for the left. But everything remained to be won, or lost, on the second ballot, scheduled for May 3. On the front page of a right-wing daily, *Le Journal,* Pétain was quoted in an exclusive interview: "Everything that is international is evil. Everything that is national is useful and fruitful. The Croix de Feu represents one of the healthiest elements in this country." He praised the La Rocque movement for its ideals: defense of the family, "moral and spiritual improvement of youth." When asked for his position concerning the following Sunday's ballot, he declined to reply. The French crisis, he said, was not material but spiritual, and a new "mystic" was necessary.[7]

Then and later, Pétain's relations with La Rocque and his followers were ambiguous. In the mid-1930s La Rocque had enemies not only on the left (which saw in his organized, disciplined veterans' movement a precursor of Fascism) but on the extreme right as well, for here La Rocque was considered too moderate, too respectful to the Republic and its government.[8] There were elements in the Croix de Feu program to which Pétain could adhere, an echo of his own experience in the Doumergue cabinet, of his suspicions of the Freemasons, left-wing parties, and parties in general. And when the Croix de Feu, after being banned by the Popular Front government in 1936, became the Parti Social Français, it came up with a slogan: "Work, Family, Fatherland," which Pétain would remember when it came time to proclaim the principles of his own regime in Vichy.[9]

In that feverish year of 1936, some were prepared to see Communist plots, Masonic conspiracies, everywhere. One day, Pétain's aide Conquet relates, an "important person" whom he identifies as J.B., and who may be Joseph Barthélemy, one of Pétain's justice ministers in Vichy, walked in with a "most secret" report revealing the structure of the Communist Party and its plans for revolution. Alfred Conquet's own feeling was that the Popular Front was overloaded with Jews. He says that Pétain refused to attend the July 14 Bastille Day parade in the official grandstand because "The first rows will be filled with all those politicians who for twenty years have been advocating anti-militarism, renuciation, surrender. . . ."[10]

It is in this context, in this atmosphere of fear of the unknown, that the activities of Loustaunau-Lacau must be placed. Responsible for political affairs in Pétain's Invalides headquarters, this officer had set up an organization of his own which he called the Corvignolles Secret Service. Its purpose was to combat subversion, particularly within the army. Later he would claim that he did not inform Pétain of the existence of his organization, despite the fact that an early recruit was Pétain's closest aide, Léon Bonhomme. Why hadn't Loustaunau informed his chief of what he was doing? Not only to protect him, but also (he said in 1945) because Pétain was imprudent and opportunistic, always favoring the stronger side.[11]

XVI

THE NEXT WAR

In the second half of the 1930s decade, the chief concern of Marshal Pétain and his staff was military preparedness. So many records of those years are self-serving, and where Pétain is concerned, so ardently pro or violently against that it is difficult to define responsibilities. Fortunately we now have access to the secret papers covering those years, so we have a fair idea of what was really being thought and said. Thus, in a secret session of the High Military Committee under the chairmanship of Premier Flandin on January 9, 1935, we have Pétain pleading once again for an increase in air strength, complaining of bad faith on the part of some people that was delaying progress in civil defense—notably in cities with Communist or Socialist mayors.[1] In a second meeting of the High Committee the same month, he warned that the next war would not last four years, "because it would call into play such material means, and cause such demoralization, that the conflict could not last more than several months." He expressed concern at German rearming and suggested that France occupy its fortified frontier positions right away. To Laval's question, "Must we envisage the possibility of France fighting alone?" he replied affirmatively.[2]

The argument as to Pétain's responsibility for the inadequate state of French forces at the outbreak of the Second World War will probably never end. Later, Air Minister Pierre Cot, who sat alongside Pétain at many of these planning sessions, was to say that the marshal exercised "a sort of intellectual dictatorship" on military thinking. He blamed Pétain for not objecting to the general orientation of French military policy but made no specific charge that Pétain flatly opposed a buildup.[3] One could argue that Pétain's views were not in all respects adapted to the war Hitler would wage, but he was not alone in France in failing to anticipate Nazi tactics. Would the war have gone differently if Pétain's pleas for a strong, offensive air force and a unified command to make maximum use of it had been heeded? The question is at least as valid as the ones that have been put.

Much has been made of the preface he wrote for a book by General Narcisse Chauvineau with the provocative title: *Is an Invasion Still Possible? (Une invasion est-elle encore possible?).*[4] In November 1937, General Laure had warned his former chief of the danger in endorsing Chauvineau's thesis that a continuous defense line would protect France from being overrun. With Pétain's approval, his chief of staff Colonel Vauthier replied to Laure that because current doctrine was again favoring offensives, and France was obviously not going to be the aggressor, the only way to stop the enemy at the outset of the next war was to wait for it on an organized battlefield. Pétain felt that his support of Chauvineau would be a way to challenge the thinking that was taking France back to the worst days of 1913. But the old man made one concession: He agreed that it would be better to stress the notion that the continuous-front strategy was applicable only "at the commencement of operations."[5]

When a copy of Chauvineau's book turned up on his desk, General Gamelin later recalled, he asked the cabinet of Defense Minister Daladier (who by now was also premier) how it happened that the book was allowed to appear. "We couldn't stop publication of a book prefaced by the Marshal," he was told.[6]

In April 1937, Pétain celebrated his eighty-first birthday; statistics tell us that three-quarters of all men born when he was were already dead.[7] We have further statistics for that year, concerning the marshal's income. He earned 136,755 francs as marshal—something like 200,000 francs in today's currency.[8] That year he took out an annuity with the Confederation Life Association of Toronto by making a single payment of £3,177; he was to receive from this policy £600 annually. The source of the initial sterling sum was never clarified, and in 1945 the public accountant who audited his finances for the High Court concluded: "Thus to counter the risks of inflation, then threatening, the Marshal—without a personal fortune—sought to consolidate his situation and guarantee his old age."[9] "If the government maintains the same rate of spending," a worried Pétain wrote to his wife that year, "it will be futile for us to watch our own budget."[10] (The date was July 11, just a fortnight before he was to receive the first semiannual installment of his Canadian annuity.)

Loustaunau-Lacau records that the marshal spent a good part of the same summer inspecting frontier defenses. During a twenty-eight-day tour they covered nearly every inch of the Maginot Line, which Loustaunau saw as a monumental fiasco, and apparently Pétain was not far from agreeing. Thus, when a general indicated that he had placed his best battalions in front of the forts to protect them, Loustaunau thought, "That's the limit! They spent billions to build forts to save human flesh and they're covering them with flesh to save their cement!" And Pétain confided to him, "I've heard a lot of stupidities in my military career but none like that one."[11]

XVII
MUNICH

The election of a new president of France to replace Albert Lebrun was not due to take place until the spring of 1939 (the president was then elected by the Chamber and Senate sitting together as the National Assembly), but a full year before that his friends were promoting Pétain's candidacy. For president or for premier—Pétain in power in any case. His adviser Henry Lémery as early as March 1938 lobbied for the old marshal's appointment as premier to replace the fallen Camille Chautemps.[1] Blum got the job, although he lasted less than a month, giving way to Daladier. As for the presidency, Laval considered Pétain his very own favorite horse for that post.[2] "My office is jammed with people who are trying to get me to accept functions which I don't want and which would represent a crushing responsibility for me," Pétain wrote a friend in March 1938. "I have a desire for independence and freedom which doesn't concur with the plans they have for me."[3]

One of the things he did that year was to draw up a will, or a revised will. Only the codicil has been found. It contains a phrase that was to be remembered: "My dearest wish is to be buried in the National Cemetery of Douaumont," he declared, "or close to this cemetery." He had, he said, resisted the intention of Verdun to erect a statue in his honor, but if that town persisted in its desire after his death then he wished it to be the equestrian statue by Cogné. He also declared that he had left no memoirs, "for I have always noted that their authors, overly inclined to justify their errors, take liberties with truth which make them quite indulgent for themselves and very severe for everybody else."[4]

That year too the Nazis completed their annexation of Austria, after which Hitler turned his attention to another weak neighbor; pressure against Czechoslovakia built up all summer and fall. "I hoped to leave Paris Monday evening," Pétain wrote Eugénie on September 9—she was already at Villeneuve-Loubet—but "events don't allow it." If the situation prevented him from coming at all—"for we must think of everything"—he would give instructions on how to harvest the grapes. But on the following day he was more reassuring. "Talks have resumed and in the end the Czechs will give in." On September 14 he wrote to his wife: "I don't believe that we can be dragged in to the Czechoslovak brawl. Not unless our leaders lose their heads."[5] Neither the French nor the British were dragged in just then, for at a meeting in Munich at the end of that month Prime Minister Neville Chamberlain for Britain and Premier Edouard Daladier for France, in the presence of Benito Mussolini, accepted Hitler's demand for a portion of Czechoslovak territory. Chamberlain returned to London with the assurance "I believe it is peace for our time. . . ." (And, he added, it was a "peace with honour.") From then on Hitler could assume that the Western Allies were not going to interfere with his plans for Europe.

Charles de Gaulle had not forgotten the book he had written with Marshal Pétain, or for Marshal Pétain. And when a publisher asked him to do a study of the military profession, de Gaulle, now a colonel commanding a regiment of tanks, responded that he lacked the time but suggested publishing that manuscript he had worked on a decade earlier.[6] On August 2, 1938, de Gaulle took up his pen to inform his onetime protector that he intended to publish the contested manuscript under the title *France and Its Army (La France et son armée)*. Since the work had been carried out under the older man's "impulsion," de Gaulle asked him to sign a preface; he even enclosed a draft of one.[7]

The reaction was sharp. Pétain snapped that he was "deeply astonished" that Colonel de Gaulle planned to sign a book that Pétain had ordered him to write. He reminded the author in a letter of August 4, 1938, that it was when de Gaulle had announced that the work was his literary property that Pétain had "taken the decision to lock it in a drawer." And now de Gaulle thought that he could publish it simply by informing Pétain that it was happening. "The work I assigned you was a staff study," he insisted. "I consider that this work belongs to me personally and exclusively."[8]

Most of the book, objected de Gaulle on August 18, had been written after his departure from Pétain's staff, and even the section actually written for Pétain had been heavily revised, so that the book's "literary, historical, philosophical nature" now made it anything but a staff assignment. And in the eleven years since Pétain had put an end to their association, many things had changed. "I was then 37 years old; now I am 48. Morally I have been injured—even by you, Marshal, I've lost illusions, abandoned ambitions." He was gradually becoming known for his ideas, his style; he could no longer remain incognito. Still, he wished to acknowledge Pétain's contribution to the conception of the book, if only Pétain would allow him to do that.[9]

The two soldiers met in Paris on August 28.[10] De Gaulle was persuasive, the old man yielded; on September 5, Pétain offered a draft dedication for the book that acknowledged Pétain's "advice in the preparation" of four chapters. Taking Pétain's draft as nothing more than a suggested draft, de Gaulle embellished it in the book as published:

TO

MONSIEUR

LE MARÉCHAL PÉTAIN

WHO WISHED THIS BOOK TO BE WRITTEN,

WHO WITH HIS ADVICE GUIDED

THE WRITING OF THE FIRST FIVE CHAPTERS,

AND THANKS TO WHOM

THE FINAL TWO ARE THE HISTORY

OF OUR VICTORY.

Pétain protested—directly to the publisher, Plon. This dedication represented a veritable breach of trust, and he demanded its suppression.[11] De Gaulle saw Pétain's reaction as "a little intrigue of the Pétain clan" without importance and advised Plon to reply to the marshal "in a way which is most polite in form but evasive in content." There would always be time, should the book be reprinted, to defer to the "so-called wishes of the Marshal."[12]

The controversy over *La France et son armée* was not to be forgotten. It would be evoked again and again by the marshal; it would be described by General de Gaulle. In later retellings it was graced with colorful details, sometimes to the advantage of one of the antagonists, sometimes to that of the other.[13] De Gaulle's book as published contains a stirring tribute to the victor of Verdun: "Above all, a chief appeared who taught the army the art of the real and the possible," begins a paragraph on Pétain's leadership. "From the day one had to choose between ruin and reason Pétain was promoted." The author speaks of the marshal's "lucid personage," his "critical spirit."[14] De Gaulle's dedication to Pétain was removed from reprintings of this book after the liberation of Paris.

In November 1938, Pétain traveled to Metz for the twentieth anniversary of the entry of French troops into the liberated Lorraine. He painted a grim portrait of present-day France, which had "allowed most of the advantages of our victory to escape." The French had let themselves be lured by "material pleasures and desires." France's decline was due to "the abandonment of all spiritual life in the framework of the nation, for the world is governed by ideas."[15] He told a congress of the National Veterans Union: "It's our very lack of seriousness which is the cause of our divisions."[16]

In December he was in Villeneuve-Loubet. His friend Marie-Antoinette Pardee remembered one of their conversations: Seated before a pile of letters, Pétain told her: "Look, they want me to take power, as if they didn't know that I don't want it at any price and that I desire my independence." She asked him if by taking power he might not "restore the situation and perhaps avoid war," to which he replied: "I know nothing about politics." Politicians detested him, he explained; he didn't know why, for he had never played politics. Then: "Well, yes I do know, and I'll tell you: I bother them, I'm still alive. But when they have brought France to the end of the abyss, and we are on the eve of catastrophe, I'm the one they'll look for."[17]

When the call came, it was an unexpected one. General Franco's armies had taken Madrid and all Spain; Pétain, as a military man and an ally of the Spanish generals during the Moroccan war, seemed the right person to serve as France's first ambassador there; his prestige, as well as his relations, might help Franco to forget that the French had not been on his side. As the minister of foreign affairs of the period, Georges Bonnet, later explained it: The point was to reconcile France and Spain before war broke out with Germany.[18] In his meeting with Bonnet at the Foreign Ministry, Pétain posed three conditions: "First, I want to deal directly with you. Second, I want a new car. Finally, I want no women in the embassy." Bonnet smiled. "Your wishes are easy to satisfy." Pétain then took a blank sheet of paper from his briefcase and waited for instructions. Bonnet was moved to see this prestigious old man seated before him with pen poised over paper, like an earnest pupil; from time to time Pétain would say: "Speak more slowly so I can write it all down." Bonnet explained the need to keep the Spanish frontier friendly in the event of war, and of keeping communications open to North Africa. France was also anxious to obtain strategic materials from her southern neighbor, notably pyrites for explosives.[19]

When the appointment was announced, on March 2, 1939, a right-wing daily quoted Pétain as saying he would find in Franco one of the best pupils of France's War College, and "the dearest companion" in the joint French-Spanish pacification of Morocco.[20] Another rightist periodical published an interview in which Pétain was quoted as calling Franco "a great mind." He was "calm and ponderate"; the French could trust him.[21] For the left, Pétain was too good for Franco. "Sending Marshal Pétain to Burgos [temporary capital of Franco Spain] will shock . . . as if it were in bad taste," wrote Léon Blum. "The noblest, the most humane of our military chiefs is out of place alongside General Franco."[22] And when Pétain actually reached Spain, the Communist organ in Paris was quick to report Franco's reluctance to receive "the illustrious soldier"; the paper saw a humiliation to France in the act of allowing "its most honored soldier to wait until a disloyal general decides to see him."[23]

France had just then recognized General Franco's regime, a *de jure* recognition preceding the establishment of formal relations. On February 25, 1939, French diplomat Léon Bérard and General Francisco Gomez Jordana, Franco's foreign minister, had signed three documents: a declaration affirming both countries' intentions to maintain friendly relations; a promise by France to return gold, arms, and equipment that had belonged to or had been ordered by Republican Spain, along with livestock brought into France, cargo and fishing vessels, art treasures, cash, stock, and other valuables; and a pledge by both parties to prevent on their respective territories any activity directed against the other. These were documents that Pétain had not seen, of which he was not even aware when he agreed to serve in Spain, documents that he said "deeply surprised him," for they gave up gold and war matériel, for example, with nothing offered in return.[24]

Just prior to taking up his assignment in Spain, Pétain apparently disappeared from circulation for a week, a week that he spent incognito in Normandy, in an inn noted for its table. He was accompanied by an unidentified woman who drove him there in a small open car and whom he introduced as his "cousin"; later, the innkeeper described her, and the description fitted that of Jacqueline de Castex.[25]

At first, the new ambassador and his staff had to take up quarters just over the border at San Sebastián, in an elegant villa surrounded by gardens. Eugénie Pétain stayed on the French side, in Hendaye, and drove across to Spain each day to see her husband; later, she remembered that they could still hear the shelling of the last battles in the Civil War.[26] Pétain discovered that he was going to enjoy a singular advantage as ambassador, for the War Ministry unearthed an old decree that allowed the combining of a marshal's pay with a civil appointment. So in addition to his annual indemnity of 150,000 francs as marshal (plus 30,000 francs for expenses), he was to receive an ambassador's salary of 141,000 francs, with an additional 640,800 francs as a representational allowance.[27] It would be a "fat" year, he informed Eugénie; they'd be able to "put some comfort and order in our affairs"; the new assignment "came at the right time."[28]

XVIII
SPAIN

In a first comprehensive report to Daladier, who was now both premier and minister of national defense and of war, Ambassador Pétain set forth Spanish demands. The Franco government claimed that France owed it compensation because of previous hostility, and what the Spaniards wanted was the warships that the French had interned in Bizerta. Pétain recommended giving back the fleet as the most efficacious way to restore confidence. It was important to counterbalance the influence of Germany and Italy, and return of the fleet would also encourage Spain to take over responsibility for refugees still in France. Daladier agreed.[1]

Soon the new ambassador was ready to provide his government with an overall view of French-Spanish relations. He reported that he had been received courteously but coolly; until proved otherwise, every Frenchman was suspect south of the border. The Spaniards blamed France for having supported the "reds," which Pétain agreed had been the case. Pétain told Daladier that in any case France should have used its bargaining position—possession of Spain's gold, for example—to oblige Spain to take back its refugees ("who weigh heavily on our finances, on our defense, and on the people of our southwest provinces").[2]

The first encounter with Franco, when it came, was glacial. The generalissimo hardly opened his mouth.[3] Much later Pétain was to recall that Franco had stood up during their whole meeting and didn't even invite the old marshal to sit; after the audience the Spanish leader didn't accompany him to the door, so he had to find his own way out.[4] Eugénie Pétain remembered that when she and her husband showed themselves in public in those first days, local inhabitants would turn their backs or even spit in their direction.[5]

In a dispatch to Daladier in April, Pétain repeated his conviction that even if the Bérard-Jordana accords were draconian, entered into on the French side to protect the country from having a belligerent Spain on her border, it was essential to apply them loyally. Otherwise, anti-French elements in the Franco government would block execution of the political engagement contained in the agreement.[6] "I still think that in case of international conflict the Spaniards will sincerely try to remain neutral," the ambassador reported to Paris after a meeting with Foreign Minister Jordana. "But as long as the attitude concerning us which reigns in many circles hasn't evolved, as long as a veil of forgetfulness isn't thrown over the resentments nourished with respect to us and on the services rendered by Rome and Berlin to the nationalist cause, we cannot dismiss the possibility that the Spaniards will want to harm us in the event of war."[7] There was good cause to worry about war now. After the Munich pact Hitler had moved troops into Czechoslovakia, setting up a protectorate there in March 1939. In the same month he occupied Memel, which had been taken from Germany after the First World War, and was then under Lithuanian control. And Germany was now demanding that Poland turn over another lost territory, Dantzig, then under international supervision; soon enough the demand was to become a *casus belli*. Germany's hand was soon to be strengthened by the neutralization of the Soviet Union: On August 23, 1939, the two nations signed a nonaggression pact which would lead to the dividing up of Poland when the Germans launched their invasion on September 1.

* * *

Although far off in Spain, Pétain was much in the thoughts of his political friends back in Paris. Some felt that Daladier had sent him to Spain because he was jealous of his popularity. Members of Parliament who favored Pétain's candidacy for the presidency (the elections to be held in April 1939) had empowered Gaston Henry-Haye to speak for them; Henry Lémery was also active. "I see that there is a lot of excitement concerning the presidential election," Pétain wrote his wife on March 21. "I'm going to be careful not to be involved in this affair, the very idea of which horrifies me." He wrote his political adviser General Brécard, enclosing a statement declaring that he was not a candidate and added to Brécard: "I am firmly resolved to resist all pressures which might be exercised to try to change my mind." He could best serve his country, he added, by carrying out his mission to Spain, not by accepting "a function absolutely contrary to my aptitudes and my desire of independence."[8] In any case, Albert Lebrun agreed to stand for reelection and was returned to the Elysée Palace without difficulty. But there is considerable evidence that Pétain listened to—if he did not encourage—political friends who wished him to take power. The ambiguity of Pétain's attitude was such that the very existence of these contacts was later taken as evidence of a plot against the Republic.

Thus, Henry Lémery later admitted that he had gone to see Pétain in San Sebastián, apparently with Pétain's political mentor Raphaël Alibert, and had argued that if the situation in France further deteriorated, Pétain would have to be prepared to head the government. When Pétain protested that he didn't know how he would deal with such a situation, Lémery drew up a list of persons who could be ministers in a Pétain cabinet; he quotes Pétain's reaction: "The whole thing's a joke."[9] And embassy councillor Armand Gazel was to remember that Ambassador Pétain twice showed him lists of cabinet ministers he would appoint if he headed the French government; both lists contained the names of Pierre Laval and Henry Lémery. Gazel, who was himself a career diplomat, did not consider Pétain's comments on these lists in the nature of a plot against the government and remembered that Pétain would tell him, "The politicians are trying to use me. They're making a mistake."[10]

A journalist who talked to Laval shortly after the beginning of the war remembered that Laval also saw Pétain as a head of government. "Contrary to what they say I'm not associated with Pétain," he said, "but I saw how respectful Göring was to him in Crakow at the funeral of Pilsudski. I'm aware of his prestige. His name would draw the best and most energetic men we have." When the journalist objected that he had seen Pétain in Spain and found him truly too old, Laval reportedly replied, "That's without importance. What would we ask of him? To be a mantelpiece, a statue on a pedestal. His name! his prestige! nothing more."[11]

In that same period—the date was September 8, 1939, just a week after Hitler attacked Poland—Daladier called Pétain to Paris (it was the ambassador's first trip home since he had left for Spain the previous March). The premier asked Pétain to join his cabinet, but he declined, evoking the problems that remained to be dealt with in Spain. In reality, Pétain confided to intimates, he had no confidence in Daladier as a war leader and did not approve of some of the ministers Daladier had chosen to serve alongside Pétain.[12] Which ministers? Apparently the presence of radical leader Edouard Herriot bothered him most, and he had posed another condition for participation in a Daladier cabinet: an immediate agreement with Italy.[13] The political gossip was that Laval had gotten to Pétain before Daladier, and convinced him to refuse to serve with Herriot; Laval would also have pleaded the cause of Italy.[14] (Although Italy had already signed a friendship treaty with Germany, it did not join the war; in fact Mussolini waited until France was about to surrender to Germany to abandon nonbelligerence.)

"I have been asking myself for a long time what is the best way to render service to the nation," Pétain wrote his aide Paul Vauthier in January 1940. "I've come to the following conclusion: my physical strength doesn't allow me to support the weight of a government post and so I abandon the idea." But there was still the army: Perhaps he could be useful there, to deal with problems involving morale. "But if nothing is asked of me," he concluded, "I'll go back to plowing."[15] This was the period of the *drôle de guerre,* the "phony war": France and Britain were engaged in a global defense against the challenger, Nazi Germany, in mainland Europe, in the Mediterranean basin, North Africa, and the Middle East, but the two sides were taking up or building up positions; there had been little fighting until now.

In a sense, by serving as French ambassador to Franco he was already performing a role in national defense; the subject came up every day. He wrote Henry Lémery that "the Spanish press is still subject to German influence"; he was trying to counter it, but the Germans disposed of considerable funds for the purpose of bribery.[16] But by October 1939 the ambassador was able to report to Daladier that "the tide is turning in our favor"; there was less hostility to France now, and the announcement in the previous August that the Germans and Russians had signed a pact facilitated his task by opening the eyes of many Spaniards to the true nature of Hitlerism. He did not believe that France would have to fight Spain in addition to her other enemies. Henceforth the main job was to develop French-Spanish trade and to convince Spaniards, "by an enlightened but discreet propaganda, that France's fight is a continuation of the Nationalist cause in the Spanish Civil War." In this message to Daladier, Pétain also requested that he be replaced, for he wished to return to France to participate in high-level military deliberations, where he could utilize his World War I experience; he was prepared, he said, to carry out missions in the front or rear.[17]

Daladier preferred to keep Pétain in Spain; as he explained it later, he wanted the old man as far as possible from Pierre Laval.[18]

XIX
MAY 1940

That Pétain knew his job was not finished is suggested by the telegram he sent his Foreign Ministry on January 3, 1940, pleading for immediate execution of commitments made to Spain. If France did not deliver the needed wheat and carry out the other terms of the accords, Spain would not supply France with explosives; indeed, Spain would turn against France.[1] His feeling about the war, and the way it was being managed, comes out in a letter he wrote on the same day to his Paris liaison officer, Colonel Henri Pellissier de Féligonde, reporting on the mail he was getting from France that described "a notable lack of resolution in the government, which usually prefers words to action." Pétain himself felt that life in France had become "too easygoing. . . . To stimulate energies, there is nothing like suffering."[2] Receiving the French colony in the salons of his embassy for a New Year's party, he expressed somewhat more optimism, urging his fellow citizens "to patient efforts in all fields of endeavor, to hasten victory." He also said: "Under the wise leadership of General Franco Spain is recovering after the ordeal of a civil war which was the most horrible of all wars"; he urged his audience to help Spain in its renaissance, which would be a "work of justice and friendship."[3]

Later in January he visited Paris again; he told General Joseph Georges (who had been his chief of staff in Morocco and now commanded France's crucial northeast theater of operations) that his visit had been "incognito," that he had seen friends as well as the military establishment and learned a lot about the "poor organization" of the army command, which he described as "anarchy." But he advised Georges to stick to his job all the same.[4] Back in Spain, he was visited by an old friend and fellow academician, Louis Gillet, who reported what he saw for readers of the daily *Paris-Soir*. Gillet described the embassy, a late-nineteenth-century mansion decorated with Gobelins tapestries. And the ambassador: "At 85 [sic] he looks 60. . . . His body, invulnerable to age, seems composed of fresh snow, or of marble bathed in ambrosia." Spaniards tell him: "You can't imagine what miracles the Marshal has created here." Even Franco admired him. Gillet hears about the considerable distribution of material aid to the population: "the Marshal's trucks" were a familiar sight in Madrid. Pétain himself felt that France's best propaganda in Spain would be victory in the war against Germany. To that Gillet added: "Meanwhile, for Spain, Pétain is our propaganda."[5]

Still, this man of marble had private feelings. He would have liked to be in Paris, where momentous things were happening; but he would have liked to be in Villeneuve-Loubet too. From Spain, in the middle of his preoccupations with the local situation and the far-off war, he wrote to his friend Marie-Antoinette Pardee about the condition of the roof of his beloved Ermitage. (He seemed to know more about it than she did, and she lived nearby.) The roof needed replacement, "a job which can't be done in my absence, but I can't spend in south France the two months required for it."[6] Writing to Bernard Ménétrel, then in uniform, of the possibility that the doctor could obtain leave to visit him in Madrid, he said: "The month of April would be favorable. But watch out for the Boche! It's possible that all leaves will be cancelled at that time."[7]

Friends continued to beseech him to return to France, arguing that the situation required that he be there.[8] The press joined in; the newspaper campaign in behalf of this providential man was not to let up as long as the Third Republic lasted.[9] "In Paris everybody is talking about you, of your coming back, of the various deals being made to bring you into the government to strengthen its weak spine," one of his intimates reported from the capital (this on April 7, just a day before Germany was to begin its invasion of Denmark and Norway, both of which would be completely overrun before the fall of France in June). "They don't care what you might feel about it; they say you've got to do this, do that . . . etc."[10] He wrote Eugénie on April 4 to inform her that he might soon be called back to report on Spain, but meanwhile he wanted her to know that she was right to tell people that he hadn't changed his mind: He wished to take part in war planning, or nothing. But he added: "I don't want to be in Paris during parliamentary debating, because I want to avoid the makers of cabinets." The next letter, on April 7, suggests where the pressure was coming from now: "I'm astonished by the insistence of P.R. after what I told him." So it was the new premier, Paul Reynaud, who sought Pétain's participation in the cabinet. But Pétain repeated that he could be useful only on the War Committee, "and I won't change my mind."[11]

While in Spain, the ambassador managed to remain in touch with an organization he had helped create, the French Information Center, based in New York. After the war began, a meeting was held in Paris, taking advantage of the temporary presence there of some members of the board such as André Maurois, to discuss future activity. It was agreed that while much could be done by the New York group to help France, it was vital to avoid giving the impression that the center was an official propaganda agency. They would be able to reach American public opinion through the sixty American citizens on the sponsoring committee, personalities such as Clarence Dillon, Walter Lippmann, Roy Howard, Eugene Meyer, Henry Luce, and Nicholas Murray Butler. Moreover, there would be an exchange of information with the French government's information department: The French Information Center would provide reports on American opinion and suggestions for pro-French propaganda campaigns. In a communication to the center's directors, Pétain expressed satisfaction with the group's plans, complaining only that he was being asked to obtain the demobilization of René de Chambrun (Laval's son-in-law) so that he could manage the center's activities;

Pétain offered the countersuggestion that René's father Adalbert, who was in New York anyway, could handle affairs there.[12]

But the calls from Paris could not be ignored forever. Pétain returned to Paris—traveling with his houseguests, the Bernard Ménétrels—and was received on May 1 by Paul Reynaud, who offered him a cabinet post as minister of state. Pétain apparently accepted, although this was not made public, asking only to be allowed to return to Madrid to clear up urgent business.[13] Surprised by Reynaud's choice, the premier's private secretary soon understood that what Reynaud wanted was Pétain as a counterweight to his defense minister Daladier and his general in chief Gamelin; the old man's "daily hour of lucidity" could be useful; furthermore, left-wing politicians liked Pétain.[14]

Before returning to Madrid Pétain spent over a week in Paris. On May 5 he called at the Admiralty for a long talk with François Darlan, commander in chief of the Navy. Later, when he was Pétain's number two in Vichy, Admiral Darlan disclosed that Pétain had said to him that day: "We have to stand shoulder to shoulder. Can I count on you?" Darlan replied affirmatively but a year later confessed that he had not immediately seized the full meaning of the question.[15]

Pétain finally left for Spain on May 9. Perhaps it was now that he solicited a final audience with Francisco Franco. As the generalissimo remembered this meeting, he tried to persuade Pétain not to accept new responsibilities. "You are the symbol of victorious France. . . . You risk becoming the hostage of French surrender. . . . You are marching toward sacrifice." Pétain replied that he knew what to expect, but he was now eighty-four years old and had nothing to offer his country except himself. In making this sacrifice he could be useful to France.[16]

On May 10, the day that Neville Chamberlain turned over the British cabinet to a new prime minister, Winston Churchill, the Germans attacked in Belgium and the Netherlands, launching a drive against France's reputedly impenetrable northeastern frontier on May 13; by the sixteenth they began the penetration of the Ardennes with Panzer divisions and intensive air attacks. Before that day was over, Paul Reynaud had picked up his option on Philippe Pétain. The coded telegram arrived in Madrid at noon: Pétain's presence in Paris was necessary because of the gravity of the situation. The ambassador left by automobile at 8:30 the following morning, at Hendaye boarded a night train, to arrive in Paris at 8:00 A.M. on May 18. At 10:00 he was back in Reynaud's office.[17]

In Reynaud's view, the war command had to be changed radically now. Gamelin had to go, but Georges, who was felt to be equally responsible for the German breakthrough, would not replace him. Reynaud told his private secretary Dominique Leca that what he needed was "a name which sounded, and resounded well" for a demoralized army. The choice fell to Maxime Weygand, no young man himself (he was seventy-three). But for Reynaud, who would soon be taking over the National Defense and War cabinet post from Daladier, "Reynaud and Weygand" would have an impact that "Daladier and Gamelin" did not have.[18] Pétain was offered the title of vice-premier; he hesitated, but Reynaud insisted on an immediate reply so that he could announce the appointment over the radio that evening.[19] In his radio message Reynaud warned that the situation was grave, that the enemy had enlarged its pocket south of the Meuse River. "Here is the first decision that I have just taken," he announced. "The victor of Verdun, the man thanks to whom the attackers of 1916 did **not** pass, thanks to whom the morale of the French army was reaffirmed in 1917 to make victory possible, Marshal Pétain returned this morning from Madrid, where he rendered so many services to France." Pétain was now "at my side" as minister of state and vice-premier, "putting all his wisdom and strength at the service of the country." And he would stay "until victory."[20]

Reynaud seemed to have achieved the desired effect. "Pétain is the sublime and victorious resistance of Verdun," declared Wladimir d'Ormesson in *Le Figaro*. "France has an immense impression of security." The Socialist *Populaire* saw the cabinet revamping—which also brought in Georges Mandel, once Georges Clemenceau's right-hand man, as interior minister—as raising the nation's potential for making war "to the highest level."[21] On the front page of *L'Action Française,* Charles Maurras greeted Pétain's advent with a "Finally!"[22]

Reynaud's new team had little time to organize itself. Weygand arrived from Beirut, where he had been in charge of operations in the Mediterranean theater, on May 19; he agreed to replace Gamelin at the head of France's armies but warned Reynaud: "You won't be surprised if I can't guarantee victory, nor even give you a hope of victory."[23] On the following day, after sounding out the high command, Weygand described the situation to Reynaud and Pétain: The entire north of France was in a state of collapse; although he was working out a line of defense with General Georges, all communications with the front were cut off, except via the British through London.[24] Pétain and Reynaud then joined the other ministers at the Elysée Palace for a cabinet meeting. It was at the close of this session that Pétain is supposed to have said: "We should use traveling pigeons." A remark that was later taken as a sign of his senility, suggesting that the old man was unable to comprehend what was going on around him. But in context, after what Weygand had reported concerning the interruption of communications with French troops in the north, it may have been less incongruous; and the minister who recorded it thought it said something not about Pétain but about French inadequacies.[25]

Pétain had set up his civil and military staffs in the offices that he had not abandoned during his service in Spain, on the Boulevard des Invalides. He lived with the Bernard Ménétrels at their Avenue de Montaigne apartment, dining out with Bernard.[26] Although Ménétrel had been mobilized at the outbreak of war as an army doctor with the rank of lieutenant, Pétain persuaded him to accept reassignment to his own staff as his personal physician, pointing out that this too was national service.[27] Now Pétain was able to talk, if only by telephone, with Jacqueline de Castex, who had remained at her castle in Normandy; she was "rather anxious," she confessed, but she would hold on "with your marvelous love to support me." During her exodus she cautioned Philippe to avoid signing his letters to her and to use the less intimate *vous* form of address.[28]

Now his circle of intimates expanded by one. The diary of aide de camp Bonhomme for May 19 indicates a meeting between Pétain and Raphaël Alibert.[29] Pétain asked him to become his private secretary, as director for the civil cabinet. During the relatively brief period he held this post Alibert said that he had little to do, later claiming that in conversations with Pétain he sought to persuade him to leave the Reynaud government, in which he served only as a "flag."[30]

Some of those who came into contact with Pétain in those feverish hours later remembered his impassivity, his torpor, functions of advanced age. Old General Mordacq, he who had been Clemenceau's secretary for military affairs, was struck by Pétain's "sluggishness." When Interior Minister Mandel decided to organize a military police force to combat home-front defeatism, he told Pétain about it over lunch, since Pétain had dealt with a similar problem in 1917. But, Mandel confided to a friend that evening, he could get nowhere with the old man. "Pétain is senile. He doesn't seem to understand." What Pétain had told him was that he would oppose any new organization, for the war minister "must have done whatever was necessary." Mandel was also to remember that during crucial cabinet meetings Pétain seemed to doze, breaking silence only to make statements not directly related to the subject under discussion.[31]

But it was Pétain, so Reynaud tells us, who insisted on meeting Reynaud and Weygand each morning. The problem, adds Reynaud, was that this brought him face to face with two senior officers who ganged up on him; both Pétain and Weygand felt that France must accept an armistice if defeated in battle in mainland France. When Reynaud reminded them that France had pledged not to separate herself from Britain, Pétain replied: "You place yourself on the international level and I, on the national level." Pétain thought it essential to keep the army intact to maintain domestic order. But after the boost to the nation's morale brought about by the arrival of Pétain and Weygand, could Reynaud destroy this new confidence by dismissing them? He had to keep his difficulties with the two senior officers to himself, he later said, so as not to allow the story to spread—as far as Berlin.[32]

Meanwhile, Pierre Laval was also busy. At the Senate's Commission on Foreign Affairs on May 24 he attacked Daladier, who was felt no longer to enjoy sufficient authority as war minister, declaring: "We need Pétain."[33] Behind the scenes Laval appears to have been still more active, telling his Italian contacts that France needed a direct link to Hitler. He felt that a Pétain-Laval government would be in a position to ask the still-neutral Mussolini to intervene with Hitler; as its reward, France would help Italy replace Britain as the dominant Mediterranean power.[34]

XX

THE FALL
OF PARIS

The offensive of the Germans through Belgium, southwest toward
Paris, west and northwest to the Channel, drove a wedge not only
between the French and British armies but into their alliance. The
British were losing ground in the north where the French counted
on them; it was as if an effort of will could compensate for the
inadequacy of Allied forces in the face of the German onslaught.
General Edward Spears, liaison officer in the First World War,
now Prime Minister Churchill's liaison with the French, bore some
of the brunt of French anguish, notably at a May 25 meeting with
Reynaud, Weygand, Pétain, and Darlan.[1] Spears found Pétain
friendly but silent; he seemed not to have heard what was being
said.[2]

That evening an all-important war council brought together
President Lebrun, Premier Reynaud, Pétain, and the war ministers, Weygand, Darlan. Weygand presented a detailed analysis of
the situation which concluded that France had committed "the
immense error of going to war without having either the matériel that it needed nor the military doctrine it needed." It would

probably pay dearly for this imprudence. Reynaud replied that France had to save the honor of the army with a fight to the finish. But what if the French armies were dispersed and destroyed? asked President Lebrun. It was agreed that Britain would have to be consulted before France accepted a German peace proposal. Already on May 15 the Dutch army had capitulated; the Belgians were to lay down their arms later that week.

It was now that Pétain made his single recorded intervention. He asked whether there was a "complete reciprocity" in the obligations of France and the United Kingdom. The latter had committed only ten divisions to the battle while France had engaged eighty, and the comparison should be made not only of the military effort of the two nations, but of "the suffering which awaited them."[3]

Next day, a Sunday, General Spears called on Pétain at the Invalides. Pétain informed him that he was determined not to interfere with Weygand's command, although he would not hesitate to pose questions. He was convinced that the situation was catastrophic; he saw no way out. Yet Pétain remained calm; he didn't react to Spears's evocation of Churchill's pledge to resist. Later the same day, at the end of another meeting with Spears, Pétain asked if he was aware that Weygand feared a revolutionary uprising in Paris. Pétain also told Spears that sixteen French generals had been relieved of their commands, which Spears took to be Pétain's way of saying that bad choices had been made since he ceased to have responsibility for the army.[4]

At noon—we are still on that busy Sunday—Pétain called on Paul Baudouin, undersecretary of state in the premier's office, as well as secretary of the War Committee. He told Baudouin that he did not think France should pursue the war to the bitter end; that would be too easy, but it would also be stupid, criminal. He hoped that at least part of the French army could be salvaged, led by a few officers to keep order; without this, a true peace wasn't possible. He confessed that he hadn't slept all night after the last War Committee meeting. And Baudouin says there were tears in the eyes of the old man as he told him what a frightful ordeal it was, in his eighty-fifth year, for him to be obliged to serve his country in these horrible circumstances.[5] At 6:00 P.M. he met Weygand, to talk about the eventuality of an armistice.[6]

That same day Reynaud was in London, telling Churchill, Lord Halifax, Anthony Eden, and other British leaders that if the battle of France was lost, Pétain would advocate an armistice.[7]

According to Weygand's memoirs, he met Pétain during the morning of May 28. He wished to be certain that "no difference of opinion existed between us" before sitting down to write a crucial memorandum for Premier Reynaud. In this document Weygand began by explaining that despite the resolution to defend present positions to the death, it was his duty as commander in chief to examine all hypotheses. It was possible, in view of the enormous imbalance between the German attacking force and the Allied defense, that the Germans would break through and rapidly attain the country's vital centers. Even though it was hoped that Britain would throw new forces into the battle, and in view of the defection of the Belgians (who had asked for an armistice the previous evening), it was important that the British know that France might have to give up the fight.[8]

Pétain read Weygand's draft on the twenty-ninth and informed him: "I see nothing to add, for the moment. . . ." But he thought that the British should be notified as soon as possible and invited to come to Paris.[9] At the morning conference in Reynaud's office that day, after Weygand handed in his paper, Pétain announced that he approved it and congratulated its author. When Reynaud suggested the preparation of a redoubt with its back to the sea—the Brittany peninsula, Weygand agreed to study the question and Pétain endorsed the idea; at the close of the session Reynaud told Baudouin how happy he was that Pétain and Weygand were partisans of resistance. He felt that the Germans would offer an armistice "contrary to honor"; the Brittany redoubt would help France avoid that.[10]

Another view of Pétain's feelings at this time comes from his Spanish contacts, and in a roundabout way. On June 3 the German embassy in Madrid sent Berlin a telegram based on information received from "Wilhelm," the code name for Spain's foreign minister Colonel Juan Beigbeder Atienza. The information had come from the Spanish ambassador in Paris, José Felix Lequerica y Erquiza, who informed Madrid of "another long conversation" with the marshal, who had told him that a coup d'état would be necessary to bring him to power. President Lebrun, who was merely a "servant of the political parties," would not resist if Pétain demanded the transfer of his powers. It was a question of time. Pétain also told Lequerica (says Lequerica) that he was sorry he had not returned to France a month earlier, for then he could have prevented the collapse of Belgium. Pétain thought the situation grave but not desperate and actually showed the Spanish ambassador on a map the line from the Somme to the Maginot Line, along which he thought resistance was still possible. But Pétain did not really sound optimistic, complaining of lack of British support; at this time the bulk of the British forces, with some of their French allies, had been evacuated across the Channel from the beaches of Dunkirk, an operation which had begun at the end of May and was completed by June 2. (The German Embassy in Madrid reported to Berlin on June 5 that a Spanish source in Paris claimed that if the German army approached Paris, Lebrun would resign in favor of Pétain; Pétain and Weygand would then tell the French people that the cause of their military catastrophe was the Popular Front, and that a separate peace with Germany was essential.) [11]

We know something of the marshal's life in Paris from a letter he wrote his wife on June 4. He was still living with the Ménétrels, beginning each day with a massage or heat treatment, often with the two combined. He took lunch daily at Chauland, a convenient restaurant off the Invalides esplanade—where prices had doubled. "I make do, although my financial situation is quite diminished because of my change of status." He couldn't say much more. "One must be prudent by letter as well as by telephone." [12]

If we know more it is thanks to the memoirists of that desperate time—General Spears, for instance, who describes his encounters with Pétain in detail. On June 6 he called on the marshal at the Boulevard des Invalides, hoping to restrain Weygand in his intention to break away from the alliance to seek an armistice. Spears found Pétain friendly enough, and the deafness "so apparent at the morning sessions of the War Committee" had disappeared, along with his "surly, expressionless mask." He "almost" smiled; his face was "almost" animated. But Pétain drew his visitor over to a map to demonstrate the hopelessness of the military situation. He spoke bitterly of the politicians and school-teachers who—rather than the generals—were responsible for the coming defeat. He also attacked de Gaulle, who had just been taken into Reynaud's cabinet as undersecretary of state for national defense. "His vanity leads him to think that the art of war has no secrets from him," said Pétain, and then described the history of the writing of *La France et son armée,* complaining of de Gaulle's failure to acknowledge his role in its creation. "Not only is he vain, he is ungrateful."

Spears brought the conversation back to the war. Hoping to stir the French to resistance, he evoked Joan of Arc, but that only led Pétain to begin a hunt for a speech he had once delivered in Rouen on the Maid, and then Pétain proceeded to read it. Spears felt "sadness now based on pity for a very old man for whom I had, till so recently, felt the deepest affection and regard." He saw Pétain now as "infinitely pathetic," and felt that France was "fading out on an old man's tremulous evocation of a heroic past." He stopped Pétain before he could read another speech aloud, this one on French peasants; he tried to return to the subject of Weygand and the armistice but failed to get through. Pétain showed him a model of Cogné's sculpture of Pétain on horse-back—the one he hoped would be erected in Verdun after his death. And then Spears left, convinced that "Pétain's natural pessimism had already led him to accept defeat."[13]

Next day, Pétain called on Paul Baudouin to ask him to intervene with Reynaud so that de Gaulle did not attend their morning conferences; he told him too about *La France et son armée.* "He is arrogant, ungrateful, and spiteful," Pétain added.[14]

The Germans would soon be in Paris; it was time to evacuate the capital. On June 9 (the day the Germans overran Rouen, just eighty-five miles downstream from Paris), at the morning conference with Reynaud, Pétain read out a note opposing the departure of the government "at the very moment when the dominant concern should be to preserve the moral and intellectual heritage of the country"—so reads Paul Baudouin's summary, for the original note was not kept.[15] At five o'clock that Sunday at a cabinet meeting, after hearing Weygand's report on the military situation, President Lebrun asked if Pétain wished to comment. (Lebrun had observed Pétain to be half-asleep, prostrated.) "I have nothing to say," the marshal replied. Lebrun thought to himself that if Pétain had been brought into the cabinet to contribute a spirit of resistance it had been an error, for he seemed oriented in the opposite direction. The cabinet decided that the government would leave Paris, the various ministries to be installed at previously agreed locations along the Loire River.[16]

Pétain left the capital by automobile that night. Near the forest of Fontainebleau south of Paris they found traffic slowed by Sunday picknickers returning home late.[17] At two in the morning the Pétain party reached Briare, one hundred miles from Paris and temporary seat of General Headquarters, then went on to Gien, where the marshal was given a bed in the railway station. Next day he was put up at the prefecture in Nevers; on June 11, the castle of Saint Armand in Puisaye was his host.[18]

On the eleventh, there was a morning meeting at the castle of Vaugereau near Briare with Reynaud and Weygand. On the previous day, Norway's King Haakon had ordered an end to resistance to the German invading forces; closer to home, Mussolini had at last entered the war against a battered France. While the premier and the marshal walked in one part of the estate park, Weygand was in another part of the same park telling an emissary of the military governor of Paris that he was declaring Paris an open city. Weygand then informed Reynaud and Pétain of what he had done; they neither approved nor disapproved, he later remembered. At that instant they received word that Churchill was en route to Briare for a meeting of the Supreme War Council; the site chosen was the castle of Muguet, which was more spacious than Vaugereau.[19] When Churchill arrived he recognized Reynaud, Pétain, Weygand, and others, including "the relatively junior General de Gaulle"; the British prime minister also remembered that the castle possessed only one telephone, and that was in the lavatory; it was kept very busy. We also have an account of de Gaulle's arrival for that momentous session. Seeing Pétain in a corridor de Gaulle saluted him (they hadn't met since their discussion of *La France et son armée* in 1938). "You're a general!" Pétain exclaimed. "I don't congratulate you. What good is rank during a defeat?" "But *monsieur le Maréchal,* you received your first stars during the 1914 retreat. The Marne victory followed a few days later." Pétain grumbled, de Gaulle tells us, "Not the same thing." And de Gaulle felt that Pétain was right.[20]

The meeting began soon after Churchill's arrival: Reynaud, Pétain, Weygand, Georges, de Gaulle among French participants; Churchill, Eden, General Sir John Dill, Spears for the British. Churchill made it clear that his country would pursue the struggle come what may. He did not exclude the possibility of a reversal of the situation as in the last war, during the battle of the Marne or after the German attack in March 1918 when as a cabinet officer in the David Lloyd-George government he happened to be at Pétain's side. He recalled how Pétain had restored the situation (Churchill tactfully omitted mention of Foch), and how Clemenceau had declared that he would fight before Paris, inside Paris, behind Paris. After Weygand warned that the analogy with the Great War could not be taken too far, Pétain put in that in 1918 the French had been in a position to dispatch forty divisions to the front. Finally Churchill asked whether it would not be possible, should coordinated defense prove unfeasible, to fight a guerrilla war to gain the months necessary for American intervention to take effect. "That would be the destruction of the country," Pétain objected, and Reynaud agreed with him.[21]

Anthony Eden found Pétain "mockingly incredulous" when Churchill promised that if necessary Britain would pursue the war alone. At dinner Eden sat next to the old marshal and found conversation difficult, Pétain clearly preoccupied with the destruction of his country.[22] When they left the table and sat with coffee and brandy, Reynaud told Churchill that Pétain had informed him that he felt France had to solicit an armistice now, and that he had written a paper on the matter he wished Reynaud to read. "He has not handed it to me yet," added Reynaud. "He is still ashamed." "Thus we all went unhappily to bed in this disordered château or in the military train a few miles away," Churchill closes the day.[23] Next morning Churchill and Eden were chatting in the sun with Reynaud before breakfast when Pétain appeared. "He looks buoyant this morning," Reynaud commented. "There must be some bad news." (Eden adds: "There was.")[24] During the morning meeting the British promised to examine the possibility of increased air support. Churchill expressed the hope that if there were a change in the situation the French would let the British know at once, so they could come back to discuss future moves.[25] General Spears recalls a long talk he had with Pétain that morning—their last. Pétain said that an armistice was now inevitable, and he blamed the Popular Front for lack of preparation. He scoffed at the idea of pursuing the war from French possessions in Africa, advised Britain to seek peace as well, for it would not be able to stand up to Germany for more than a month. "It's a catastrophe," Pétain concluded, "a rout." Later that day, reconstructing the conversation, Spears felt that Pétain had sounded satisfied.[26]

Back in London the same day (June 12), Churchill reported the results of his mission to the War Cabinet. He described Pétain as "a dangerous man at this juncture," adding that "he had always been a defeatist, even in the last war." In a message to Roosevelt this "former Naval Person," as his transatlantic messages identified Churchill, warned that "the aged Marshal Pétain, who was none too good in April and July, 1918, is, I fear, ready to lend his name and prestige to a treaty of peace for France."[27] That same afternoon the French government convened outside Tours, at the castle of Cangé overlooking the Cher River, temporary residence of President Lebrun.[28] Weygand opened the meeting with a grim description of the retreat. "The time for another armistice has arrived," he concluded. Reynaud asked him what that would do to France's relations with the British and the Americans, and what about the last-ditch stand in Brittany, in French colonies in North Africa, black Africa, the West Indies? He warned that Germany's terms would be harsh, and that in any case the French would have to keep their promise to the British not to sign a separate peace. Pétain spoke briefly to express his solidarity with Weygand. The meeting broke up at 11:00 P.M.[29] Then Pétain returned to his new temporary residence, the castle of Nitray near Azay-sur-Cher.

On June 13 Churchill was back, to meet Paul Reynaud in Tours. The two heads of government agreed to send an urgent appeal for help to Roosevelt. Earlier that day, driving along the Cher River toward Reynaud's residence at Montrichard, Finance Minister Yves Bouthillier had stopped off at Nitray to call on Pétain and found the marshal alone in the grand salon, a sheet of paper on the heavy table in front of him. Pétain said this was a statement he intended to read to Churchill that day. "Weygand is right, we have to do what he says," Pétain added. At that moment the door opened and a young officer entered, snapped to attention, and saluted. It was Bernard Ménétrel. "He's just good for taking your temperature," joked Pétain, but then asked Ménétrel to remove his cap and read the statement.

Pétain was not to have the opportunity to read it to Churchill. The British group, after the meeting with Reynaud at Tours, drove to the airport for their return to London.[30] Reynaud informed his ministers that his sole act in Tours was to appeal to Roosevelt for active intervention; only after a reply came from Washington would a decision be made concerning an armistice.[31] At that time, of course, the United States was still neutral, although with a heavy wink in the direction of the one-time allies of Western Europe. In November 1939 the U.S. neutrality act was amended to permit arms sales on a cash-and-carry basis; Lend-Lease shipments were not to begin until the spring of 1941, and the United States would not have a conscription law until September 1940.

Now, as the French cabinet assembled, Weygand announced that he had been informed by military headquarters that the Germans would enter Paris the next day.[32] Pétain rose to deliver the statement, which Bouthillier had already listened to. The sky was cloudy, night was approaching; the old marshal found it difficult to read in the center of the room, so he walked to a bay window, found a seat there, and resumed his reading.[33]

If the government failed to ask for an armistice, Pétain warned, French soldiers might cease to obey orders and panic. Establishing a redoubt for a last-ditch stand was not the answer, for that would be only a temporary expedient. And to abandon the French mainland would be to desert, to deliver France to the enemy, to kill its soul; this would make its rebirth impossible. What he called "the revival of France" would issue from the soul of the nation, which soul could be preserved only by staying rather than reconquering the country with Allied cannons. He preferred to stay and accept the suffering that would result. "The French renaissance will be the fruit of this suffering." So the question was not whether the government would or would not ask for an armistice but whether it would ask for that armistice—or leave the territory of the French mainland. "I declare, concerning myself, that in the government or out if necessary, I shall refuse to abandon the mainland. I shall remain with the French people to share its sorrows and its misery." Only an armistice, he concluded, could assure the survival of "eternal France."[34]

"That is contrary to French honor," exclaimed Reynaud.[35] Weygand had some harsh words for the government's indecision, which he said was imposing useless sacrifices on the troops; he added that as far as he was concerned he would prefer to stay in France as a prisoner, with irons on his legs, rather than abandon the country; he then asked permission to withdraw.[36] "Gen. Weygand walks out slamming the door," Léon Bonhomme told his diary.[37] The meeting broke up late. "Everybody is tired, on edge," noted Paul Baudouin.[38]

XXI

A PÉTAIN CABINET

Just as the evacuation from Paris to widely dispersed castles and manors along the Loire had been planned in advance, the withdrawal south and west to Bordeaux had also been planned. The Pétain party left Nitray for Bordeaux at 2:00 P.M. on June 14. We know from Léon Bonhomme's diary that Raphaël Alibert of Pétain's civil staff and General Henri Bineau, who with Charles Brécard made up the military cabinet, joined the group before it left Nitray; and that evening in Bordeaux the marshal dined with Bernard Ménétrel and Bonhomme at the Hôtel Splendide. Bonhomme even tells us that in passing de Gaulle saluted the marshal.[1] De Gaulle adds to that: "He shook my hand, without a word. I would never see him again."[2]

De Gaulle also delivers some judgments on his former protector. "Too proud for intrigue, too strong for mediocrity, too ambitious to be a climber, he nourished in his solitude a passion to dominate." Now a lifetime of suppressed desire would "burst forth without limits; on one condition, nevertheless: that he accept the disaster as a stepping stone to his glory. . . ." For de

Gaulle, age had corroded the older man's character, had delivered him over to the manipulations of men clever enough to make use of him. And he concludes, "Old age is a shipwreck." To France's misfortune, Pétain's old age would identify itself with the shipwreck of France. The morning after shaking Pétain's hand for the last time, de Gaulle left for Brittany to look into the co-ordination of local defense forces, then embarked at Brest on a destroyer for Plymouth and London, where he was to discuss the transport of French troops to new fighting positions. The armistice found him there in an atmosphere of calm before the storm, for the Nazis had not yet put together an invasion plan for the Channel crossing and the takeover of the British isles; the Luftwaffe onslaught was still many weeks away.[3]

Soon everybody who counted in French politics was in Bordeaux, crowding the best hotels and restaurants, congregating at the city hall where Mayor Adrien Marquet (known to Pétain ever since their cohabitation in the Doumergue cabinet) presided, at the prefecture, or simply out of doors on public squares and promenades. The first notable event here was an afternoon session of the cabinet on June 15, during which Reynaud suggested doing what the Dutch had just done: They had negotiated a military cease-fire, leaving their government free to carry on the war in exile. Pétain agreed to step out of the cabinet meeting to explain to the waiting Weygand that such a solution would not be contrary to the honor of the army. He returned a quarter of an hour later to say that he had not convinced the commander in chief. It was then that Camille Chautemps offered a compromise: Ask the Germans for terms, and when these terms prove unacceptable, public opinion will understand why the government prefers to pursue the war from abroad. Reynaud recorded the vote: thirteen for the Chautemps proposal, six against. The premier turned to President Lebrun to announce that he was resigning; Lebrun rejected his offer firmly. Reynaud then informed the British of the decision of what he called "the cabinet majority," asked for their advice, pledged that in no case would the French fleet be surrendered.[4]

In Churchill's estimation, when Reynaud appealed to Pétain to persuade Weygand to accept a cease-fire, "he could not have chosen a worse envoy."[5] We know from Weygand's subsequent statements with what strong feelings he resisted the idea of a cease-fire; for him it meant the dishonor of capitulation.[6] Meanwhile, Raphaël Alibert was warning Pétain that his presence in the war cabinet misled public opinion. As Alibert remembered it, Pétain promised that he would resign at the next morning's cabinet meeting.[7] Among other intriguers in those hours, Reynaud's companion Hélène de Portes, a partisan of an armistice and admirer of the marshal, apparently tried to convince Reynaud that he should yield his job to Pétain.[8]

June 16, 1940: The first cabinet meeting on that fateful day began at eleven in the morning at the prefecture. Reynaud announced Roosevelt's reply: The United States could offer material help, but not military intervention. Meanwhile, the British were holding France to the promise not to negotiate separately with Germany. Pétain rose to read his letter of resignation: Only an end to hostilities could save the nation; the government's stalling would result in the definitive abdication of French sovereignty. He refused to be associated with that. "Ah, you're not going to do that to us, not now!" exclaimed Lebrun. The marshal was persuaded to postpone resigning until Reynaud had seen Churchill again; a second cabinet meeting was planned for five that afternoon.[9] But as time passed it became clear that Churchill was not coming back to France for another meeting. On the other hand, the British—in order to save what could be saved, and above all to keep the French fleet out of Hitler's hands—did offer to merge the two countries into a Franco-British Union; henceforth—under Churchill's proposal—France and the United Kingdom would form a single and indissoluble nation, with a single constitution and citizenship, a single military command, and Britain would assume its share of French war damage. De Gaulle read the offer to Reynaud from London by phone.[10]

At five Pétain joined the other ministers to hear Reynaud describe the British merger proposal. Chautemps saw it as relegating France to dominion status, and Pétain thought it simply delayed the French request for an armistice. Declaring that he spoke for himself and the high command, he rejected the idea that the army capitulate in the field. So the Chautemps proposal to ask Germany for armistice terms was once again the order of the day.[11] The debate was heated, but it was clear that the majority of the cabinet favored Chautemps' plan. Reynaud spoke up: He could not, he said, be the one to ask for terms, for he had signed an agreement with Britain not to negotiate separately with the enemy. "But there is someone here who . . . is most qualified for that task," he is quoted as adding. "I shall therefore place the resignation of the cabinet in the hands of the President, and he will ask Marshal Pétain to form the new cabinet."[12]

In Lebrun's view, Reynaud was the premier and had to remain premier. When he called in the presidents of the Senate and Chamber, Jules Jeanneney and Edouard Herriot, to ask for their advice on who could replace Reynaud, they replied in unison, "Reynaud." But Reynaud refused to be the one to ask the Germans for armistice terms. "Then who?" asked Lebrun. "That's your business. You won't have trouble finding someone," Reynaud is supposed to have said. "Marshal Pétain told me this morning that he had his cabinet in his pocket."[13] As he walked through the parlor where his ministers waited, Reynaud informed them: "Marshal Pétain is forming a government."[14] The marshal was then eighty-four years old.

Accounts conflict of how Pétain's first cabinet was put together. What is clear is that he did have a list in his pocket. Significantly, he did not seem to know much about some of the proposed ministers on his own list, for Lebrun remembered having to tell Pétain something about them.[15] Pétain had been warned, notably by Lebrun, that the choice of Pierre Laval as foreign minister would be a gratuitous slap in the face for the British, an unnecessary compromising of future relations with the United States as well as the United Kingdom. So he asked Paul Baudouin to take the job, leaving the Justice Ministry to Laval. But when Laval heard of that he closeted himself with the old marshal and ten minutes later came out to say that he was getting Foreign Affairs after all. Then Weygand and François Charles-Roux, secretary-general of the Foreign Ministry, called on the marshal, repeating the warning about what Laval's appointment would do to relations with Britain. So once more Pétain reversed himself. On hearing that he was not going to get the Foreign Ministry, Laval refused to join the cabinet in any post.[16]

General Weygand, while holding on to command of what remained of the army, received the Ministry of National Defense in the Pétain cabinet; Yves Bouthillier kept Finances, and a number of other ministers were simply carried over from the Reynaud government. When a couple of them made the point that this armistice cabinet should be one of "sacred union," Pétain agreed to take in one or two Socialists, adding ("with a mischievous look," a witness noted), "I'd prefer a single Socialist if possible." In fact, two were found, Albert Rivière and André Février, and it was understood that Socialist leader Léon Blum approved the appointments.[17]

The new team lost no time in contacting the Germans (via Spanish ambassador Lequerica) and the Italians (via the papal nuncio). On June 17, Pétain went on the air at midday with his first message to the French people. "At the request of the President of the Republic, I assume the leadership of the government of France starting today," he began. "I offer myself to France to attenuate its misfortune." Expressing his sympathy for those fleeing from the north, he said, "It is with a heavy heart that I tell you today that we must cease hostilities."[18] This phrase caused consternation, for it sounded like a cease-fire order. An attempt was made to limit the damage by revising the statement for the press: "We must try to cease hostilities."[19]

Churchill dispatched a personal message to Pétain and Weygand: "I wish to repeat to you my profound conviction that the illustrious Marshal Pétain and the famous General Weygand, our comrades in two great wars against the Germans, will not injure their ally by delivering over to the enemy the fine French fleet. . . ." He urged that it be sailed to safety in British or American ports. The same night Churchill broadcast a message to his own people: "We shall defend our island home, and with the British empire we shall fight on unconquerable until the curse of Hitler is lifted from the brows of mankind."[20]

"So here is Pétain, the glorious soldier, thrown into the political arena, with total lack of experience and in what circumstances!" Senate president Jeanneney noted in his diary when the morning news announced the formation of the new government. "The Marshal has contempt, if not scorn, for the political world. And now he becomes the prey of the worst politicians. . . ."[21] In fact, Jeanneney would be proven right in a matter of hours. Someone got to Pétain that morning and convinced him that Georges Mandel, interior minister in Reynaud's government, was engaged in an armed conspiracy against the government; the

marshal signed an order for the immediate arrest of Mandel and
General Jules-Antoine Buhrer, chief of staff of colonial troops.[22]
Mandel, born a Rothschild, had been a constant target of the extreme right (although a moderate in politics) and, of course, of
anti-Semites; now the former aide of Clemenceau was considered a leading member of the war party. The arms in question turned out to be rifles legally possessed by the Ministry of
Colonies.[23] On hearing of the arrests, Pétain's new ministers
Charles Pomaret and Ludovic-Oscar Frossard requested an audience. "If you were not our glorious Marshal," Pomaret later
remembered telling Pétain, "I would say that you acted irresponsibly." Pétain had Mandel and Buhrer brought to him.
"I'm sorry for you, Marshal," Mandel said, "for being at the mercy
of your associates, and I'm sorry for my country for having you
as its leader." Pétain agreed to write a letter of apology; he began, "After the explanation given to us . . ." but Mandel refused to accept that. "We gave you no explanation and I wouldn't
stoop to doing it." Pétain began the letter a second time; after
describing the motive for the arrests, he declared: "I have acquired the conviction that this denunciation had no basis and had
the character of an incitation to disorder. I ask pardon and sincerely hope that this unfortunate affair will have no other consequences."[24] Pétain told Charles Pomaret: "Today you've taught
me a lesson of prudence that I won't forget!"[25]

On the following day, June 18, Charles de Gaulle took his place
before a BBC microphone to tell France, if in a still feeble voice,
that she was not alone, that she had an empire and an ally, that
the war was not over. In Bordeaux there had been a morning
cabinet meeting to hear Weygand describe the irresistible advance of the Germans. There was talk of armistice terms, and a
resolve that whatever the Germans demanded, they would not
get the fleet.[26] "I consider it my duty to remain with the French
people," Pétain declared to his ministers; "whatever happens, I
won't leave."[27] Perhaps the most significant meeting of that day
was the "meeting of the four presidents," Lebrun, Pétain, Jeanneney, Herriot. When Pétain repeated his determination not to
leave France, Jules Jeanneney asked him whether he agreed that
the president of the Republic should not be taken prisoner. "De-
cidedly yes," Pétain replied. But the president could not make
decisions without the countersignature of a minister; therefore

the government would have to be wherever the president was. From that evolved the suggestion that Pétain remain in France, as he wished to, while delegating power to his vice-premier Chautemps, who would operate in French North Africa with the president and other key cabinet members. Pétain promised to consult the cabinet about this the next day.[28]

The Germans kept the French waiting for their reply, but we know that Hitler told Mussolini during a meeting in Munich on June 18 that his plan was to keep a French government on French soil. It was important not to pose armistice terms that might be rejected, for in that case the French would go abroad to continue the war. It would also be wise to have a French government in France to handle the administration of the country, rather than oblige the occupation army to do that. Furthermore, said Hitler, an agreement with the French would neutralize the French fleet, keeping it out of British hands. Hitler was even willing to allow the French to keep their ships in a neutral country such as Spain.[29] France's armistice government, in Hitler's view, would make it possible for Germany to pursue the war against the United Kingdom; its first mission would be to assure the security of French African colonies from the British and the Gaullists.[30] (Germany's need for Pétain was such, the Italian ambassador in Berlin reported home on June 21, that a false report of Pétain's resignation had caused an unhappy reaction in Germany.)[31]

On June 19 the French got word through the Spanish ambassador that the Germans were ready to talk about the armistice. The transfer to Algeria of the president and some of the cabinet was still very much on the agenda, and Pétain agreed to facilitate their departure. Meanwhile, the British were busy in Bordeaux, seeking guarantees that the French fleet would not be handed over to the Germans. At a meeting on the night of June 19 in the presence of Admiral Darlan, Pétain confirmed to Lord Lloyd, the colonial secretary, that France would keep its ships out of enemy hands.[32]

Next day Pétain returned to the airwaves to announce that he had asked for an end to hostilities. "We shall learn our lesson from the lost battles," he went on, returning to a favorite theme: "Since our victory [of November 1918], the spirit of pleasure has dominated the spirit of sacrifice." The French had "made demands" more than they had "served"; they had avoided "effort," now they were facing "misfortune." "I was with you in the glorious days," the marshal told his people; he would be with them in "the somber days."[33] At nine that morning there had been a cabinet meeting; impressed by an attack on the city the previous night, most ministers indicated a desire to leave at once. Pétain opposed the idea, but it was agreed that an evacuation to Perpignan would be planned so that the government would be close to Port-Vendres, from where it could sail to North Africa. Later that morning Pétain, Weygand, and Baudouin received General Charles Huntziger, who represented the French side in the armistice negotiations. Pétain instructed him to break off negotiations with the Germans if they demanded that the French turn over the fleet, in whole or in part, or insisted on total occupation of the mainland, or of any of the colonies.[34]

It was agreed that President Lebrun would leave Bordeaux for Perpignan at 2:30 that afternoon; then the departure was postponed.[35] There is a mass of testimony that Raphaël Alibert, acting for Pétain or on his own initiative, was responsible for the postponement. Apparently he informed Lebrun that the Germans had not yet crossed the Loire; then, returning to Pétain's office at the prefecture, he used Pétain's letterhead to issue an order to ministers not to leave Bordeaux under any pretext.[36] On his side Pierre Laval—perhaps at the urging of, or in coordination with, Alibert—was organizing a veritable parliamentary lobby. Under the leadership of Laval and of the Bordeaux mayor, Adrien Marquet, a fellow member with Pétain of the 1934 Doumergue cabinet, the group (which someone called the Bordeaux Commune) reached a consensus: The government must not abandon the mainland. At Laval's urging a delegation of deputies and senators called on Pétain to protest the planned departure of Lebrun and the cabinet; Pétain interrupted their spokesman to say that he had delayed Lebrun's departure and expected to have further information to announce the next morning which would make a departure unnecessary; he had a mischievous expression and even winked when he said this, a witness remembered.[37] Next day, when Baudouin asked what attitude Pétain would adopt with regard to Lebrun should he leave, Pétain replied: "It's very simple. I'll have him arrested."[38]

On that night of the twenty-first, General Huntziger telephoned Weygand to dictate German terms. They were harsh, Huntziger observed, but not contrary to honor; the Germans did not ask for the fleet.[39] Joining Pétain, Darlan, Baudouin, Bouthillier, and Alibert in Weygand's drawing room at the military governor's residence to read the German terms as a typist dashed them off from Weygand's notes, diplomat Charles-Roux watched as one of the group traced the German occupation zone on a map. The Germans were keeping not only Paris but the whole Atlantic coast. "If those are German terms, we'd better leave for Africa!" he exclaimed. "Again!" replied Pétain, raising his arms as if to implore the heavens. Charles-Roux took that to mean: no point in reopening a closed matter.[40]

The scene in Bordeaux was not anarchy, but close enough to it. Deputies, senators roamed the temporary government offices seeking news. Senator Jacques Bardoux noted: "The disorder is total." He attended an informal session of the Senate to hear Laval's expression of faith in Pétain: "We can trust him in these days of mourning. He won't write a page of history which will dishonor us." Afterward Laval told Bardoux that he would be willing to take part in negotiations with Italy, where he was well connected, if he were appointed minister of state and vice-premier. Bardoux made sure that Alibert informed Pétain of this.[41] "He has a lot of people behind him," explained the marshal, when Reynaud expressed surprise at reports that Pétain was going to take Laval into his cabinet.[42]

When Baudouin showed up at the prefecture for the cabinet meeting on the morning of June 23, Pétain told him: "I've just come from the President's office. I had a lot of trouble getting him to sign the two decrees." "What two decrees?" "Those appointing Laval and Marquet ministers of state." Laval simply had to be inside the cabinet, Pétain explained, for his intrigues would be less dangerous there than if he created an outside opposition.[43]

On the previous day, receiving news of the armistice—the whole European continent except for Spain and Portugal was under Axis control now—Winston Churchill addressed both his own nation and France to express his sorrow and surprise. A free government, he said, would not have accepted conditions that placed France and its empire at the mercy of the Axis. Now, at the cabinet meeting, the ministers had to react to that and to the angry departure of British ambassador Sir Ronald Campbell the previous day. Laval argued for breaking relations with the United Kingdom then and there; Baudouin says that he, Weygand, and Darlan were prepared to resign if relations were severed. Pétain approved Baudouin's draft telegram to the British expressing disappointment at the lack of sangfroid in their reaction to the armistice and assuring the old ally that their alliance held firm, that neither France nor its fleet would be used against them.[44] Later that day (June 23), Pétain made a public reply to Churchill: The Englishman could be the judge of his own country's interests, but not of France's, and not of French honor.[45]

With Laval inside instead of out, the Bordeaux government could begin to develop an ideology. It was apparently Laval who introduced the notion of investing Pétain with full legislative authority.[46] Alibert, who himself was often seen as the guiding spirit of the Vichy state, later claimed that Laval came to him on June 25 with a proposal that the Senate and Chamber be convened jointly as a National Assembly, in order to empower Pétain to draw up a new constitution guaranteeing the rights of the family, labor, the fatherland. Alibert submitted the idea to Pétain, insisting (with Laval's approval) that the old marshal remove himself from debate on the matter so that his prestige and authority would remain intact whatever the Assembly decided. The old man agreed.[47] The evolution toward a regime stripped of democratic principles and democratic guarantees was accompanied by what seemed a widespread revulsion against the Third Republic, helped along by official propaganda. Thus, the radio controlled by Pétain's government launched a campaign against those ministers and deputies who had actually sailed to Morocco, despite the fact that the government had arranged their departure.[48]

Emmanuel Berl, man of letters, eclectic journalist and gregarious personality of the 1930s, had been editor of the cultural-political weekly *Marianne* and had friends on the right as well as the left. Even the fanatical anti-Semite Charles Maurras saw him as a "well-born" Jew. The day after Pétain's cabinet was formed Berl was invited to Bordeaux—he later could not recall who issued the invitation—to edit Pétain's speeches. And he edited—he says he actually composed—the much quoted Appeal of June 25, in which Pétain sought to justify the armistice.[49] It was a reasoned explanation of how the enemy's might had overcome the French; it did not fail to stress the severity of the armistice terms but argued that honor had been saved. No one would take over French ships or planes; the government remained free, France would be governed by Frenchmen. Now France had to think about the future. "A new order begins." Life would be hard, but Pétain did not intend to fool the French with deceitful language. "I hate the lies which have done you so much harm. The earth doesn't lie. It remains our recourse." Words—Berl's or Pétain's or someone else's—that were to become themes. This speech concluded with another, already familiar refrain: "Our defeat is due to our laxities. The spirit of pleasure-seeking destroys what the spirit of sacrifice had built. I invite you to an intellectual and moral revival first of all."[50]

But a premier was more than a moral guide. From the first day the old man was overwhelmed with detail. "I am deaf and I'm exhausted by the efforts I make to hear what is said," he confessed to his minister Baudouin on June 25. Next day Baudouin observed Pétain more closely at the cabinet meeting which lasted all of three hours and decided that the premier, although surprisingly well preserved for his age, did not have an intellectual resistance equivalent to his physical strength; if his bearing remained erect, his memory, his willpower, showed his years.[51] Henceforth, each in turn, the members of his government were to discover what Baudouin now knew, and each would make use of the information in his own way.

So the hours that followed brought about two changes: a new division of responsibility in the government, in the form of a smaller cabinet, and a more ideological one. Camille Chautemps worried about the fascistic tendencies that were becoming manifest in the cabinet under Laval's inspiration.[52] Yet one of Laval's most vigorous opponents in the cabinet, Maxime Weygand, was circulating a memorandum of his own composition beginning: "The old order of things, that is to say a political regime of Masonic, capitalistic and international compromises, brought us where we are today." He advocated a new way of life summed up in the words God, Fatherland, Family, Labor.[53]

By that time the Germans had arrived. Under the armistice, Bordeaux as an Atlantic port belonged to them. It was time for the government to migrate once again, deep into continental France. The first site chosen, Clermont-Ferrand, already crowded with refugees from the north, could not provide lodgings and office space for all the ministries, parliamentary services, and foreign missions that required them, even when the migrants had spread out to Royat, La Bourboule, and other nearby localities. When the suggestion was made that only Lyons was large enough to serve as seat of the displaced government, Pétain rejected the idea, for his old Radical Socialist nemesis, Edouard Herriot, was its mayor. The choice narrowed down to Vichy, less than forty miles from Clermont-Ferrand, a town of large hotels and hardly much else.[54]

XXII
CHIEF OF STATE

The town scarcely contained 25,000 inhabitants, but each year it took in seven or eight times that number of patients for short or long stays. Vichy was the resort town par excellence, where grand hotels stood side by side like row houses; the vital center consisted of the thermal baths and fountains, casinos, hotels, and tearooms surrounding a large park. Ministries and their annexes, official residences and embassies were all to be within minutes of each other on foot. At the heart of it all was the bright facade of the Hotel du Parc with its balconies of wrought iron, on the edge of the park with its covered walkways and tall plane trees, facing the Moorish cupola of the principal thermal establishment. This grand hotel was to be the residence of Marshal Pétain, premier at the beginning of July, chief of state of post-Republic France for the next four years; it was Pierre Laval's quarters too, and the exile home of the Foreign Ministry. A more modest establishment, the Pavillon Sévigné (a historic domain that once gave shelter to the marquise herself), served as the marshal's ceremonial office and meeting place.

Even before the government was settled into its wartime capital, the basic tenets of its political philosophy were being drawn up. In Clermont-Ferrand on June 30, Laval outlined a plan to convene the Chamber and Senate together to vote a new constitution. There is testimony (the memoirs of Paul Baudouin) that Pétain resisted at first; he would have preferred simply to suspend the legislature, for this did not seem the right time to reform basic French institutions.[1] Next day, Pétain accompanied Laval to explain the constitutional proposal to the president but Lebrun noticed that Pétain remained silent.[2] A few hours before that, Pétain had lunch with the American ambassador, William C. Bullitt. After telling Bullitt that "it would be a good thing for France if the parliamentarians who had been responsible not only for the policies which led to the war but also for the relative unpreparedness of France should be eliminated from the French government," Pétain said he felt that the very system of government had to be changed. In his view the Germans were going to try to reduce France to a mere province of Germany, while the United Kingdom would be crushed rapidly. One of the chief causes of the collapse of the French army, the marshal told the American ambassador, was that reserve officers who had been educated by unpatriotic and Socialist schoolteachers had deserted their men. He intended to dismiss every politician connected with the Blum government.[3]

Calling on Laval in the Clermont-Ferrand prefecture of July 1 (the government would begin the transfer to Vichy that afternoon), Senator Bardoux was assured that Laval's constitutional reform would win a majority. "I've been doing the work of a mole for days and days," Laval told him, arguing that a stronger government would be in a better position to negotiate with Hitler. He regretted that Pétain did not like the idea of punishing prewar politicians. "I hope to get him to that point gradually. But he's an old man, he's difficult to maneuver."[4] Next day at the Hotel du Parc, Pétain presided at a meeting of key cabinet officers that ratified Laval's reforms. "The Marshal clearly supported" Laval, Paul Baudouin remembered.[5]

For the moment, questions such as what to do with the detested leadership of the Third Republic seemed to be the only ones that the armistice cabinet could deal with. Disarmed, with no apparent means of exercising authority and uncertain communications, it hardly seemed capable of wielding power. And now, at the very outset of the Vichy era, the disarray of the government was aggravated by a blow from an unexpected source. Although the French were determined to keep their fleet out of German hands, the British were less confident that they would be able to do so. On July 3 a British task force approached Mers-el-Kébir, a naval base on the Algerian coast, with an ultimatum to the French fleet moored there: Sail out to fight alongside us, sail to a British port for internment, sail to a French port in the West Indies, or scuttle. The French admiral relayed the message to Vichy in abridged form: He reported that he had been ordered to scuttle, not that he had the possibility of sailing to a French port in the Western Atlantic; the order came back from the Admiralty to resist. The British opened fire, damaging or sinking most of the vessels, killing nearly 1,300 sailors.[6]

"If the Marshal hadn't possessed his robust good sense . . . if he hadn't been surrounded by men who knew how to keep cool at a time of misfortune," remarked one of these men, Mers-el-Kébir would have transformed the armistice, moving France to Germany's side.[7] Pétain's official complaint against the "hateful aggression" took the form of a note to Franklin Roosevelt. He was setting the case before the American president, "whose active friendship for France will not, I am sure, fail my country in the cruel misfortune from which I have undertaken to extricate it."[8] Darlan and Laval both favored a French surprise attack on the British Mediterranean fleet, but Pétain resisted; that decision was postponed, but meanwhile it was agreed to break off relations with Britain.[9] (In a talk with Mussolini on July 7, Hitler expressed satisfaction for the way he had dealt with the French fleet in the armistice agreement: now France and Britain had become enemies.)[10]

On July 8, after nearly a week of informal lobbying and public debate, Laval spoke before the deputies in the Petit Casino, a nondescript structure on a side street near the park. He presented the cabinet's plan for a "new regime, audacious, authoritarian, social, national"; capitalism would disappear in favor of a "new order."[11] On July 9 at 9:30 A.M., the Chamber held its first official session in the elegant white and gold decor of the Grand Theater of the main casino. It was opened by its president

Edouard Herriot, and in these words: "Our nation has rallied in
its distress to the side of Marshal Pétain, in the veneration his
name inspires in all of us. Let us take care not to trouble the accord that has established itself under his authority." The old
Radical Socialist warned that France would now have to "reform, to render more austere a Republic that we had made too
easy. . . ."[12] That afternoon in the same hall, the Senate heard
its president Jules Jeanneney: "I certify . . . to Marshal Pétain
our veneration and the full recognition due to him for the renewed gift of his person."[13] After both houses voted for the
principle of constitutional reform, they were convened the next
day, July 10, as a National Assembly. It began with a closed
morning session to which Laval presented a letter from Pétain
authorizing Laval to represent him at the Assembly, confirming
also that the government's proposal "seems to me necessary to
assure the welfare of our country."[14] Laval made it clear that the
proposal was "the condemnation, not only of the parliamentary
regime, but of everything that was and can no longer be." He
blamed anti-Fascist opposition for having prevented a prewar alliance with Mussolini, then praised Germany and Italy both for
having "restored the idea of fatherland."[15]

It was clear that Laval had won the Assembly over; the opposition was buried. "Don't fool yourselves," he said at one point,
"we're now living in a dictatorship."[16] At two o'clock Jules Jeanneney formally presided over the public session of this Assembly,
which was asked to approve a "unique article":

> The National Assembly accords all powers to the
> Government of the Republic under the authority
> and the signature of Marshal Pétain, for the pur-
> pose of promulgating, by one or several decrees, a
> new Constitution of the French State.
>   This Constitution should guarantee the rights
> of labor, of the family, and of the fatherland.

The vote was 569 to 80; the Assembly ended at 7:10 P.M.[17]

If the game was Laval's until now, henceforth Pétain could
make it his. We have Laval's insistent denials of responsibility for
the form taken by the constitutional decrees that were now to be
signed by Pétain one after the other, decrees that began with the

regal phrase, "We, Philippe Pétain, Marshal of France . . ."[18] An insider later claimed that these decrees were drafted by Laval with Raphaël Alibert.[19] In any case, three of them were signed that evening, following the Assembly vote. The first had "We, Philippe Pétain, Marshal of France" assuming the functions of chief of the French state, simply casting aside—or overlooking—the existence of a president of the Republic. The second accorded this chief of the French state "the totality of government power," responsibility both for making the law and carrying it out, the sole restriction being that he could declare war only with the consent of Parliament. The third decree adjourned the Senate and Chamber, which could meet again only on the convocation of the chief of state. Watching the marshal sign the three decrees, Laval was heard to say, "And that's how you overthrow the Republic."[20]

During his own trial in 1945 Laval was to testify that one day, exasperated by Pétain's use of "this personal power," he asked him, "Marshal, do you know the extent of your powers? They are greater than those of Louis XIV, because Louis XIV had to submit his edicts to Parliament." Pétain agreed.[21] Yet the testimony of Pétain's own entourage generally concurs with that of his secretary-general, Charles Brécard: "Mr. Laval presented a decree for the Marshal's signature; the latter refused it; Mr. Laval came back a second time, the Marshal refused again. And then some evening, after an exhausting day during which the Marshal received many people, he was presented with the decree he had refused the day before and in his fatigue he signed it."[22]

Pétain took to the air on July 11 to explain how he would use his new powers. He had set up a cabinet with twelve ministers, and he would appoint governors of the large provinces. "We shall construct an organized France, where the discipline of subordinates responds to the authority of chiefs, with justice for all," he promised. They would "create elites" and "give them command," doing away with "international capitalism and international socialism," for they had been in secret alliance all the time. This did not mean giving up the "powerful driving force of profit," nor the reserves accumulated by savings.[23] Later messages spelled out the grand lines of the "new order," soon also to be called "National Revolution."

It was Pétain's intention, so he told his foreign minister Paul

Baudouin, to leave the question of his succession to the cabinet. But Laval did not see it that way.[24] Constitutional decree number four, then, provided that should Pétain be unable to exercise his functions before the ratification of a new constitution, Laval would assume these functions with complete authority.

Each morning Pétain presided over what became known as a *Petit Conseil* in a narrow room adjoining his office in the Hotel du Parc: There would be Laval, new Justice Minister Alibert, Baudouin, Finance Minister Bouthillier, Interior Minister Marquet, Defense Minister Weygand, with Admiral Darlan; this meeting would discuss problems connected with the armistice and other urgent concerns. The formal cabinet sessions were held in a larger room at the Pavillon Sévigné, officially the residence of the new chief of state but where he preferred not to live.[25] Indeed, the Hotel du Parc was soon the center not only of government but of France itself. "Once you crossed the birdcage of a lobby, you bumped into the most horrid solicitors in every staircase, every elevator, every corridor," an early visitor recorded, regretting that the chief of state "was reduced to planting his flag over a vulgar dormitory for tourists."[26]

A memorandum written in the first year of the Vichy regime, perhaps by Bernard Ménétrel, warned of leaks of information from the seat of government. "The Hotel du Parc is extremely 'sonorous,' " it read. "From one door to the next, and especially from one floor to the next, one can overhear conversations perfectly, especially by telephone." Vichy was a "microcosm," and the "hunters of news" who "haunted" the Parc Hotel could, by bits of information gathered here and there, "piece together an important piece of information." The telephone was dangerous, for the Germans were listening; it was regrettable that "the French have lost the habit of secrecy, they no longer know how to conspire." The writer goes on to suggest how to "orchestrate" the dissemination of false information.[27]

At the Parc, Pétain and his entourage had taken over a whole floor, with offices and living space for Ménétrel, Bonhomme, and other close aides; Laval and his staff occupied another floor, Foreign Affairs two others.[28] Pétain's own quarters occupied a corner suite facing the Rue du Parc and the Rue Petit, his reception room-office offering balcony views of the park and the thermal establishment. The adjoining room was his bedroom, which also contained a small bathroom behind a frosted-glass panel. First-time visitors were often surprised by the small dimensions of these rooms and by the simplicity of their furnishings. Downstairs, at least in the earliest period, the seat of power continued to serve as a resort-hotel restaurant, and patrons of the famous Chante-cler restaurant passed through the lobby to get to their tables. In the grand salon space was reserved for the marshal to take coffee with guests, while everyone else could watch.[29] In those early disorganized months of Vichy he took his meals behind a screen at the rear of the main hotel dining room.[30]

At least his financial situation improved. Henceforth his salary, combined with a special account for travel, receptions, and other official expenses, came to 300,000 francs monthly or some $48,500 in U.S. currency. There was also a 15,000-franc salary as a member of government (which he refused at first and then accepted, apparently at Laval's insistence). To that was added his marshal's pay: 25,000 francs monthly. In 1940 his declared earned income totaled 963,828 francs; in 1941 it was 1,893,300—over $250,000 in U.S. currency—and remained at that level during the following Vichy years. (In 1938, declared salaries amounted to 151,012 francs; in 1939, 158,512 francs.) And the chief of state also had the use of "special funds," secret and unaccountable, amounting to 220 million francs for the total Vichy period and dispersed at the marshal's discretion by his secretariat. His improved situation allowed him to undertake long-needed renovation of the Ermitage and to acquire new parcels of land for his Villeneuve-Loubet estate (some two million francs were deposited to his wife's account in Antibes).[31]

XXIII
PÉTAIN'S MEN

"He is very secretive," noted Weygand. He understood the staff system as he found it in the army: he needed, in each of the principal fields of governmental activity, men who enjoyed his confidence. But he did not like to reveal what he was thinking, preferring to reach decisions in private conversations and then to make them known in more formal meetings such as cabinet sessions. His coldness, causticity, the sharpness of his replies Weygand attributes to shyness. The general also observed something else: The marshal tired quickly of his aides, confidants, advisers. He got rid of them as soon as he found them harmful or useless. This aspect of his behavior was not conducive to the formation or the work of a team, which demanded confidence and continuity.[1]

There were those, like his personal adviser René Gillouin, who worried about the extent to which Pétain was influenced by his circle, especially by those who spoke in loud voices. It sufficed for Raphaël Alibert to affirm in a biting tone: "That's impossible, Marshal," for Pétain to retreat.[2]

Alibert, the adviser on political strategy of the 1930s, was one of the first civilians to be admitted to the inner circle when the marshal joined Reynaud's cabinet in May 1940. Alibert served as justice minister from July 1940 to February 1941. According to memoirs written in exile by Pétain's private secretary, Henri Du Moulin de Labarthète, Pétain felt that he owed his power to Alibert as well as to Laval, Alibert, "a man of high moral values, but a violent and impulsive man." He had not succeeded in politics, and his defeats in successive legislative elections between the wars were well known, but he knew his constitutional law.[3] "I felt it indispensable to break with the principles of the previous regime; I felt it necessary to reestablish the notions of authority, order, respect, and discipline," Alibert explained in a postwar justification (in which he denied having been Pétain's *éminence grise*[4].)

In his talks with journalists, Alibert made it clear that he considered the Vichy regime more in terms of its domestic possibilities than its foreign ones; the triumph of the Vichy revolution was more significant than the nation's military defeat.[5] In private he didn't hide his scorn for the Republic, his preference for restoration of the monarchy.[6] It was he, so his peers tell us, who was largely responsible for the ideological content of that first year in Vichy. He was an early advocate of Vichy's measures against the Jews and pushed for other changes whose effect was to align Vichy with the totalitarian regimes—the introduction of corporatism, for example.[7]

Charles Brécard, another political adviser of the marshal in prewar years, joined the staff in June 1940, first as aide to Alibert, then as undersecretary of state to the premier.[8] In the first Vichy months he was secretary-general of Pétain's personal staff, yielding this job to General Émile Laure on Laure's return from German captivity.[9] There was Léon Bonhomme, of course, ever the faithful Bonhomme. Despite his flirtation with Loustaunau-Lacau's conspiracies, he was far from agreeing with everything Pétain did or said now, but he admired his old chief as a human being and remained loyal. Privately he said of Pétain, "He'll get us all shot."[10]

Du Moulin de Labarthète: brilliant, distinguished, parodoxical; in his person one encountered, without apparent friction, the extreme ideas of the left and of the right, an observer noted.[11] "I need friends around me," Pétain told Du Moulin when he was brought to Vichy by André de Gorostarzu, who had been air attaché in the Madrid embassy and was now a member of Pétain's military staff. He didn't have more confidence in Du Moulin than in anyone else, Pétain explained, but at least he knew and could recognize him. Henceforth Du Moulin would direct the civil staff, Brécard the military staff.[12]

René Gillouin was an Alibert recruit, and one of his jobs was to draft speeches for the marshal. "I don't want to be made to say things that I wouldn't have found by myself," Pétain told him. When they had a disagreement over a text, Pétain called in Lucien Romier, another adviser for whom he had particular affection—"my child," he called Romier, who resided just above Pétain's room at the Parc, and who was given an official appointment as minister of state in February 1941. (Romier was a historian and economist, author and former director of *Le Figaro*.)[13] His poor health was blamed for excessively prudent advice, and thus for reinforcing Pétain's passivity.[14]

There was an outer circle as well as an inner one. It certainly included the curious erudite Bernard Faÿ, who was not only Vichy's choice as administrator of the National Library but the guiding spirit of the new regime's campaign against the Freemasons, which included both a vigorous propaganda effort to link Masons, Jews, Communists, and Gaullists, and a painstaking purge of Masons in government, public life, and the school system.[15]

And what to make of the "Synarchie," a term used to describe members of the Pétain circle who had come from business and banking, and who were accused of seeking to dominate the regime as a state within a state? A number of Vichy officials, allied with extremist politicians and journalists, put forth the claim that these business and banking leaders belonged to the Jewish banking system or sought to protect Jewish interests.[16] A lengthy report on the Synarchie which circulated in Vichy identified a number of officials past or present as belonging to it, among them Paul Baudouin, Jean Bichelonne (secretary-general for Industrial Production and Foreign Trade), Yves Bouthillier, René Gillouin, Henri Du Moulin de Labarthète, Pierre Pucheu (then secretary of state for industrial production), and banker Jacques Rueff. Four were in Pétain's entourage, five were ministers or secretaries of state, fourteen high-level functionaries, and so on. They were to be accused, among other things, of responsibility for the removal of "revolutionary" National Socialists—Alibert,

Laval, Marquet—from the cabinet.[17] Bouthillier, one of the alleged conspirators, remembered that Pétain handed him a report on the Synarchie containing allegations against him, but while smiling.[18] Perhaps the last word on the Synarchie can be given to the worldly Du Moulin de Labarthète, who doubted that it was a true conspiracy. Here was simply a group of top-level businessmen who thought that men who knew how to run industry could run a country too.[19]

"I had foreseen everything," Laval was quoted later, "except that France would be run by a doctor."[20] The reference was to the most controversial member of the circle, perhaps because he was the most intimate and the longest lasting: Bernard Ménétrel. On one hand he has been attacked as a Rasputin, or a Florentine intriguer; on the other described as ingenuous, "an astonishing illiterate, a singular blunderer."[21] He was called Pétain's *éminence grise*—another one—but seemed not to mind the term, although he said he wasn't one.[22] The story circulated that he was Pétain's illegitimate son;[23] it made more sense to say he was "in a sense the child he never had."[24] As a matter of fact, Pétain did have a son, actually a stepson, born of Eugénie and her first husband. Pierre Dehérain, or de Hérain as he would call himself, had been a draftee in Morocco during the Rif war in 1925; he was called up again in 1939 and sent to the front; after the armistice he worked in the film industry in Paris and on the Riviera. During this period his companion was Odette Stirn, of Belgian Jewish origin. He had met Odette before the war when she was twenty-one and he nineteen, and Eugénie wouldn't allow them to marry. She married someone else (a French Jew) and had a child, but she waited until after the Liberation to divorce her husband. During the occupation Odette lived in southeast France under false papers. She found a job in Clermont-Ferrand, which allowed her to visit Eugénie Pétain at the Parc Hotel in Vichy. But although Pétain knew of her existence, she didn't meet him at the Parc; their first real meeting was to be at the Ile d'Yeu.[25]

We know how Pétain coopted Lieutenant Ménétrel in May 1940, convincing him that he would best serve his country by keeping Marshal Pétain healthy. At Vichy, Ménétrel joined Pétain's aide de camp Bonhomme in the personal secretariat of the chief of state. Bonhomme was responsible for Pétain's living and working quarters, his automobiles. Ménétrel handled charitable donations and, above all, propaganda; this included censorship of anything concerning the person of the chief of state.[26] Ménétrel's influence grew each time a member of the inner circle departed. Significantly, his room at the Parc adjoined that of his chief. (Once, when Ménétrel was away, his deputy Paul Racine took over his room; from the bed, Racine remembered, he could actually hear the marshal, also in bed, drumming on the wall.) To reach Pétain's office there was an official channel, via the secretariat and a corridor, and the Ménétrel way: from his room to Pétain's bedroom and then to his office.[27] He had a solid build, was well fleshed out, rapid, quick-tempered; he was also described as mischievous and sly by those who liked him;[28] by others, as a practical joker, an overgrown student, agitated, always in a hurry; his was the coarse, brutal humor of a medical student. He was the court jester. But he alone, the same witness noted with respect, could enter the marshal's rooms at any time of day or night.[29] It is certain that he watched Pétain's health as a mother did her child's, putting warm water into his wine, observing his food intake and his sleeping hours. His treatment included the hot-air method already described, "tonic" injections, bleedings.[30]

Ménétrel arrived in Vichy with a reputation as an enemy of the Republic, a right-wing nationalist; he had sympathized with movements like the nationalist-extremist Jeunesses Patriotes.[31] His anti-German attitude was apparently accompanied by hostility to the anti-German resistance. Thus, Vichy historian Robert Aron tells the unattributed story of a resistance leader who called on Pétain in 1942. Pétain went to the door, looked through the keyhole, said, "Bernard isn't there? Then tell me, how's the Resistance doing? Do you need anything?"[32]

Some who evoke the doctor's influence on his patient speak not only of Ménétrel's anti-German sentiments but of an underlying anti-Semitism.[33] Pétain's adviser Gillouin thought that the marshal's failure to resist anti-Jewish decrees proposed by his advisers might have been due to Ménétrel's influence. He quotes Pétain's wife, who explained why she could not intervene on behalf of Jewish friends: "I couldn't act without Bernard knowing about it and when you speak of Jews in front of him he sees red."[34] Ménétrel kept a file of pathetic letters from French Jews who were asking for protection or exemption from anti-Jewish regulations.

One such letter bears the notation of Ménétrel or of a member of his staff: "A Jewish story"; another: "I prefer to help prisoners of war"; a third: "File: Jew typical of his race" (Jew and typical were each underlined).[35]

Ménétrel also corresponded with doctors all over France, some of whom served as an unofficial information network. In one exchange with an old friend of his father, Ménétrel complained that he had compromised the position in which his father had left him, lost his clientele; to another he explained that he endeavored to be a devoted doctor to the marshal, a conscientious secretary, a chief of propaganda, a director of charitable works that had already assisted 5,000 families in both zones. Could one still believe, he asked, that he had time "to engage in Machiavellian schemes and to be a damned soul or evil angel?"[36]

When a friend who had been a military doctor and who had a Jewish grandfather (although he had been married to the niece of a priest in a Catholic church) wrote Ménétrel to say that he wished to do useful work after demobilization, Ménétrel warned him (in August 1940) that anti-Semitism was growing, that it failed to discriminate between good and bad Jews. Ménétrel assured his friend that he did not share these feelings. "There is nevertheless one feeling I do have," he went on; "it's that too many bad Jews had unwisely taken up too much room and importance in French public life, and they were among those responsible for leading us into the catastrophe where we find ourselves." He didn't know what measures Vichy would be obliged to take but insisted that "our adversaries" were not dictating Vichy's policy on Jews. French anti-Semitism was "an absolutely spontaneous movement of desperate people."[37]

Du Moulin de Labarthète accused Ménétrel of setting up a "Marshal's police force" and later of advocating, via the creation of an order known as the Francisque, whose members wore a badge, a "party of the Marshal."[38] We shall see him at work screening visitors, listening at doors, ready to intervene to protect the chief of state in his own way. "You're like a cat," Laval is said to have told him. "You can be swung by your tail and flung away but you land on your feet."[39] Did Pétain really say, in his Ile d'Yeu prison, that he had been badly advised at Vichy, and that his greatest mistake was to be surrounded by kids, whose leader was Ménétrel?[40]

XXIV

THE SHAPING
OF THE STATE

From the day of the British attack on the French fleet at Mers-el-Kébir, Admiral Darlan began planning revenge. His hope had been to bomb the British fleet at Gibraltar, using aircraft based in Morocco, and Pétain was said to have approved the plan despite the opposition of his foreign minister Paul Baudouin, who did not think an act of hostility toward Britain would relax the rigors of Germany's harsh treatment of France. On July 16, after sleeping badly for thinking of the planned attack on the British, Baudouin slipped in to talk to the marshal at 9:30 A.M., and in the absence of Darlan and Weygand he won the argument; Pétain authorized him to telephone the two military chiefs to cancel the operation.[1]

The same morning there was a different sort of challenge. General Huntziger, who headed the permanent French delegation to the armistice commission in Wiesbaden, arrived in Vichy with a veritable ultimatum: The Germans demanded air bases in Morocco, use of the Tunis-Rabat rail line, French North African ports, and French cargo ships for carrying German soldiers and equipment to North Africa; for the Axis attack on the British sphere of influence in North Africa and the Near East was now under way.[2] Pétain was determined to resist. It was agreed that the French reply would take the form of a letter to Chancellor Hitler from the marshal himself. In it, Pétain referred to Mers-el-Kébir, where France "sealed with the blood of its sailors" her promise to the Germans to protect her fleet. For this reason, he went on, he had been hurt by the German request. If France looked forward to a suspension of certain clauses of the armistice to allow her to take up arms against "British aggression," the German demands concerning North Africa would result in turning over part of France's empire to Germany.[3]

Pétain's old friend Bernard Serrigny, now a senior representative of the oil industry, came to see the marshal on July 26 and spent over an hour with him. They talked of the German invasion of the British isles, which was expected shortly; Serrigny noted that Pétain felt that the Germans were ready and would succeed. The friends also discussed the return of the government to Paris, which Pétain favored because "a part of France escaped him." Serrigny warned that this move would place Pétain in the hands of the Germans but this did not convince him. Pétain brought up the matter of sanctioning those responsible for France's defeat, saying he had impressive files against individuals such as Daladier and Gamelin. Serrigny agreed that public opinion expected prosecutions, but he hoped they would be limited to a few exemplary cases such as Gamelin, Blum, Cot, and Mandel—if they were guilty. Don't, he insisted, create a new Dreyfus affair. The marshal listened to his advice with attention; Serrigny found him lucid, "youthful."[4]

For the time had come to punish those "responsible"; if Vichy could not do much about its foreign enemies, it could act against its domestic ones. "They're trying to get me to prosecute the main people responsible for our present plight," Pétain told Jules Jeanneney on July 23. Jeanneney warned that Hitler would benefit from any effort to create new subjects of discord among the French, especially if the trial supported the Nazi claim that France was responsible for the war. "Yes, that's true," replied Pétain. "I haven't forgotten that. . . . But can I resist?"[5]

At least some of the pressure was coming from Alibert. He

had drafted and then lobbied for a decree (signed on July 23) which stripped French nationality from those who had left France between May 10 and June 30, a measure that affected prominent Jews, leading Third Republic politicians. The parliamentary passengers who had sailed to Morocco (on the *Massilia*) in the belief that they would be carrying on the war from there were treated as deserters, and a number of them were interned. It was announced that all naturalizations effected since 1927 would be reviewed, and those considered undesirable would lose French citizenship.[6] In August and September further decrees limited the practice of medicine and law to those born of French fathers, and although the word "Jew" wasn't mentioned in them, the measures were applied with particular severity to Jews.[7]

Constitutional act number five of July 30 set up a Supreme Court of Justice qualified to try the highest government officials, including the president. This was the Court of Riom, which held its inaugural session in that town (twenty-seven miles from Vichy) in the presence of Minister Alibert on August 8.[8] The trials of former Third Republic leaders, despite all the precautions taken to keep them within bounds and to prevent public knowledge of damaging testimony, proved a boomerang. Although an attempt was made to avoid placing blame on the prewar policies of Pétain or Weygand (by limiting the investigation to the period since March 1936), the accused Third Republic leaders were able to turn the tables on their accusers.[9]

Still, Vichy was not to be punishment alone. There would be an ideology, but which one? Whose? A group of prewar extremists including Marcel Déat and Gaston Bergery suggested to Pétain the concept of a single party, which would promote the ideology of the new French state. Pétain, his secretary Du Moulin tells us, was tempted by the proposal before rejecting it. His objection was not that the single party represented incipient Fascism, but that it might revive the party spirit, and Pétain was adamantly opposed to that.[10]

Instead, the marshal encouraged the development of a party that was not a party, the French Legion of Veterans, conceived as the unique organizational framework for the propagation of the ideology of the new regime. Founded by a decree signed on

August 29, with Pétain as president (usually called "The Chief"),
the Legion eventually became the umbrella organization not only
for war veterans, who were still a major factor in the country,
but for all Frenchmen "wishing to associate themselves with veterans to serve the principles of the National Revolution."[11] Its
official publications were filled with evocations of the person and
the thought of the marshal, homilies on the role of the chief, regime propaganda; Legion offices distributed color portraits of
Pétain, his statuette in plaster (in a choice of colors), posters,
postcards (six different views of the marshal), pamphlet biographies, pencils containing his portrait, as well as pins, tie clips,
badges. From its headquarters in Vichy's Hotel Thermal it distributed tracts with titles such as "The Legion Against Bolshevism," "The Legion Against Gaullism," "The Legion Against Jewish
Power," "The Legion Against the Freemasons."[12]

The first secretary-general of the Legion, Xavier Vallat, who
announced himself as legionnaire number two (after Pétain), went
on to become Vichy's first commissioner of Jewish questions. In
the pages of a Legion magazine he proclaimed: "Anti-Semitism
is always and everywhere a simple phenomenon of legitimate national defense."[13]

The new regime's doctrines were expounded in Legion meetings and publications, but also in the marshal's own speeches,
drafted by members of his entourage, including Yves Bouthillier, René Gillouin, Henri Massis, Émile Laure, and Jean Fernet.[14] Corporatism, a system based on an idealization of the roles
of capital and labor—like those other themes: new order, national revolution—was to align Vichy with existing authoritarian
regimes. In August 1940 a decree calling for committees of organization set the stage for a reorganization of the economy on
corporate lines; in the minds of the ideologists of Vichy, govern-
ment-regulated industry and a labor force inspired by love of work
and country would become "the pillars of these corporations on
which the French count for a large part for the renaissance of
the fatherland."[15]

Pétain summed up his philosophy of government in a document which he called Principles of the Community. Here he
stressed the duties of the citizen: "work and courage, discipline
and obedience to law." The "spirit of collaboration" had to re-

place the "spirit of demanding things"; private interest had to be
subordinated to public interest. Every community needed a chief,
who should be "honored and served." The state, extension of the
family, must be strong. Another thought had it that "neither birth
nor fortune confer the right to command," for "the true hierarchy is that of talent and merit."[16]

The literature of the time and postwar memoirs describe the
day-to-day routine, conjure up the atmosphere of the transformed watering place. The precise Du Moulin de Labarthète,
writing from Swiss exile, had the leisure to record many observations. About the indigence: the frayed clothing of high officials, the cooking—notably of potatoes—done by their wives on
electric burners in their hotel rooms, the absence of private cars.
Pétain received many visitors, seven or eight a day, those unable
to obtain appointments often being invited to lunch. Decrees were
signed, and death sentences; Du Moulin says that Pétain signed
the latter without hesitation, for he felt that it was not he but society that had sentenced the guilty; clemency might itself be
criminal, but pity would be cowardice.

Lunch brought together a dozen or more guests—Laure, Ménétrel, Bonhomme, Du Moulin among the regulars, with civil and
military staff officers taking turns, and old friends like Serrigny
when they were in town. Here Pétain was at his best: "gay, at times
brilliant," was receptive to suggestions, to warnings. He played
jokes, told old barracks-room stories. In the afternoons he took
drives outside town, returning to his office for more appointments; each evening Laure and Du Moulin saw him for a final
briefing and to have him sign papers. Before dinner there was
half an hour to relax with the children of the Ménétrels and of
the Séguins (the grandchildren of Jacqueline de Castex). Dinner
at eight was limited to eight or ten guests: friends who happened
to be in town, the Brécards, the Romiers. Then half an hour at
the coffee table, the coffee being camomile tea.[17]

Admiral Fernet lets us glimpse the regular 11:00 A.M. meeting of Pétain's advisers in the early months of Vichy; it was usually held in his own office (the small drawing room adjoining his
bedroom). There would be Weygand, Laval, Baudouin, Bouthillier, Darlan, sometimes Alibert. The cabinet meeting was held

three or four times a week in the ground floor grand salon of
the Pavillon Sévigné. Fernet remembers that Pétain liked it to be
an orderly meeting, hated interruptions—which usually came from
Laval. His hearing deficiency, less severe than some had suggested, nontheless made it difficult for him when several persons
spoke at once. Fernet tells us, regretting it, that ministers got into
the habit of calling on Pétain separately to discuss their problems
and submit suggestions, which led to a certain lack of cohesion
and competing influences. Pétain listened to all who came to see
him and received summaries of the thousands of letters received
each day.[18]

As for this mail: Denunciations represented a high proportion of it. Most were anonymous and concerned alleged Communists, Freemason leaders, civil servants with poor records, or
it might be a question of a simple citizen who wasted gasoline, a
teacher alleged to be a nudist and who encouraged her girl pupils to meet boys. Indeed, most often the targets were teachers (the
alien element in smaller towns and villages). But there was even
a denunciatory letter from a French resident of New York—in
fact, it was an ordinary postcard—to demand the removal of a
French commercial attaché posted to that city—an "incompetent,
notorious Freemason." Brécard alerted the Foreign Ministry, and
the man was recalled.[19]

The denunciations became so overwhelming that Pétain's staff
informed the press and information service in September 1940
that it was receiving too many of them, and that they were "often
motivated by vengeance, hate or jealousy." For the sake of public
morality it would be better to limit this practice. It was suggested
that a press or radio statement make it clear that anonymous denunciations would not be taken seriously and inaccurate ones
would be punished. But the files show that anonymous denunciations continued to arrive, and to be acted on.[20]

XXV
FEELERS

It was at the beginning of August 1940 that a court sitting in Clermont-Ferrand found Charles de Gaulle guilty of treason and sentenced him to death. Much later, after his own arrest in 1945, Pétain declared that he had added a note to de Gaulle's dossier, indicating that the sentence was not meant to be carried out. It had been necessary for military discipline and to put a halt to the exodus of French officers. Pétain's note—never found—was reconstructed by him during his detention.[1]

On the evening of August 13, Pétain spoke to the French by radio. He made a hard-line doctrinal speech, carrying a warning of the stern measures to come, notably in the "purging of our administration, into which too many newly nationalized Frenchmen had inserted themselves"—a reference to immigrants, mainly Jews, who had become citizens under the 1927 law. Some of France's problems derived from war and defeat, he went on, but others "had their origins in the same causes as those which led our country to disaster, in the demoralization and disorganization which, like gangrene, had infiltrated the State."

This message also offered an indication as to what the government hoped to do to feed its population, to restore order to agricultural production, to repatriate refugees and assist in their reintegration, to demobilize soldiers and help them find a place in civilian life. Pétain offered public thanks to American generosity for sending food and clothing, thanked the Swiss too. He concluded with an attack on the prewar Republic, whose "guiding principle was to stir up reasons for irritation, legitimate or not, to the point of convincing our people, which was then one of the happiest on earth, that it was the most deprived."[2]

In the pages of the venerable *Revue des Deux Mondes,* Pétain described what he felt to be an essential element of his program: educational reform. It would stress discipline rather than individualism—for the latter was responsible for prewar abuse. It would teach respect for people, family, society, nation. Primary school would teach manual skills and avoid sterile theorizing, so that the best pupils would stay in their villages rather than migrate to the big cities. Excessive industrialization would be discouraged, the tradition of craftsmanship restored. The new France would do away with "administrative nomadism, an irresponsible bureaucracy"; there would be sports, ideals; peasants would receive a new affirmation of their dignity.[3]

On August 20, less than two weeks after the German air force launched its assault on British ships and ports which would signal the beginning of the Battle of Britain, Winston Churchill told the House of Commons: "That France alone should lie prostrate at this moment, is the crime, not of a great and noble nation, but of what are called 'the men of Vichy.' "[4] Pétain summoned his foreign minister. He wished to reply to Churchill, but Baudouin argued that a chief of state "must remain above polemics." Pétain warned that Laval would use Churchill's speech as a springboard for his anti-British policy, so Baudouin offered to attempt a more diplomatic reply to the British prime minister, which would nevertheless let the French people know that the British were refusing to lift their blockade of ship traffic between France and North Africa. In a second meeting that day Baudouin heard Darlan ask for authority to bomb Gibraltar immediately to retaliate for the blockade. Pétain agreed, but Baudouin says that he

defused the issue by offering to allude to Britain's "privileged situation" in Gibraltar in the speech he was planning.

On the twenty-second, Baudouin attended a meeting of Pétain's advisers at which General Huntziger, just off the plane from
Wiesbaden, brought a German demand for payment of an ex-
traordinarily high occupation indemnity: 400 million francs a day
(equivalent to nearly that many of today's francs). Baudouin records that he and Bouthillier insisted that a French protest against
this exorbitant demand be made public; Laval objected, and Pétain agreed with Laval. After the meeting Weygand and Baudouin sought Pétain's approval of publication of a protest against
the German takeover of Alsace-Lorraine; Pétain accepted the
protest but strenuously refused to allow it to be publicized. Baudouin replied, so he tells us in his memoirs, that their silence made
them "accomplices of the Germans." On August 30, when Laval,
back from a visit to German headquarters in Fontainebleau, said
that he would favor war against Britain, no one in the cabinet
agreed with him. Pétain offered the opinion that France should
remain neutral in the war between Britain and Germany.[5]

Relations with Britain remained precarious through the four
Vichy years, but until the Americans landed in North Africa in
November 1942, Pétain's personal preferences kept U.S.-French
contacts alive and often friendly. In a talk to American journalists in Vichy, Pétain assured them of France's faithful friendship
and expressed appreciation for America's "magnificent generosity" to France's refugees. He promised that France's recovery
would "astonish the world. It will become what it should never
have ceased being, an essentially agricultural nation." And he
painted a picture of a country true to its traditions of craftsmanship, discipline, Christian morality; like the democracies of the
Western Hemisphere it would respect "the human person, the
cult of the family, of the community, of the fatherland, the love
of justice and of humanity. . . ."[6]

A letter to President Roosevelt dated August 27, 1940, begins: "France is today experiencing the most tragic hour of its
long history." Three fifths of its territory was occupied; two million prisoners remained in Germany; millions of refugees who
fled France's most fertile farmland awaited repatriation. His government's chief concern, Pétain told Roosevelt, was to help the

French support their burden, and he appreciated U.S. material aid that served that purpose.[7]

"A Jew," Du Moulin de Labarthète quotes his marshal, "is never responsible for his origins; a Freemason always is of his choice."[8] Pétain's intense, lifelong distrust of the Masons has already been described; his was a conviction shared by many right-wing Frenchmen, notably by followers of Action Française. The belief that the Third Republic had been evil, that it had been responsible for France's decline and then for its fall, and that the Masons were the secret rulers of that Third Republic dominates Vichy rhetoric, and the marshal's. "Politics and Freemasonry . . . it's the same thing," Pétain confided to a visitor; "together they brought us down."[9]

A decree dated August 13, 1940, outlawed secret societies and confiscated their possessions. Government employees were required to declare under oath that they never belonged, or no longer belonged, to the Freemasons (and promise never to join). Another decree actually called for publishing the names of Freemasons in the *Journal Officiel,* while a ban on holding public office already applicable to Jews was extended to Freemasons.[10] (Pétain's private secretary says that there were 100,000 Freemasons in France in 1940, of whom 46,000 were active dues payers.)[11]

It is generally agreed that Raphaël Alibert was the architect of the anti-Masonic decrees.[12] Then their philosopher was certainly Bernard Faÿ, in charge of an ambitious program of officially sponsored propaganda, including the maintenance of a library and a museum, traveling exhibits, and periodicals.[13] He ran the Service of Secret Societies which published the monthly *Les Documents Maçonniques.* In this journal, evoking his own twenty-year anti-Masonic crusade, he reported a conversation with the chief of state. When Faÿ described the difficulties inherent in pursuing the war against the Freemasons, he says that Pétain replied: "You must not hesitate. The Freemasonry is the chief cause of our misfortune; it lied to the French and gave it the lying habit. And it is lies, and the habit of lying, which led us to where we are now." Far from diminishing their efforts, Pétain told Faÿ, they must augment them, "without ever letting ourselves become tired."[14]

There are as many explanations as there are witnesses to Pétain's cabinet revamping of September 6, 1940. What is clear is that ministers who had parliamentary backgrounds were dropped, with the exception of Laval, while the ranks of the technocrats were reinforced. "Parliamentarians irritate me," Pétain told Du Moulin. "They make me waste precious time. And then, they aren't very popular. . . ." "Laval also, Marshal?" No, he would keep Laval. Laval "is no better than the others," but he had been useful. Even Henry Lémery, minister of colonies, had to go, for the Germans didn't appreciate his West Indian origins, and Pétain himself now wondered (or so Du Moulin tells us Pétain told him) whether he hadn't been a Freemason. And a nonparliamentary minister, Weygand, was replaced. (Weygand became Vichy's governor of French Africa.)[15] It hadn't helped Weygand's case that he had recently shouted at Laval, during a cabinet meeting, "You roll around in defeat like a dog in shit."[16]

After the Second World War, during and especially after Pétain's trial, much was said about Vichy's contacts with the British during the occupation years, contacts that could only have been secret, considering that France was occupied by a nation at war with Britain. On one side are those who dismiss Vichy-London contacts as without consequence, on the other, supporters of Pétain who claim that he actually approved one or more secret understandings or treaties. The evidence is confused by the presence of a number of unofficial emissaries, and of the tendency of such persons to inflate their roles. The most significant talks, the talks with the most potential, were those held in Madrid between Vichy's ambassador Robert de La Baume and his successor François Piétri and the United Kingdom's Sir Samuel Hoare. These encounters were not to produce permanent agreement, but while they lasted they prevented a bad situation from becoming worse. Thus, in hopes of winning over French West Africa, de Gaulle's Free French, assisted by a British task force, attempted to seize the port of Dakar on September 23; the attack failed and there was loss of life and of ships, and a new level of animosity between the former allies. Pétain not only gave the order to resist the attackers but this time authorized Darlan to proceed with his plan to bomb Gibraltar.[17]

In Madrid, meanwhile, La Baume called on Hoare on September 27 with a message from Vichy to the effect that if the French were not to be driven entirely into German hands, Britain had to allow the passage of supplies from the colonies to the French mainland, on a French pledge that the supplies would not reach the Germans. From London, Foreign Minister Halifax instructed Hoare to tell Vichy that Britain was prepared to talk to the French despite such hostile acts as the firing on British warships at Dakar (for the British had entered the port with a request for negotiations), and even despite the bombing of Gibraltar. But Halifax also warned that Britain would retaliate against further hostility and would not cease to support de Gaulle. He asked for guarantees that French colonies would not fall into German or Italian hands; after receiving this assurance, Britain would consider lifting the blockade. Vichy replied that the French would not be the aggressors, but if Britain wished a relaxation of tensions it would have to reconsider its support of de Gaulle. In any case, Vichy would cede neither colonies nor fleet to Britain's enemies. The reply disappointed London, but the dialogue was pursued.

On October 25, Halifax sent Hoare a message from His Majesty George VI to Marshal Pétain: The date is significant, for Pétin had met Hitler the previous day. "Reports are reaching me of an attempt by the German government to secure from you undertakings that would go far beyond the terms accepted by you at the time of the armistice," the king told the marshal. He was confident that Pétain would "reject proposals that would bring dishonor to France and grave damage to a late Ally." Pétain replied with a reminder of the "aggressions" of the British fleet and British support for "Frenchmen rebel to their country." France would not carry out an unjustified attack, he said, but would know how to protect "with honor" the essential interests of the French nation.

Following Pétain's radio message of October 30 announcing the principle of collaboration with Germany, Halifax cabled Hoare to ask where Vichy now stood on a *modus vivendi*. Hoare replied that the French embassy in Madrid had not heard from Vichy, but feared that Laval intended to sign a treaty with Germany and then attack French colonies which had declared for de Gaulle. Finally on November 11, Hoare reported the French government's position: France would protect its empire against both de Gaulle and the Germans. Disappointing, commented Halifax, but in present circumstances Vichy was unlikely to commit anything useful to paper, "or indeed, anything which would be exposed to objection by the Germans."[18]

One might also recall Louis Rougier and his mission to London, for postwar memoirs are filled with accounts of it, some stressing the significance of this attempt to deal with Churchill behind Hitler's back, others pointing to the ambiguity of Rougier's assignment and its failure to produce tangible agreement. Rougier, a well-traveled economist and philosophy professor, went to Vichy in mid-September 1940 to inform the government that he had a way to get to London secretly and could go there to argue France's case against the blockade.[19] Rougier has Pétain telling him: "Make sure to tell the British that I hold nothing against them. I made only one speech against Churchill, but he had attacked French honor and I had to reply." Pétain was most concerned that the British leave French ships and bases alone.[20]

Rougier arrived in London on October 22; these were the worst hours of the Battle of Britain, when hundreds of Luftwaffe bombers hit London in a single night; thousands of civilians died; and hospitals, churches, and monuments were destroyed. He met Halifax the next day and Churchill the day after that. After arguing Vichy's case, he says that agreement was reached on the blockade; the British also promised that when they attacked the Vichy regime on the radio they would not attack the marshal personally. But that day Pétain met Hitler at Montoire. As he expected, Rougier was called in to see Churchill again; he paints a picture of an exasperated Churchill, convinced that Pétain had signed a treaty with Hitler. Churchill asked Rougier, says Rougier, to help convince Weygand to rebel against Vichy; Britain would supply arms so that Weygand could pursue the war from North Africa. On October 28, before Rougier's return flight to Lisbon, he drafted a résumé of his talks, which he called a protocol. He claims that Churchill personally corrected his text.[21]

For their part, the British categorically denied (when Rougier's claim was published after the war) that a gentleman's agreement was approved with Vichy; the meetings with Rougier were seen on the British side only as an exchange of views. The Foreign Office went so far as to say that Rougier falsely declared that his notes for a forthcoming "Conversation with Weygand" were a record of his past "Conversation with Churchill," simply by blocking out Churchill's name.[22]

Yet on his return to Vichy on November 8, Rougier handed a report on his London talks to Pétain, who apparently remarked, while showing it to Du Moulin with a wink, "This should make de Gaulle lose a lot of sleep!"[23] Later, Pétain would tell his High Court interrogators that he had "negotiated a treaty which had to remain secret" with Churchill; he dates it as contemporary with his meeting with Hitler and says it showed what the meeting with Hitler really represented for France. . . .[24] On the British side, we have Churchill's later explanation that he received envoys from France in the hope of inducing some of Vichy's ministers to carry on the war in Africa. He received Rougier "not because I or my colleagues had any respect for Marshal Pétain, but only because no road that led to France should be incontinently barred."[25] Rougier himself, in a memorandum to Lord Halifax, presented Vichy's position on a number of points, one of which was the recommendation that "The British Government . . . should not make Communists, Socialists and Jews speak on the wireless."[26] An agreement could hardly have been reached between the author of this recommendation and His Majesty's wartime government.

XXVI
MONTOIRE

On October 11, Pétain issued what his aide Du Moulin de Labarthète was to describe as a "doctrinal message." It began with a
merciless attack on the "weaknesses and blemishes of the former
political regime" which had brought France to its present plight.
The "new order" would not allow the French to return to past
errors which had cost so dearly, yet it would not represent revenge for the "events of 1936" either. It would not be "a servile
imitation" of foreign experiments—the allusion is to Nazism and
Fascism—although "some of these experiments have their meaning and their beauty." Every people must develop its own regime. "We must, tragically, achieve in defeat the revolution which
in victory . . . we could not even imagine." France would have
to free itself of its traditional "friendships and antagonisms." Pétain proceeded to outline a foreign policy for his new order, and
here the term collaboration was introduced. "France is prepared
to seek this collaboration in all fields, with all neighbors." If Germany could "dominate its victory," France would know how to
live with her.

On the domestic side, Pétain's speech described his regime as a hierarchy that rejected "the false idea of the natural equality of man" in favor of equality of opportunity.[1]

But, of course, it was the foreign policy of the new order that caused immediate concern. The American mission in Vichy, in the person of chargé d'affaires H. Freeman Matthews, reported as much to Washington. "Thus the struggle within the French Government continues," he concluded, explaining that the Laval forces were working for total acquiescence to Germany, while opposing Laval were weak and uninfluential friends of Britain. And in the middle were the marshal and his entourage, who were willing to forget the past but insisted that Germany must do her part in return.[2]

Montoire—the summit meeting of Pétain and Hitler—may have been Hitler's initiative, but Pétain too wanted a meeting. He had made personal contact with the Germans through a man he believed had good relations in Germany, and this at the end of August 1940. René Fonck, born in 1894, had been the first French ace in the Great War, personally credited with bringing down seventy-five enemy planes. On September 15, Vice-Admiral Fernet reports, Pétain asked him to transmit a message to Fonck, then in Paris, containing the code: "Please give me news of your parents in the Vosges." Apparently this was to set the colonel moving to seek Hermann Göring's help in setting up a meeting with Hitler.[3] We have independent evidence in German envoy Otto Abetz' memorandum to Berlin of September 16, in which he reported Fonck's request, in Pétain's name, for a meeting between the marshal and the Führer.[4]

Soon after that, Pierre Laval was informed by Abetz that German foreign minister Joachim von Ribbentrop was coming to France and wished to meet him. The Germans drove Laval from Paris to Tours, across the Loire to a region he didn't know; then and there Abetz let him know that he was going to meet not only Ribbentrop but Adolf Hitler. *"Merde, alors!"* exclaimed Laval— "I'll be damned!" would be a suitable equivalent.[5] The Hitler-Laval meeting took place in the Führer's railroad car at the Montoire-sur-le-Loir station on October 22. The German account of it has Laval assuring Hitler that Pétain shared his feeling that sincere and unreserved cooperation with Germany was France's only salvation (while Laval personally hoped France could enter Germany's New Order). Hitler expressed the desire to meet the marshal, and Laval accepted in Pétain's name.[6]

After this meeting Hitler proceeded by rail to Hendaye, where he met Spain's dictator Franco. Hitler told Franco that there were two tendencies in France, a Fascist one represented by Pétain and Laval, and an opposition that hoped to carry on under-the-table dealings with the British. If with French aid he could win the war faster, Hitler said he was prepared to accord France better peace terms.[7]

Montoire was the smallest of towns, with old fortified walls and medieval vestiges. But the backdrop for the meeting of the German chancellor and the chief of the French state was something else. A garden had been planted in haste in front of the small railway station; a red carpet led from the station to Hitler's car. Why Montoire, which was not even on a main line? Because the station was near a tunnel; the train could move inside quickly in the event of air attack.[8] It was getting dark as Pétain's party drove up. The marshal was ushered through the station to confront Hitler, Ribbentrop, and Field Marshal Wilhelm Keitel. Pétain offered his hand, and Hitler apparently said, "I am happy to shake the hand of a Frenchman who is not responsible for this war." Pétain said, "Fine, fine, I thank you."[9]

Du Moulin de Labarthète and Ménétrel accompanied their chief but were kept out of the historic meeting in Hitler's railroad car. The only complete record existing comes from the German side, a record written for immediate use by the Nazis and therefore probably as accurate as they could make it. Hitler's interpreter was convinced that Hitler, Göring, and other Nazi leaders genuinely respected the old marshal, for he incarnated France's military traditions. Hitler was neither triumphant nor (as some French sources later suggested) intimidated.[10]

As they took their places in Hitler's parlor car, the interpreter observed Pétain. His features had seemed pale as they stood outside on the platform; now they heightened in color, indicating emotion, interior tension showing through the "mask of impassivity."[11] Hitler opened by expressing regret that he was meeting Pétain under such circumstances, and so late. But this talk would also be a reply to Pétain's July letter. Pétain told Hitler that he was pleased by Hitler's welcome, despite the sad atmosphere. He described his position as tragic: He had always opposed war with Germany, which is why (he said) that he had been sent off to Spain. And now he had to atone for the faults of past French governments.

Concerning cooperation with Germany, he regretted that it had not begun earlier, before the war. But perhaps there was still time to regain what had been lost, thanks to the British and their bad behavior since the armistice. France would not forget the British attacks at Mers-el-Kébir and Dakar, nor that bad Frenchman de Gaulle (who had been sentenced to death). Since Hitler had done France the honor of seeking her cooperation, Pétain went on, the reconquest of the dissident African colonies could be the terrain for practical application of this cooperation.

Hitler replied that despite Pétain's opposition to the 1939 war it had been declared all the same, and France had to take responsibility and share costs. He outlined plans for the conquest of the United Kingdom, indicating that he wished to associate France in this combat. Pétain said he was not yet able to define the limits of French cooperation but favored it in principle. He praised the German armament program and Hitler personally; he had never known anyone with so much confidence in himself and his people, accomplishing such great things. Hitler summed up: Pétain was agreeing to cooperate with Germany, the means to be worked out case by case. Pétain asked for favorable peace terms, and Hitler agreed to that.[12]

The Germans came out of the Montoire meeting certain that they knew what "cooperation" meant: the French would help in the war against Britain. So Ribbentrop reported in a top-secret telegram to Germany's ambassador to Italy.[13] That the Germans expected more from Montoire than they actually obtained is suggested by a draft protocol prepared by them for signature by Hitler and Pétain, calling for French support for the war against Britain, permission for France to increase military strength to defend its colonies; after the defeat of Britain, France would receive territorial compensation. Apparently this draft protocol wasn't even seen by Pétain.[14]

At Montoire, Pétain made two requests of Field Marshal Keitel: that his longtime aide General Laure be released from captivity, and that he himself be allowed to visit a camp containing French war prisoners.[15] The next morning he joined a German convoy to visit such a camp near Amboise. "Will they keep us here or take us to Germany?" a prisoner asked Pétain. "My friend, I hope that it will not be long. You have held on for three months. You'll hold on for a few more weeks. Have you any children?" "No, Marshal." "It's a pity; I hope you'll catch up for lost time." Du Moulin, who overheard this, remembered that the poor prisoner was floored by Pétain's remark. The visit had been useless; the men would soon be transferred to Germany.[16]

"Historical Document" was the headline in *Le Petit Parisien* to introduce the photograph of Pétain shaking hands with Hitler.[17] On October 30, Pétain used the national radio to explain Montoire to the French. He said that he had gone there "at the Führer's invitation" but without pressure, and had received no *diktat*. "A collaboration was envisaged between our two countries. I accepted it in principle. The ways and means will be discussed later." He added: "It is with honor and in order to maintain French unity, a unity ten centuries old, in the framework of a constructive activity of the new European order that I have today entered the way of collaboration." Thanks to this decision, France's suffering would be lightened, the condition of prisoners improved, occupation charges reduced. This collaboration, a sincere one, was his own decision. "I alone will be judged by history."[18]

René Gillouin remembered asking the marshal what effect Hitler and he had had on each other. "He had none on me, but I had a lot on him." Gillouin suggested that Hitler's having fought as a corporal at Verdun might have something to do with that, and the marshal agreed.[19] As it happens, we know what Hitler thought, or what he was willing to say that he thought, about Montoire. He told Mussolini, at a meeting at Florence's Palazzo Vecchio on October 28, that in contrast to Laval, Pétain seemed a "very decent, reliable character." He didn't hesitate to believe Pétain's assurance that he had always opposed the British and had opposed France's entry into the war. Pétain was no opportunistic politician, pursued Hitler; he was furious against de Gaulle and considered his behavior a blot on the honor of the French officers' corps, a blot erased by the death sentence pronounced against him [20]

We have an account of the atmosphere in Vichy just then (on October 29), by a veteran chronicler of the marshal's career, his World War information officer Henry Bordeaux, who was invited to lunch by Pétain that day. Bordeaux observed that the parlor adjoining the Parc Hotel dining room was unheated, and Eugénie Pétain entered in a fur coat ("tall, heavier, with a new dignity and effusive cordiality"). Pétain followed, in a light overcoat which he removed despite the chill ("he remains magnificent and in keeping with his great destiny"). A handful of guests gathered at the round table, Alibert and Fernet among them. The food was excellent, fish, wild boar on a chestnut purée, although Pétain himself had chicken.

Pétain told Bordeaux that Hitler had been extremely courteous, while he had been "icy." "I wasn't treated as a loser; I wouldn't have accepted that."[21]

Baudouin recalls that he ushered the Portuguese ambassador into Pétain's bedroom at ten the next night. Pétain asked the ambassador to inform Portugal's President Antonio Salazar that he wished Churchill to know that in no case would he authorize an act of hostility against Britain; collaboration with Hitler would never be military. The recourse to the Portuguese allowed Pétain to keep this message out of hearing of the new foreign minister, Pierre Laval. (Laval replaced Baudouin as foreign minister after Montoire.)[22]

To Weygand, who loyally reported British attempts to win him over, Pétain wrote: "You were right not to reply to the letters of Churchill and Halifax, who were curious to know the purpose of my talks with Hitler. I was able to tell them, for it is the truth, that we only discussed the principle of collaboration." Pétain repeated that he had limited himself to asking for improvement of the condition of prisoners, of food supplies, interzone communications, doing away with the frontier that separated the German and Vichy zones of France, "etc." Perhaps the matter of collaboration would come up again, Pétain went on, but he'd see to it that it was confined to economic questions and the defense of French Africa, to the exclusion of an attack on Britain.[23]

A week later, Pétain sent Weygand a copy of the reply received from Churchill. In this "personal and most secret" message, the British prime minister announced that if in the near future the French government decided to move to Africa or to resume the war against the Axis, Britain would help it defend North Africa. The British air force was growing in strength, and the French and British fleets together would control the Mediterranean. The United Kingdom was ready, Churchill added, to engage in secret staff meetings with French military representatives. Delay was dangerous; the Germans were capable of a surprise attack in the Mediterranean at any time.[24] Churchill had just circulated a memorandum to his cabinet: "Pétain has always been an anti-British defeatist, and is now a dotard. The idea that we can build on such men is vain." But French opinion and German severity might force Vichy to change its line, so contact must be maintained.[25]

XXVII
THE REASONS WHY

It has become customary to blame the Germans for Vichy's anti-Jewish policy. The paradox is that Pétain's entourage refused to blame the Germans: The anti-Jewish decrees, they insisted, were devised and enforced by Pétain and his government. Pétain's private secretary Du Moulin de Labarthète affirms in his memories: "This legislation was, if I dare say, spontaneous, purely native."[1]

The only evidence of a German-Vichy understanding prior to the promulgation of the Pétain decrees comes from a contested source, Fernand de Brinon, Laval's liaison with the Germans in Paris. In his memoirs written between his conviction and execution as a collaborator, Brinon said that he had discussed the matter with Werner Best, a Nazi staff officer in Paris responsible for anti-Jewish activity; Best let it be known that the way to "protect" French Jews would be for Vichy to "take their fate in hand" before the Nazis did; Brinon says he informed Pétain and Laval as early as August 1940 that they would have to do something to save the Jews. When Ménétrel explained to Brinon that "the Marshal can't interest himself in Jews," Brinon replied that Pétain had Jewish friends himself; he tells us that Ménétrel laughed and said that the marshal felt that the Marquise de Chasseloup-Laubat and other Jewish acquaintances were a nuisance.[2]

Marcel Peyrouton, interior minister at the time, remembered that Vichy learned in late September that the Germans were planning to extend Nazi laws against Jews to occupied France. To "save the essential" for Jews and their possessions, Justice Minister Alibert was asked to draft a decree.[3] We know from the carefully kept diary of Paul Baudouin that a meeting of Pétain's cabinet advisers examined Alibert's draft on September 30. On October 1 the full cabinet discussed it for two hours; Pétain, says Baudouin, was "the most severe." He insisted, for example, on barring Jews totally from the legal and teaching professions.[4]

Pétain was not an anti-Semite, René Gillouin later observed, but like most French officers he wasn't an anti-anti-Semite either.[5] This is the most charitable explanation of the willingness of the chief of the French state to tolerate the rabid anti-Semites of his entourage, to accept their proposals for anti-Jewish regulations, to reduce to a minimum measures that would alleviate the ordeals faced by French as well as by foreign Jews. "Why does Gullouin campaign in favor of Jews?" Pétain asked the Protestant leader Marc Boegner.[6] But the same Pétain who accepted and apparently encouraged anti-Jewish measures was appalled when they got out of hand. There is testimony to the effect that when the anti-Semite Xavier Vallat was replaced as commissioner for Jewish questions by Louis Darquier de Pellepoix, a still more outspoken prewar anti-Semite, Pétain said to him naïvely: "I hope that you will succeed where Xavier Vallat did not; he didn't defend Jews sufficiently."[7] Soon Pétain will be saying to Darquier, "Mr. torturer, I hear too much about you."[8]

Pétain put his name to all the decrees submitted for his signature, rarely objecting. Naïveté or, as both sympathizers and opponents of Pétain have claimed, the helplessness brought on by age? And were the hard-line anti-Semites knowingly exploiting one or the other? The image of Pétain as shrewd and omniscient, manipulating his entourage even as they thought they were manipulating him, weakens when we seek to come to terms with Vichy's Jewish policy.

*   *   *

"We, Marshal of France, Chief of the French State," begins the decree of October 3, 1940, spelling out the Statute of the Jews. It was signed by Pétain, Laval, Alibert, and seven other ministers; it has been referred to as "the Alibert law."[9] It defines a Jew as a person with three Jewish grandparents, or two Jewish grandparents if his or her spouse is Jewish. Under this decree Jews were banned from public office, teaching, or military command; nor could a Jew be an officer of any enterprise receiving public funds. An exception was made for war veterans, and the number of Jews in the professions was limited by quota. In no case could Jews run periodicals or write for the press, except for strictly scientific publications; nor could they hold responsible positions in the film industry, theater, or radio. Exemption from these restrictions was possible, by special decree, for Jews "having rendered exceptional services to the French state" in the literary, scientific, or artistic fields.

It has been pointed out that Vichy's statute went further than a German ordinance issued just a week earlier. The September 27 German regulations defined Jewishness by religion, whereas Vichy spoke of race. Under the German measure it took three Jewish grandparents to be a Jew (which Vichy reduced to two when the spouse was Jewish). And a second Vichy decree signed by Pétain on October 4 called for something more than what the Germans were then doing: It authorized the internment of foreign-born Jews in "special camps."[10]

Du Moulin states that Pétain signed these decrees reluctantly and did what he could to attenuate the sufferings of his Jewish friends. A dozen high officials whose war service or scientific achievements were noteworthy were exempted.[11] But the decree stood. When France's Great Rabbi Isaac Schwartz protested the statute, Pétain told him: "Obedience to the law is one of the essential principles of all states and one of the indispensable conditions for France's recovery."[12] In January 1941, Pétain personally intervened to oblige the presidents of the prewar Senate and Chamber to identify Jewish members of Parliament in conformity with the statute. "My task mustn't be made harder," he told Jeanneney and Herriot. He agreed, he said, that the decree was unfair, depriving officers of their rank although they may have earned their promotions in battle. He agreed such things should be changed. "But I am facing great problems. I ask you not to make them worse."[13] Since these problems were not being caused by the Germans, the pressure on Pétain must have been coming from his entourage.

The record is a seesaw: lenience toward outstanding Jewish professors;[14] an outburst against "Masonry, Jewry, nepotism, profiteering" by Pétain, reported by Swiss minister Walter Stucki to his government in January 1942.[15] An illustrated brochure published by Pétain's office listed among the marshal's achievements "defense of the race"; in the same publication a page devoted to anti-Jewish measures was titled "France to the French."[16]

Marcel Peyrouton, who had become interior minister in the September 6 cabinet reshuffle, writes that the regional tours Pétain began in November 1940 were his idea. Pétain was free to travel throughout the Vichy zone, and it was felt that he should take advantage of this opportunity to encourage the population, as well as to collect complaints and suggestions.[17] Before the year was over the marshal had been to Toulouse, Montauban, Clermont-Ferrand, and Lyons (in November), then to Arles, Marseille, Toulon, and Avignon (December). There were motorcades, handshaking with local dignitaries, decorating of war monuments; photographs show Pétain being kissed, caressing children, saluting and being saluted. Welcoming crowds filled every available space along the lines of march and overflowed public squares during speeches and other ceremonies.[18]

For his first trip, Pétain left Vichy on November 4, spent the following day in Toulouse, leaving the next morning for Montauban, returning to Vichy on November 7. One notable relic that remains is the collection of menus of the official banquets. In Toulouse: selection of hors d'oeuvres, rolled filets of sole in a cream and mushroom sauce, roast young turkey, foie gras in a port jelly, pear custard pie; the wines were a 1934 Chablis, a 1929 Château Latour, a 1933 Château Canon; and there was coffee. In Montauban: fresh ham, filet of sole, roast partridge, salad, cheeses, fruit salad.[19]

To compose his statements and speeches, Pétain now had the faithful Laure with him again; the Germans had heeded his request at Montoire, and Laure was transferred from German detention to Vichy, where he became the chief of state's secretary-general, in fact, director of the military staff, while political affairs remained in the hands of Vice-Admiral Fernet and Du Moulin de Labarthète. In a private talk with his old chief during an automobile ride, Laure was told that Pétain had accepted his post as chief of state out of duty. He had really wished to rest, but "I think that I'll bear my cross until I die." At bottom, he said, he preferred to convince rather than issue orders, but if he were seen to be soft he feared that he'd be "fooled all day long." His temperament and the fact that he grew up away from home had given him an appearance of coldness which had proven useful. "Thus I can show a marmoreal face to those who contradict me, for I don't like to be contradicted when I've made a decision after having thought about the matter carefully." He expected to have to utilize authoritative methods unnatural to him; the armistice terms were severe, and he'd have to respect them even if this aggravated his unpopularity.[20]

On the same day (November 16), as it happens, Pétain unburdened himself to the American chargé H. Freeman Matthews. He was clearly depressed by his "enormous and tragic responsibilities." He felt that his policy of collaboration had been misunderstood in the United States, for he intended to limit it to economic affairs and not help Germany in military matters. This policy was now beginning to bear fruit, he thought, for Germany was releasing some prisoners, and he understood that communications were to be facilitated between the two zones. Pétain complained to his American visitor that the British were behaving badly. Despite that, the French had to hope for a British victory—although he personally believed that the war would end in a draw. "I have no love for the British and I shall defend French territory from them," said Pétain. "But their victory is much better for France than that of Germany. . . . They may finish by putting me in prison. I shall however never agree to anything contrary to the honor of France." Matthews went back to his office to report to the State Department that in his opinion, defeatist though he might be in some respects, Pétain would not consciously agree to anything that he felt to be contrary to French honor.[21]

XXVIII
CRISIS IN COLLABORATION

The most detailed case for the existence of secret French-British understanding has been made for what is called the Halifax-Chevalier agreement. It has even been claimed that this agreement was a secret pact between Pétain and George VI, and that the Rougier mission paved the way for it.[1] There is the sworn testimony of Professor Jacques Chevalier, dean of the faculty of letters of the University of Grenoble, who in December 1940 was Vichy's secretary-general of public instruction, that on December 4, 1940, he received the visit of Canadian diplomat Pierre Dupuy, who transmitted a personal message from an Englishman he had known since they were students together at Oxford. This Englishman was Lord Halifax, then secretary of state for foreign affairs in Churchill's war cabinet. Dupuy told Chevalier that Halifax wished "to resume contacts." According to the Chevalier version of events, Halifax did not wish the Germans to know that the British and French had an agreement, and so a state of "artificial tension" was to be maintained. Dupuy explained to Chevalier that the British wished France to hold on to its fleet and colonies, but to do nothing to take back the colonies that had joined the war on Britain's side. Thus a *modus vivendi* could be reached, allowing France to receive vital food and fuel through the British blockade. All this in secret, so the Germans would not accuse France of violating the armistice clause by which she agreed to do nothing harmful to Germany.

Chevalier called on Pétain on December 5; Pétain agreed to the British proposal, asking only that the phrase "artificial tension" be replaced by "artificial coolness." On the following day Chevalier accompanied Dupuy to see Pétain, at which time the so-called Halifax proposal was discussed in greater detail, with Pétain agreeing on all points. Dupuy left France on December 7, and two days later, Chevalier testified, he received a telegram from him reading, "All goes well," the prearranged signal that the British government accepted the agreement. Chevalier added that from that moment on, the agreement was executed for the greater good of both France and Britain.[2]

In fact, there was already a misunderstanding. We now know that the British attached little or no importance to the contact with Chevalier, that Dupuy did not even report it to London at the time; and when and if he sent a telegram announcing "All goes well," he had not even informed the Churchill government about his contacts in Vichy, let alone received its consent to conclude a pact with Pétain. What Dupuy told the British was that in his two meetings with the marshal, Pétain had assured him of his intention to resist German pressures, while convincing Dupuy that he favored British victory. (Halifax told the war cabinet that if the assurances Dupuy had obtained could be relied on, they would indicate that Britain's policy of "firm and straight language," including the threat to bomb Vichy, combined with sympathetic understanding of France's unfortunate position, was the best way to encourage French resistance, and he proposed to take advantage of other reliable emissaries as they became available.)[3]

As a matter of fact, the "Halifax-Chevalier" contact was diplomat Dupuy's invention. He had actually gone to see Chevalier on his own initiative, as a means of reaching Pétain without using an official intermediary; remembering Chevalier's old friendship with Halifax, Dupuy had said that he was calling on him "on behalf of Lord Halifax."[4] On his return to London, Dupuy drafted

a memorandum for Anthony Eden, who by then had replaced
Halifax at Foreign Affairs, reporting a proposal by Pétain, Darlan, and Huntziger for a secret meeting of French and British
blockade experts to allow vital supplies to move between France
and French Africa (including aviation fuel to allow the training
of pilots in North Africa in violation of the armistice).[5]

From London, Dupuy again utilized Chevalier to contact Pétain. He did it via the American chargé H. Freeman Matthews.
According to Chevalier's recollection, one of the documents he
received from Matthews on December 31, 1940, concerned the
blockade and gasoline; the other, French-British collaboration.
Chevalier took them to Pétain that morning, and in the presence
of the new foreign minister, Pierre-Etienne Flandin, he read and
translated them. Pétain reread the documents and then burned
them. Later that day Pétain received Chevalier alone and dic-
tated a reply, in which he agreed to the proposal on the blockade
and expressed appreciation for it; as for the second, he said "he
never received it."[6] However, chargé Matthews' telegram to
Washington of that day confirms what Chevalier remembered.[7]
As for the text concerning French-British collaboration—the one
that Pétain preferred to say he "never received"—it would seem
to be a message that Churchill admits having sent Pétain that day,
and that begins: "If at any time in the near future the French
Government decide to cross to North Africa or resume the war
there against Italy and Germany, we should be willing to send a
strong and well-equipped Expeditionary Force. . . ."[8] (Apparently this was a repeat of the message already received by Pétain
in November.)

Canada's minister to Paris, G. P. Vanier, had left France after
the defeat. He personally felt that Pétain intended to collaborate
with Hitler, and that Canada should break diplomatic relations
with Vichy. But his government was persuaded by the British to
maintain contact with Vichy in the interests of the Allied cause.[9]
On November 2, 1940, Lord Halifax sent a personal message to
Canadian prime minister Mackenzie King, suggesting that Pierre
Dupuy, Canadian chargé d'affaires then in London, visit Vichy
"to make an informal report on the present situation." The Canadians agreed, while hoping that the contact would be given no
publicity, and suggested that Dupuy could use as a pretext for
his visit the question of Canadians interned in occupied France.[10]

In response to British requests, Pierre Dupuy made three trips to France between November 1940 and July 1941, at a time when the theater of war had shifted to East Africa.

His first impression of Pétain was not a favorable one. "He looked tired and sleepy—in fact he nearly fell asleep three times at the beginning of our conversation—and I succeeded in rousing him only by loudly repeating the name of General de Gaulle," reported Dupuy. But on the three other occasions when he saw Pétain on this trip, he found "a different man," "alert, quoting accurately, quick in taking decisions, and even imposing his will on his close collaborators like Admiral Darlan and General Huntziger." Dupuy judged that it would be a mistake to conclude that the marshal was not the real master.

In his meetings with Dupuy, Pétain expressed the hope that the British would pursue the war, and win it, but claimed that he was not in a position to help, other than by resisting German pressure to use France against Britain. "I am obliged," the marshal told the Canadian, "officially to maintain the balance between both sides, but you know where my sympathies lie."[11] In a telegraphic summary of his first mission to Vichy, sent to Mackenzie King from London on Christmas Day, Dupuy offered a sympathetic portrait of Pétain and his entourage. He had found Pétain "still alert and hoping for a British victory," and recommended that the present atmosphere of tension be maintained as a "smoke screen, behind which secret collaboration between France and the Commonwealth might be possible." While Pétain and Darlan would not let the fleet fall into the hands of the Axis, the time might come when Pétain would find it difficult to resist German pressure for occupation of the colonies. But Pétain had agreed that nothing would be allowed to happen until Dupuy returned to Vichy with, it was hoped, a *modus vivendi* satisfactory to both sides.[12]

Yves Bouthillier records his morning visit to Pétain on December 2, 1940. The finance minister was determined not to have anything more to do with Pierre Laval, who had gone a step (or more) too far in collaboration with the Germans; he had agreed to cooperate on military matters in Africa and had turned over to the Germans gold held in France for the Belgian government. "Well, so you're a bit offended. . . . At your age I wasn't even a major. Am I walking out on everything?" But after a brief silence Pétain added, "Don't leave; he's the one who will leave."[13]

That afternoon it was Paul Baudouin's turn; again Pétain promised that Laval would be dismissed. Baudouin left to meet Bouthillier and Marcel Peyrouton, to plan the execution of the anti-Laval operation, but also to discuss its consequences, notably the German reaction.[14] On his side, Pétain drafted a letter for Otto Abetz to give to Hitler which announced his intention to dismiss Laval and to replace him with Pierre-Etienne Flandin; he asked the Führer's authorization. Pétain assured the German dictator that he remained "more than ever favorable to a policy of collaboration"; it was just that he objected to Laval's intrigues. General Benoît-Léon de Fornel de La Laurencie, then Vichy's delegate to the German military authorities in Paris, carried the letter to Paris on December 9 but received a telephone call from Du Moulin de Labarthète the next morning informing him that the plan had changed and he was to wait for further instructions before submitting the letter. (The instructions never came.) Later the same day, La Laurencie was called to Laval's Paris office; there a beaming Laval showed him a letter from Hitler announcing his intention to return to France the remains of the Duke of Reichstadt, the son of Napoleon Bonaparte, who had died in Austria in 1832. Laval added that Hitler wished Pétain to be present to receive the remains in Paris.[15]

The Vichy conspirators were not only after Laval; they intended to deal with Laval's ideological ally Marcel Déat at the same time. In German-occupied Paris, the French Fascist Déat had been engaged in constant propaganda warfare against the Vichy government, taking care to spare the person of the marshal. Thus on December 3, on Radio Paris, Déat read his editorial "Throw Them Out" from the previous day's issue of his daily newspaper L'Oeuvre: ". . . Marshal Pétain, despite his astonishing physical vigor, despite the sharpness of his regard . . . cannot see everything nor settle everything." According to Déat, Pétain "has abandoned the business of government to clerks promoted to cabinet positions." And these cabinet ministers were "pledged body and soul to all possible reactionary interests, in a permanent flirtation with big business, and steeped in clericalism. . . ." These "bigots," these "cads," these "troublemakers," these "notorious incompetents . . . Marshal, you have to get rid of them."[16] General La Laurencie had carried to Vichy what he described as "a voluminous file" on Déat, upon which Pétain told him, "Well, we've got to have that one arrested." Pétain sent La Laurencie to talk to Du Moulin and Peyrouton. At first they were evasive, but at last they revealed that Déat's arrest would be part of a broader operation, and they would give the general the signal by telephoning him in Paris to say: "The Marshal's wife will cross the demarcation line at 5 o'clock."[17]

On December 12, the news of Hitler's visit to accompany the remains of Napoleon II became official. Laval expressed the opinion that the Germans were being rather nice about the whole thing and offered to go to Vichy to escort Pétain back to Paris.[18] On the eve of that day, Pétain's personal typist remembered that General Laure told her: "Miss Lucet, stay with us to sort the files. The Germans will certainly be here tomorrow." She says that they burned papers all night in the Parc Hotel furnaces.[19]

Pierre Laval drove down from Paris the next morning, bringing Fernand de Brinon with him. It was Brinon who called on the marshal at noon with a letter from Hitler formally announcing the return of the Duke of Reichstadt's remains, with an oral invitation for Pétain to come to Paris for the ceremony on December 15. According to Brinon, Pétain let himself be convinced gradually; he says that Pétain already planned a visit to Rouen and Orléans; he could combine the trips.[20] (It is not impossible that the presence of Jacqueline de Castex in the neighborhood inspired the plans for a visit to Rouen; communications between the marshal in Vichy and Jacqueline at her isolated castle residence were difficult then.)

Earlier that day Pétain had assured Yves Bouthillier that he was determined not to make the trip to Paris, if only because his first appearance there should not be to preside over a French-German ceremony. But after lunch Bouthillier ran into Peyrouton, who told him that everything had changed; Brinon and Laval had won. They had to act fast. Peyrouton, as interior minister, offered to arrest Laval, but they agreed that they would have to inform the marshal first.[21] At three o'clock Peyrouton slipped in to see Pétain; he said that Pétain now had a unique opportunity to get rid of Laval, to put an end to his intrigues and his pro-German policies. Pétain replied that he preferred to see Laval leave peacefully, to avoid stirring up the Germans.

At four the anti-Laval conspirators, who had been talking in Du Moulin de Labarthète's office, marched in to see Pétain. Alibert and Baudouin were there, with Bouthillier, Peyrouton, Du Moulin, Darlan too. Peyrouton later remembered that when he brought up the arrest of Laval, the others were hearing the word for the first time. Pétain now gave him carte blanche. It was agreed that there would be an extraordinary cabinet meeting that evening at eight, at which the ministers would all be asked to resign.[22]

By now it could have been obvious to anyone that something was going on in the Parc Hotel. The stairways and corridors filled up with members of a special "hangmen's squad," as Brinon remembered them.[23] These were the shock troops of a paramilitary organization called Groupements de Protection commanded by Colonel Georges A. Groussard, apparently with the encouragement of the War Ministry; many of its members had belonged to the prewar anti-Communist conspiracy called the Cagoule, and now they served as a patriotic, essentially anti-German auxiliary of what was left of the French army.[24] Early in the afternoon of December 13, Groussard had been summoned to the Ministry of Justice by Alibert. Alibert told him: "It's been decided to arrest him. But first he has to attend the cabinet meeting, and then we have to see that Pétain doesn't withdraw the order. . . . We'll see, my friend, we'll see!"[25]

As soon as the cabinet meeting opened at eight, Pétain ("very pale," observed Baudouin) declared that he had decided to make some changes, so wanted the ministers to sign a collective letter of resignation. Pétain returned to his office, after asking Baudouin to bring him the letter when all the ministers had signed. Laval, visibly nervous, also left the meeting room; Peyrouton whispered to Baudouin that the telephones had been disconnected, troops consigned to barracks, and the police were ready to prevent Laval from communicating with the outside. Ménétrel entered the room to say that Laval wished to see Pétain alone but he was refusing; Baudouin brought Pétain the resignation letter and was told by the marshal: "What I want to avoid is a tête à tête with Laval."[26]

Pétain returned to the cabinet room—still quite pale—to announce that the resignations of Laval and of Georges Ripert, minister of public instruction, were accepted. (Ripert would be replaced by Jacques Chevalier, Lord Halifax' friend.) "What have you against me, Marshal?" asked Laval. Pétain replied that Laval was supported by the Paris press, a press that attacked the government and was inspired by German ambassador Abetz; further, Laval never kept him informed of what was going on. "Every time you go to Paris I wonder with what disaster we're going to pay for your trip. You don't have the confidence of the French. You don't have mine." Laval asked what happened to the decree that made him the marshal's successor; Pétain replied that it was revoked as of that instant.[27] On Laval's departure Pétain announced that Flandin would replace him as foreign minister and Baudouin would take over his propaganda responsibilities.[28] Then it was time for dinner. Bouthillier, dining in Pétain's company, notes that the day's events were not discussed at table, and when the wife of a friend observed: "Your day was peaceful, Marshal," Pétain replied: "Be careful, madam, it's not yet midnight."[29]

For Groussard's men were busy now. Laval's chauffeur was arrested, his car taken away, a secretary confined to quarters. Brinon was kept under guard. Were they going to arrest Laval himself? he wondered. He demanded to see Pétain. Du Moulin knocked at Pétain's door, found him in a bathrobe, calm. "So he's unhappy?" "It's no surprise, Marshal." "Too bad, he's only getting what he deserves. Tell him I'm sleeping, and try to gain time." Du Moulin went back to Laval's office and was present when a police officer came to take Laval away to forced residence at his Châteldon estate.[30]

When Alibert's office phoned General La Laurencie in Paris that evening to announce: "The Marshal's wife will cross the demarcation line at 5 o'clock"—the password for the arrest of Marcel Déat—the general was momentarily puzzled, for he had simply forgotten that it was a password: Had Pétain's wife been detained at the border crossing by the Germans? Then at last he remembered and telephoned General Laure for confirmation of the order. Laure replied: "Immediate execution." La Laurencie had Déat arrested the next morning.[31]

XXIX
THE MORNING AFTER

The problem was: What to tell the Germans? Obviously not that Laval had been dismissed and arrested because he cooperated with them. Certainly it was true that Laval was unpopular: The Pétain cabinet kept a voluminous file of complaints, including anonymous ones, that protested Pétain's association with Laval, "the most detested man in France." Laval was a traitor, a Jew, a rat, a gangster, a scoundrel, a pig—so said the letter writers, the main reproach being that he favored collaborating with the Germans.[1] In his letter to Hitler, Pétain thanked the German Führer for the honor he was rendering France by returning the mortal remains of Napoleon's son. He confirmed France's sincere collaboration with Germany but pointed out that Laval, although an advocate of this policy, no longer enjoyed sufficient confidence and authority to carry it out. His methods, attitude, and connections made him too suspect, and he would actually do harm to collaboration.[2]

On December 14, Pétain addressed the country by radio to announce Laval's departure. It was a matter of domestic policy, he said; it would not affect relations with Germany.[3] Pétain also tried to circulate a message in the German-occupied zone thanking Hitler for returning the remains, but it contained a comparison between the melancholy destiny of the exiled duke and France's own internal exile, so the Germans refused to allow it to be published in the occupied-zone press.[4]

The Germans, of course, were beside themselves. We have Ambassador Abetz' word that Hitler's first reaction was to order a march into the Vichy-controlled zone. All planned concessions, such as the liberation of war prisoners, reduction of occupation costs, relaxation of demarcation-line restrictions, were suspended.[5] Abetz lost no time in storming down to Vichy, waiting only until he had solemnly turned over the remains of Napoleon's son in a ceremony at the Invalides. He made it clear that he intended to talk to the vice-premier—Laval—as well as to the marshal, and that the Vichy-zone press must maintain silence concerning Laval's removal. But the story was out, in Pétain's radio message, in the press.[6] Of course, Abetz could act more expeditiously in Paris. He told General La Laurencie to release Marcel Déat within the hour or La Laurencie himself would be taken hostage.[7]

Abetz met Pétain on December 17 at ten in the morning. The decor was the high-ceilinged drawing room of the Pavillon Sévigné. The German ambassador told the marshal that Hitler considered the removal of Laval a personal affront and demanded his return, or else collaboration as spelled out at Montoire was over. Pétain replied that his decision was irrevocable; if Germany insisted on Laval's return, he himself would have to go. At that point Abtez stood up and asked to be excused from the lunch that had been planned in his honor; he was leaving. Pétain thereupon suggested he go over the German demands again, since most of them were acceptable. This scene, so Abetz reported to Berlin, was repeated five times.

The German ambassador expressed astonishment that he had been in Vichy for several hours and Laval was still under arrest. Pétain replied that he had not known this and on the spot ordered Laval's immediate release. But he said Laval would have to be heard out before his return to government could be considered.[8] So Laval was brought in from Châteldon (a short thirteen miles away). He insisted on seeing Abetz alone first (and made it clear to the German envoy that the majority of the cabinet would now have to be replaced). Abetz and Laval then entered a smaller drawing room where Pétain was drafting a letter to Hitler, in which he suggested—so Abetz observes—that after a lapse of time Laval could be brought back to the cabinet as minister of agriculture, say, or of labor. Abetz warned him that such action was tantamount to rejection of German demands and once more prepared to leave. This led to what Abetz described to Berlin as a lively scene between Laval and Pétain.[9]

As it happens, we have an account of this scene, for Du Moulin de Labarthète and Colonel André de Gorostarzu were next door in the grand salon and could hear what was being said—especially Laval's loud voice. "You threw me out like a valet," Laval shouted. "It's in France's interest to cooperate with Germany, in honor and dignity. . . . But you don't give a damn about honor and dignity. You're just a puppet, a bloated balloon, a weathercock which turns around in the wind."[10]

Abetz agreed to stay for lunch, after all, and to give the marshal time to consult his ministers.[11] "We've done a bad job," Pétain informed Baudouin in the Parc Hotel dining room. He said Abetz insisted on Laval's return as interior minister and the setting up of a directorate headed by Darlan, with Laval, Huntziger, and Flandin, as well as the departure of several ministers including Peyrouton and Alibert, La Laurencie's replacement in Paris by Brinon. Pétain told Baudouin that he had refused to change his cabinet, although he was ready to give Darlan the vice-premiership. When Baudouin said it would be a serious matter to put the government into the hands of a man chosen by Germany, Pétain replied: "What do you want me to do?"[12]

The cabinet agreed to try to gain time, to yield on certain points in order to avoid a break with the Germans.[13] Pétain agreed to letting Darlan run the government and to replace La Laurencie with Brinon.[14] Pétain wrote Hitler announcing these concessions but added: "My dignity and my authority would be seriously compromised if I should immediately take M. Laval back into the government." He was launching an investigation as to the actual merits of the complaints against Laval, and if the results showed that he had been deceived he would take Laval back.[15]

In reporting to Berlin on his Vichy mission, Otto Abetz thought it wise to try to describe the atmosphere of the French capital, "where several hundred statesmen, politicians, military men, journalists, and foreign diplomats have been living with their wives, in a few crowded hotels, carrying on intrigues." These people had constructed a dream world which prevented them from understanding true power relations or what was happening in the outside world. "In this atmosphere lives the old Marshal, who is becoming more and more vacillating in his decisions and who, unfortunately, is almost exclusively surrounded by persons who only flatter him." Abetz observed that after the collapse of France "the deputies could have called the generals to account fully as much as the generals did the deputies," but these "guilty generals" who had irresponsibly drawn France into the war were seeking to set up a military dictatorship with the prestige of the victor of Verdun, and with aid from the Church. If Action Française, a major influence in the cabinet, was anti-Semitic and anti-Freemason, even to a certain degree anti-British, it was above all anti-German. Abtez felt it essential to counter the bourgeoisie and the Jesuits by supporting a popular figure like Laval; Darlan, another anti-British, procollaborationist leader, should be groomed to replace Pétain as chief of state, with Laval as his premier. Action Française should be given free reign to eliminate the Jews and Masons, and then be eliminated in turn.[16]

On December 20, Pétain informed Abetz that investigation proved that Alibert and not Peyrouton was responsible for the deplorable circumstances of Laval's dismissal and Déat's arrest, and so Pétain was replacing Alibert and dissolving Colonel Groussard's Groupements de Protection. Pétain also accepted the German demand for a directorate presided over by Darlan, but it would be subordinate to the cabinet and act under Pétain's orders. Only one problem remained. Pétain had completed his investigation and found that he could not take Laval back for an indefinite period; should the Germans insist, they would complicate relations with the chief of state who, under the terms of the armistice, could choose his own ministers.

In relaying this message to Berlin, Abetz pointed out that it contradicted Pétain's promise to consider the investigation of Laval merely a formality so as to appear master of his decisions. But

Abetz was pleased to be rid of the troublemaker Alibert, and glad that a proven enemy of Britain and a friend of Laval, Admiral François Darlan, had been brought in. Furthermore, Laval's presence in German Paris would represent pressure on Vichy, while his absence from the Pétain government deprived it of the possibility of asking for German concessions.[17]

Meanwhile, Pétain was writing two more letters to Hitler. In one of them he expressed gratitude for the "noble gesture" of returning the ashes of Napoleon II (who had been deprived of his father's inheritance by the "insular enemy," Pétain reminded Hitler slyly). In the other, Pétain stood firm on the removal of Laval, evoking Laval's attack on Pétain during the meeting with Abetz in Vichy; the fact that Laval's behavior was widely known made it impossible to take him back. (In a telegram to Berlin, Abetz viewed this new letter harshly, seeing it as a retreat from the marshal's previous letter on the same issue, and making the Laval affair a test of strength. He concluded that if the Germans forced the Laval issue now, Pétain would not resign.[18]

Ironically, Abetz' long telegram to Berlin following his turbulent talks in Vichy is the first analysis we have from outside the ideological underpinnings of Vichy. Did Action Française really dominate Vichy? Indeed, its sympathizers were present and influential in the early months of the French state, and it is also true that they were to disappear in successive purges induced by Laval and the Germans. The evidence indicates a respectful relationship, and some distance, between the marshal and Action Française's leading spirit, Charles Maurras. The old Action Française leader later recalled that his first visit to Pétain in Vichy took place in the middle of July 1940, at which time Maurras made it clear that he had established his headquarters not in Vichy but far off in Limoges, so as not to compromise the Pétain regime in the eyes of the Germans (his anti-German attitude was well known).[19] Maurras was a guest at Pétain's table a couple of times during Du Moulin's tenure. ("The Marshal liked him, and knowing how deaf he was, spoke to him with his mouth against Maurras' forehead. . . .")[20]

For Maurras, Pétain's assumption of power had been "the divine surprise" (the phrase, drawn from poetry criticism, was often misunderstood to refer to the German victory).[21] A letter dated in the final months of Vichy, from Pétain to Maurras, read: "I know that those who are grouped around you are guided toward the only road the French must travel: that of national interest. You give them the best lessons every day. We all benefit from them."[22]

Pétain's political beliefs, and the doctrine behind the day-to-day action of his regime, have never been codified, unless one considers the pamphlets and books published by his own people during the four-year reign of the French state to be an accurate representation of them. "Politically the Marshal was naked," remarked Du Moulin de Labarthète. He had no sense of masses, of people. And yet, unlike the other generals of the First World War, he was a "republican Marshal." Du Moulin says he heard Pétain say, "I always believed in Dreyfus' innocence. But why did that chap defend himself so badly?" But if Pétain remained loyal to the Republic in principle, his cabinet experience of the 1930s had made him an enemy of Parliament. "Authority comes from above," he would tell Du Moulin.

He enjoyed power and its privileges, including the gifts showered on him by farmers, local craftsmen, during his travels. Du Moulin claims that when the gift-giving took on more and more importance, he protested, feeling that Pétain's enjoyment of the gift of baby lambs dressed in pink ribbons (for his farm), or even of amateur art works, were slight signs of senility. Each day that passed saw an aggravation of Pétain's weakness; France was to suffer from Pétain's obstinacy in thinking of himself as the living incarnation of the nation. Still, Du Moulin found his chief free of pettiness. He loved his country, and it was perhaps the only thing he did love; he served it as well as he could.[23]

As for Pétain's foreign policy, his adviser and apologist Yves Bouthillier challenges the notion that Pétain was playing a double game, i.e., pretending to collaborate while really working for Germany's destruction. Instead, Pétain was a "loyal adversary" of Germany. He felt that the armistice had been necessary, although this did not mean he wished to integrate France into a German-dominated Europe. Indeed, he sought to avoid signing a permanent peace treaty with Germany, preferring a policy of neutrality and of waiting.[24]

He expected that the war would end in a compromise; France

might even become the mediator. He disliked, without hating, the British, while he had "a veritable passion" for the United States of America. Du Moulin feels that Pétain's attitude was aptly summed up in his instruction: "Concerning the British, silence; concerning the Germans, dignity."[25]

"I'm sorry for future historians," wrote Du Moulin in his memoirs published in Switzerland after the war, "if they must accumulate index cards, scrutinize documents, make use of sources poisoned by blindness or fanaticism." How will they re-create the character of this man without having had direct contact? he wonders. Du Moulin gives us some hints: physical vigor, good eating and sleeping habits; there was only that weakness in the left ear. His blue eyes were still keen, although he wore glasses for reading; his other senses were satisfactory. He liked to tell stories, even naughty ones, and to tell them more than once. He possessed an impassivity that was often disconcerting, liked to tease, employed sarcasm too. He protected himself with silence, but this silence also worked against him, for it suggested duplicity. Du Moulin also tells us that his master lacked conventional goodness, for that would have been weakness. He had no gratitude to his subordinates and was untroubled when they had to leave. "I don't sacrifice people," he would say, "but no one is indispensable to me." Du Moulin found Pétain of superior intelligence, deductive, more logical than imaginative, well balanced, endowed with common sense—the peasant's common sense.[26]

To understand the marshal one must know the French peasant, Marcel Peyrouton agreed, the peasant's basic strength, his sense of the concrete, his conservative instinct.[27] Yet this image of the prudent old man who looked before he leaped is contradicted by evidence of the way major decisions were often made in Vichy, where fundamental matters, such as the anti-Jewish and anti-Freemason decrees, were approved "at the end of a cabinet meeting, in the middle of the scraping of chairs, the smoke of cigarettes," the marshal, "impressed by the attitude of his ministers," at times signing texts without reading them, so that he would wonder, some days later, how he could have done it.[28]

Pétain's secrecy, and his silence, helped him create his stereotype as a devout Catholic and grandfather of a nation of Catholics. He was praised by Church leaders; prayers were said for him;

his portrait was often displayed in churches.[29] He accorded generous subsidies to Church schools.[30] And yet he was just barely a practicing Catholic; went to mass only on important holidays or when dragged there by his entourage.[31] He went because he did not wish to offend the Church, and to set an example.[32] Although he married a divorcée and could hardly be described as faithful to Church doctrine, he was adamant about one of its tenets, refusing clemency in matters of abortion. When one of the special courts set up by Vichy sentenced an abortionist to death, Pétain as "defender of the family" and promoter of the birthrate refused to pardon her.[33] In fact, once he had signed a decree, he rarely deviated from its provisions. When, for example, Paul Valéry appealed to Pétain on behalf of Robert Debré of the Paris Medical Faculty, who as a Jew was to be excluded from teaching despite the fact that as a specialist in infant mortality he had devoted his life to saving as many French children as he could, Pétain replied that it was "impossible" for him to do anything; not that he was holding Debré's anti-Vichy attitude against him personally, but because he had made a principle of never intervening for anyone.[34]

In retirement, Vichy's justice minister Joseph Barthélemy took the time to draw a full-length portrait of the marshal. What he saw was "order, harmony, dignity." No portrait had reproduced his features with accuracy: "The Marshal has a sovereign beauty, a beauty which is the reflection of an elevated soul conscious of his mission." Barthélemy on his first meeting with the marshal was struck by the "radiance emanating from his person." He was often kind, but he could also be cool, and then he turned his visitor to ice. He stood straight, had the health of a man of fifty. He lived simply: Barthélemy mentions what a visitor even today can see, for Pétain's rooms at the Hotel du Parc have been preserved as he left them: They show a level of comfort far inferior to the luxury of grand hotels in larger cities.[35]

XXX
ADMIRALS

The scene was the garden of the Pavillon Sévigné, covered with snow on January 7, 1941, as a battalion of French marines saluted Admiral William D. Leahy, the personal choice of President Roosevelt, who had just been elected to a third term, as American ambassador to Vichy France. Leahy wore a formal coat for the occasion, an exaggeratedly high hat too (which reminded Du Moulin de Labarthète of illustrations he had seen of American Civil War days). The atmosphere was more than cordial; on the French side there was a feeling that American support, in the wake of Laval's disappearance, would open new possibilities.[1]

For his part, Leahy could see that his arrival had given a lift to Pétain's morale. The old marshal seemed to him physically and mentally alert during their noon meeting that day: "He had a splendid, soldierly bearing for one of any age, and a pair of remarkably clear blue eyes." Pétain, who wore his uniform, recalled their only previous meeting, at the Yorktown, Virginia, commemoration in October 1931. On the following day at four, Leahy and the embassy's first secretary, H. Freeman Matthews, called on Pétain in the presence of Pierre-Etienne Flandin, the new foreign minister, at the Hotel du Parc. This time Flandin did all the talking (the subject was shipping American milk, medicine, and clothing for French children). Leahy was startled by the change in Pétain's appearance from the previous day, for now he appeared (as Leahy reported to Roosevelt) "a tired, discouraged old man." After this experience Leahy sought to avoid late-afternoon meetings with Pétain, but he had no control over the hour of their appointments.[2]

The idea behind Leahy's assignment was that the United States should be represented in Vichy by someone who could talk to Pétain. General Pershing would have been the ideal choice, but he was ill; Leahy had had a distinguished career in the navy, and an aptitude for special missions.[3] In a talk with Leahy the previous month, Roosevelt explained that his main job would be to keep France "on our side," to convince Pétain that the defeat of the Axis was in France's interest. But Leahy was also to attempt to inform Pétain of things that his ministers might be keeping from him, and he was to serve as a "watchdog" to help prevent France from assisting Germany beyond what was called for by the armistice.[4] In a formal letter of instructions Roosevelt noted that Pétain occupied a unique position, both in the hearts of the French people and in the government. "In his decrees he uses the royal 'we' and I have gathered that he intends to rule." Thus, it was important to cultivate relations with Pétain, while making it clear that the United States intended to support those countries that were defending themselves against aggressors and would continue to give Britain "all possible assistance short of war."[5] It was now that Roosevelt was to affirm in a speech to Congress that the United States must become the arsenal of democracy, and to set up an Office of Production Management to facilitate the buildup of U.S. and Allied military potential; the Lend-Lease Act was voted in March despite heated opposition by noninterventionists.

On January 25, Leahy provided the president with a first roundup based on talks with Pétain and other Vichy officials. ("They have all been exceedingly polite and agreeable to me.") Leahy felt Pétain to be "remarkably capable for a man of his age," although "the burden of work which he has assumed is beyond his physical capacity." He was vulnerable to German pressure, particularly with respect to war prisoners, food supplies, and the authority of his government; he respected the armistice, although he did not wish to go beyond its terms. He would not "under any conditions" abandon mainland France for North Africa, and he did not believe that Britain could win the war. Darlan also thought the Germans would win, reported Leahy, and Flandin "leans pretty far over to the German side." Indeed, Pétain and his cabinet seemed to be molding the Vichy regime along the lines of Fascist Italy, without Italy's expansionist policy.[6]

When Leahy called on Pétain on January 29, he told him that Roosevelt had asked him to keep in as close touch as was convenient to the marshal; Pétain said he liked that idea. He added that the Germans were becoming increasingly difficult, and he was expecting new demands from them. He complained of the German-subsidized collaborationist press in Paris, of the German theft of France's food. It was a bitter thing to be defeated, said the marshal, adding with a smile: "Since I am always young I can bear it."[7] On February 6, Leahy asked Pétain to authorize Robert Murphy, the embassy's counselor, to return to North Africa to plan the arrival of American supplies; Pétain had no objection. Was there anything else Pétain wished to discuss? No, replied Pétain, but he would hide nothing from Leahy. Still, Leahy felt that Pétain might have spoken more freely if Flandin had not been present; he had walked in during their meeting.

"Admiral Darlan seems to be getting closer to the Germans and to be playing more with them," Pétain confided to Leahy on March 18. "I must watch him and I will restrain him as much as possible." The Germans were saying that Pétain was "swimming with both currents," but he had told them, he said, that he was only trying to float peacefully and to keep out of the swamp. He complained that the Free French were making this difficult. The Gaullists, Pétain told Leahy, pretended that he was secretly allied with them; on the contrary, he felt that Charles de Gaulle was a traitor.[8]

"The only two persons here who have impressed me as completely devoted to France without thought of personal advantage," Leahy wrote Roosevelt the day after that meeting, "are Marshal Pétain and General Weygand. While they possess an astonishing vitality, both are old and both are irreplaceable."[9]

A complicity of sorts developed between the marshal and the ambassador. Leahy felt that Pétain drew closer to him as his difficulties with the Germans increased, for he seemed relieved to have someone to whom he could unburden himself.[10] Cordell Hull, the American secretary of state, told Lord Halifax (who was now Britain's ambassador to Washington) that continued American and British contacts with Vichy were essential to keep the French Navy, French bases, and "all-out" French aid away from Hitler; otherwise the "Pétain branch of the French Government" would be submerged by pro-German forces led by Darlan.[11]

When Leahy called on Pétain on April 18, Pétain told him with a chuckle that he had arranged their talk to coincide with a cabinet meeting over which Darlan was presiding, so that they would not be interrupted. They discussed new German demands, particularly for an increase of German personnel in French North Africa. Pétain seemed discouraged, seemed hopeful only when he spoke of how the French were united behind him, and when he talked of the United States and its growing strength. "The Marshal certainly does not stand for defiance to German encroachments," concluded Leahy in his report to Washington, "but he does definitely represent a brake to full military 'collaboration'; he will try to save the fleet from German hands and we cannot fairly say that North Africa is yet lost."

Even in the tense months of May and June, when Vichy assisted Germany militarily in the Middle East, the meetings with Leahy continued. On June 4, Leahy told Pétain in Darlan's presence that the United States was determined that Nazi Germany be defeated. "When?" the two Frenchmen asked in chorus. Pétain said that in a sense the United States had already won the war, and it was up to that country to insist on a compromise peace. Otherwise, if the war went on, it would mean the destruction of all concerned; the United States as well as Europe would succumb to Communism. Neither Frenchman would indicate the limits of collaboration, and the American ambassador took leave of them with the feeling that Pétain was not going to resist further commitments by Darlan to the Germans.[12]

Another observer came back to town. Pierre Dupuy arrived with positive feelings; he had told the Canadian prime minister Mackenzie King that on his first visit to Vichy, Pétain had treated him like a son.[13] But this time it took him over a fortnight to arrange a meeting with Pétain. The marshal received him on February 12 at four in the afternoon, seemed in perfect health and mood. He expressed admiration for General Archibald Wavell, British commander in chief in the Middle East, and the way he had been conducting operations against the Italians in Africa. He also praised the high morale of the British, the growing strength of their air force. He told Dupuy that his position was not an easy one. "We are under the Germans' 'thumb.' They are interfering with everything, but the game is not lost, it is only difficult." He hoped the British wouldn't make it more difficult still.

Pétain assured the Canadian envoy that if the Germans transgressed the armistice terms, the French fleet would sail from mainland ports for North Africa. In confidential talks with French officers, including intelligence personnel (but not with their chiefs, who said they could not see Dupuy because he was being shadowed by the Gestapo as well as by Darlan's naval secret service), Dupuy worked out exchanges of information and aid to escaped Allied prisoners, and laid the groundwork for other forms of secret cooperation. "This time I think the French have come a step nearer to us," he concluded.[14]

Pétain engaged in a more ambitious act of diplomacy in February. He traveled to Montpelier with Darlan, Peyrouton, Laure, and France's ambassador to Spain François Piétri to meet Franco, who was returning to Spain from a visit to Mussolini in Italy. As Darlan reported the talks to Abetz, the French side affirmed that collaboration with Germany was the basis of French policy; France recognized Germany as leader of the new order. It was in France's interest that the Mediterranean be purged of British influence; Africa would be "reserved in its entirety for continental Europe," with a division of interests to be worked out subsequently by France and Spain.[15]

Back in Madrid, Ramón Serrano Suñer told the story in his own way to German ambassador Eberhard von Stohrer. The Spaniards distrusted France; Pétain acted pro-German only when necessary, for at heart he hoped the British would win. Indeed, Pétain had made it clear that he didn't think Germany would obtain total victory, for the resources of the United States and Britain were too great for that; the war would last a long time, in the marshal's view, and end in compromise.[16]

* * *

Despite the absence of Laval, the Germans were now exercising decisive influence in Vichy. Thus, Interior Minister Peyrouton, as well as Justice Minister Alibert, both considered responsible for Laval's dismissal, had to go.[17] In *L'Oeuvre,* published in German Paris, Marcel Déat used his front page to denounce "little doctor Ménétrel, a dubious character, an Action Française fanatic whose only regret is not to have shot those he held at his mercy for several hours. Admiral Fernet, unlikely mixture of Jesuit and Maurrassian . . . general Laure, who was brought back from Germany but doesn't show the slightest gratitude for that . . ." All of them, said Déat, took advantage of the marshal's ignorant good faith.[18] On the following day Déat went further, with a personal attack on Pétain himself. "This large and robust body, this marmoreal face, have marched into History, but can no longer make it." And so "the valets command," while Pétain clings to power. But: "A nation cannot attach its collective destiny to a curve too clearly drawn of declining vitality."[19]

At the request of Laval, Pétain agreed to meet him in secret; the place chosen was La Ferté-Hauterive near the demarcation line separating the German-controlled and Vichy zones; to avoid observation Pétain and Du Moulin de Labarthète slipped out of Vichy by automobile, as if for a short drive, then boarded the special train of the chief of state.[20] There are two accounts of that meeting, Du Moulin's and Abetz' (which the German ambassador certainly got from Laval). The reports agree that Pétain opened the meeting with an explanation of why he had let Laval go: his unpopularity, his methods, his failure to keep Pétain informed. Laval argued that his methods reflected his intuitive and empirical nature, and they had made possible the Montoire meeting with Hitler. They discussed the statement to be released concerning this meeting; Pétain refused to express confidence in Laval or to commit himself to Laval's return to power. Laval observed that the operation seemed to have been conceived as a two-part affair: reconciliation first, reintegration later. Pétain replied that the two elements might be separated by a certain length of time.[21]

In forwarding the report of the La Ferté meeting to Berlin, Abetz added the suggestion that Laval be set up as a minister of Vichy in Paris, which would serve both to protect him and to allow Germany to bring direct influence to bear on Pétain through him. Hitler didn't accept the proposal. The diary of the chief of his general staff, General Franz Halder, notes for January 28: "Führer has made a decision to the effect that he does not want to have Laval in the French Government. He is to remain in Paris and be available as an opponent of Pétain." Collaboration had ceased to exist, and Hitler would so inform Pétain. Laval was to be kept in readiness for the setting up of a future government, should Weygand make common cause with the British and de Gaulle.[22]

Just after the Pétain-Laval encounter, but before Hitler could have received a report of it from Abetz, the Führer met the duce in Bavaria. Hitler remarked that the French did not inspire him with confidence, but he did not think that Pétain, Weygand, and the others had a precise plan; they simply did not wish to join the Axis. But Hitler did not intend to force Laval on the Vichy government; doing so might arouse North Africa to resistance against mainland France. Laval was collaborating with the Germans, Hitler added, if only in hatred of Vichy. In Hitler's view, Pétain was unable to keep up with the maneuverings of his cabinet. Generals usually don't have political experience, and Pétain was an old man. Vichy was in the hands of Action Française, the clergy, and the reactionaries, the same combination that surrounded Franco.[23]

The Germans may have lost Laval for the time being, but thanks to pressures and promises they soon had a Vichy government satisfactory to them, under the leadership of Admiral Darlan. He was Pétain's vice-premier, but also minister of the navy, minister of foreign affairs (evicting and replacing Flandin), minister of the interior (Peyrouton's old job). On February 10, 1941, Pétain signed a constitutional decree providing that in the event of his inability to carry out his functions, Darlan was to replace him.[24]

Just before Darlan's takeover, however, Pétain had reinforced his grip on the Vichy establishment with a constitutional decree providing for an oath of fidelity to the chief of state by high-ranking officials. He could punish them with detention in a fortress or simple house arrest, by his own decision.[25] For his part, Darlan discovered an aspect of government of which he had ap-

parently not been aware. He began to receive heaps of denunciations, either directly or via Pétain's staff. When he complained,
General Laure explained that the marshal received an average of
1,500 letters each day, which in addition to professions of loyalty
contained information and complaints. "This correspondence
represents, in the Marshal's view, a source of information of great
value, for it informs him not only about the general state of
opinion, but about the work of civil servants and the functioning
of the administration." Some of this information, said Laure,
helped in decision making.[26]

That April Pétain celebrated his eighty-fifth birthday. Precisely on April 26 a telegram was received from Washington, D.C.,
signed by General Pershing: "May you have many more years to
serve your great country."[27] We know from an observer of the
Paris scene what some were saying about this old man. "Pétain
preaches a return to the soil. At his age he could show us the
way." In another story an old woman in Vichy waits for the marshal to pass on the street. "Oh, how handsome he is!" she ex-
claims. "And he walks all by himself!"[28]

Just before his birthday he had another visit from Bernard
Serrigny. He had talked to mutual friends in Paris who felt that
the old man ought to be told what was being said about him; Laure
agreed that Serrigny should be frank, for Pétain now listened only
to flatterers, a sign of age. "Your prestige, Marshal, has declined
considerably in Paris." Pétain himself hadn't had that impression
in traveling through the Vichy zone. When Serrigny explained
that after a pro-German statement by Darlan (to the effect that
Germany had been more generous than Britain), followed by Pétain's affirmation of total confidence in Darlan, Pétain's portrait
had disappeared from Paris shops from one day to the next. Pétain replied that he hadn't even known about Darlan's statement.
After describing renewed German demands for authorization to
cross the Vichy zone to attack Gibraltar and close the Mediterranean, Pétain said to his former aide: "I've definitely decided to
leave, when I feel the time is right."[29]

XXXI

MILITARY COLLABORATION

Early in 1941, Pétain had taken a moment off to settle a private matter. In fact, he had very little to do about it, for Eugénie Pétain went up to Paris with his proxy and in the chapel of the archbishopric of Notre Dame, on March 7, she was married religiously to Henri Philippe Pétain, marshal of France.[1] (This was made possible by the Church's annulment of her previous marriage to François Dehérain.)[2] It has been said that Pétain could have accomplished this act in his own suite at the Hotel du Parc in Vichy, but by using a proxy he avoided not only unwanted publicity but the obligation to confess.[3]

There would be plenty of opportunity for public gestures in 1941. In a speech to factory workers from the balcony of the city hall of Saint Etienne on March 2, for instance, he outlined a philosophy of cooperation between workers and factory owners, who through new organizations to be set up by decree would join together to resolve problems in the direction of social justice. He attributed a share of responsibility for the class struggle to capitalists because of their egoism and lack of comprehension; without necessarily giving up their profits, they would have to understand what their duties were as men and as Frenchmen.[4]

In April he made a speech of a different kind; it was his first public attack on the resistance. Defending the unity of the empire, defending his government against "a subtle, insidious propaganda inspired by Frenchmen," he denounced "the leaders of the dissidence" for dividing the French, for allowing French blood to flow. "There aren't several manners of being faithful to France," he declared, puncturing the notion that both Gaullists and Pétainists were serving France.[5]

In Pau, on April 20, he addressed French farmers, outlining social and educational reforms that would make agriculture the economic underpinning of the new France.[6] On May 1 he drove to Commentry, heart of an industrial region not far from Vichy, to declare that henceforth the first of May would be a symbol of unity and friendship, rather than of division and hatred as in the past.[7]

Later that week he was able to make a different sort of journey, the first since the fall of France. From May 5–10 he was in Villeneuve-Loubet; returned in October for nearly a week; and then in March, May, and September 1942 for a total of sixteen days that year.[8] We have a photograph taken during the first visit, in which Pétain is dressed not as a country gentleman but as a statesman, standing alongside other formally attired personalities such as the newspaper publisher Léon Bailby, the bishop of Nice, and the *préfet* of the Alpes-Maritimes district.[9]

In this year of consolidation of the French state two projects received priority: drafting a constitution, and launching the consultative assembly set up by decree in January under the designation National Council. Indeed, when Pétain asked Joseph Barthélemy to replace Raphaël Alibert as minister of justice, he wrote out in his own hand that the veteran law professor and jurist was to be "Secretary of State for Justice, Legislation, the Constitution, and the National Council," although, Barthélemy writes, the following day he found that the last three responsibilities had been stricken from his title.[10] In Vichy, Barthélemy discovered himself in a "Louis XIV state" where Pétain was the chief, the constituent (empowered to write and to proclaim his own constitution), the legislator; and under one of the constitutional decrees Pétain signed, he was also a judge. Barthélemy also learned that Pétain considered the writing of the new constitution to be his private domain, his personal prerogative. Based on difficult talks with Pétain and with Darlan, Barthélemy drafted a constitution, discussed it in private session at the Council of State, and then handed it to Pétain, who decided to submit it for advice to the National Council. And when this council died on the vine, so did Barthélemy's draft constitution.[11]

Du Moulin de Labarthète says that the National Council had been Flandin's idea, offered as a demonstration that the overthrow of Laval had not been a reactionary pronunciamento, since there would now be a consultative body on which the government could lean. But when the list of appointees to the council was released, half of them turned out to be former members of Parliament. Not only that, but Flandin's old party and his former political colleagues were present in force. Pétain exploded, says Du Moulin, and in these terms: "You've gotten me to appoint 90 members of Parliament, nearly all of them discredited. You want to give them a salary. You intend to convene them with pomp. All you are doing is to revive, behind my back, the prewar Chamber. I don't want that under any circumstances!"[12]

Pétain's most notable intervention in the National Council was his speech of July 8, 1941, concerning his draft constitution. "The electoral, representative, majority-vote parliamentary regime which has just been destroyed by the defeat," he said, "was condemned a long time ago by the general evolution of thought and developments in most European countries, and by the proven impossibility of reforming it." And so the French state that would result from Vichy's national revolution would be "authoritarian and hierarchical," based on rule by elite at every level of the social scale. He was opposed to voting even on the municipal level; in his view (expressed in a June 17 speech to the council), the government would appoint mayors, while provincial assemblies would be composed "on a corporative basis"; only later on, when the mentality of the nation had changed, could elections be reintroduced into municipal affairs.[13]

Concurrently with these constitutional matters, the French state created a new framework for the elimination of Jews from public life and the professions. A decree Pétain signed on March 29, 1941, set up the Commissariat Général aux Questions Juives— literally, the Commissary General for Jewish Questions. It was a measure concerning which he showed no enthusiasm, if we accept what Admiral Darlan told Ambassador Abetz. Pétain hesitated, said Darlan, for he did not wish to harm French-born Jews, especially those with distinguished war records. Despite Pétain's reluctance, Abetz told Berlin, it was best to let the French set up their own agency, thanks to which the anti-Jewish campaign would acquire a certain legitimacy, and the Germans would then be able to bring pressure to bear on it from their zone.[14] Abetz assured Berlin that in Xavier Vallat, of Pétain's French Veterans Legion, Vichy had a first-rate commissioner for Jewish questions (he cited Vallat's prewar anti-Semitic campaign against Léon Blum).

Vallat's was a threefold job: executing French regulations concerning Jews, harmonizing these regulations with German ordinances applied in the occupied zone, and preparing new decrees. But since Darlan had been able to win Vallat's appointment only in the face of strong opposition from Pétain, Abetz felt it advisable that Vallat proceed gradually in drafting new measures so as not to place himself in open opposition to the marshal.[15]

Vallat himself told Werner Best, responsible for Jewish affairs in the German high command in Paris, that Pétain had given him instructions to expand the October 1940 anti-Jewish decree to include the professions and business, but also to watch over the takeover of Jewish businesses to prevent abuses that could be exploited by pro-Jewish propaganda. But Pétain seemed to have refused to help the Germans by accepting foreign Jews whom the Germans wished to send to the Vichy zone for internment.[16]

On June 2, 1941, the chief of state signed a new Jewish statute. Applicable to all of France, this decree at the same time hardened the restrictions contained in the 1940 statute and offered some compensatory derogations. On the same day, a second decree signed by Pétain called for a census of Jews. On July 22 a third decree, "in order to eliminate all Jewish influence from the national economy," provided for the takeover of Jewish businesses and property by the commissioner for Jewish questions.[17]

Repression and prison were indeed to take on increasing importance in year two of the Vichy regime. It was the year when a Special Criminal Court was established to deal with economic crimes, such as hoarding or failing to respect price controls, and the year of the Special Section attached to regular courts to punish Communistic or anarchistic activity.[18] The leaders of the Third Republic were held without trial in the Fort du Portalet, on a cliffside in the Pyrenees. When Senate president Jules Jeanneney sought a meeting with the marshal to protest the detention of Georges Mandel under particularly harsh conditions in the Ardèche region, Pétain replied by letter: "Mr. Georges Mandel is held by a considerable segment of French public opinion to be one of the chief persons responsible for the pro-war policy which led us to disaster." Jeanneney replied that Mandel had not been indicted for any crime and so should not be treated worse than if he had been. And, he added, if it was legitimate for public opinion to denounce, it was up to the appropriate jurisdictions to establish guilt. Soon after that, using his new judicial power under constitutional decree number seven, Pétain sentenced Mandel to detention in the Fort du Portalet.[19]

Witness after witness came away from meeting the marshal with recollections of his vow never to collaborate—never to collaborate on military matters—with the Germans.[20] But this vow was to receive a severe challenge in May 1941. Britain was fighting a German-fomented uprising in Iraq; Germany wished to utilize France's Syrian colony as a base of operations. On May 3, Darlan was summoned to Paris to consult with Abetz, who offered a simple bargain: Vichy was to accord military support to the Germans in the Middle East war; in return, Hitler would make concessions on occupation policy and assist France's buildup to protect her colonies against the Gaullists.[21] On Darlan's return to Vichy, Pétain wrote Hitler to express pleasure that the Führer was going to meet Darlan. "I see in this gesture your desire to associate France in the construction of the European order which is developing. I wish to assure you that this is my desire as well."[22] Darlan lost no time in instructing Vichy's high commissioner in Syria, General Henri-Fernand Dentz, to grant "all facilities" to German airplanes transiting Syria to fight the British.[23]

Darlan then met Hitler in Berchtesgaden, the Führer's Bavarian Alps retreat, on May 11. His own report has him telling Hitler that French-German collaboration was not only a consequence of defeat but "an ineluctable historical necessity." He added that Pétain intended to lead French policy in this direction "without detours or second thoughts."[24] We have a witness to Pétain's thoughts at the very moment Darlan was talking to Hitler. The old man was nervous, noted Admiral Leahy, and apprehensive about what Darlan would bring back from Bavaria. Leahy warned Washington in a long telegram that France was moving toward greater collaboration with Germany and that Pétain would offer no resistance to German demands unless they included "voluntary active military aid." The Germans might indeed use Vichy France, as well as Mediterranean ports and the colonies as bases in future.[25]

On May 15, Pétain took to Radio Nationale once again for a message to his people, announcing the Darlan-Hitler encounter without revealing what was decided. He asked the French "to follow me without reservations on the paths of honor and of national interest," for if France succeeded in the negotiations then under way, it would "overcome its defeat and preserve its rank as a European and colonial power."[26] On the same day he dispatched a more portentous message to General Dentz in Syria. Darlan had already ordered Dentz to give the Germans base facilities, gasoline, and other supplies. Pétain's telegram confirmed his intention to pursue collaboration with the Germans "without reservations" while defending Syria; Dentz would thus be showing, "in conditions I know to be politically and materially delicate, the measure of your desire of collaboration in the new order."[27]

On May 28, in Paris, Darlan and Abetz drew up and signed what became known as the Paris Protocol, which gave Germany air, sea, and surface facilities in Syria; arms, other supplies, and intelligence on British movements. In North Africa, Vichy offered use of the Bizerta naval base, ships and rail transport, war matériel; in French West and Equatorial Africa, the Germans could utilize Dakar and eventually receive naval and air facilities. Vichy in turn was authorized to reinforce its own strength in these areas to resist British and Gaullist attacks. Germany also allowed Vichy to arm itself to prepare for possible war with Britain or the United States, and would also make political and economic concessions to help Vichy justify eventual war with Britain and America to the French people.[28]

All available accounts agree: It was Weygand who saved the day.[29] "I'll fire on the Germans," he warned Darlan, "rather than execute your orders."[30] When Weygand threatened to resign his African command, Pétain argued: "Even if you abandon Africa you'll be responsible, and more than ever, for what happens." Weygand then suggested a delaying tactic: Ask the Germans to spell out their concessions. And then he returned to North Africa, but not before repeating his warning to Darlan: "If someone wants to come to Bizerta I'll shoot him into the sea." He also called on Pétain before he left, to find the marshal relieved that the crisis had been resolved without the need to break with Darlan, and so to have to call back Laval. Pétain promised that he would no longer authorize Darlan to act alone.[31]

Then, on June 8, a Sunday, Du Moulin de Labarthète was roused at eight and told to report to the chief of state. In bathrobe, unshaved, hollow-cheeked, Pétain handed him a message from General Dentz, commenting, "It's war!" The British had attacked Vichy's forces in Syria. "We've got to defend Syria," Pétain told Darlan, for if not, the Germans would take over North Africa. Darlan drafted an order to Dentz to resist. "I don't want another armistice," Pétain told Du Moulin, "I want to kick the British out." (Du Moulin warned him that he couldn't do that with German help.)[32] That same day Pétain signed a message denouncing the British-Gaullist attack, pointing out that France had not been the first to open fire against her former ally. "You are fighting for a just cause," he told his troops.[33] It was the battle for Syria, and not Germany's surprise attack on its recent ally, the U.S.S.R., launched on June 22, which was to preoccupy Vichy in the following weeks.

XXXII

THE PERSON
OF THE MARSHAL

A story that made the rounds in Vichy in 1941, at least in whispers, was that the British had secretly offered to inform Pétain of the itinerary of a flight de Gaulle was planning to the Middle East, so that Vichy France could shoot him down, and thus rid both Vichy and Churchill of a nuisance; Pétain was said to have rejected the offer.[1] The legend that some bond stronger than their enmity united the two leaders died hard. Another frequently heard story was that de Gaulle would say to London visitors, speaking of himself and the marshal, that France "needed two strings for its bow."[2] In his memoirs de Gaulle acknowledges the fact that most Frenchmen in mainland France felt that Pétain was acting craftily, and wrongly thought that he was secretly in agreement with the Free French chief.[3]

The evidence suggests that no such agreement, whether or not it was advocated by persons on either side, was ever seriously considered or accepted by Pétain and de Gaulle. When an overture to this effect was made by a third party, de Gaulle would dismiss it by attributing the initiative to that "sly old man": "Of course he would like people to believe that he is in agreement with us in order to obtain some benefits from it."[4] On his side, Pétain appeared quite adamant in opposition to overt or covert cooperation with the Free French leader. "He's a viper I clutched to my bosom," he would say of de Gaulle.[5]

"I don't think History will turn up another example of so much propaganda created in France for the benefit of a man," Pierre Laval would write in his cell while awaiting trial in 1945, referring to the pro-Pétain campaign in the Vichy press, radio, and films; the reverential anthem "Maréchal, We are Here"; the medals; the organizations (such as Friends of the Marshal).[6] Surely the busiest of the propaganda factories was the one operated right inside the Hotel du Parc, and by Pétain's aide, doctor, and friend, Bernard Ménétrel. ("The title of doctor is rather starchy for him," wrote the marshal's best-known hagiographer. "He's the Marshal's friend, a friend who is like a son. He loves the Marshal, that's his reason for being; he watches over him, that's his function.")[7] Ménétrel recruited a printer whose job was to produce "personal propaganda," for Pétain desired that a distinction be made between what he believed and what the government or the Germans would like him to believe.[8] A former jeweler was also hired, assigned to "artistic censorship," which meant making sure that Pétain's features were properly reproduced on the gifts the marshal offered when necessary, such as medals and Sèvres porcelain.[9] It was this jeweler who designed the Francisque medal—a double-bladed war hatchet whose handle was a marshal's stick—given to faithful followers of the marshal's ideology.[10]

Little was left to chance. In April 1941 the Secretariat General of Information made that clear in its "Permanent General Instructions for the Press." No information could be published on Pétain and his wife without prior clearance; all works of art representing Pétain's features, whether photographs, drawings, paintings, engravings, sculptures, or stamps, required preapproval by censorship headquarters. Subsequent advisory notices dealt with specific problems: The press was not to mention a certain visit to Pétain by Ambassador Abetz, nor Pétain's relations with French volunteers who fought in German units against the Soviet Union, or even Pétain's presence at Vichy horse races.[11] All lectures that dealt with Pétain, anywhere in France, had to be approved by his staff; all speeches by officials alluding to Pétain had to call him "The Marshal of France, Chief of State" (although subsequent references could abbreviate that to "The Marshal").[12]

On two Thursdays a month, formal audiences took place during which delegations and privileged individuals could—to cite a typical program—"greet the Marshal, give the Marshal a present, give the Marshal a book of which he is the author, give the Marshal a souvenir manufactured by war prisoners, submit a gift created by pupils, offer the Marshal some lacework." There were children, veterans, widows with children, scouts, picturesque groups such as the fishmongers and flower vendors of Marseille.[13] Ménétrel's propaganda office—called Bureau de Documentation—even published a small book to celebrate these audiences: "And always, at that instant, the identical touching scene repeats itself. . . ." There are some seconds of silence as the Victor of Verdun enters. "A minor mystery whose explanation is discovered by observing the faces of the visitors. They seem stupefied by this apparition, so marvelous that it seems unreal. . . ."[14]

His staff kept a log of gifts that Pétain offered to important visitors, from Baccarat crystal vases; bronze or biscuit medals with his image designed by the sculptor who did his equestrian statue, François Cogné; to knives, scissors; cigarettes in packs of ten, twenty, or one hundred; busts, engravings.[15] Obviously the press was filled with photographs of the marshal's tours of France, his visits to farms and workshops. Du Moulin noted that the Information Secretariat produced bulletins on Pétain's popularity, and they were always up in the 85–95 percentages; but if we believe Du Moulin, even Pétain was skeptical: "They lie to me, as they lie to all chiefs of state."[16]

The censors of private mail and telephone calls, in addition to watching for evidence of subversion, recorded favorable references to their chief. As late as January 1944, when the censors registered 583,415 opinions in 2,336,120 letters opened in that single month, as well as 23,998 opinions heard in 92,100 telephone conversations, and 12,426 opinions in 1,573,761 telegrams, the French still seemed to like the marshal. There were 1,840 expressions of confidence and faith in him, 55 of compas-

sion, only 46 of hostility. Examples of confidence: "In this horrible situation the marshal is our ray of hope." "He's the one who
will negotiate with the Americans." Of compassion: "Poor Marshal! They're taking all his friends away." Of hostility: "One always finds excuses for old people.—He'll need them."[17]

Vichy produced a remarkable variety of books, booklets, leaf-
lets, calendars, almanacs concerning Marshal Pétain, as well as
biographies tailored to different reading levels. Children's books
were not overlooked, and this category included illustrated biographies—even coloring books (one such assured children that
"these beautiful pictures . . . are the nicest you've ever received
as a present"). Obviously the propaganda content was not overlooked, although tailored to the reading level. Thus, in one biography Pétain is depicted sitting beneath an oak tree, promising
to "put things in order and to separate the good from the evil."
"And, as he spoke, all the horrible bugs, all the spiders, all the
termites, all the vermin who had done so much harm to France,
left the soil of the fatherland in great haste."[18]

XXXIII

REASSURING HITLER

The changed atmosphere in Vichy after the Syrian campaign became clear at once to Canadian diplomat Pierre Dupuy. This time, on his third and final visit, and although he stayed from July to September 1941, he could not get in to see Marshal Pétain at all. Du Moulin de Labarthète explained that Admiral Darlan had to approve all such audiences, and Darlan was not going to allow this emissary of the despised British to talk to the chief of state. Through René Gillouin, Pétain let Dupuy know that he was unhappy about this, but he already had so many reasons for conflict with Darlan that he didn't wish to add another. But he passed word to Dupuy that he was still seeking to gain time with the Germans; as proof he cited his refusal to grant base facilities in Bizerta. Dupuy in turn let Pétain know that Darlan's veto of contact between them would lead to a further decline in his government's confidence in Vichy.[1]

Admiral Leahy was also seeking to keep in touch with the marshal, although what he observed gave him no reason for optimism. He saw the likelihood of a German move against the

Mediterranean, worried that since Vichy had ceded Indochina to Japan it would hardly be likely to refuse French Africa to Germany. He felt, so he told President Roosevelt by letter on July 28, 1941, that the old man was "surely if slowly being manoeuvered into a position where his only purpose will be to hold the loyalty of the French people and to make speeches to school children and veterans."[2]

The evidence is that Pétain and his entourage cared very much what the Americans thought. On August 2 the marshal received the visit of a general staff officer, André Poniatowski, who had just been to the United States. Pétain learned with surprise that the American press was attacking him, and when Poniatowski told him that the United States would surely enter the war, Pétain replied that he was getting the opposite picture from his ambassador in Washington, Henry-Haye, who thought that America's economic and social problems were too grave to permit that. Pétain was also astonished by the difference between the arms-production figures Poniatowski gave him and those he had from Henry-Haye. He expected that the United States would concentrate its attention on North Africa. "If only we know about it in time, so we can take advantage." That was exactly what Poniatowski—a member of the underground army resistance—wanted to hear. When Pétain asked if the Americans understood why he had to oppose the British-Gaullist attack in Syria, Poniatowski was evasive. But he also noticed that the old man had ceased to listen. Fatigue? A way to evade delicate questions? The visitor couldn't decide.[3] The U.S. commitment to the Allied cause became clearer, in any case, with the mid-August meeting of President Roosevelt and Prime Minister Churchill on a ship in the Atlantic Ocean, when the two leaders proclaimed the Atlantic Charter containing a joint program of peace aims which included a pledge to restore sovereignty to countries which had been deprived of it by force.

In September when Leahy called on Pétain he found Darlan present, a Darlan who spoke as if he intended to resist German military demands in Africa. Both Pétain and Darlan complained of Gaullist radio attacks; it was clear that Pétain bitterly resented criticism of his own person. "Please tell the President," said Pétain, "that so long as the British tolerate de Gaulle and his activities, there can be no better understanding between them and ourselves." Once more he alluded to de Gaulle's former employment on his staff, as "a viper that he had warmed in his bosom."[4]

Another diplomat kept as close to the marshal as one could in those days, the papal nuncio Valerio Valeri. Valeri reported to the Vatican in September that he had taken coffee with Pétain after a lunch given at the Hotel du Parc for the diplomatic corps. In the presence of Spanish ambassador Lequerica and Brazilian ambassador Louis Mattins de Souza Dantas, Pétain explained that although Britain and America accused him of "sailing" toward Germany, Germany accused him of "sailing" toward England, in reality "I don't sail, I float." Valeri understood that to mean that Vichy had adopted a policy of waiting, tied to events. Since the German attack on the Soviet Union in June, France had been moving closer to the United States.[5] Later that month Pétain expressed the fear that when Germany had achieved its goals in the Soviet war, it would offer France a separate peace. (By this time the German steamroller offensive was approaching Moscow, preparing the siege of Leningrad; much of the Ukraine had been conquered.) "I hope," Pétain told Valeri, "that the terms will be such that I can't accept them." But he still seemed impressed by German military success and thought that the United States could step in to arrange a compromise peace. "If England didn't accept it, she'd be crushed," said Pétain, who blamed the British for everything that had happened to France, which was why he didn't have the slightest sympathy for the United Kingdom.[6]

In his relations with the Holy Office, Pétain hoped to get something more than moral support for his foreign policy. Through his ambassador to the Vatican, Léon Bérard, he also sought information on the Church's attitude to Vichy's anti-Jewish decrees. Bérard reported that no one in the Vatican criticized or disapproved the Vichy measures; the Holy Office asked only that Christian marriage be respected, and that the precepts of justice and charity be remembered.[7] Obviously Pétain communicated these assurances to his commissioner for Jewish questions, Xavier Vallat.[8] But when he repeated them to the nuncio, the reaction was more lively. The nuncio suggested that Bérard's was a rather simplistic summary of Vatican policy, to which Pétain replied jokingly that Valeri might be out of step with his own superiors; he suggested that the nuncio read Bérard's report. When Valeri did, he discovered that it was less categorical than Pétain had suggested it was. In reply to the nuncio's oral criticism of Vichy's anti-Jewish regulations, Pétain said that he too deplored some of the measures, but they had been drawn up under the pressure of the occupying power, and he didn't see how he could revoke or modify them before the end of the war. (The Holy Office, replying to Valeri's report of his talk with Pétain, observed that Bérard's dispatch on Vatican policy had been well balanced and agreed that Pétain himself was using it in an exaggerated way.)[9]

On August 12, 1941, Pétain had made another attempt to define the ideology of the French state. "I have important things to tell you," his speech began. He warned of the "veritable malaise" which had attacked the French people—"worry," "doubt," "false rumors and intrigues," "calls for disobedience"; he blamed London radio but also "certain French newspapers" for adding to the confusion. The French were urged to accept collaboration with Germany, for that country was engaged on its eastern front in "the defense of a civilization." He asked Americans not to worry about France but to try to understand his country. France's difficulties, he explained, were above all the result "of our delay in constructing a new order, or more precisely in imposing it." He accused "partisans of the former regime and servitors of trusts" for having delayed implementation of the national revolution. The former included "the Freemasons, political parties stripped of their supporters," civil servants still attached to the old order or to foreign interests. "If France doesn't understand that it is obliged by the force of circumstances to change its regime, it will stand before the abyss into which Spain had almost disappeared in 1936, before being rescued by its faith, youth, and sacrifice." The marshal would punish selfish capitalists, would tighten the reins of command. "Authority no longer comes from below. It is only that which I confer and delegate."

He went on to announce a series of decisions: a ban on the activity of political groups, an end to parliamentary wages, disciplinary sanctions against those who falsely declared they were not Freemasons, a ban on government employment for Free-

mason leaders, a reinforcement of the police, and a tightening
of economic controls. Finally he announced that he would personally sit in judgment on "those responsible for our disaster."
For that purpose he had created a Council of Political Justice to
make recommendations to him by October 15, He would save the
French once more, this time from themselves.[10]

The speech was obviously a bombshell. All that the American
diplomat H. Freeman Matthews could find in it that was positive
was the absence of a concrete plan for collaboration. Otherwise,
it showed Vichy to be the Fascist state par excellence, he thought.
It would be harder for the United States to maintain relations with
Vichy from now on.[11]

In his speech Pétain had had a good word for his French Legion of Veterans: It remained "the best instrument of National
Revolution." The Legion now began to open its ranks to all good
citizens, whether war veterans or not; its name was lengthened
to French Legion of Veterans and of Volunteers of the National
Revolution. "I accept this new name," Pétain told the legionnaires in a speech at the end of August, "which will expand your
field of action."[12] On the day he made his speech in the Vichy
stadium, a declaration of loyalty to Pétain and to Darlan was read
which denounced "past disorder" when "anti-national Marxism,
alien Judaism joined together in a monstrous alliance to under-
mine the state and France."[13]

As if Vichy's own efforts to embrace Fascist goals were not
enough, the French Fascists in Paris, encouraged by the prox-
imity of the Germans, were now to lend a hand. In July 1941 a
coalition led by Marcel Déat, Jacques Doriot, and their respective
movements created a Legion of French Volunteers Against Bolshevism, whose function was to recruit Frenchmen to fight
alongside the Germans on the Russian front. It soon had the endorsement of Darlan, who told Fernand de Brinon that Vichy had
no objection to the new Legion's recruiting activities, although it
would not provide material aid to the venture unless the Germans indicated that they would like to see France represented in
the war against Communism. From the outset young volunteers
were told that the Legion was endorsed by both Pétain and Hitler. They wore German uniforms with a shield bearing the French
colors and the word "France."[14]

Pétain's endorsement took the form of a message to the Legion's commanders. "On the eve of your forthcoming combats," he wrote them, "I am happy to know that you do not forget that you hold a part of our military honor. . . . In participating in this crusade led by Germany . . . you contribute to protecting us from the Bolshevist peril."[15] "What were you thinking of, Marshal?" General Laure asked him. "I didn't read the text." "And how did you dare sign it?" "Brinon told me that there were brave people over there, good Frenchmen, who didn't like Germany, but who were fighting the Soviets out of conviction. Should I have discouraged them?" Du Moulin de Labarthète says that Laure had tears in his eyes at this point, and he himself was speechless. He adds that he tore up the draft of a speech he had written for Pétain on agricultural corporatism. "If you think that after what you've just written that any message from you will have the slightest influence on the country, you're fooling yourself badly." "Get out, both of you!" Pétain replied. "I don't want to see you anymore."[16]

The resistance was also hardening. On August 21 a German soldier was shot in Paris. The occupying authorities demanded that the French deal with what they described as Communist terrorists, or they would arrest and shoot hostages. At an extraordinary cabinet meeting in Vichy, Interior Minister Pierre Pucheu presented a draft decree that established special courts to try subversives and sentence them to death, although the previous maximum penalty for such crimes was five years. Pétain approved: "Order is the essential thing." When at a second cabinet meeting Pucheu read a German note approving the draft, Pétain was heard to say, "It couldn't be better." Pétain signed the decree, and within days the new Special Section sentenced three persons to death, although they had already received relatively minor sentences for the same acts; three other defendants escaped death penalties, but on German insistence they were retried by a new court set up by still another decree, and were then sentenced to death as well.[17]

On October 20, Pétain drafted a letter to Hitler to mark the first anniversary of their meeting at Montoire. He praised the majesty of the German leader's gesture. "The victory of your arms over Bolshevism now offers the possibility that this collaboration will affirm itself in works of peace. . . ."[18] But even as this letter was being readied for signature, relations between the Germans and Vichy took a tragic turn. Another German, this one an officer, was shot by an underground fighter in Nantes. The Germans ordered the execution of fifty hostages in Paris, Nantes, and Châteaubriant, announcing that another fifty would be shot if the murderers of the officer were not discovered in forty-eight hours. Pétain returned to the air with an appeal to the French: France had laid down her arms and did not have the right to take them up again to shoot Germans in the back. He asked his listeners to help find the killers, in order to save the hostages.[19]

The next day—October 24, 1941—Du Moulin de Labarthète was summoned to his chief's office at 7:00 A.M. The marshal was waiting for him, pale, badly shaved. He had just learned of the killing of the first fifty hostages. "We can't stay here any longer," the distraught old man, his eyes filled with tears, told Du Moulin. But how to protest? "I've been thinking about that; I didn't close an eye all night," Pétain replied. "I must go to Paris to offer myself as a prisoner." He would be the single hostage instead of fifty.

The cabinet ministers were called in. Some approved, but the opposition to the gesture overwhelmed Pétain; he was convinced that one must not yield to impulses of that kind.[20]

Ambassador Abetz received from a member of the cabinet—Pucheu—a copy of the radio speech Pétain had wanted to make; it would have been addressed over the heads of his listeners to the Führer himself. "If you refuse to hear my voice and if you need further hostages and victims," the draft said, "then take me. I shall be at the demarcation line at Moulins at 2:00 P.M., where I shall consider myself your prisoner. . . ."[21] Abetz personally felt that the French were only pretending to be shocked at the German executions of hostages; actually they took "secret pleasure" in them because the hostages were Communists. He thought that Pétain's draft message to Hitler could be a bluff to extort cancellation of the execution of one hundred additional hostages.[22]

According to General Laure's unpublished memoirs, it was he who had drafted this message to Hitler. Pétain read it at dawn on October 24, first thought that it was too sentimental, but then told Laure: "That's fine. We're going to pack a few light bags.

You and Ménétrel will accompany me." Laure had tried in vain to prevent Pétain from informing his chief ministers. Finally it was decided not to publish the letter but to send Pucheu to Paris to seek a delay in further executions (fifty hostages had been shot that morning in Bordeaux; fifty more were waiting in Nantes). Laure told Pétain's ministers—Darlan, Lucien Romier, Henri Moysset, Pucheu—"You, sirs, carry the heavy responsibility of having stopped the Marshal from a march that he began this morning with a resolute and courageous step."[23]

On November 12, War Minister Huntziger was killed in an air crash. Abetz came to Vichy for the funeral and called on Pétain. He carried a letter from Hitler dated November 10, which replied to Pétain's salute to Montoire. Hitler regretted that French-German cooperation had not been as fruitful as it could have been; but if all French prisoners hadn't been returned, it had to be realized that France had declared war in the first place. Hitler knew that Pétain had been shocked by the execution of hostages, but it was Hitler who had the right to be shocked, because of the killing of innocent German officers.

Pétain took Hitler's letter seriously, noted Abetz; he promised that the French would do all they could to prevent further attacks on German soldiers. He added that since the armistice there had been no single act of the Vichy government—Mers-el-Kébir, Dakar, Syria, Indochina among them—that had not been directed against Britain. The French had done everything they could to support Germany's war effort but needed to satisfy public opinion concerning future relations with Germany. On his side, Abetz stressed the need for Weygand's recall from Africa.[24] On taking leave, Abetz left behind Roland Krug von Nidda, who would henceforth be his representative in Vichy.[25]

XXXIV

THE DOUBLE
GAME

In his August 12, 1941, speech Pétain had said that he would
personally judge the Third Republic's leaders. He would do that
by invoking a decree he himself had signed, constitutional decree number seven, which gave him judicial power, and by ap-
plying it retroactively to cover officials not subordinate to him but
preceding his reign. For the Riom court had not been able to prove
the guilt of the defendants. Pétain's hastily conceived Council for
Political Justice delivered a finding on October 14 to the effect
that Pétain had the sovereign right to try the same defendants
by himself.[1] This meant the group on trial in Riom on the charge
that they were responsible for the war, or for lack of preparedness for war—notably Daladier, Blum, and Gamelin—as well as
others not on trial because not implicated in prewar military policy: Paul Reynaud, Georges Mandel.[2]

On October 16, Pétain spoke on the national radio network
to announce that the Council for Political Justice had recommended, unanimously, that Daladier, Blum, and Gamelin be detained in a fortress; he was dispatching them to the forbidding

Portalet in the Pyrenees. But these "simple political sanctions" would not bring a halt to the Riom trial, he added. As for Reynaud and Mandel, the "majority" of the council had recommended their detention as well, and he had so ordered. The "court system, with its prudence, its slow ways, its meticulous procedure, had aggravated the country's dissatisfaction," he said, which was why he had decided to act directly.[3]

Maxime Weygand, one of the spiritual founders of the French state and still a believer in its ideology, remained outspokenly anti-German. In a letter to General Laure on November 2 he made it clear where he stood: He hoped, he said, that there was no truth to the rumor that Bizerta or another African port would be delivered to "our enemies."[4] On November 16, Weygand was summoned to Vichy by the marshal for "decisions of the highest importance."[5] Pétain informed him that Darlan was saying, "It's either he or I." The suggestion was made that Weygand return to North Africa with civil duties only, giving the military command to General Dentz. Weygand refused; Pétain commented, "I expected that."[6] Weygand told Laure that Pétain would either have to fire him or confirm his confidence; he would not accept a compromise assignment. Pétain confided to Laure, "What can I do against these insistent German demands? I'd like to try to have it out between soldiers with Göring, who I'm told is more understanding than the Führer, but they say a meeting with him is impossible as long as Weygand keeps his post."[7]

On November 18, Weygand was called to Pétain's office again. Pétain showed him a report sent by Brinon of a meeting of Vichy representative Jacques Benoist-Méchin with the German command in Paris: Benoist-Méchin had been warned that Hitler was quite irritated at the delay in getting rid of Weygand. "The Weygand case is settled," concluded Weygand, when it became clear that he was not going to be defended by the marshal or his cabinet. As Pétain walked him to the door he mumbled something; Weygand caught only the word "noble." That evening Pétain told him something else: that he would not be able to reside in Africa, or even return there to say farewell to his men. Later, Weygand was also to learn that Pétain had given orders that he was to live in southern France but not too close to the sea, and not where he might receive too many visits.[8]

When the protests were heard, they were late and in vain. François Valentin, director-general of the Legion of French Veterans, asked for an immediate audience, accompanied by other legion officials. "One day, Marshal, they will spit on your portrait, they'll burn Villeneuve-Loubet down."[9] Du Moulin de Labarthète says he was present at that meeting, and he claims to be the one who shouted, "Everything's collapsing around you, Marshal. . . . Have you considered the people's waking up, its anger? If you continue your best friends will be shot, your bank account will be cleaned out, you won't be able to recognize the ruins of Villeneuve-Loubet." "All that at once?" responded Pétain, jaw extended, hard eyes. "You're all over-excited. You're the plotters. I should have you arrested."[10]

The day after Weygand's ouster, Admiral Leahy called at Pétain's hotel headquarters. He was able to see Pétain alone, the only witness being Douglas MacArthur II, who was third secretary of the American embassy and Leahy's interpreter. Leahy told Pétain that his submission to German pressure on Weygand might lead the United States to cut off economic aid to French colonies, for the Americans might consider that the Axis now controlled the region. Pétain explained that he had been forced to choose between the welfare of his people, threatened by Germany, and Weygand. But he continued to deny the Germans the fleet and military support. Leahy found Pétain "very much distressed," saying repeatedly that he was a prisoner. The Germans were ruthless; they had threatened, had Weygand not been dismissed, to occupy all of France and live off the country—thereby starving the French.

Leahy was not convinced. On returning to the embassy that evening, he dispatched a cable suggesting "a complete revision of American policy," cutting off economic assistance to Africa, even recalling Leahy himself "for consultation," and a radio campaign. But American Secretary of State Cordell Hull preferred to give Pétain another chance and to see what could be salvaged; Leahy accepted the idea of trying to exercise "a restraining influence" on the marshal.[11]

Leahy's reply to Hull was dated November 22. On the same day he wrote a personal letter to Roosevelt containing a harsher judgment. "While one may be fully justified in looking at the difficulties of the Marshal's ending years with understanding sympathy," wrote Leahy, "it seems necessary to reluctantly relinquish what was perhaps only a faint hope that it might be possible for me through friendly personal relations and pertinent advice to give some semblance of backbone to a jellyfish."[12]

But the meeting that Pétain had been wanting could now take place. On December 1, at Saint-Florentin in the Yonne district, Pétain encountered Field Marshal Hermann Göring. Photographs showed both the French and German marshals in full regalia, Pétain with a cane, Göring with a marshal's stick.

En route to the meeting Göring remarked to an aide, "In twenty minutes I shall have finished with the old gentleman."[13] As they began to talk he assured Pétain of the respect in which he held him; had Pétain exerted more influence on his nation at a critical moment, he said, there would have been no war. Pétain handed Göring a note requesting concrete information on the objectives of French-German cooperation, reminding the Germans of France's wish to build up her armed forces, asking for a decrease in occupation costs and other servitudes. Göring protested that this note hadn't come from Pétain but from his government; he turned to Darlan and asked how he could have offered a paper that turned everything upside down, as if Germany and not France had been beaten. He complained of the anti-German atmosphere of Vichy. Pétain replied that the French could gain influence over anticollaborationists only if the seat of government returned to Paris from the provincial town where it was located. He warned of the British threat to French colonies, which France could defend if Germany authorized a building up of military strength.[14] French reports of the meeting do not differ significantly from the foregoing, which was the Germans'. They do say that when Pétain presented his demands to Göring, the German commented that to show them to the Führer would be to render ill service to Pétain and his government. "You demand very important concessions," Göring is quoted, "but in exchange you offer nothing. You don't even speak of helping us against the British!" Darlan's files contain a report on the lunch that followed the meeting in Göring's parlor car. Göring: "To sum up, we have to help you defend your colonies." Pétain: "And if you plan to take Syria back, we'll certainly march with you."[15]

Less than a week later, the United States entered the war. After a succession of easy victories in Asia, the Japanese had turned their attention to the Pacific power that blocked the way to further expansion of their so-called Greater East Asia Co-Prosperity Sphere, with a devastating surprise attack on the U.S. fleet at Pearl Harbor on December 7, 1941. Japan's success in Hawaii opened the way to conquest of the Philippines, Malaya, and the Dutch East Indies. The United States quickly declared war on Japan, as well as on her European partners, Germany and Italy. A witness remembers that the event seemed to stir the marshal from his lethargy; he ordered large maps of the Pacific and spread them on his table, asked Du Moulin de Labarthète to keep a record of the progress of American armament.[16] Pétain told Leahy he hoped to maintain existing relations, but warned that if Germany demanded that Vichy break with the United States it could force a decision by starving France's civilian population.[17] Calling on Pétain on December 14, Leahy made a specific request: that the French not employ their ships based in the Caribbean and that they be disarmed; U.S. defenses, he explained, required that only American ships operate in those waters. Darlan rejected the request: The vessels were there to protect French colonies. Leahy felt that Pétain was more sympathetic to American interests, but he wasn't at all sure that the marshal would offer effective resistance to further German pressure.[18]

The American request had come in the form of a personal message from Roosevelt to Pétain, and Leahy had soon heard from "our friends in the Vichy Government" that it had given the marshal sufficient courage to tell his foreign minister that no agreement should be made with the Axis concerning American relations without his approval.[19] On December 30, Leahy saw Pétain and Darlan together, to express concern about the delivery of French gas from North African stocks to Axis troops in Libya. On their side, the Frenchmen raised the matter of the Free French seizure of the Saint Pierre and Miquelon islands off Canada. Leahy cabled Cordell Hull that "The Marshal appeared fatigued and even older than usual and Darlan as usual maintained control of the French statements of attitude and policy."[20]

On New Year's Day 1942, Pétain spoke on Vichy's national radio to sum up France's plight. After appealing to Germany to attenuate its pressures, he turned to the home front, where he noted conflicts between Frenchmen on either side of the demarcation line. In a clear allusion to extremists who were sniping at Vichy from German-controlled Paris, he attacked "those who in the press and on the radio, abroad and in France, undertake abject roles of disunity, and all those in this country who stoop to calumny and denunciation." He had harsh words both for the black market and the "systematic disparagers of the National Revolution." His conclusion was more personal: "In the partial exile to which I am obliged, in the half-freedom left to me, I try to do my duty. . . . Help me."[21] ("We're taking a big risk; we're going to be rapped on the fingers," Pétain told Du Moulin. "So much the worse or so much the better! I'm beginning to have enough. And Leahy will approve what I've done.")[22]

The speech was recorded in secret, making use of technicians known to be reliable. But at the last minute Pétain read the text to Darlan, who ordered the man in charge of broadcasting to efface "partial exile" and "half-freedom" from the recording. The sound engineer stood firm, reinforced by two of Du Moulin's men to help guard the studio until the scheduled broadcasting time. So the speech was heard. It was published in the Vichy-zone press, but the Germans kept it out of the Paris dailies.[23] We know from Vichy's files that Fernand de Brinon phoned from Paris to report the "painful impression" certain passages made on the Germans; it wasn't going to make Otto Abetz' job any easier, warned the subservient Brinon.[24]

Public opinion, if we believe the reports sent to Vichy by prefects in the German zone, was impressed by the speech; it had brought about "a deep change of opinion with respect to the Marshal's government and especially to the person of the Chief of State, whose popularity has risen more than ever." The prefects felt that the very fact that the Germans had censored it augmented the impact of the speech.[25]

On January 5, Ambassador Abetz was received by Hitler for a two-hour meeting. In Abetz' report to Ribbentrop on this talk, he explained that he had told the Führer that "Pétain is a kind of idol, like Hindenburg," though he didn't consider either Pétain or Darlan a great man. He didn't think Vichy would declare war on Britain or the United States unless they attacked first; Pétain would do it with regret, Darlan with enthusiasm.[26]

A week later, Leahy was back at the Hotel du Parc with a message of sympathy from President Roosevelt. Giving it to Laure to read, Pétain commented: "This arrives at the very moment that I'm solicited in the opposite direction by the Germans." Laure expected Pétain to maintain good relations with the United States at any price, while holding on to Germany's goodwill, even if this seemed a double game. If double game there was, thought Laure, the preponderance of sympathy was for the American side.[27] Roosevelt sent Leahy a personal message suggesting that he speak to Pétain, or to Weygand, to convey "some thoughts." He wished the French "to realize that the President of the United States is about the best friend they have." But now that it was engaged in the war, the United States considered any help to the Axis as a hostile act; should the French make concessions in their zone or in the colonies, the United States would consider this to be "playing the German game." But if Vichy resisted, the Americans would support its resistance.

Leahy showed Roosevelt's message to Pétain in Darlan's presence, pointing out that he had frequently given expression to most of its content, the new element being the possibility of American military support. Pétain replied that his government would resist invasion by the British, the Gaullists, the Germans—or the Americans. Leahy took away a negative feeling; the United States couldn't expect Vichy's help in keeping the Axis out of French Africa.[28]

XXXV
THE RETURN OF LAVAL

In Paris, of course, the hard-liners had a different complaint. Marcel Déat, apparently after speaking to Spanish ambassador Lequerica, concluded that the marshal's entourage was influenced by Admiral Leahy, that Pétain believed in an American victory. Jacques Benoist-Méchin, ostensibly Vichy's man in Paris, told Déat "that Vichy is rotten with treason, that people like Du Moulin de Labarthète are British agents, that the Admiral [Darlan] is mediocre and the Marshal a dodderer, with bright flashes from time to time, and fine bearing."[1] In a tract published by Déat's movement, called the National People's Rally, under the title "Vichy Against the Marshal," the Paris collaborationists sought to attack Pétain's government without openly attacking the marshal himself. Each page contained a comparison of what "The Marshal said" and what "Vichy has done." Vichy was dominated by trusts and clerics; there was an atmosphere of denunciation and terror, social policy was paternalistic, agricultural policy favored large landowners.[2]

Visitors to the Hotel du Parc offer a confused picture, difficult to synthesize. When a former deputy, Camille Fernand-Laurent, called on the marshal on February 3, 1942, Pétain expressed distaste for a number of his subordinates, including commissioner for Jewish questions Xavier Vallat. When Fernand-Laurent observed that Vallat was only carrying out the measures of persecution that Pétain had signed, the old man replied: "Look, you know very well that I'm a Christian like you, that I think exactly the way you do. If they give me the time I'll arrange all that." He seemed ready to believe that the Russians would get the better of the Germans; he confided that he was counting on the Americans. "Marshal," the visitor concluded, "those who love you pity you." "Pity me, indeed, for I've gotten myself into quite a mess!"[3]

Two days later Bernard Serrigny was in town. Pétain told him that relations with Germany hadn't improved since his meeting with Göring; if anything, they had worsened. But Pétain was glad to hear of the British defeat in Libya, for he had feared complications had the Germans and Italians been driven back to Tunisia. That evening during a tête-à-tête, Serrigny protested Pétain's endorsement of the French Legion of Volunteers fighting with the Germans on the Russian front, for, he argued, the armistice didn't oblige Vichy to help the Germans in that way. Pétain replied: "But I really believe in the Bolshevist threat to France."[4] He spoke at a time when the Red Army's winter counteroffensive continued to push the Germans back, although the latter remained firmly positioned inside the frontiers of the Soviet Union and would soon be launching a spectacular new offensive.

Since Pétain failed to assure the United States that no further military support would be given to the Axis, President Roosevelt informed the marshal through Leahy that he was asking the American ambassador to return to Washington "for consultation." Leahy himself applauded this manifestation of toughness on the part of the Department of State; in a message to Roosevelt he recommended that sympathy for Pétain and for France should not lead to exaggerated concern for French sensibilities when the future of civilization was at stake. In a follow-up report to Under-Secretary of State Sumner Welles on March 4, Leahy wondered whether in the interests of the war effort America should continue to support the marshal rather than "the dissidents." He felt the United States should not be bound to Vichy. Welles, in his reply, pointed out that the United States was already helping the Free French. He felt that relations with Vichy and with the Gaullists were compatible; by maintaining contact with Vichy, it was hoped to "strengthen those elements which are loyally resisting the extension of German influence."[5]

On February 4, Pétain joined Darlan and other ministers at the first national council of the Legion of French Veterans. "The French citizen of 1942 has many more duties than rights," he told the gathering. "He doesn't even have veritable rights except to the extent necessary to accomplish his essential duties." Promising that the Legion would henceforth be more closely associated with the government, he concluded: "You are not authority, but you must represent the vigilant and permanent protector of authority."[6]

But this Legion dear to his heart was about to acquire a dangerous auxiliary. The Service d'Ordre Légionnaire (SOL) was a shock troop, receiving not only political indoctrination but physical training in order to create an "acting elite" for the marshal's national revolution.[7] This SOL acquired a chief who would be heard from: Joseph Darnand. By June, Pétain had authorized his appointment as permanent representative of the Legion to the chief of government (who by then was Laval again).[8]

On March 3, British planes bombed the Billancourt industrial complex outside Paris: The British air force was now ready for the offensive, and saturation attacks on German cities would begin in spring. Pétain wished to attend the funeral of raid victims, but he was persuaded by his entourage to abstain;[9] instead, Justice Minister Barthélemy read the marshal's angry message at the graveside. "History has already passed judgment on the criminal aggression by a former ally who allowed our soldiers to face death alone and then, two years later, with cold resolution sent our innocent civilians to the same death."[10] "I have a feeling," Pétain commented to Du Moulin, "that we are plunging into the fog."[11]

And the Riom trial was going badly; it was clearly a burden to Vichy now. Once, when someone suggested the likelihood that the defendants might escape, Pétain was heard to murmur, "We'd be well rid of them." Pétain confided to his justice minister that he agreed the trial had boomeranged; a way had to be found to bring it to a close.[12] Vichy was shaken, for example, by former Premier Edouard Daladier's vigorous courtroom defense of himself and his prewar policies, for Daladier did not forget to talk about Pétain's own role in strategic planning, Pétain's arguments against fortifying the Belgian frontier, Pétain's defense of reductions in the defense budget and in the length of military service when he was minister of war in 1934; Daladier also reminded the courtroom of Pétain's preface to the book titled *Is an Invasion Still Possible?*, adding that the book had since been removed from military libraries to avoid embarrassing the marshal.[13] In his own defense, Léon Blum pointed to the Riom court's arbitrary decision to punish only those faults committed after 1936, when in fact the Nazis took power in 1933 and Pétain was war minister in 1934.[14]

The best evidence that Vichy was appalled by the trial and its revelations is the stream of instructions issued to the press to protect "the person of the Marshal and . . . his policies." It was forbidden to mention that Pétain had been war minister in 1934, that he had at that time failed to convene the Supreme War Council, had recommended against fortifying the Ardennes, and so on.[15]

It has been said that the trial was finally abandoned by German order.[16] And, in fact, Abetz favored shutting down the proceedings, reporting to Ribbentrop that the French were now aware that they had made a monstrous error—with respect to the French public, to the Germans and to "enemy propaganda."[17] What actually happened was that the French on their own initiative decided to suspend the trial in April 1942 (using Easter as a pretext). Pétain felt that the trial was arousing hatred among Frenchmen.[18]

The return of Pierre Laval began with a visit to the Hotel du Parc by Laval's son-in-law René de Chambrun, on March 24, 1942. Chambrun was in Bernard Ménétrel's room when Pétain walked in; it was a surprise to the marshal, but he readily accepted the idea of listening to the "serious, confidential things" that Laval wanted Chambrun to tell him.[19] The Pétain-Laval meeting took place on March 26 in the Randan forest with Ménétrel as sole witness; Du Moulin says that Pétain wished to keep the very fact of the meeting secret from Darlan, as well as from members of his own entourage.[20] So at the beginning it was not a German demand at all, Laval's return; it was Laval's personal coup, and it succeeded (thought Du Moulin) because Pétain had already decided that Darlan was on his way out, and because Darlan misplayed his hand with the Americans and the Germans.

On the subject of Darlan's personal popularity, or the lack of it, Pétain had only recently told Weygand the story of an official visit to Toulon. The marshal rode in an automobile alongside Darlan to cries of "Long live Pétain!" Suddenly during a silence a lone voice shouted, "Long live Darlan!" and Pétain turned to the admiral to say, "Are you a ventriloquist, Darlan?"[21]

There was a more formal meeting with Laval at the Pavillon Sévigné on April 2. An observer, Laure's deputy Georges Féat, overheard part of Laval's overture to the marshal: It was a warning about "the frightful dangers that hung over France."[22] A few days before that (March 30), Leahy called on the marshal and in the presence of Darlan delivered an American statement warning that if Laval were brought back to the government "in any controlling position" the United States "would be obliged to discontinue its existing relations of confidence . . . with the French Government at Vichy." Pétain replied that he didn't enjoy making decisions that were personally disagreeable to him, that the French did not like Laval, and that he was not in a hurry to decide. Leahy expressed his personal opinion that Laval's return would cause a break in American relations with Vichy; as he rose to leave, Pétain said that he hoped Leahy had not already begun to pack his bags.[23]

Apparently when Darlan overplayed his hand, the crisis came to a head. He called in Roland Krug von Nidda, Abetz' man in Vichy, and showed him the American threat to break relations if Laval came back. Likely, Darlan simply wanted to prove to the Germans that it wouldn't be *his* fault if Laval was not taken into the cabinet. If so, the scheme boomeranged, for Krug von Nidda quickly informed Abetz, who happened to be at Hitler's headquarters at the time. And the Germans were not going to allow the Americans, with whom they were at war, to decide that a friend of Germany couldn't enter the Vichy government. France now had to choose between Germany and the United States, and Hitler would draw the consequences if France decided the wrong way.[24]

On April 8 an Italian diplomat paid a formal visit to the marshal at the Parc. Pétain told him: "It has been two years since I assumed the duty of governing France, a difficult job . . . considering my age and the fact that this is not my field. I ask myself each day if the decisions I make are just or erroneous; it's difficult, believe me, to choose the proper path when there are several possible choices—it's like walking in a field where there is no path at all. You have to have a moral compass. . . ." He went on: "Everyone has confidence in my wisdom, but am I really wise? And wisdom isn't enough; you must have authority. Do I have it? In any case I must share it with a guardian angel who is not always easy to live with." The chief of state was severe in his comments on the British, whom he blamed for the situation in which the French found themselves; he expressed anger at the bombing of Paris, and fear that Vichy might also be bombed. "Can you imagine the situation I'd be in if they bombed these hotels?" He concluded: "We are on the eve of great and perhaps decisive events; we must accept our destiny and hope that France will come out of them without too much destruction. As for me, I don't know how or when my life will end, but I already know that it will have been a very tormented life."[25]

A still friendlier witness, the outgoing education minister Jérôme Carcopino, also describes the old marshal—he would be eighty-six in a fortnight—at an afternoon meeting on April 11. Carcopino found him unrecognizable: hollow features, earthen color. He had aged years in a matter of days; he was visibly in a state of depression. "Ah! The Germans are still so strong!" he exclaimed. "They can still do us so much harm!" Saying this, he raised his arms slowly and then let them drop as if in exhaustion.[26]

Indeed, the evidence is that Laval had managed to terrorize the old man with his description of the horrors in store for France. In his own memories, Laval says that he had learned of these horrors from Göring during a secret meeting in Paris the previous month.[27] Nothing less than that, and the threats from Hitler conveyed by Brinon and Abetz, could explain the abrupt about-face that would now occur.

* * *

While lunching with friends at the Cercle Interallié in Paris on April 15, Bernard Serrigny received a phone call asking him to come down to Vichy immediately. "It's an order!" When he arrived at 8:00 P.M., Féat was waiting for him at his hotel, to explain that Pétain's staff had met in Bonhomme's office and unanimously agreed to call on Serrigny to help block Laval's return. He was assured that there had been no ultimatum from Berlin but only a palace maneuver, with René de Chambrun utilizing Ménétrel to create a favorable climate (Ménétrel apparently accepting in order to play a role, and perhaps out of a desire to show Laval that he had no responsibility in the ouster of Laval in December 1940).

Serrigny felt that all one could do now was to limit the damage, possibly by keeping the army, the police, and foreign affairs out of Laval's hands, and prevent the Déats and Doriots from entering the government. He saw Pétain only at lunch next day, after Pétain had seen Laval, but Pétain assured him that nothing had been decided; he was to see Laval again that afternoon. "He was imposed on me," Pétain insisted. "I'm going to give him so much responsibility that he'll collapse under it." He concluded: "We'll know in October if Germany can win the war. At that time we'll have to decide."

Pétain also told Serrigny that he was letting General Laure go, for he lacked "a political mind."[28] In his unpublished memoirs, Laure says that he felt then that Pétain had given in because he was no longer strong enough to resist the persistent Darlans and Lavals. By turning the government over to Laval, he would be rid of responsibility while holding on to his personal prestige for what use it might be to the country. Laure thought that Pétain would have done better to withdraw altogether, but he also knew that Pétain would consider that to be desertion.[29]

Another who was to leave now was Admiral Leahy. He was recalled on Laval's return, delaying departure only because of his wife's illness (when he finally left for the United States in early May it was with Mrs. Leahy's remains). His final meeting with the chief of state was cordial, so he reported to Washington. Pétain had professed sincere devotion to the United States and promised that France would never furnish armed assistance to Germany.[30]

Constitutional act number eleven, signed by Pétain on April 18, 1942, provided that the effective control of domestic and foreign policy was in the hands of the chief of government, responsible to the chief of state. The four secretaries of state, Fernand de Brinon, Jacques Benoist-Méchin, Admiral Charles Platon, Paul Marion, attached directly to the new chief of government, were as committed to collaboration as Laval himself was. A well-known fanatic, Louis Darquier de Pellepoix, took over the post of commissioner for Jewish questions. The Swiss envoy Walter Stucki saw it as symbolic that a heavy iron gate was installed between the floors of the Hotel du Parc occupied by the chief of government and the chief of state.[31]

XXXVI
FIGUREHEAD

If we believe the reports from the prefects of the German-occupied territories, the Laval restoration did not affect the prestige
of the marshal.[1] But it is possible that the resolution of the crisis
only increased the scorn of the Nazis for Vichy. Hitler felt that
Pétain was simply too old to govern. His authority derived from
his prestige, but it was as if one would give an important role to
an old singer, consoling oneself with the recollection that thirty
or forty years earlier he had had a golden voice. The Führer told
his intimates that he admired Pétain personally and felt that he
was a loyal collaborator, but thought it useless to talk to him now.
The problem was that there was no one else in Vichy, not even
Laval, who could make clear decisions. Vichy's was a phantom
government, and only the German occupation army held France
together.[2]

On June 11, 1942, at its headquarters in Vichy's Hotel Thermal, leaders of the French Legion of Veterans met in the presence of the new chief of government, Pierre Laval. After a lunch
given for them at the Hotel Majestic, next door to the Parc, Pé-

tain arrived. When the ovation had subsided he said: "There is no longer a dark cloud between us. Mr. Laval placed his trust in me on his return. We shook hands, and now we march hand in hand." He made it clear that it was Laval who made policy now. But there was "perfect communion of our ideas and our acts."[3]

It is possible to follow Philippe Pétain in the first weeks of Laval's return through the impressions of visitors. There is another pathetic snapshot from the departing Carcopino, who joined other outgoing cabinet and staff members for a dinner with the marshal on April 20. At one point Carcopino heard the old man mutter to his aide Bonhomme: "Yes, Laval seems very content with himself today. It doesn't change the fact that on the 13th of December [1940] I gave him a nice kick somewhere." But as he retired from their company, Pétain told his guests: "You can pity me, because as you all know I'm now nothing more than a man overboard."[4] Indeed, when Serrigny next showed up, on May 13, he discovered that the old marshal no longer had anyone in his immediate circle who could warn him of potential danger, a serious matter considering Laval's dexterity. Serrigny found that Pétain was losing both his hearing and his strength of character.[5]

In a report to Berlin on June 1, Otto Abetz summarized talks his envoy Rudolf Rahn had just held in Vichy. The French had evoked the likelihood of an Anglo-American attack on the North and West African coasts; Pétain had called Rahn to his office twice and both times expressed concern about Allied military action. He even suggested French-German preventive measures, and Abetz observed that this was the first time the French were taking the initiative in suggesting German military intervention in the colonies. Pétain added, so reported Abetz, that should the British and Americans attack mainland France, it would be the duty of the French government to offer Germany the help of the French army, perhaps by taking responsibility for the defense of a small sector of the Atlantic coast.[6]

Yet Jean Jardel, who replaced Laure as secretary-general of Pétain's staff, remembered Pétain telling him as he took office, presumably in the second half of June, that Germany had lost the First World War because it had two fronts, and was losing the Second World War for the same reason.[7] Serrigny heard Pétain say something like that during their afternoon together on

June 19. Serrigny had joined Pétain on a visit to the small castle
of Charmeil, overlooking the Allier River a few miles from Vichy, which was to be Pétain's summer residence. The modest
structure had been renovated for his stay, and in their visit Pétain didn't spare his visitor a single bathroom; Serrigny remembered what Laure had told him: that in aging, the marshal—
formerly unconcerned with comforts—was increasingly preoccupied with the material advantages of power. Still, observed
Serrigny, the castle's lawns had become potato fields. As they
separated, Pétain said that he had heard that Serrigny believed
a British-Russian victory was not far off. Serrigny replied that he
believed Germany would suffer internal collapse under the weight
of Russian victories and Allied bombing. "I'm not far from having the same opinion," replied Pétain.[8]

This was the year that Germany's anti-Jewish policy intensified in occupied Europe. Soon there would be the mass arrests
and the deportations, while the French state expended little effort to resist the tide. Some of the protests got as far as the marshal, especially when the bearer of bad news was someone as
important as Protestant leader Marc Boegner. On January 18,
1942, after calling attention more than once to the suffering of
France's Jewish population, Reverend Boegner called on Pétain
and came away convinced that the chief of state was genuinely
upset about the consequences of Vichy's anti-Jewish decrees; yet
Pétain believed himself powerless to prevent or to repair these
injustices.[9]

There is a documented case of resistance: Pétain's letter of
June 12 of that year, addressed to Fernand de Brinon, which
called attention to the "painful situation which will be created in
certain French families" if a recent German ordinance requiring
Jews to wear yellow stars was applied "without it being possible
to obtain natural and necessary exceptions." Pétain wrote that he
was sure that the Germans themselves understood that certain
exemptions were indispensable.[10]

But as German tactics in dealing with Jews became more precise and harsher, the hesitations of Pétain and his entourage began to take their toll. Because there was no firm determination
to resist, what protests there were had little effect. Thus, when
Laval at a cabinet meeting on July 3 announced that he had ordered a census of Jews in the Vichy zone so as to be ready to

distinguish between French and foreign Jews "when the time came" (and added that "particular measures" could be envisaged for Jews who arrived in France after September 1939), Pétain raised no objection, commenting only that the distinction between French and foreign Jews was "just and will be understood by public opinion."[11] What Laval meant by "when the time came" was the German plan to ship all Jews east, the first step in the final solution. We now know that far from trying to stop this, Vichy worried only that in seizing and deporting non-French Jews in the German-controlled zone, the Nazis might forget to take non-French Jews residing in the Vichy zone—for Vichy wished to get rid of them.[12]

On July 10, at another cabinet meeting presided over by the marshal, Laval reported his exchange of views with General Karl Albrecht Oberg, commander of the S.S. in France. Laval informed the ministers that Oberg would probably limit his "initial demands" to alien Jews, of whom it was estimated that 50,000 had arrived in France since the beginning of the war. Laval added for humane reasons he had insisted that Jewish children be "authorized" to accompany their parents who were being taken away by the Nazis.[13] It was now that the spectacular mass arrests began in Paris. Pétain was quickly informed of them, if only by a letter from Cardinal Emmanuel Suhard, archbishop of Paris (Pétain promised to take up the matter in the cabinet, but there is no record of any such intervention).[14]

A delegation of the World Alliance of Young Men's Christian Associations was received by the marshal, led by Donald A. Lowrie, president of a committee of private groups assisting internees. When they called attention to the persecution of Jews and to the massive deportations of July and August, they had the feeling that Pétain lacked freedom of action. During the entire meeting an aide replied in Pétain's place. Pétain accepted their note protesting the deportations and promised to reply in a week, but the reply never came.[15]

On June 22, 1942, Chief of Government Pierre Laval outlined Vichy's relations with the Axis in a radio speech. A new Europe would come out of the war; Germany was "in the process of waging gigantic battles" to establish it, and France would have her place in this new Europe. "I am hoping for a German victory," he added, "because without it Bolshevism will move in everywhere tomorrow."[16] Laval had first planned to say, "I believe in German victory and am hoping for it," but when Charles Rochat, secretary-general of the Foreign Ministry, protested, Laval offered a compromise, striking out "I believe." Rochat warned that the remaining verb—hope—was even stronger. Pétain replied that since Laval was not a military expert, for him to say "I believe" was ridiculous, but he agreed that "I am hoping" could remain.[17]

A former minister, Jean Berthelot, on a return visit to Vichy, discovered that Pétain was now rather taken with Laval. When he expressed surprise, Pétain told him: "You see, Laval is very considerate. He comes to see me often and keeps me up to date on everything."[18] Public opinion, at least in the occupied zone, seemed to go along with that. Thus, an under-prefect reported that "the present policies of the government are accepted first of all because Marshal Pétain chose them, and for many Frenchmen this is enough, but also because Laval is considered a man of fine qualities, deeply patriotic. . . ."[19]

On August 19, 1942, a Canadian unit, with British air support, landed at Dieppe to test German coastal defenses, a test that cost both Canadians and their British allies dearly in men and matériel. But this commando raid engaging thousands of men had been a first testing of German Channel defenses, a chance for the Allies to try out the tactics which would be successful farther west along the Normandy coast two years later. In his memoirs, Henry Lémery reports that on hearing of the raid Pétain remarked, "If it's a battalion, we must throw it into the sea. If it's an army, we must open our arms to it and enter the battle at its side."[20] It was not an army.

Just prior to the landing, Laval had informed Ambassador Abetz that Pétain wished the Germans to know that he was ready at any time to discuss joint military action in the event of British operations on French soil.[21] And on August 22 a telegram was sent from Vichy to Fernand de Brinon in Paris for transmission to Hitler:

> After a meeting that I have just had with Laval and because of the latest British aggression, which this

time was directed against our soil, I propose to envisage the participation of France in its own defense.

I am ready to examine the means for this intervention if you accept the principle of it.

I beg you, Chancellor, to consider this message
as the sincere expression of my desire to have
France contribute to the protection of Europe.[22]

The telegram was signed "Pétain," and duly transmitted by
Abetz to Hitler. On August 24 the Paris press published a second
telegram, this one signed by Pétain and Laval together, congrat-
ulating the German commander in France, General Karl-Hein-
rich von Stulpnagel, "for the victory achieved by German troops
which, by their defensive action, allowed the rapid mopping up
of French soil."[23] This second message has been contested (the
claim was made that Pétain did not know that Laval was sending
it),[24] but at the time it was transmitted from Vichy to Paris and
from Paris to Berlin, no one contested the authenticity of Pétain's telegram to Hitler himself. An investigation subsequently
carried out by the High Court for Pétain's trial convinced the
prosecution that Pétain's offer of military cooperation with Hitler was authentic.[25]

On August 30, Pétain made a personal appearance in Clermont-Ferrand at a gathering of the French Legion of Veterans;
before a crowd estimated at 30,000 drawn from surrounding districts, he talked once again about national revolution. "A sect
flouting the most noble of sentiments is pursuing, under the cover
of patriotism, its activity of treason and revolt," he declared. A
reference to the Freemasons, the statement was placed at the top
of the September issue of the Vichy-sponsored anti-Freemason
monthly *Les Documents Maçonniques*. Pétain continued: "Too many
French people look backwards and think it is still possible to return to the easygoing ways of the former regime: professionals
of elections who have lost their privileges, big businessmen blinded
by their egoism, trusts anxious to regain their dominance, government officials who are often passive, if not hostile." But he
promised that "a page of our history has definitively been
turned."[26]

Georges Villiers was mayor (an appointed official) that summer when Pétain visited Lyons. As he remembered it, Pétain won over local officials by telling them, "I'm truly sorry for you. If you have to read and apply all the notes and directives that I'm asked to sign for you, that must give you plenty of worry."

But when he toured the Hôpital de la Charité with Villiers and they were alone in a long corridor, the marshal suddenly grabbed Villiers' arm and asked him in a trembling voice, "Where are we? What am I doing here?" The mayor understood that such incidents frequently occurred in Vichy, and Pétain's absences sometimes lasted awhile. So he replied, "You are Marshal Pétain and you're visiting the Lyons city hospital. Don't be afraid, I'm with you and we're going to see the nuns who take care of children." Soon Pétain was able to say: "Ah! Now I feel better, my friend. Let's go on." Villiers remembered feeling that there was a danger for France in having a leader of that age.

That night, when Villiers accompanied the marshal to his sleeping car, an old general leaning on a cane greeted Pétain. "Well, Marshal, I'm not sure where I shall be at your age."

"At my age, you'll be dead," replied the marshal.[27]

XXXVII
NOVEMBER 1942

A remarkable letter can be read in the seized archives of the chief of state of Vichy. It is on the letterhead of the secretariat-general of Marshal Pétain, chief of state; it is dated September 1, 1942, and signed by naval captain Georges Féat. Addressed to Dr. Bernard Ménétrel, it calls him down for "the frighful harm that you are doing to the Marshal and to France." The letter goes on: "You have, my dear doctor, magnificent qualities, but you have a serious defect, a pride which has amplified each day since you managed to get rid of those who were in your way." It identifies those who had been in his way: General Laure, Henri Du Moulin de Labarthète; in their absence Ménétrel had tried to take charge of French policy, had sought to denigrate everyone else who was close to the marshal, to remain alone with him "against Germany." But Féat went on to say that Ménétrel's pride had betrayed him, for the Germans and their French friends were not intimidated by him, and fooled him every time. Between April 1 and September 1, the balance sheet would show "defeat all along the line, successive abdications. . . ."[1]

It was true that things had changed. And with the forced departure of so many members of Pétain's entourage, of so many cabinet ministers who had also been his advisers, Ménétrel had indeed taken on more of the role of *éminence grise* that had long been attributed to him. Outside France, things were rapidly worsening for the Axis. The war had moved to its first climax in North Africa; in September, the British launched an attack on Madagascar that was to make the island an Allied base. The German advance continued into the Caucasus, but was slowed down at Stalingrad, Stalingrad which was to mark the end of the German offensive and the beginning of the end of the war on the eastern front. In mainland France, the Germans pursued their forced-labor campaign, disguised as an exchange between young workers and prisoners of war, ineffectively resisted by Laval; and pursued the Germanization, the Nazification of Alsace-Lorraine, despite Vichy's protests (unpublished).

In October, Georges Clemenceau's son Michel called on the marshal. He had just seen Georges Mandel, who, of course, had been close to Clemenceau and was now imprisoned in the forbidding mountain fortress of Portalet; Clemenceau had come to beg the marshal's indulgence. Before he was taken in to see the chief of state, Clemenceau was taken aside by Bonhomme—now Lieutenant Colonel Bonhomme—who confided, "Since you're going to see the Marshal to tell him what's happening on the other side of the line, tell him what's happening here." Bonhomme went on to explain: "The Marshal doesn't trust the people around him, he doesn't believe them. He remains seated at his table for hours at a time, probably dreaming about grave matters of war, diplomacy, and politics, but he really doesn't seem to be interested in what's happening around him."[2]

The same month, Bernard Serrigny was in town again. He had not expected to have a tête-à-tête with Pétain, but it was his old chief himself who initiated it. When Pétain complained about Laval, notably blaming him for the deportation of French workers to Germany, Serrigny warned him against making changes in his government, for that could only result in the entry of still more pro-German ministers such as Doriot, Déat, and Benoist-Méchin. Better to keep Laval, who spoke like a collaborator but continued to defend France's interests, for he had been able to keep the deportations of workers on a small scale. "We'll soon have to consider a switch in policy," Pétain said suddenly; Serrigny couldn't believe his ears. Pétain thought it necessary to prepare a "national government" and was already thinking about candidates.[3]

During the night of November 7 to 8, the Americans and British began their long-planned landing along the Algerian and Moroccan coasts. Operation Torch, engaging 650 ships and 100,000 troops, was the first significant Allied attack on strategic territory. It had been prepared in great secrecy. Shortly after midnight the first troops touched shore, east and west of Algiers, east and west of Oran; in Morocco, near Casablanca, at Port Lyautey and Safi. They met resistance from Vichy loyalists in some places, received support from local resistance movements. The invasion was announced in a radio message from Franklin D. Roosevelt: The Allies sought no permanent territorial gains.

Much depended on Vichy's response to Torch. Because the mainland French, and Pétain himself, preferred the United States to Britain, it was agreed by Churchill and Roosevelt that the Americans would not only supply the bulk of the forces but would have greater visibility; even the message drafted to inform Pétain of Allied objectives was to come from Roosevelt and not from Churchill. But the Allied leaders put their heads together to write it. Churchill complained that Roosevelt's first draft to "My dear old friend" was "too kind." Pétain's "stock must be very low now," and the Gaullists would be offended by such language. Roosevelt agreed.[4]

The message was delivered to Pétain's office at 4:00 A.M. by S. Pinkney Tuck, American chargé d'affaires. It emphasized France's humiliation by Germany, the threat to France's colonies. To anticipate German action, Roosevelt announced, he had decided to send powerful American forces to North Africa to cooperate with local Vichy officials.[5] At 9:10 that morning—November 8—Tuck called on Pétain and, in the presence of aides Jean Jardel and Bernard Ménétrel, handed over his translation into French of Roosevelt's message. The marshal had a reply ready: "It was with amazement and sadness that I learned during the night of the aggression of your troops against North Africa. . . . You invoke pretexts that are unjustified. You imagine intentions on the part of your enemies which have never been transformed into acts." He reminded Roosevelt that he had promised to defend France against "any aggressor whoever he may be." And he concluded: "We have been attacked, we'll defend ourselves." He had given the order to do so, he declared.[6] He showed this order to Tuck.

A witness to the meeting—Jardel or Ménétrel—later noted this exchange between Pétain and Tuck: "Admiral Leahy must be as sad as I am about what has happened, don't you think so?" "I am certain that he is not, Marshal, because we have only one goal, the defeat of Germany."[7]

Then a strange thing happened. As Tuck rose to leave, old Marshal Pétain took both his hands in his own and looked at Tuck "steadfastly and smiling," as the younger man reported immediately by cable to Washington. "[The Marshal] accompanied me to the antechamber and turned briskly back to his office humming a little tune."[8] Tuck lost no time before telling the other members of the small American mission what he had heard. It was clear to them all that Pétain was expressing his satisfaction with the Allied landing.[9]

But whatever he felt, Pétain endorsed the orders to resist the Anglo-American invaders on that and the following decisive days. That afternoon he presided over a cabinet at which Laval formally announced that "America has attacked us," and proposed that it be made clear that the United States had broken relations with France by this act. Laval said that the Germans wished to send Luftwaffe planes to southern Italy, employing French airfields along the way; Pétain agreed to allow them to do so.[10] The German embassy in Paris wired Berlin that night that Laval, in reply to a question by its Vichy representative Krug von Nidda, said that he personally favored a French declaration of war against the United States and Britain, while Pétain, because of his age, had been too exhausted to consider the matter. By the end of the cabinet meeting, Laval told the German, Pétain had no longer been able to follow what was happening. Laval hoped to bring him around and wished to discuss the question personally with Hitler.[11]

Now begins one of the most curious episodes connected with the Allied landing. Although no documentary evidence has been

found, there is testimony from the chief actors in this episode
that a series of secret messages was sent by Pétain to Darlan in
Algiers (Darlan had gone there when his son was stricken with
infantile paralysis, and by "odd and formidable coincidence," as
Churchill put it, had been present when the Americans and British landed.)[12] By endorsing Darlan's support of the Allies, these
secret messages from Pétain contradicted what Pétain was ordering Darlan to do publicly. Thus, on November 10, on learning
that Darlan was negotiating with the Americans, Pétain sent an
open message that disavowed him, but (by using a naval code
which the Germans didn't know) followed it up with a secret
message explaining to Darlan that he was trying to gain time. In
the absence of physical evidence that this and subsequent secret
messages were exchanged between Pétain and Darlan, de Gaulle
and his followers have cast doubt that they really existed.[13]

Weygand was alongside Pétain now, talking about what to do
when the Germans crossed the demarcation line to invade Vichy
France. That move was expected, but what could an unarmed
France do? The discussion among Pétain, Weygand, and Admiral Auphan of an armistice in North Africa was interrupted,
Auphan remembered, by a message from Darlan (on the morning of November 10), reporting that he had ordered a suspension of hostilities against the Allies; Auphan says that Pétain,
Weygand, and he himself were pleased by that.

But now Laval was getting his wish: He was off to Berchtesgaden to meet Hitler. Pétain decided to do nothing pending the
outcome of that meeting. In those frantic hours, Auphan reports, Pétain's office was "a forum, or rather a marketplace, where
everybody shouted and argued with passion."[14] It is now, to satisfy Laval, that Pétain issued his statement: "I gave the order to
resist the aggressor. I maintain that order." It was immediately
broadcast over Vichy's radio. But it was followed, says Auphan,
by a secret message to Darlan informing him that the order was
necessary because of the negotiations then under way. "Received
and understood," Darlan replied. Auphan also claims that in the
evening, when Laval informed Vichy that he had accepted the
principle of a German landing in Tunisia, Pétain took Auphan
aside to ask whether he had the means to put Laval under wraps;
Auphan said he could do it if Pétain gave that order in Laval's

presence. And he proceeded to set up a commando of tough marines, but their services were not to be called upon, for the Germans arrived the next day.[15]

The British desert victory at El-Alamein coincided with the consolidation of the Anglo-American landings on the North African coast. "This is not the end," Churchill told his people. "It is not even the beginning of the end. But it is, perhaps, the end of the beginning." To protect the Mediterranean coast from another Allied landing, the Germans crossed the demarcation line on November 11, investing what had been the "unoccupied" zone under Vichy control. Pétain protested the action in a meeting that morning with Field Marshal Gerd von Rundstedt, calling it incompatible with the armistice convention, and issued a message beginning: "I thought I had lived the darkest days of my life. . . ."[16] The message was ordered to be read over the radio, although hard-line collaborationists managed to reduce the number of times it was repeated.[17] It was the first time, Weygand later recalled, that the outside world was informed of a French protest. Within hours Weygand himself was arrested by S.S. troops and sent to detention.[18]

The German invasion also affected the status of other enemies of the Reich. From Fort Portalet, Georges Mandel wired Pétain: "To keep me in Portalet . . . means delivering me to the enemy. I wanted to warn you of this so that it is well noted for history that you will eventually be responsible for this crime." Mandel was taken by the S.S. to Germany; in 1944, when Philippe Henriot, the collaborationist propaganda chief, was assassinated, the Milice of Joseph Darnand obtained custody of Mandel and murdered him.[19] Paul Reynaud, also in Portalet, wired Pétain: "Will you deliver your former chief to the enemy?" And then, when the Germans came for him, he scrawled over a large sheet: "Marshal, At the moment when you deliver me to the enemy I say to you, Long Live France!"[20]

Pétain himself, Auphan later recorded, considered leaving Vichy for North Africa that day but felt he had to wait to see what Laval was able to get from the Germans.[21] Many witnesses offered evidence of Pétain's feelings about staying or leaving; Pétain is said to have told Henry Lémery: "The first duty of a chief is not to abandon his troops. My troops are the French people. I promised them solemnly to stay with them in these difficult times. I can be prevented from keeping my promises, but not persuaded to violate them voluntarily."[22]

On November 12, General Georges was received by Pétain, whom he urged to fly to Algiers at once, to rally the French around him. "But what will happen to France if I leave?" He feared that all-out war would result, with the devastation of North Africa. "I gave myself to France and I can't without reflection take back my promise."[23]

In the presence of Otto Abetz and of Laval on the afternoon of November 11, so Ménétrel's notes tell us, Pétain said: "If public opinion detaches itself from me there'll be anarchy. My prestige is necessary to you. . . . You'll simply have to accept my ways, my protests." After the departure of his visitors, Pétain received Gabriel Auphan and told him that French commanders in Africa would be asked to continue to resist "to the limit of their means."[24]

Immediately after that there was a cabinet meeting, at which Laval gave an optimistic report on his encounter with Hitler. Pétain did not protest the decision to issue a statement confirming Vichy's resistance to the Allies.[25] But on November 13, Pétain agreed to Darlan's appointment as his representative in Africa, on condition that Laval accept the idea; Laval in turn asked the Germans for their opinion. Once more the secret channel was used to inform Darlan that Pétain was personally in agreement with him, as was Laval, but that the Germans had to be consulted before a decision was reached. But that allowed Darlan to announce that he was taking power as high commissioner; he ended his broadcast with a "Long live the Marshal!"[26]

We know from Ménétrel's notes—notes he apparently made during the November 1942 crisis but at no other time in Vichy— that matters came to a climax on the morning of November 16, during a meeting with Laval in Pétain's office. The subject was Germany's demand that France declare war on the Allies. Since Vichy could not declare war without parliamentary consent, it was suggested that a statement be issued recognizing that a state of war existed because the United States had declared it.[27] At this point, if we rely on what Laval subsequently reported to the Germans, Pétain said he would like to retire; he was tired. When Laval replied that he too was tired, the question was dropped. But then

Laval demanded full powers so that he could negotiate with the Axis without referring back to Pétain each time.[28] In a second meeting that day, Pétain agreed to "this sort of abdication" if there were German compensations. He also expressed the wish that his concession of power to Laval not be made public, but it was explained to him that the whole point was that the nation be told that he had relinquished responsibility.[29]

That day a message issued in the marshal's name denounced Darlan, reacting to a statement by the admiral that the chief of state was unable to make his private feelings known. Pétain accused Darlan of entering into relations with the invaders, of having disorganized the resistance and broken troop morale. He stripped Darlan of all authority.[30]

Then came the moment for passing power to Laval. "I never saw the Marshal so heavy-hearted and sad," Joseph Barthélemy remembered of that cabinet meeting on November 17. "His marble face was this time spotted red. His features were drawn . . . he didn't try to hide his emotion."[31] In a letter addressed to Laval that day, a formal assignment of power that was to be kept secret, Pétain informed his chief of government that he was delegating the promulgation of laws and decrees for an indeterminate period, while reserving the right to take it back, and this under three conditions: that Laval not engage France directly or indirectly in war—only Pétain could do that, and only with the consent of Parliament—that Laval guarantee the personal and material security of Alsace-Lorraine refugees and political detainees; that he respect France's spiritual traditions in protecting religious and philosophical convictions, the exercise of religion, rights of the family, youth movements, respect of the human person. A final paragraph made it clear that Laval would not have the power to issue constitutional decrees.[32]

Henceforth Pétain would be kept out of cabinet meetings, simply because he was not informed that they were taking place. He became something of a constitutional monarch, pronouncing words he was told to pronounce. He was said to have less power now than Third Republic presidents in that he did not even have to countersign decrees, such as the one stripping Darlan of French citizenship, or instituting the compulsory labor force to be sent to Germany. When Barthélemy told the marshal that Abetz was saying, he "is as troublesome as indispensable. We can't do anything without him. We can't do anything with him," Pétain replied: "You see that I can still resist." Barthélemy notes that Pétain's entourage received this reply in silence.[33]

On November 19, at the request of the Germans, the marshal addressed the French by radio. "Military leaders in the service of a foreign power have refused to obey my orders," he began. "Generals, officers, noncommissioned officers, soldiers of the army in Africa, don't obey these unworthy chiefs. I repeat the order to resist Anglo-Saxon aggression. . . ."[34] He confided to Admiral Auphan: "The Germans demanded that I begin with a statement that doesn't please me at all. I had to accept. But the order I give to continue the battle against the Anglo-Saxons is without value because it's only a speech and the speech hasn't been supplemented with an official order."[35]

Before dawn on November 26, the Germans moved to seize the French fleet at the Toulon naval base. This move was expected, and by prearrangement the French command carried out orders to scuttle the ships. Pétain's aide Jardel tells us that he went to see the marshal at 7:00 A.M., found him getting out of bed, and told him that, with this evidence of the bad faith of the Germans, Pétain had to leave now. "I gave my word to the French that I would not leave; I don't want to abandon them," he says the marshal replied. "Perhaps my glory will suffer, but I won't abandon them. In any case, the path of duty is not the easiest one. For me the easiest path would be to leave."[36]

The final month of that year only confirmed Pétain's passive role. On December 5 he signed a letter to Hitler, in reply to Hitler's announcement that he was disbanding the French army. "I can only yield to this," said Pétain, going on to concede that the forces that Germany had allowed France to maintain after the armistice were no longer "disciplined and obedient." He assured Hitler of the continuing loyalty of the French government.[37]

In a secret speech to the House of Commons on December 10, Churchill sought to explain what was happening in France. French notions of authority, however absurd they seemed, caused even those Frenchmen who admired de Gaulle to believe that power was "vested in the person of the antique defeatist" Pétain.

So that even those following Darlan's orders in North Africa could believe that they were obeying the marshal, for Darlan had convinced them that he was carrying out the marshal's real wishes. "In fact," said Churchill, "if Admiral Darlan had to shoot Marshal Pétain he would no doubt do it in Marshal Pétain's name."[38]

But it was Darlan who was to be shot, not on Pétain's orders, and exactly on whose has never been established; historians argue that the young man who fired the pistol was carrying out a plot of the Gaullists or of the Count of Paris, and both parties have denied it.[39] At year-end Pétain issued another disclaimer in his own handwriting, published in photographic reproduction in the Vichy press: Because of his former responsibilities, Darlan had been able to claim that he exercised legal power. But for Darlan's successor, Henri Giraud, no such ambiguity was possible; General Giraud, Pétain affirmed, had no legal authority.[40]

In a Christmas message, broadcast on December 24, Pétain reminded the French of his promise in June 1940 to remain with them; he had kept his promise. He asked his listeners to remain "dignified in sorrow." And he concluded: "At this hour when it seems that the ground is missing under your feet, raise your eyes to the sky; you will find there enough stars so as not to doubt the eternity of light and to place your hopes where they belong."[41]

Was this a sly reference to the stars of the American flag? Members of Pétain's inner circle said so, and at least one of them reported Pétain's remark, "I hope that the French will understand the allusion to the Americans."[42] A prefect reported that the marshal's Christmas message had inspired a new confidence; the consensus of occupied-zone prefects was that affection and respect for the old man remained "solid."[43]

XXXVIII
PRIVATE LIFE

Whenever possible in this book not only the date of an encounter with Pétain is given but the hour as well, for much has been said about the marshal's lucidity, about the number of hours in a day when it could be counted on. There is an astonishing range of testimony, from assurances that Pétain was always in perfect physical and mental condition to accounts of his failures. Members of his entourage would comment, "Tonight the marshal is all right," or "Today the marshal is not quite right," meaning that he was tired.[1] During the crisis month of November 1942, Admiral Auphan had observed his exhaustion: The marshal's intellectual faculties were not diminished, however. Care was taken not to wake him during the night. Yet, remembered Auphan, toward the end of this period he appeared worn out; Auphan adds that it was because he felt at the end of his strength that he turned over his powers to Laval that month.[2]

In his diary Marcel Déat seemed to enjoy recording signs of Pétain's incapacity: "a state of mental non-resistance . . . long hours of absence and . . . on some days the situation becomes tragic" (January 1941). Déat's informants included Darlan ("the Marshal is no longer in a condition to rule"), Benoist-Méchin ("the Marshal still has his power of judgment, but is losing his will"), Brinon ("the Marshal is losing his memory more and more").[3] Obviously foreign visitors, particularly diplomats, were concerned with the health of the chief of state. The Americans felt that he was "better in the morning," although they did not know to what extent his apparent absences were due to fatigue, to what extent to despair; but it did seem that Pétain was always aware of what was going on.[4]

The evidence is that the venerable marshal was conscious both of his great age and of his resilience. Concerning the first, he drew up another will in Vichy, signed and dated March 21, 1943. It left all his property, without exception, to his wife Eugénie; she was also to be responsible for seeing to the donations specified in this will and in future codicils. He left the Ermitage to the Marshal Pétain Foundation, although Eugénie could make use of it as long as she lived. Half the balance in his bank account would go to half-brother Antoine or to Antoine's heirs, but of this sum his two surviving sisters would each receive 100,000 francs. The other half of the bank account would go to his nephew Paul Pomart or his heirs. Bernard Ménétrel would receive all his holdings in British pounds or American dollars, while Ménétrel and other friends were to be given certain souvenirs. Ménétrel was made executor with full powers, and in a separate note dated May 16, Pétain requested that following his death Ménétrel "sort his papers and destroy those which seem to you opportune to suppress."[5]

Madame Pétain was not admired by many of Pétain's associates at Vichy. At times the reaction was one of intense dislike, and her enemies took pleasure in signs that the marshal didn't enjoy having her around either. Her son Pierre was equally detested by some of those who frequented the Hotel du Parc; it was said that Ménétrel was jealous of him. There was gossip about his debts, his work in the movie industry, his motorcycle, his Jewish mistress.[6]

Pétain treated material possessions with a certain disdain now. The evidence is of a man keenly appreciative of comforts—good food, much attention, and even ceremony—but no longer concerned about money. He and his staff disposed of 32 million francs annually, which could be used any way Pétain desired—for bribing the press, for charity.[7] On the death of General Huntziger, for example, he sent the widow 600,000 francs to help her buy a house.[8] In a sense he didn't have to be concerned about money because he now had at his disposal all the money in the national treasury and could be generous in its disbursement. His administrative aide Antoine Alart remembered that when he called the marshal's attention to heavy expenses and suggested he reduce costs to reduce the drain on his personal account, Pétain replied, "What should I do with the money?" Discovering that he received the expenses for his official household in advance, which was traditional before the war, Pétain told his finance minister Bouthillier: "I don't want to receive money in advance for work I haven't done." Pétain's wishes were followed, although it meant that Alart had to take an advance from secret funds to meet current obligations and then reimburse these funds when the quarterly expense payment was received.[9]

But then there were the impressions of Lyons mayor Georges Villiers, who lunched with the marshal one day, perhaps in 1942, and was invited to join him at the public audience. Villiers watched as the visitors filed by, obviously awed by the presence of the marshal; some had tears in their eyes as they handed over their gifts, usually objects they had made themselves. Pétain watched them pass without a gesture, without a word. Villiers says that he could not help protesting, suggesting that Pétain say something—at least thank you; he notes that Pétain was astonished by his suggestion, for in his mind the donations were natural because they were made to the savior of the country.[10]

Although Pétain's tax declarations show that payments of his annuity in British currency ceased during the war, there is evidence that the funds continued to be transmitted in the first years after the armistice. News of the payments got out and became a matter of controversy in London, where the chancellor of the exchequer, Sir H. Kingsley Wood, justified the transfers as an exceptional arrangement, authorized because Pétain was a head of state, and because the contract was with a Canadian company—Canada having maintained diplomatic relations with France. In the House of Commons, the chancellor explained that the Ca-

nadians were making the £600 annual payments to a British bank
which credited the sum to an account held in the name of the
Morgan Bank in Paris; Morgan was paying the money to Pétain
in francs. A member of Parliament commented that continuing
to make these payments "tends to irritate the public temper."[11]

During a winter visit to Pétain's Ermitage, Henry Bordeaux
had seen work going on to enlarge the house. Pétain explained
the project to Marie-Antoinette Pardee in a letter of December
25, 1940: It was a small addition to the house which would improve the look of the back of the building, and he was changing
the heating system so that there would be more heat in cold
weather. Finally, he had added a gardener to the staff. "A beautiful dream," he concluded. "Who knows when it will come true?
How I'd like to be ten years younger, to carry out all the fine
plans I have. . . ."[12]

Many of the marshal's old friends—who were, in a sense, his
family, the family he preferred—had gravitated to Vichy, or were
there because what was left of French authority was there. Jacqueline de Castex wasn't able to visit the Hotel du Parc very often;
most of the time she remained lonely, but loyal, in her Normandy castle residence. But her daughter Renée was in Vichy with
her husband Jean de Séguin, a diplomat attached to the Foreign
Ministry right there in the Hotel du Parc. The Séguins lived a
floor below the marshal; Jean, in charge of the American section
of his ministry, would have preferred to leave Vichy but stayed
because of his wife's attachment to the old man; it was to compromise his career. They had three children, one Pétain's god-
child; the marshal would visit them in the evening, go out with
them on Sundays. Once when Jean de Séguin suggested that Pétain leave Vichy for Morocco, the marshal replied that this would
be cowardly, for he had made a gift of his person; by staying he
felt he was preventing worse demands on the part of the Germans. "If de Gaulle could understand that," Pétain added; he
made the remark that de Gaulle was the sword and he the shield.
When Séguin refused the Franscique medal of fidelity, Pétain told
Renée, "He was right! He was right!"[13]

There were also the Jacques Rueffs: Christiane, born of the
Marseille Vignat family, was the daughter of friends of Marseille
garrison times; financial expert Jacques received an exemption

from the anti-Jewish statute.[14] The memoirs of Du Moulin de Labarthète detail reunions, at Pétain's table, of many of his officer companions of the First World War.[15]

But is it possible that the old marshal, who ruled over Vichy from the age of eighty-four to eighty-eight, continued to have sexual affairs? Later, much later, he told his jailor that he had made love for the last time in 1942 (when he was eighty-six), and he seemed to be confirming the story that the young woman involved had written to thank him. Pétain is quoted, "You have to be experienced for that. It was probably the last time I made love. And yet, how many young women and girls in Vichy made advances. . . ."[16] There is also the story of an evening in 1942 or 1943 when René Bousquet, secretary-general of the police, was summoned to the Parc Hotel because the marshal was in trouble: He had a woman in his room, and the husband was marching back and forth outside on the street.[17]

XXXIX

ANOTHER CRISIS IN COLLABORATION

"As you understand perfectly, I am not the happiest of chiefs of state," Pétain wrote Émile Laure in a New Year's letter at the beginning of 1943. "Troubles follow troubles, almost without interruption. I try to act as if things weren't so bad. My calmness, which is only appearance, impresses my entourage and visitors, who adopt the same attitude, and this is best for us all."[1]

How well Pétain was acting is demonstrated by the observations of Bernard Serrigny later the same month. The war on the Germans' eastern front was accelerating—the Soviets were on the offensive after stopping and defeating German forces at Stalingrad; an Anglo-American invasion of France was becoming more certain. But when Serrigny dined with the marshal at the Parc, he found him "of a disconcerting serenity"; although Léon Bonhomme was "floored," not a word was uttered about current events. Serrigny decided that it was henceforth useless to attempt to stir the poor old man.[2]

In his note to Laure, Pétain had indicated that he hoped to visit southern France before the end of January. What happened to that hope shows his status at that moment even more forcefully than the observations of his visitors. For the Germans were not going to allow him to get close to the Mediterranean coast again. During the night of January 10, the Italian foreign minister received a call from Ribbentrop's office to inform him that the Germans considered the travel plan suspicious. Was Pétain planning to slip away to Algeria? The Nazis issued immediate orders to their Vichy forces to watch the marshal carefully, and he was advised not to try to leave.[3]

The planned trip was put off, but Pétain was to try again. Thus, the Italians learned early in March that, without informing either Laval or Krug von Nidda, Pétain had sent Bernard Ménétrel directly to General Alexander von Neubronn, senior German military authority in Vichy, to ask him to intervene at the highest level of the military command so Pétain could visit the Ermitage; von Neubronn simply informed his political counterparts, and nothing came of it.[4]

On March 11, Krug von Nidda talked to Minister of State Lucien Romier, who, after a long illness, had spent all the previous day with Pétain. Romier, whom Krug von Nidda believed to be a positive influence on Pétain from the German point of view, had found Pétain restless; he was irritated by Laval's increasing independence, as if Laval and not he were the father of the French. According to the German's report to Berlin, Romier hinted that they had better watch Pétain carefully, for he might use a visit to Villeneuve-Loubet as a way to escape to North Africa. Romier was quoted as saying that he believed the military people in Pétain's entourage to be the most dangerous; of the civilians Ménétrel was the worst, for Pétain really listened to him. Romier thought that Laval might also exercise a favorable influence, taking Pétain's "senile vanity" into consideration, by increasing Pétain's participation in the government. Krug gathered from Romier's hints that Pétain might still be in touch with the British through intermediaries. Pétain seemed to wish French-German peace treaty negotiations to develop to the point where they would represent pressure on the British, requiring them to revise their policies.[5]

The Germans were getting reports that Pétain maintained contact with General Giraud, now civil and military commander in North Africa under Anglo-American sponsorship, as well as with the Americans, although *not* with the British or de Gaulle;

and that Pétain's entourage was preparing his escape to North Africa, where he would go if allowed by the Allies to keep his power. The source of these reports happened to be Laval, who also promised to keep the Germans informed of Pétain's travel plans. In the presence of S.S. Brigade-Führer Karl Oberg, Ambassador Abetz met with Laval and the police chief, Bousquet, at the Nevers prefecture on March 11 to plan heightened surveillance of the marshal. Bousquet suggested substituting his own police for Pétain's personal bodyguard; Laval offered to find rooms for two German security officers on his own floor of the Parc, on the pretext that they were there for Laval's protection. The Germans reinforced their troops surrounding Vichy, patrolled the Parc at night, kept in touch with what they felt were reliable contacts in Pétain's entourage. Laval told the Germans on March 17 that Pétain agreed to let him be responsible for his personal protection but threatened to leave the Parc if Laval had it guarded by Germans.[6]

Whatever feelings he may have harbored about internal resistance now, Pétain had, in fact, relinquished power to Laval. It was Laval who facilitated the deportation of young French workers to Germany, who stepped up the production of factories working for the Germans.[7] But Pétain himself presided over another manifestation of the hardening of his regime: the transformation of Joseph Darnand's special police of the Service d'Ordre Légionnaire—the Legion's protection squads—into the Milice Française. Unlike the Legion squads, which were responsible to the marshal, the Militia was subordinate to Laval, and its chief was later to take an oath of loyalty to Hitler as an officer of the Waffen SS. Darnand later testified that Pétain must have known about the oath, but it didn't prevent Pétain from receiving him each time he requested an audience, although Pétain's watchword, he admitted, was "prudence."[8]

The Militia was launched at the Hotel Thermal in Vichy, Legion headquarters, on January 5, 1943. In his speech Pétain made it clear that, contrary to rumor, he remained the Legion's "only chief," and confirmed the organization's role as "the best instrument of National Renovation." In foreign affairs it was the Legion's task to "make the French understand that they were not to discuss nor to judge this policy, for which they do not possess sufficient information. They must, like yourselves, trust me." Then, after defining Darnand's Legion squads as "the young and dynamic force of the Legion," he explained that to facilitate its task he was giving it a certain degree of autonomy. Henceforth, under Darnand, it would be attached to Chief of Government Laval as a national militia.[9] It was the point of departure for one of Vichy's most contested activities, the killer squads that were to track down resistance fighters and other dissidents in the name of order and anti-Communism.

Once more, resistance to the Germans on foreign matters seemed disconnected from Vichy's behavior on the domestic front. Each new concession narrowed the differences between the French state and the Axis. Did Pétain comprehend the contradictions?

On April 4 he addressed his people by radio to "speak to you of France, of its present distress, of its future." He blamed their hardships on the Free French, whom he called "rebel chiefs . . . responsible for your difficulties, for the war and the defeat." He warned that "if the peace that these bad Frenchmen are waiting for consists in returning to prewar political, economic, and social mores, France will not rise again." Once more he invoked his domestic reforms, the attempt to create harmonious capital-labor relations in the spirit of corporatism. But institutions could not be transformed unless souls were. "Communist barbarism if it conquered would destroy our civilization and our national independence forever," he declared, concluding: "The survival of France won't come from outside; it's in your own hands."[10]

When Bernard Serrigny heard from Pétain's staff that relations between the marshal and Laval were worse than ever, that the Germans had wanted Pétain to stress collaboration and hostility to the Anglo-Americans in this speech but he had refused, Serrigny thought that as it was, the speech had been bad enough. Pétain complained of the bombing of Paris: He felt that the Americans had dropped their bombs at random, which is why he had denounced the attack as "a totally unjustified aggression." Serrigny pointed out that, on the contrary, the raid had been aimed at the Renault factory and at German antiaircraft batteries (for Serrigny, Pétain's reaction proved that he was misinformed about events). At lunch, when a prefect told the marshal how much he was admired by workers, Serrigny broke in to say that 95 percent of workers in occupied France were hostile to him, that a speech the marshal had delivered at Saint Etienne on labor harmony was more likely to ignite class struggle, and that neither workers nor their employers liked the Labor Charter which Pétain had been promoting.[11]

During that month of April, relations between Pétain and Laval worsened. Laval wasn't surprised and let the Germans know that he anticipated an attempt by Pétain to dismiss him again.[12] On April 28, Hitler addressed a formal letter to Pétain: He had been told that the marshal wished to get rid of Laval but was not sure whether it was Laval's collaboration with Germany and Italy which was at the origin of this intention. He hoped that the reports were not true, but if they were, he wished it to be clear that Germany would not allow a repetition of the events of December 1940. Pétain replied the following day: The reports "have no basis in fact." He added that he would not tolerate "that anyone in France prevents me from pursuing the domestic renovation of the country . . . in harmony with a foreign policy which is the only reasonable one."[13]

Pétain celebrated his eighty-seventh birthday that April. Jokes about his age continued to circulate. From Vichy, Maurice Martin du Gard reported the tale of Pétain traveling alone in a train; when asked for his ticket, he replied that he didn't have it. "That's nothing," the inspector told him, "you can simply buy another." Still looking for the ticket in his pocket, the marshal replied, "What bothers me is that my ticket told me where I was going."[14]

But in May, when the head of the Catholic Institute of Paris called on Pétain he found him "alert, flexible, with good reactions, an alert mind, a well-preserved soldier." They were together from eleven in the morning until three in the afternoon, and he never saw the old man falter, Monsignor Jean Calvet noted on the very day he talked to the marshal. He also jotted down some of the things he heard Pétain say. "People come to see me to ask for favors. . . . They don't come to talk about France. And yet that's the only thing that matters. The country has to be cured. Politics and Masonry—they're the same thing—have brought us where we are." He complained of traitorous civil servants, incapable prefects. "The Freemasons have put on a false nose. They still run things." The Germans weren't letting him carry out the domestic policy he desired; Laval wasn't letting him carry out his foreign policy.[15]

In the latter half of 1943 a new note crept into Pétain's relations with the Germans. For the first time acts of protest, beginnings of conspiracy against the occupying power, took concrete form. If as late as the month of April his cabinet aide André Lavagne had not been able to win his approval for formal protest to Hitler against the forced Germanization of Alsace-Lorraine and the harassment of Alsatians and Lorraines in other parts of France,[16] Pétain was at last moved by reports he was receiving concerning the harsh treatment of French Jews by the Germans in the Drancy camp near Paris. "The Marshal was pained by the facts reported to him," his staff secretary-general Jardel informed his counterpart on Laval's staff. If these facts were accurate, Pétain wished Laval to intervene at once to "put a stop to the special treatment applied to French citizens some of whom have committed no other crime than to be Jews."[17]

But Germany's own intentions were becoming clearer: the Germans now insisted that Vichy strip the protection of French citizenship from Jews who had been naturalized under the law of August 1927. So a new decree was drawn up and even signed by Laval, but was disapproved by Pétain (and even Laval was later to withdraw his signature). "By its collective nature," Pétain wrote Brinon on August 24, "this text does not allow the Marshal to discriminate among individuals some of whom may have rendered service to France." Such a law would create disturbances, and the government had enough trouble as it was maintaining order. "The Marshal wishes to point out that he has given sufficient proof of his desire to cooperate with Germany to prevent any doubt about his desire to handle the request of the occupation authorities in the best possible manner." Pétain explained that he accepted the principle of reviewing naturalizations and had even ordered that the work be hurried up; he added that he regularly signed decrees stripping individuals of French citizenship and was now ordering that all such cases be brought to completion as quickly as possible.[18] Brinon thereupon traveled down from Paris to see Pétain and reported that he did not really object to further denaturalizations, even agreed to deliver non-French Jews to the Germans, but could not accept a "global action" that linked these denaturalizations to deportations. Some of the Jews involved had served France well; for "his interior tranquility" he desired to examine each case individually.[19]

Persons who worked with Pétain at Vichy or behind the scenes have come forward since the war to testify to more serious acts of revolt, or intentions to revolt, on the part of their chief. Thus, Gabriel Jeantet, whose memoirs describe a connection between Pétain's entourage and the French resistance and even to the anti-Hitler plots of the German army, told of the mission of Paul Dungler, an Alsatian resistance leader, to Algiers, where he hoped to obtain support for his movement so that it could assist future Allied landings in France. Before his departure for North Africa, Dungler was called in by Pétain, who, in the presence of Ménétrel, asked him to see Generals Giraud and de Gaulle. "Tell them that I transfer to their persons the oath that the French have given me. . . . Tell them that I suggest that the three of us meet as soon as Paris is liberated, under the Arch of Triumph, where I'll transfer my powers to them; they are the only legitimate powers. And I'll retire to my house in Villeneuve-Loubet." Pétain also explained how Dungler could get to North Africa via Gibraltar with Ménétrel's help; and, in fact, Ménétrel gave Dungler a secret contact in Toulouse, who in turn helped him get to Spain, from where he traveled to North Africa via Gibraltar. But when Dungler told his story to Giraud, the general snapped: "I forbid you to tell anybody about this . . . I forbid you absolutely to tell it to General de Gaulle." In fact, he never did mention his meeting with Pétain to de Gaulle before his return to France, via parachute from an American plane.[20]

On September 3, the French Committee for National Liberation in Algiers adopted a resolution signed by de Gaulle and Giraud, which accused Pétain and his ministers of treason and pledged to bring them to justice. On September 8, Krug von Nidda suggested to Pétain that the resolution offered an opportunity for a radio and press campaign against the Free French. But Pétain replied that he would not stoop to polemics with the chief of the dissidents; better to kill them with silence. He thought that the Algiers attack was de Gaulle's revenge for having been sentenced to death by Vichy; if de Gaulle announced it just then, it was because his exile government had not been fully recognized by the Allies.[21]

Colonel André de Gorostarzu, then convalescing in southwest France, was summoned to Vichy (so he declared after the liberation), to be told by the marshal that he wished to renew relations with Roosevelt's circle of advisers, especially with Leahy.

Gorostarzu was to go to Portugal on the pretext of pursuing his convalescence and there make contact with the Americans. This he said he did, through a Colonel Robert A. Solborg of the Office of Strategic Services. At first Pétain's chief concern was to make known to Roosevelt the text of his draft constitution. Gorostarzu said the Americans in turn asked him to inform Pétain that they wished him to prepare to pass his powers to a new French government to be set up after the Allied landing; under the American plan, so Gorostarzu records, Pétain was to move to a Loire valley castle such as Chambord or Chenonceaux to be ready to be liberated by the Allies, who would thus liberate France's legitimacy. On his way back to Vichy, Gorostarzu was arrested by the Germans but managed to slip out of their control and deliver his message to Pétain. Without giving a definitive reply to the American suggestion, Pétain indicated that he intended to remain chief of state. "I have only the Germans to protect me now," he explained.[22]

Henry Bordeaux's last visit to the marshal was in July 1943. He called at the Parc on July 10 at six in the evening and found the old man physically the same: still erect, although "the eyes are sad and the face grave, almost severe." When Bordeaux informed his friend that he had been offered the chairmanship of a Comité France-Amérique, Pétain began by advising him to refuse because of the American bombings: Better to leave the organization inactive until they needed the United States, when the time came to negotiate. But then he changed his mind. "Despite the bombing America still shows itself as a friend, if I judge by Admiral Leahy."

Pétain expressed some gloomy thoughts. Russian victory meant Communism, British victory the return in France to the old regime, which had brought defeat. But German victory would mean subordination. American victory? But the United States was an ocean away. "What will happen to the country after me? At least I'll have left a doctrine that could have saved it." He showed Bordeaux his draft constitution, explaining that it had the approval of the papal nuncio, of all clergy "except those democratic priests who have done so much harm"; it was also opposed "by all the high-lifers and partisans of the Third Republic." The text of the draft, from which Bordeaux was able to copy some passages, guaranteed freedom and dignity, freedom of conscience and teaching, of thought and association, and protected private property. The president of the Republic, to be elected for a ten-year term, would have extensive authority; there would be a Senate and a Chamber, the latter elected by universal suffrage.

At dinner that evening, a quiet affair bringing together Eugénie Pétain (whom Bordeaux found heavier) and members of Pétain's staff including Ménétrel, the talk was of Louis XIV, whom Pétain admired as a chief of state, of Napoleon, of the French Academy. Afterward Pétain took Bordeaux aside to say, "Pierre Laval still believes the Germans will win. But Hitler will lose in Russia as Napoleon did. The Allies are far from being ready. If only they will avoid attacking France." When Bordeaux replied to this that the Allies would liberate the nation, Pétain expressed the fear that they would destroy a lot of cities, kill many people. He hoped instead that they would attack Berlin via Salonika, Budapest, and Vienna. It was important, he added, that the Allies get to Berlin before the Russians.[23]

Did Pétain tell Brinon, as the latter claims, that he was pleased at the German defense of Europe against Bolshevism?[24] We do have a personal report by Field Marshal von Rundstedt of his own meeting with Pétain in late August, a meeting initiated by the marshal and held at his summer residence in the castle of Charmeil. During their tête-à-tête Pétain complained of the parachuting of British agents, who were carrying out sabotage, and of an attempt to destroy the harvest. In these cases French and German interests were identical, said Pétain, and he requested authorization to give his police modern weapons so they would be able to deal with the saboteurs. He also expressed the wish that Germany would issue a statement on France's role in the new Europe, a request that Rundstedt endorsed in his report to Berlin; he felt it would reinforce Pétain's position to the benefit of Germany's military operations.

Then Pétain and Rundstedt were joined by Laval, Charles Rochat, Jean Jardel, Ménétrel, General von Neubronn, and Krug von Nidda. Pétain promised, in the event of an Allied landing in France, to issue a proclamation asking the French not to attack German troops. Rundstedt told Berlin that he felt the requirements of Pétain and Laval were legitimate; it was desirable that the Germans satisfy them in the interest of Germany itself.[25]

XL
CONSTITUTIONAL CRISIS

The evidence is convincing that Pétain believed he could make a lasting contribution, war or not, by giving France a new constitution to replace the despised Third Republic. Starting in spring 1943, the best minds of his entourage were put to work. They took as a point of departure the Barthélemy draft and sought to reconcile Pétain's conception of the state with French traditions. Vice-Admiral Jean Fernet remembered that the drafters had to exercise patience to convince the marshal of the need for universal suffrage, if only to conform to national habit.

Pétain showed most interest in the articles concerning representation of the professions, and he was also interested in the reorganization of the provinces, in which governors would wield power locally. One achievement of the drafting committee was in obtaining the marshal's consent to call the nation a Republic once again. Pétain signed the draft on January 30, 1944.[1]

Concurrently with the ambitious constitutional project, Pétain and some of the same advisers were busy on a shorter-range plan to deal with the marshal's succession. Under existing decrees, Laval remained next in line to the chief of state. To evict him from the government might bring a severe German reaction, even Pétain's arrest; to deal with that eventuality it was necessary to have an alternate center of power in readiness, which could if necessary operate in secret.

Yves Bouthillier, with other advisers including Admiral Auphan, came up with the idea of a secret act of succession. It was drawn up as a constitutional decree, signed and dated by Pétain on September 27, 1943, and provided that if Pétain was unable to carry out his functions before the ratification of the new constitution, the country would be led temporarily by a college consisting of Auphan, Bouthillier, Weygand, and other dignitaries. A final article abrogated the decree that had designated Laval as Pétain's successor.[2]

A note of explanation signed by Pétain pointed out that five different decrees had dealt with his succession, showing that it was an error to tie the designation of a chief of state to the fluctuations of politics. He also explained that the college was a temporary expedient; in the event of his permanent absence from power, the college was to give Parliament the powers that had been turned over to Pétain in July 1940.[3]

The balance of the year was occupied with the strategy and tactics of dumping Laval. This was hardly a secret to the Germans. On the eve of the crisis, on November 7, according to Brinon, Pétain asked what the Germans would think of a cabinet reorganization. "Obviously," Brinon replied, "that depends on the people involved."[4] On November 11, Auphan noted, it was Yves Bouthillier who succeeded in convincing Pétain to take the first step by signing still another succession decree (since the secret decree of September 27 was considered not to exist); this decree of November 12 returned the constituent power to the Senate and Chamber, and abrogated all measures taken since July 10, 1940, which limited the rights of the National Assembly (the Senate and Chamber meeting together).[5]

It was agreed that Pétain would explain this change in a radio broadcast to the nation on November 13. Before making this speech, however, Pétain thought it wise to read it to Laval, and this on the evening of November 12. Apparently—Auphan wrote—Laval seemed to approve it. But he also said that the

Germans had to be informed, and Pétain duly notified Krug von Nidda (on the morning of the thirteenth) that he would deliver the speech by radio that day. The German response was to occupy the radio studios with troops, along with the offices of the *Journal Officiel* (which would have published the decree).[6] That evening Pétain read a formal protest to Krug von Nidda: Brinon had told him that the Germans would use force to prevent the broadcast; Pétain yielded to that. "But I declare that until I am allowed to broadcast my message I consider myself unable to exercise my functions."[7]

Still, the message was to get out, disseminated in France and even abroad by the marshal's entourage.[8]

And on Sunday, November 14, Pétain abstained from the flag-raising ceremony, an absence that was noted, as his staff's record of the November crisis documents. For the crisis went on. Pétain argued to Laval that the succession act was directed not against him but against the Gaullists in Algiers, to safeguard the legitimacy of the Vichy regime. Romier, Rochat, and Bousquet helped Laval rewrite the succession decree's language so that Laval retained power in the event of Pétain's death, but the marshal stood his ground. He still intended to publish and to broadcast his speech and his own act of succession.[9]

The war of nerves was observed by a visitor from Paris, former minister René Belin. They were in Pétain's office at the Parc, and Pétain had begun to tell Belin about his problems when an attendant burst in to announce Laval. "Stay, you'll see what more he wants from me," begged the marshal, but Belin preferred to leave by the door leading to Ménétrel's room. He did hear Laval's first words: "Marshal, I've been working for you this morning; here is the text that I suggest. . . ."

In Ménétrel's office Belin found the doctor with Lucien Romier. When he explained why he had left Pétain's office, they looked at each other and Romier said, "Someone has to be there." "Yes, yes, go in," replied Ménétrel. "I cannot," Romier said; he was ill (and didn't have long to live; he died on January 5 of the new year). So Ménétrel went in. Romier confided to Belin, "Laval is diabolical. . . . He sees the Marshal four times a day. . . . When Laval asks him to do something he doesn't want to do, Pétain throws him out the first day. The second day he listens to him but refuses. The third day he questions him and doubts. The fourth day he gives in. You have to wind up a watch without a spring constantly. I'm at the end of my rope. . . ."[10]

Clearly Pétain was more isolated than ever. He leaned on Ménétrel more than ever. "I'm not a politician," Ménétrel told Maurice Martin du Gard, "but even if they apply burning cigarettes to the soles of my feet I won't abandon the Marshal!"[11] Another old friend tried to help. Serrigny tells us that he had stayed away for some time, certain that Pétain could not shake off the influence of Ménétrel either. But on November 20 he had received an official-looking envelope with the text of the banned speech and decree, accompanied by a copy of Pétain's November 13 protest to Krug von Nidda. Serrigny and friends in Paris agreed that he should take up his pilgrim's stick once more. On November 23 Serrigny saw Pétain, who confirmed that the banned speech and decree had been directed against de Gaulle as well as Laval; Pétain showed bitterness as he explained that after seeming to accept the modification, Laval had informed the Germans about them. Henceforth, said Pétain, he considered himself a prisoner and refused to sign papers. Serrigny replied that the public was not aware of this; he must let everyone know, instead of continuing to carry out his functions. "Perhaps, but for the moment I have to show myself, or else they'll say that I am ill."

Serrigny pursued: The marshal had a last chance to act, especially since the Gaullists of Algiers had not yet convinced French opinion. He must get rid of Laval. Pétain replied that in such a case, as Berlin had warned him, the Germans would rule France with a *Gauleiter*. "Think of the suffering that would result for the French." "You think of the French too much and not enough about France, Marshal." After more such talk, ending inconclusively, they went down to dinner. When they had finished eating, Pétain fell asleep.[12]

The German response to Pétain's unspoken November 13 message took some time in coming, but when it did come it left no ambiguity about the state of Germany's relations with Vichy. In a letter from Berlin dated November 29, Foreign Minister von Ribbentrop expressed surprise that an act of such importance had been submitted to the Germans so short a time before publication. He took note of Pétain's announced intention not to exercise his functions and to resign if the decree and speech continued to be banned, as well as of "certain reflections" heard in Pétain's immediate entourage which were in open contradiction to the policy of collaboration. Hitler, to whom Ribbentrop had reported all this, refused to allow the Parliament which had declared war on Germany to decide on a successor. Hitler demanded that in future all laws be submitted in advance to the Germans, that Laval reorganize the cabinet to reinforce collaboration, and that Pétain support these measures; Pétain must also purge the administration of those who were preventing "recovery." Hitler had been generous in allowing France to continue to have a government after its defeat and expected the French to cooperate in Germany's war effort. The only guarantee of order in France was the German army, and it would know how to protect German interests.[13]

Abetz, accompanied by Brinon, personally brought the letter to the marshal on December 4. Pétain asked for time to think about it.[14] Next day Abetz demanded that Pétain indicate at once whether or not he would resume his functions; the Wehrmacht did not wish to face an Allied landing with a chief of state who had partially resigned and who was in public conflict with the Germans. Pétain handed Abetz a *note verbale*, in which he agreed to resume his responsibilities as chief of state within the limits he exercised them before November 13, "on condition that no publicity or comment is given to this decision."[15] The press was informed that it could report that Pétain had received Abetz and that he did not resign, but *not* that he had resumed his official responsibilities.[16]

German strategy succeeded. Pétain not only stayed on but agreed to sign a reply to Hitler drafted by Brinon, apparently on the basis of an earlier draft by Abetz himself.[17] In this letter, dated December 11, Pétain expressed the desire for reconciliation between Germany and France, and promised "total support" for a new Laval cabinet, asking only that its members be "good Frenchmen" and that they not be persons who had shown hostility toward him in the past. Pétain would also welcome a new envoy whom Ribbentrop was sending to Vichy.[18]

The envoy was Minister Cecil von Renthe-Fink, and he was to be Pétain's watchdog (Pétain called him his jailor).[19] Abetz submitted a list of persons in the government who were undesirable, some of whom were to be arrested or deported, while representatives of a new breed of extremists were brought into the government: Militia chief Joseph Darnand as secretary-general for the maintenance of order, and Militia spokesman Philippe Henriot as information minister.[20] Jardel was sent to Paris, while Laure and other close advisers were arrested and deported. Adviser Romier had died, adviser Henri Moysset was asked to move out of Vichy, and Ménétrel was told to confine himself to medical matters. It was now, too, that Lieutenant Colonel Léon Bonhomme, Pétain's aide de camp since the 1920s, was killed in an automobile accident. When Admiral Auphan, surprised to have escaped the roundup himself, came down to see the marshal at the beginning of January 1944, he found the old man morally and intellectually alone.[21]

Cecil von Renthe-Fink took the occasion of the New Year for his first meeting with Pétain. Pétain sought to have a witness present, the son of a former ambassador who happened to be available, but Renthe-Fink insisted that their meetings were to be different from those between the chief of state and foreign chiefs of mission: They must remain strictly private. (As Jacques Bardoux heard the story from Bernard Faÿ, the former ambassador's son was pushed—and punched—until he left the room. "Go, my boy," Pétain murmured to him.)[22] "Despite temporary absences of memory, which are at times invented, he is in general in possession of all his mental forces," Renthe-Fink reported of Pétain to Berlin. The marshal promised to submit cabinet changes and other decisions affecting relations with Germany before they were taken. Still, Renthe-Fink concluded that in view of the deep personal differences between Pétain and Laval, it would be difficult to "neutralize" the marshal. But from the German point of view, he thought, there was an advantage in this, in that it was unlikely that Pétain and Laval would agree on a policy detrimental to German interests. Further, despite a certain "senile stubbornness," Pétain was not closed to objective arguments.[23]

To Jean Tracou, new director of Pétain's civil staff, Renthe-Fink seemed engaged in a deliberate policy of isolating the chief of state. Indeed, Tracou's first impression of the Parc, "this barracks for bathers," was that the hotel was a kind of prison, as well as a microcosm reflecting and amplifying all the differences between Frenchmen.[24] "The prison closes in around us," Pétain himself wrote Marie-Antoinette Pardee on January 11. "Then this war will never end! . . . I knew that a defeat would have disastrous consequences, but I didn't think that our misfortunes would go on for so long."[25]

One thing the Germans wanted now was Vichy's support in the event of an Allied landing on the French mainland. General von Neubronn called on Pétain on January 4, 1944, with a letter from Marshal von Rundstedt stressing the need for French cooperation. (Renthe-Fink reported that Pétain was "less fresh" than on previous visits, but the old man did promise to relay instructions to his prefects.) From Paris, Abetz recommended that Pétain's message to the French people on the Allied landing be prerecorded, so that Pétain would not have the excuse, when the day came, that he was sleeping or ill.[26] Pétain informed von Rundstedt on January 20 that Laval, as chief of government, would issue appropriate instructions on measures to be taken and attitudes to be observed, adding that he would be ready with an appeal to the French when the invasion came.[27]

There is testimony that Pétain resisted new German demands, levied on Laval by Gauleiter Fritz Sauckel, for the dispatching of one million French workers to Germany and another million to be sent to strengthen French coastal defenses.[28] But Sauckel himself reported to Hitler that Pétain and his government "largely accepted" his request for an increase in working hours from forty to forty-eight weekly, with the development of forced labor in France and in Germany. Pétain had only objected to sending French women to Germany, and wished women from eighteen to twenty-five to be employed only in their own homes. Since even this represented considerable progress, Sauckel told Hitler, he accepted. The French would also apply the death penalty to those who sabotaged the forced-labor program.[29]

Abetz cabled Berlin on January 22 that the purge on Pétain's entourage and the presence of Renthe-Fink had made Pétain cautious. Abetz' informants agreed that Pétain sounded more positive on German-French relations, believed that Germany would be victorious, and that France should help Germany.[30]

XLI
THE SPRING OF 1944

Laval's new government was indeed a cabinet of hard-liners. His aide Jean Tracou remembered seeking to persuade Pétain not to attend cabinet meetings in protest against the nominations of Darnand and Henriot; Laval supported the idea: "Let me do the dirty work, Marshal. Remain above all that."[1]

Early in his tenure, Tracou witnessed an extraordinary encounter between his chief and Laval. Laval made the point that France's present misfortunes were to some extent Pétain's fault, for Laval (with Lémery and Alibert) had wished the marshal to become president in 1939; he could then have prevented the outbreak of war. Laval quoted Reynaud: "Who are the three men responsible for France's misfortune? Daladier, for having appointed Pétain ambassador to Madrid, Reynaud for making him a Minister, and Laval for making him Chief of State." Laval told Pétain that he was aware of having treated him badly: He should have seen him more often, but he hadn't dared to, for he would have seemed to be trying to impose himself. Pétain agreed that Laval had let him down, for he hadn't been prepared for politics; he was too old. He could have done useful things at the time of the First World War. "But now I'm an old man and my memory is going. You're stronger than I am." "Anyway, all that is the past," said Laval. "As long as you are here, nothing is lost." And Tracou heard Pétain's reply as the seal on a new alliance: "My friend, henceforth I won't do anything without you." When Laval left, Pétain told Tracou: "He has a hard life; he's doing what he can. I want to help him."[2]

In Paris the chronicler Galtier-Boissière noted in his diary "the latest from Vichy": "Do you know that the Marshal is dead?" "No, since when?" "It happened three months ago, but his entourage kept it from him."[3]

Certainly, at the beginning of 1944, the marshal seemed removed from day-to-day reality. Laval held executive power and presided over an advisory cabinet group, while Pétain was titular chief and no longer even signed decrees. He received visits from high-level civil servants, kept his diplomatic contacts and the right to pardon. The layout of the Parc remained as before: a floor for the Foreign Ministry, another for Laval, another for Pétain, the top floor for ministers and senior officials.[4] The ground-floor dining room and adjoining salons were the marshal's domain, decorated with Francisque emblems in every conceivable material: stucco, bronze, crystal; on curtains, furniture, tableware. There were usually a dozen persons at table—Ménétrel almost always, Tracou or his new aide Louis-Dominique Girard three times a week each.[5]

The new members of the staff, Tracou and Girard, found Ménétrel disconcerting, although the latter would later feel that his role as court jester had been necessary to help rid Pétain of nuisances or to turn the discussion away from delicate matters.[6] Tracou was convinced that the curious machine Ménétrel kept in his office—presumably this was the equipment for oxygen injections—really hid a radio transmitter. Medicine was Ménétrel's "camouflage," for in Tracou's flattering description, the doctor was, above all, an adversary of collaborationism and of the Germans. His friends pardoned his impish ways, for they knew his loyalty.[7] Another friendly source describes Ménétrel's role as the marshal's watchdog, guarding his chambers, keeping out the undesirables, intimidating the bothersome, even at the risk of irri-

tating his chief. He kept the door open between Pétain's rooms
and his own, and let it be known that he was listening. Sometimes Pétain closed the door, but at other times it was Pétain who
opened the door.[8]

If we credit wartime testimony, Pétain deplored the violent
behavior of Darnand's Militia, which had become the French
auxiliary of the Nazi police. One day, during a formal audience
in the ground-floor salon of the Parc Hotel, Tracou has Pétain
walking up to a group of young men in uniform. "What is that
uniform?" "The Militia, Marshal." "Ah! How many Frenchmen
did you kill this week?" According to Tracou, Pétain was particularly understanding with respect to the maquis—the resistance
bands composed in part of young men seeking to avoid forced
labor in Germany. Hearing of a grouping of 500 maquisards on
the Plateau de Glières in Haute Savoie, against whom Laval intended to act on the pretext that the Germans would do it if he
did not, Pétain reportedly said: "I'd like to be able to go to see
those young people. . . . We must try to bring them back without harming them."[9]

But in Pétain's office that same month—February 1944—the
entourage, and presumably at the marshal's order, was dealing
with the problem in another way. In a memorandum dated February 29 it is noted that "Terrorism appears to be growing. . . .
We must try to carry out simultaneous operations in all the critical zones. . . . The Marshal calls attention to the gravity of this
situation. . . . Since Mr. Darnand certainly has the confidence of
the occupation authorities, a solution ought to be found."[10]

Darnand's solution, it was already clear, included torture and
summary executions, carried out by his Militia alone or in cooperation with the Germans.[11] That Pétain was aware of this is
claimed by the faithful Tracou, who has Pétain requesting of
Darnand (who by June was secretary of state for the interior) that
he control the violence of his Militia.[12]

The same ambivalence existed with respect to that other German auxiliary, the Legion of French Volunteers. Renthe-Fink insisted that Pétain receive Lieutenant Jacques Doriot, together with
Captain Jean Bassompierre and Lieutenant François Gaucher, who
were on leave from the Russian front for a propaganda and re-

cruiting tour. When they arrived in Vichy on March 14, accompanied by Laval and Brinon, Tracou has Pétain receiving them coolly: "If I say anything at all to you you're going to use it in the press for your propaganda." He pointed out that France was not at war with the Soviet Union. Had the Legion been a French unit, he could have encouraged it; as it was, few Frenchmen approved of it. Bassompierre, visibly upset, exclaimed that he had joined the unit only because Pétain had encouraged it in 1941; Pétain replied that the situation had changed since that time. He asked Tracou to issue a statement that avoided encouragement.[13] But in the press Tracou's "the Marshal expressed interest" became "expressed great interest"; his request to be kept informed of Legion action and of its losses became: "He asked to be kept informed of the activity of the Legion of French Volunteers against Bolshevism."[14]

Certainly, the hardest pill to swallow for the marshal's entourage was the arrival of Marcel Déat, the Déat who, from the inception of the regime, had been attacking Vichy as insufficiently Fascist, insufficiently collaborationist. When Pétain agreed to Abetz' request that Déat become part of the government, a member of Pétain's staff protested: Pétain hadn't opposed Déat only because he was a collaborationist—for after all, Pétain had already accepted and even appreciated the entry of Henriot and Darnand into the government. But it was a matter of "personal dignity."[15] Apparently stiffened by his staff's protests, Pétain sought to resist: He told Renthe-Fink that Déat had soiled all he held dear, and that if Déat entered the cabinet Pétain himself would leave. But Renthe-Fink warned Tracou that Berlin would not be moved by Pétain's threat to resign; Tracou shows us a Pétain getting ready to withdraw, sorting and destroying papers, even talking about the consequences of resignation for his personal financial situation. But the next day, March 12, he told Tracou: "I have thought about it a lot during the night, and I've decided not to leave because of Déat. But we're going to have to be more prudent than ever and even become crafty—something I've never been." Déat was appointed by Laval alone, and Pétain refused to countersign the decree; on March 16 Déat became minister and secretary of state for labor and national solidarity, with control over welfare payments—a job Pétain had tried to keep from him.[16]

A report sent by Minister Stucki to Berne on March 20 reads: "The Marshal hopes he will not live a long time, for the burden has become insupportable to him, and every visit by the Führer's new special envoy von Renthe-Fink costs him a year of his life."[17] But the day after that report was sent, André de Gorostarzu brought Pétain a message from Roosevelt. In Tracou's account of it, the Americans wished Pétain to remove himself entirely from activity; when the Americans arrived they would bring him out of his retreat. Pétain told Gorostarzu that it would be unpardonable for him to leave France in the hands of dangerous men whose actions he could moderate by remaining. He was still the only legal power in France. Besides that, the Germans would never leave him free; they would deport him.[18] And when the director-general of his guard, General Jean Perré, sought permission to resign—since with his new power Darnand might requisition his men—Pétain replied that only Perré could protect him, adding: "I'm not leaving, so you can certainly stay." Pétain also told him that he needed his personal-protection force for the day when he would reverse policies; he encouraged Perré to double his troop strength, then 6,000 men.[19]

In public he continued to put the best possible face on events. At a reception of a delegation of mayors on April 22 (at 4:30 P.M.), Pétain was once more the joker, enjoying his ability to surprise. When one mayor boasted that he represented the region of former President Émile Loubet and asked Pétain what he thought of that, Pétain replied: "God! I have nothing to say; I'm polite!" When another mayor explained that he had been billeted at Pétain's Ermitage during the war, the marshal responded: "Ah, you're the one who drank my wine and broke my dishes! I ought to call my wife down to talk to you." He became more serious when another member of the delegation told him that the Germans had shot several persons in his town. Pétain asked for the names of the families so that he could make amends. Finally he addressed all the mayors together, advising them not to "become excited" by taking sides in the war. "We are surrounded by impossible people. The Germans and the English who are bombing us are impossible people right now."[20]

According to Tracou, the surprise visit to Paris that week was General Brécard's idea. Brécard, now grand chancellor of the

Legion of Honor, had written that the city was tense after the Allied bombing which had killed 500. But Pétain's staff feared that if the visit were announced too far in advance, the Militia and other pro-Fascists would mobilize, and the marshal would be obliged to review their parade. The Germans agreed to remain in the background during the visit and allowed Pétain's own people to handle censorship of the Paris press during the trip. Just before they set off, Tracou was summoned to Laval's office. "Although I'm the Chief of Government I learn by chance, thanks to the German police, that the Marshal is leaving in a few hours for Paris. . . ." Finally it was agreed that Laval would be present, with Cardinal Suhard, to greet Pétain at the entrance of Notre Dame Cathedral.

When Tracou asked Pétain if his wife would come along, he replied that she didn't seem to want to, so he hadn't insisted. But Eugénie Pétain told Tracou that Pétain hadn't even suggested that she come.

The trip was made by car. At Melun they stopped for the night at the prefecture, and Pétain talked to children assembled outside the iron gate. "Who's in a cage? Who's a prisoner? Is it you or me?" When the children screamed, "We are!" Pétain replied: "We are all prisoners, you as well as I." Next morning, April 26, they drove on to Paris, arriving at City Hall at 9:30. The vast square was deserted. Then at the entrance to Notre Dame, just as Pétain was about to go into the cathedral, Renthe-Fink and two German officials drove up with Brinon. Louis-Dominique Girard warned Brinon that Pétain did not wish to see any Germans on the square and ordered a police commissioner to escort them inside.

By now the people of Paris were becoming aware of the presence of the marshal. The cathedral began to fill up as a mass for the dead was recited in the presence of families of victims of the Allied bombing. As Pétain left the cathedral, a crowd acclaimed him. The party returned to City Hall for a lunch with Cardinal Suhard and other distinguished guests. Tracou remembers having been called to the telephone to be told by Renthe-Fink that loudspeakers were being set up on the square in front of the building; Tracou replied that no speech was planned; there was no advance text. The crowd—and photographs show that it covered most of that large square and adjacent avenues—was now chanting, "To the balcony!"[21] The press was present in force and Pétain's speech was recorded, but there are a number of versions of what he said. A commentator for Radio Paris, Roland Tessier, who recorded the speech for broadcasting that evening, later claimed that Pétain began: "Ladies and gentlemen, I've come to pay you a visit. I arrive from Vichy, where I'm held prisoner." But when Tessier brought the recording to the studio, the German censor had him remove the "I arrive from Vichy" sentence, and even the typescript version found in Vichy's files lacks that phrase.[22] Pétain went on to say that he had come "to solace you for all the sorrows which hang over Paris." His own copy of the speech has him add: "But it's only a first visit. I do hope I shall be able to come to Paris without being obliged to give notice to my guardians. . . ."[23]

Renthe-Fink, Tracou says, was furious. "You are personally responsible. This text won't appear in the papers."[24] (In fact, it did not. A totally different text was printed.)

The Pétain party went on to the Bichat Hospital, where the marshal visited bombing victims, then across Paris ("on a bed of flowers," says Tracou) to Pétain's apartment on Square de Latour-Maubourg, where he received friends, such as former Spanish ambassador Quiñones de León.[25]

A typical headline was the one Le Petit Parisien spread over its front page the next day:

THE MARSHAL ACCLAIMED
BY THE PEOPLE OF PARIS

AT NOTRE DAME THE CHIEF OF STATE, PREMIER LAVAL AND CABINET OFFICERS ATTENDED A CEREMONY IN MEMORY OF FRENCHMEN MASSACRED BY THE ANGLO-AMERICANS.[26]

XLII
NORMANDY

We have it from Pétain's staff director Jean Tracou that the marshal's guardian angel, Cecil von Renthe-Fink, made his first request that Pétain denounce the resistance on February 25, 1944; the struggle to wrest such a declaration from him lasted two months; Renthe-Fink won. Pétain objected that in order to conserve his authority he had to avoid offending public opinion, but Renthe-Fink pointed out that French opinion was that Pétain secretly sympathized with the resistance; by his silence he was assuming a heavy responsibility. "You have to be with us, and say it clearly," the German envoy insisted in early April, warning that if Pétain did not act, then Hitler would revise his policy toward France. Several drafts were prepared, one by Tracou and another by Philippe Henriot; at the insistence of Renthe-Fink a phrase was added: "When the present tragedy comes to an end and, thanks to the defense of our continent by Germany, our civilization is definitively saved from bolshevism, the hour will come when France will regain and hold its place."

Again according to Tracou, even General von Neubronn, asked

for his opinion, told Pétain that if he were a Frenchman he could not accept that.[1] On April 19, Pétain apparently drafted a note (with no indication of its addressee): "If I make the speech as it is, I may cause a revolt; it's a responsibility I cannot accept because of the disastrous consequences that may result."[2]

On April 21, Renthe-Fink informed Tracou that Berlin had instructed him to warn Pétain that if he continued to refuse to make a statement the situation would become "very serious." Pétain told Laval: "Everybody tells me it would have a deplorable effect. I know that the nuncio, when he heard I wouldn't make the speech, thanked God." Then it was his birthday, and his visit to Paris. After that, on April 28, Renthe-Fink attacked again. Von Ribbentrop, he said, was waiting. The speech was broadcast the same night.[3]

In its final form Pétain's declaration was a detailed indictment of the resistance, which he said was in the hands of "masters without scruples" who were guilty of "odious crimes." The resistance claimed to be working for the liberation of France. "This alleged liberation is the most deceptive of mirages." He warned that anyone, government employee, soldier or simple citizen, who participated in a resistance group was compromising the future of the country. "It is in your interest to maintain a correct and loyal attitude toward the occupation troops." He appealed to youth and their parents, farmers and workers and veterans, to ignore the calls of the resistance. Then came the phrase about Germany's defense of Europe.[4]

The reaction was as predicted. Apparently only Joseph Darnand really approved the speech, saying that it had a good effect on his Militia.[5] Pétain himself asked Swiss minister Stucki whether he too condemned Pétain because of the speech. When Stucki replied that he had failed to understand some of the language, Pétain burst out: Stucki had no idea of the pressure to which he had been subjected; he had lost his former advisers and had no political experience of his own. He knew that most Frenchmen thought he should have flown to North Africa or resigned in 1942; it had been the most serious conflict of conscience he had ever known, but he still believed that he had been right to stay.[6]

Now, at Renthe-Fink's request, Pétain was moved to a country castle not far from Paris, at Voisins near Rambouillet. It was a sumptuous place, with vast salons, a dining room all in gold and marble, in a splendid forest setting. Renthe-Fink was never far away, and on Pétain's first morning there (May 8), there were visits from von Neubronn, Abetz, and Brinon.[7] After a visit from Philippe Henriot, the Paris press published an editorial in which Henriot declared: "But Paris, heart of France, suffers the monstrous assaults of the Anglo-American 'liberators,' and to affirm his sympathy for Parisians, the Marshal has come here."[8]

There is a touching note in an anonymous account prepared by his staff about Pétain's stay in Voisins. On May 9, just two days after his arrival, Ménétrel returned to Vichy. On May 10, Pétain asked four times if Ménétrel was returning that day. On May 11, the marshal again asked for his doctor a number of times—asked anyone he met; at dinner he commented that Ménétrel seemed to have been absent for at least a week, which prompted his wife to say that this was "very kind" for Bernard, and she would tell him that. (Ménétrel returned on May 12.)[9]

Hearing that Pétain was cut off from the outside world, Serrigny phoned the castle and was invited to Voisins on May 19 with General François Anthoine, another World War I comrade. They found a barrier at Rambouillet where the road to Voisins began, a German guard post, more German police along the road and at the entrance to the property, and a park full of plainclothesmen. When the two retired generals got out of their car, Pétain threw himself at them and kissed them with emotion; apparently they were the first friends he had seen since his "internment" (Serrigny didn't feel that the word was too strong).

Yet to Serrigny, the marshal seemed "quite intoxicated" by the Germans. He praised the hard-line propagandist Henriot (at this Ménétrel raised his eyes; the doctor was anticollaborationist now, thought Serrigny, who also felt that the conversion had come late). Pétain was being criticized, so Serrigny warned, for having said in his April 21 speech that the Germans were protecting France. "But that's what I think," replied Pétain; it caused Serrigny to wonder if Pétain was in possession of all his faculties.[10]

Field Marshal von Rundstedt came to see Pétain and invited him to visit German coastal defenses. Pétain replied, so Tracou reports, that he preferred to save the visit for after the battle, so he could see how the fortifications held up. Next day Renthe-Fink complained of Pétain's reaction: von Rundstedt had been disappointed, for he had asked Hitler for this authorization and thought he was offering Pétain an "agreeable surprise." Instead, Tracou said he convinced Abetz that it would be safer to have the marshal visit Rouen, to commemorate the martyrdom of Joan of Arc in that city. Abetz thought the idea excellent; to honor Joan was to defy the English. They drove up in a convoy to find the old Norman capital in ruins. The crowd was subdued, but it was present. Pétain confided, "If they keep comparing me to Joan of Arc they'll burn me at the stake."[11]

Pétain took advantage of being in the neighborhood to drive over to Caumont Castle, where Jacqueline de Castex was living with her daughter Hélène. Afterward Pétain told a member of his staff: "Not a word to Mrs. Pétain about all that!"[12]

Something seems to have gone wrong with German decision-making with respect to the marshal's transfer to the northern zone. At whatever level the choice of Voisins was originally made—apparently to keep Pétain in German power at the crucial moment of the expected Allied landing—it seems now that the move did not please Hitler; he wanted Pétain back in the center of France before the Allies attacked across the Channel. Pétain had arrived at Voisins on May 7, but two days later, we know from captured German telegrams, Abetz had already told Renthe-Fink that Berlin wished Pétain to return where he came from.[13] He was offered a choice among three castles in the region of Vichy. The Pétain party left Voisins May 26, with plans for a detour via the eastern provinces. In Nancy a crowd waited on the Place Stanislas as the chief of state drove up for a flag-raising ceremony; the Germans kept their distance, Tracou recorded, and allowed the French flags to fly alone. Pétain appeared on a gilded balcony equipped with microphones, once more to speak without a text prepared in advance. Tracou quotes him: "It wasn't easy to come to see you today; it was necessary to negotiate it, but I managed to escape from my guardians." The crowd cheered. As two German planes flew low above the crowd, Pétain added: "And there are some who weren't invited to our party." Renthe-Fink informed Tracou that he had banned any reporting of this speech, so he and Tracou worked on a statement that would give the visit to Nancy a "European significance.[14]

Tracou also describes the six arduous weeks of negotiation with

Renthe-Fink to arrive at an acceptable text which Pétain was to record in advance for broadcasting on the day the Americans and British touched shore in Normandy. There were ten drafts. Finally a text was approved which Pétain recorded on March 17; it was broadcast on June 6, when the Allies landed in Normandy: "The German and Anglo-Saxon armies have come to grips on our soil. France thus becomes a battlefield." He called on government officials and other workers to remain at their posts, warning the French not to commit acts that would lead to tragic reprisals. "Don't listen to those who, seeking to exploit our distress, would lead our country to disaster." Should the German army take special measures in the combat zones, the French were to accept that necessity.[15]

For the Anglo-Americans under the command of Dwight D. Eisenhower had at last landed on French soil, after long weeks of preparations in secrecy, postponements, and apparent success in misleading the waiting Germans as to precisely where along the Channel coast they would attack. American and British paratroopers began to drop over Normandy shortly after midnight on the night of June 5–6; at dawn Allied forces that had crossed the Channel on thousands of vessels hit the coast south of Cherbourg, the beaches north of Bayeux and Caen; following General Eisenhower on radio broadcasts beamed to France, General de Gaulle urged his countrymen to facilitate the Allied advance.

The atmosphere in Vichy was feverish on June 6. Pétain was just back from Voisins; there was fear that resistance forces might attack the Hotel du Parc, so he was asked by the Germans to move to his new quarters, the castle of Lonzat, that very night. Actually the castle was pleasant in its isolation, as well as being easy to watch and to defend. In addition to the French police inside the residence and 200 soldiers of Pétain's personal guard in the surrounding park, an estimated 1,500 German troops and an armored detachment formed an outer circle.

Each evening after dinner Pétain would doze on the terrace overlooking the Allier River, would go to bed at ten and wake up at five, read and work until nine, when his aides would come in with maps to report on the military situation. During one such conference Ménétrel warned Tracou not to speak so loudly, then dropped to the floor and perceived feet moving away from the other side of the door. Tracou installed an office in a tower where the walls were six feet deep. "You want to lock me up already," Pétain told him. "I have a great fear of detention. I couldn't survive it."[16] When he arrived at the Hotel du Parc each day, his military staff was ready with more maps of the Normandy battle.[17]

On June 11 the marshal was asked by the Germans not to go in to Vichy at all, but to spend his days as well as nights at the castle.[18]

He continued to receive his beloved Legion regularly, notably Xavier Vallat and Director-General Raymond Lachal. At their request for guidance on how to deal with the resistance on the one hand and the Militia on the other, he released a message to legionnaires on June 14, which included the admonition: "We are not at war; your duty is to maintain a strict neutrality. I do not want a fratricidal war."[19] The Germans, predictably, were upset; they asked that the message not be publicized, for it would confuse the Militia and affect the morale of those responsible for order. Philippe Henriot issued a directive: All statements, even those from the marshal's office, had to be submitted to him first. A member of Pétain's staff, Henri Yvan, was actually arrested by the Militia for giving Pétain's message to the legionnaires to the radio service before showing it to Henriot. When Pétain protested, Darnand's office replied that the arrest had been ordered by Henriot; Henriot, when finally located, said it was Darnand's affair. The matter raged over a long day; Pétain refused to leave his office at the Parc until Yvan was released; finally he was.[20] Four days later Pétain was sending a message of condolence to the widow of Philippe Henriot, who had been gunned down by a resistance commando in his Paris residence.[21]

Without responsibility for governing or even for making policy, Pétain was left in Vichy's final months with a morale role, a function of his own remaining energy and of the tattered remnants of his entourage. We have Tracou's word that Pétain protested firmly, if ineffectively, against the atrocities committed by the Germans, notably the cold-blooded murder of 642 inhabitants of Oradour on June 10 (where the men of the village were shot, the women and children locked in the church before it was set on fire). "You burn our villages, you kill our children, you profane our churches, you cover your country with shame," Tracou quotes Pétain as telling Renthe-Fink. "You're a nation of savages." Pétain said he intended to protest directly to Hitler, but Renthe-Fink warned him that his credit was low in Hitler's entourage and he'd better submit the letter to Renthe-Fink first. Pétain did write such a letter, Tracou remembers, and, when Renthe-Fink refused to accept it, sent it through von Neubronn.[22]

Visitor Maurice Martin du Gard, who was granted an audience with the marshal on June 17 at 4:30 P.M., reports that at eighty-eight, Pétain showed no new wrinkles; in fact, he seemed to have fewer than before. His complexion seemed healthy. "In his blue eyes, gravity and mischievousness alternate; his voice, without being full, has almost none of the hesitations which annoy the listener when he speaks on the radio." He seemed to fill out his suit jacket; the visitor knew that he was eating well (that day he had given his third diplomatic lunch since his return from Voisins). Why couldn't he live another fifty years? wondered the visitor. "An extraordinary and seemingly innocent selfishness protects him." He continued to thrive on crowd response.

Pétain complained that he lived in a glass house, under surveillance. He refused to preside over the cabinet, but now he no longer knew what was going on. Of de Gaulle he exclaimed: "He's a man with terrible ambition! More arrogant than anyone I ever met, a liar impossible to live with, making trouble wherever he goes." When Martin du Gard spoke of the prewar republic and its Parliament, Pétain attacked with some vivacity: "They did nothing for the people. They gave them words and alcohol."

Would Pétain leave the helm of state? "I didn't leave in November 1942; I'm not going to leave now." It would have been cowardly to leave; what would have happened to the French? He protected Alsatian refugees, Jews, Communists; if he had gone, the Nazis would have killed all the Jews. He expressed the hope that the achievements of his national revolution would survive: the labor charter, the reorganization of agriculture. "We must create unity through work, and make a fine nation full of children, farmers, artists!" He gave his visitor a de luxe edition of his speeches and autographed it before escorting him to the door.[23]

XLIII
LAST WEEKS OF VICHY

By the beginning of July 1944, Vichy had taken on the atmosphere of an abandoned capital; it was clear that important events would no longer occur in this place. The future of France was being decided in the north and in the west as the Allies consolidated their hold on Normandy; it would be settled in Paris. But Paris had no time to spare for Marshal Pétain: That became obvious early in the month when Laval asked Abetz whether Pétain could go there and Abetz replied that Hitler opposed the transfer. The story was spreading that Pétain and the government would be moved east. When Pétain asked Renthe-Fink about that, the German replied that this was a tall story. Pétain told Renthe-Fink that he would leave Vichy only to go to Paris. If the Americans got to the capital, so would de Gaulle. "I have to be there to have it out with him and defend those who followed me."[1]

In a talk with Tracou on the terrace at Lonzat on July 14, the marshal delivered himself of some thoughts. "It is regrettable that de Gaulle is inadequate, for at bottom we have the same ideas. . . . I can't do anything more for France, my job is over. . . .

We'll be put in prison, they'll try to dishonor us, but I have confidence in the judgment of history." One thing was clear: Tracou himself had to go. He had become persona non grata to the Germans; even friendly General von Neubronn didn't dare compromise himself by talking to Pétain's aide, and Renthe-Fink simply wouldn't have him around.[2]

We have the testimony of Swiss minister Stucki as well as of Tracou—who had not yet left Vichy—that when the German high-command assassination plot against Hitler failed on July 20, 1944, Pétain refused to send a message of sympathy to the Führer.[3] Actually the Pétain files contain such a message: "I condemn the criminal plot of which Your Excellency was the object. I beg you to accept my congratulations for having escaped it." Was this only a draft, never sent?[4]

We are less than a month away from the end of Vichy, and it would be interesting to know whether old Philippe Pétain had a clear understanding of how the battle for France was developing, and of what was likely to happen, and unlikely to happen, at its climax. Many former members of his entourage, many friends, were thinking about these things for him, sometimes in the conviction that they were doing so at the marshal's request or with his knowledge and approval. The history of this time is obscured by postwar memoirs and other testimony designed to convey the impression that there was a meeting of minds between de Gaulle and Pétain. But how can one know, in a clandestine contact, for instance, that the party claiming to speak for the Free French is really speaking for them, that the party claiming to represent the point of view of the marshal really knows it?

Jean Tracou recalled that an agent of the Free French Central Office of Intelligence and Action asked through an intermediary what Pétain's attitude would be if de Gaulle returned to France with American backing. Pétain replied that he himself wished to set up a government of national union which would bring together both resistance fighters and those who did not resist but were not compromised by collaboration; then, after a period of transition, he would withdraw as chief of state. A new question came back from the Gaullist agent (says Tracou): What would be the role of de Gaulle? The marshal is said to have replied that de Gaulle would be chief of the future government.

Tracou says that a friend of Pétain in contact with the resistance
came to Lonzat for further talks. "The interest of France re-
quires that I shake the hand of General de Gaulle," said Pétain.
"I'll shake his hand."[5]

Probably, the friend who was going to serve Pétain as an intermediary with the Gaullists was his former minister, Admiral
Gabriel Auphan, who on August 11 was handed a letter signed
by Pétain empowering him to represent the marshal before the
"Anglo-Saxon" high command in France, "and eventually, to make
contact for me with General de Gaulle or his authorized representatives, for the purpose of finding a solution to French political problems, at the moment of the liberation of the country,
so as to prevent civil war and reconcile all Frenchmen of good
faith." Auphan was to consult Pétain before taking decisions, if
possible; if not, he had Pétain's confidence "to act for the best
interest of the country, provided that the principle of legitimacy
that I incarnate is maintained."[6] Auphan did seek to make significant contacts in Paris, but failed. In his memoirs he blames
this on resistance leaders who did not wish to see a reconciliation
that would have robbed them of the fruits of their efforts, i.e.,
good jobs in postwar France.[7] The best evidence is that the
Gaullists were unprepared to accept Pétain's condition—expressed in his letter empowering Auphan to speak for him—that
"the principle of legitimacy that I incarnate" be maintained.[8]

Meanwhile Pétain was delivering himself of an unprece-
dented indictment of Darnand's Militia. A letter of August 6 to
Laval began: "For several months many reports have called my
attention to the harmful activity of the Militia." He reminded Laval
that he had previously warned him of this situation and had hoped
for an improvement in the behavior of "this political police," but
there had been no improvement—"quite the contrary." The
"courageous behavior" of the Militia did not excuse its faults:
collusion with the Germans, the burning of farms and entire villages, murders, abductions, thefts. Pétain added that the Militia
had killed Georges Mandel and probably Jean Zay (a Popular
Front minister jailed by Vichy), that it carried out acts of torture
that caused Vichy's jails to resemble those of the "Bolshevist
tchekists."[9] Darnand himself replied, in language that he later
summarized in this fashion: "Over a period of four years I re-

ceived your compliments and congratulations. . . . And today, because the Americans are at the gates of Paris, you begin to say that I'm going to be a blot on the history of France? You could have started sooner."[10]

On August 11, Pétain invited Walter Stucki to dinner at Lonzat Castle, an exceptionally melancholic dinner, the Swiss diplomat recalled. Then, in a tête-à-tête, Pétain told him: "My closest collaborators and myself are no longer sure of our lives. At the very least we are going to be arrested and interned for a long time somewhere." Their documents would be taken away or destroyed. He wished Stucki to be his witness, ready at any hour of day or night to observe what was taking place. Stucki agreed and from then on took careful notes each evening.[11]

At the same time, preparing for whatever might happen, Bernard Ménétrel handed an envelope to Antoine Alart, head of the secretariat staff, and warned him not to let it fall into the hands of the "Boches." Alart took the envelope to his quarters at the Pavillon Sévigné and hid it in the lining of one of his wife's coats. It was unsewed and removed in the presence of police investigators in September 1944 and found to contain photographic negatives of three documents: Pétain's handwritten explanation of why he sentenced de Gaulle to death; the August 11 letter empowering Auphan to represent him; and a letter signed by Pétain requesting Gabriel Louis Jaray, a government official and member of the Comité France-Amérique, to contact American diplomatic authorities in Switzerland so that Pétain's intentions would be known at the moment of liberation, "in view of the safeguard of the principle of legitimacy that I incarnate." Jaray was given the mission of finding a solution that would prevent civil war in France, "relying on the high authority of President Roosevelt."[12]

On his side, Laval was also making preparations. On August 12 he drove to Nancy and picked up Edouard Herriot, who was under house arrest there, to take him back to Paris. Next day Pétain talked to Laval's assistants in Vichy about the advantages and disadvantages of his joining Laval in Paris. Was the chief of government planning to convene the National Assembly? Would Pétain's freedom be guaranteed if he went to Paris?[13] Laval was unable to guarantee that the marshal would be received well. As for his safety, he would indeed be better off in Paris; if he depended on his personal guard in Vichy, "it's as if he were already in the maquis." [14]

Meanwhile Pétain's entourage had informed Stucki that they were considering sending an emissary to the American commander in chief Dwight D. Eisenhower, with documentary proof that Pétain was France's number-one resistance fighter, and to suggest that the marshal set up a new government with persons acceptable to the Allies. Under this plan Pétain would also denounce the armistice with Germany, provide military and police forces to the Allies, and order a general mobilization. He would then turn his powers over to the Parliament that had been sent home in July 1940. Stucki's reaction was that it would be difficult to execute this plan in the presence of the Germans, and that in any case he did not think the Americans would accept it. It would be best for the marshal, so Ménétrel told Stucki, if by one means or another he could put himself in the hands of the Forces Françaises de l'Intérieur (FFI), the Gaullist secret army. [15]

It was an interesting comment for Ménétrel to have made just then. Genuine contacts were taking place at that moment, and with genuine resistance leaders. Thus, an officer attached to Pétain's personal staff, Captain Paul Ollion, had sought out "Mazières," the Free French regional commissioner of the Republic for the Auvergne, who was based in Clermont-Ferrand. "Mazières" was Henry Ingrand, a physician, who after early resistance activity and arrest by the Germans managed to reach that region. Pétain's emissary assured Ingrand that talks had already taken place between Pétain and Eisenhower's general staff, as well as with de Gaulle's entourage. Pétain feared that he might be abducted by the Militia or by the Germans, and offered to place himself under the protection of the FFI and to issue a statement to the effect that he was retiring and wished the French to follow de Gaulle. Pétain was concerned with legitimacy, explained his emissary, and hoped to avoid a situation where de Gaulle would simply be brought to power by the Americans. Thus, even while under FFI protection he wanted to be able to pursue his negotiations with Eisenhower and the Gaullists.

Ingrand/Mazières asked for time to think about the proposal, and a new meeting was set for August 18. Ingrand now proposed that Pétain place himself in the hands of the FFI, to be kept under armed guard; he must make no preliminary statement nor communicate with the exterior. He could bring three or four persons with him and, once under FFI control, could prepare a text to submit to the Free French government, which would decide what use to make of it.[16]

On August 19 it was the turn of "Satine," actually Octave Grasset, an employee of the Youth Ministry, who described himself as a counterespionage agent in touch with the Interallied General Staff (Ingrand was able to verify his credentials immediately by radio message to London).[17] According to the report that Ingrand immediately dispatched to Free French headquarters in Algiers, "Satine" came with a proposal for direct negotiations between Pétain and de Gaulle "in view of an eventual transmission of the legitimate powers which were given to Marshal Pétain by the National Assembly." In reply, Ingrand repeated to "Satine" the only proposal he was authorized to make: Pétain would place himself under FFI control and be interned. The emissary handed over an aide-mémoire, which summed up Pétain's status:

> To understand the position of the Marshal one
> must consider that
> —the Marshal is a prisoner,
> —the Marshal is isolated,
> —the Marshal is an elderly man who, although in
> possession of all his faculties, cannot pursue a sus-
> tained effort without rest periods. . . .[18]

As it happened, the Free French in Algiers received a full report of Pétain's proposal only on August 21, by which time de Gaulle had left North Africa for the French battlefield. Jacques Soustelle, director-general of Special Services, dispatched a reply rejecting any tie with Vichy; if Pétain was taken into custody by the FFI, he should be held for trial.[19]

Which way would Pétain go? On August 14 he had informed the director-general of his guard, General Jean Perré, that he feared abduction by the Germans and wished to take refuge in a castle in the mountains to the southwest, from where he would contact the Allies when the time came. He asked that a group of

volunteers be ready, dressed as civilians, for his escape. When time
passed and nothing happened, Perré warned Ménétrel (on August 18) that it was now or never. The doctor replied that if they
could not escape they would resist. In an atmosphere of growing
tension the Germans began flying low over Vichy on the nineteenth; it was clear to Perré that this was designed as a threat.
He learned that night that to avoid the bombing of Vichy, Pétain
had given up the idea of defending himself with arms. Perré went
to the Hotel du Parc at once and, after a lively argument with
Ménétrel, managed to see the marshal. He informed him that the
guard was ready to resist. "Too late! I've made my decision," the
old man replied. Perré unpinned his Francisque medal and placed
it on the desk, and asked that the marshal give him his freedom.
Pétain rose from his armchair, picked up the medal in his left
hand, placed his right on Perré's shoulder as he walked him to
the door. "Take it back," he said, his voice heavy. "I give you your
freedom. Good luck."[20]

XLIV
DEPARTURE

Until the last moment, the Paris option seemed to be available. Walter Stucki reported that Pétain was receiving conflicting advice about the matter.[1] Soon, however, it became inevitable that when and if the marshal left Vichy his direction would be eastward. On August 17 Renthe-Fink informed him that he must leave at once. In a note that Renthe-Fink handed Pétain (and which Stucki copied immediately afterward), the German informed him that the Reich accepted the principle of a session of the National Assembly. But in view of military developments, there was a danger that Vichy would be cut off from the north of France. Thus, Pétain would now have to leave, together with those members of his government still in Vichy. Pétain replied that he could not take so serious a decision without consulting his chief of government.[2] But Laval, who had apparently hoped to call the Assembly into session in Versailles, ready for the arrival of the Allies, had himself been ordered to leave Paris, with his government. In the late evening of August 17, before Pétain could get a message to him, Laval was picked up by the Germans and driven out of

Paris with a Gestapo escort.[3] Not a moment too soon, for the city
was up in arms, as local resistance groups prepared to liberate
the city. In just over a week Paris would be theirs, as the Allies
arrived with Free French General Leclerc in the vanguard.

At 10:00 A.M. on August 19, while Walter Stucki was in Ménétrel's office, Pétain walked in and spoke in the Swiss diplomat's
presence of his negotiations with the resistance. Pétain suspected
that Laval was betraying him once again, but Stucki replied that
he didn't think so; he was certain that Laval was a prisoner in
Belfort on France's eastern border. Stucki then learned from the
Germans that Pétain was going to be asked to leave for Belfort
immediately; his refusal would signify a rupture of the armistice.
And then Pétain learned officially from Renthe-Fink that Laval
and his government were indeed in Belfort, "new temporary
capital of the French government." Pétain was given a solemn
promise that he would remain on French soil.

In reply, Pétain handed the German envoy a memorandum
informing him that Laval had promised to exercise power only
in Vichy or in Paris, and that if anyone ever said he was exercising power elsewhere it would be untrue. If Laval was in Belfort,
unless he informed Pétain of a change of attitude, it had to be
considered that he was not there as chief of government. Renthe-
Fink left, furious.

To Stucki, General von Neubronn admitted that he had orders to take Pétain to Belfort that night, using all the force at his
disposal, but he added that the execution of this order was the
heaviest task he had ever been asked to carry out. That afternoon at five, Pétain told the Swiss minister: "I don't have the right
to let the women and children of Vichy be bombed so I can enter
history with more glory." It was agreed that the guard would be
given orders not to fire unless the Germans did; the doors of the
Hotel du Parc would be shut, the iron gates lowered, the access
to the marshal's apartment locked. The Germans would have to
pass through the line of guards and remove the barricades one
by one.

At 8:30 P.M. Stucki and the Vatican representative Valeri, who
had been called to the Hotel du Parc by Fernet, were escorted
into Pétain's office. Renthe-Fink and von Neubronn were already there and were visibly surprised by the arrival of the dip-

lomats. Pétain told the newcomers that the Germans had been playing a game with Laval and himself; he couldn't leave Vichy under such circumstances. He had been threatened with violence, and if he yielded it would only be to this violence. He wanted the diplomats to make sure that the truth become known.

The German position was summed up in a final note from Renthe-Fink: For his own protection Pétain was being taken to Belfort, where Laval and the government were waiting; they would have appropriate facilities there, and the diplomatic corps could join them. The military situation had worsened since Renthe-Fink's first notification of the move. "In consequence," the letter concluded, "the government of the Reich has given instructions to effect the transfer of the residence of the Chief of State even against his will."[4]

That night Stucki warned von Neubronn that taking the marshal into custody would involve more than simply sending an officer to the hotel at seven in the morning. To avoid bloodshed, he begged the German general to remain in Vichy that night and to make certain that proper tools were available to break down the doors and gates; he hoped that the weapons on both sides would be unloaded. Von Neubronn agreed, as had the marshal's men.

For these last moments of Vichy, Stucki remains the most thorough and reliable observer. He was on the street in front of the Hotel du Parc at 6:45 A.M. on Sunday, August 20, for that was when the action was to take place (so von Neubronn's aide de camp had informed him). The building was already surrounded by S.S. troops. With a special pass obtained in advance, Stucki walked up to the swinging door, barricaded from inside; the guards in the lobby allowed him to enter. He observed that the heavy gates at the bottom of the stairs between the second and third floors were also closed and guarded; again he was allowed through. On Pétain's floor he found some thirty persons— members of the marshal's staff—in front of the old man's rooms, and then from a balcony he looked down to observe the arrival of a German detachment to take up positions in front of the hotel. The Germans asked to be admitted; receiving no reply, they broke down the front door with crowbars. Stucki went downstairs to watch as the Germans crashed through the first and then the second iron gate, using their crowbars again. The German major in charge asked the commander of the guard which door was Pétain's; the French officer indicated the door but then took up a position in front of it. "I'm sorry, the Marshal is resting. No one has the right to disturb him." The German withdrew, but a few minutes later General von Neubronn arrived and politely persuaded those blocking the door to stand aside. He then had a noncommissioned officer break the thin-glass-panel entrance to the marshal's suite with a single kick, shattering the glass; once inside the corridor, a soldier lifted the inner door from its hinges. Von Neubronn entered Pétain's bedroom.

Stucki couldn't follow but learned afterward from Ménétrel's wife, who was inside, that Pétain was seated on a chair dressed in shirt and trousers, tying his shoelaces. Von Neubronn accepted the old man's request that he be allowed to finish dressing.[5] At 7:45, von Neubronn's aide de camp asked Stucki to have Pétain hurry, but at Ménétrel's request he was allowed to have breakfast. In Ménétrel's office, Stucki and Valeri were shown another note from Renthe-Fink delivered the previous day, suggesting the persons who should accompany Pétain to Belfort; Mrs. Pétain said that she would also go. Pétain walked in, impressing Stucki for being as calm and unruffled as he had ever seen him; he gave the diplomats copies of his formal protest to Hitler. It began by recalling his pledge not to leave French territory, which had allowed him "in the loyal respect of conventions, to defend French interests." He accused Hitler's envoys of using "arguments contrary to truth" to convince him to leave Vichy, and now they were using violence. He raised "a solemn protest against this act of force which places me in the impossibility of exercising my prerogatives as chief of the French state."

After shaking hands with members of his staff, he got into the elevator. Downstairs, a company of the personal guard presented arms; Stucki noted that hardly any of the men were dry-eyed.[6] It was raining hard as Pétain left the building, so the crowd was small but enthusiastic, and their singing of the *Marseillaise* seemed particularly moving to Stucki. The convoy of automobiles, escorted both by the Germans and six motorcycles of Pétain's own guard, drove off quickly.

At ten that morning Stucki was given a copy of Pétain's proclamation to the French people.[7] In Paris, at one that afternoon, Admiral Auphan received a delayed radio message from Ménétrel, asking him to announce Pétain's departure and to release the proclamation (which had been sent to him earlier). Auphan had the text reproduced in thousands of copies; it was also posted on the walls of Paris.[8]

We know from Henri Massis that it was he who drafted this proclamation. Ménétrel had asked him to write it twelve days earlier and gave him two pages of notes to guide him.[9] The message reviewed Pétain's efforts over four years to protect the French from the worst. Everything he had accepted or submitted to, willingly or against his will, had been for the protection of his people. He had not been able to be their sword any longer, but he had wanted to remain their shield. "In some circumstances, my words or my acts may have surprised you. Learn now that they hurt me more than they hurt you. I suffered for you, with you." But now he was being taken away by "our adversaries." He asked the French to "follow those who will give you the assurance of leading you on the path of honor and in an orderly manner." He reminded the French that order must reign, and since he represented it legitimately, he was and would remain their chief. He asked the people to obey him and, as well, those who followed a policy of reconciliation and renovation.[10]

While the Pétain motorcade was making its way north, preparations went on in Vichy for an orderly takeover by the Free French. Stucki obtained a promise from the Germans not to send troops through the city during their retreat, and the Germans still stationed inside Vichy left during the night of August 24; the FFI began their entry the next morning.[11] Leading figures of Vichy were rounded up; a court-martial was installed in the lobby of the Parc.[12]

In Moulins, a brief stop, Pétain left instructions with the prefect of the Allier district: He wanted a message sent to his staff back in Vichy to make sure that his rooms remained "in the disorder in which they were on his departure; that is, not to sweep them up, to leave even the broken glass on the floor, not to cover up traces of the break-in and if possible to photograph the damage."[13] The party stopped at Saulieu for the night, lunched the next day at the Dijon prefecture in the company of a sober collection of local dignitaries; that night they were in Belfort. Laval was there to greet the marshal and to warn that a new German-sponsored government was in the process of being formed, with hard-liners such as Doriot, Brinon, and Darnand.[14]

Next day, in one of a continuing series of memorandums addressed to Pétain during his exile, designed to keep him aware of what was happening around him, Bernard Ménétrel wrote:

> . . . The Marshal is in Belfort, Prisoner of the Germans. Premier Laval is also Prisoner of the Germans and there is really no longer a government. . . .
>
> He has no further official activity and must await better days before acting again.
>
> Above all he must refuse all political combinations and all public manifestations of any kind (new government with Déat, Brinon . . . proclamations, speeches, etc.) . . .[15]

On August 24, Pétain was moved to the castle of Morvillars outside Belfort, under the protection of a battalion of *Feldgendarmerie;* the Germans controlled all exits.[16] It was the home of Louis Viellard, but he was in the underground resistance. Viellard's wife, an acquaintance of Pétain, was his hostess. She warned the marshal that she herself belonged to the resistance. "You? It isn't possible." "Why not? Marshal, there aren't only terrorists in the resistance." "They never told me . . . They never tell me anything." Pétain insisted that his hostess dine with him in his "prison"; she agreed, provided that neither Laval nor his ministers were invited. One day Pétain asked her if her resistance contacts could get a letter to General de Gaulle, for he wished to negotiate a transfer of power. Mrs. Viellard agreed and gave the letter to a courier, but a complicated liaison through Geneva could not be carried out.[17]

On August 25—the day French and American troops entered Paris—Pétain issued a "decision": For the time being he would accept only his wages as marshal of France.[18] Henceforth, Ménétrel noted every significant event in Pétain's daily existence and continually summed them up. These reports were for the immediate use of his chief, but surely they were also intended for history.[19]

With the marshal refusing to cooperate, the Germans turned to a more reliable instrument, Fernand de Brinon. Since Brinon had served in Paris as delegate to the Vichy government, he and the Germans decided that he should continue to exercise this function. In a meeting with Brinon on August 31, von Ribbentrop encouraged him to deal with administrative affairs, working with those of Laval's ministers who had joined his "delegation." (Laval himself was no longer in the good graces of the Germans and was remaining aloof.) Von Ribbentrop hoped to see the formation of a new government presided over by Jacques Doriot, with Pétain remaining as chief of state. Could Brinon accomplish that? Brinon felt that the marshal could not be persuaded to accept such a thing. In that case, von Ribbentrop replied, Pétain would simply have to be eliminated. But Brinon felt that it would be difficult, without Pétain, to maintain an appearance of legitimacy.

On September 1, Hitler received Doriot, Brinon, Darnand, Déat, and Paul Marion, to whom he expressed the hope that they could save their nation. He also hoped that they could persuade Pétain to accept their cabinet, for a government always gained strength by being covered with legality; the Führer reminded the Frenchmen that he himself had gained power through a delegation of authority from Hindenburg.[20]

Back in Belfort, Brinon asked for a meeting with Pétain and was refused. Ménétrel informed him that the marshal was no longer exercising his functions and therefore could not "extend the powers of anybody." But in view of the importance of the matter, Pétain did not object to Brinon continuing to deal with civil internees.[21] Then, on September 6, Renthe-Fink announced to Pétain that Belfort would soon be part of the war zone, so that he would have to go to a safer place—in Germany—and at once. The marshal refused but was told that he would be expected to leave the next morning at six. Before their departure, Pétain's staff secretary-general, General Victor Debeney, handed Renthe-Fink another protest for Hitler: Pétain had received the assurance that in all circumstances he would remain on French soil, and now that agreement had been broken.[22]

In Paris, meanwhile, Admiral Auphan was still trying to honor the trust vested in him by the marshal. On August 27 he wrote to Charles de Gaulle, now installed as chief of the provisional government in Paris, and saw that his letter actually reached de Gaulle through the good offices of General Alphonse Juin. Auphan said that it should be possible "to find a procedure respecting the dignities of Marshal Pétain and General de Gaulle both, and allowing, by their reconciliation, the setting up of a government of national union desired by the entire French people."[23]

De Gaulle was not surprised by Auphan's appeal. He was aware of the contacts between Pétain and Free French representative Henry Ingrand. "What an end! What a confession!" thought de Gaulle. "Thus, in the disintegration of Vichy, Philippe Pétain turns toward Charles de Gaulle. Thus comes to an end the frightful series of surrenders under which, in order to 'save the furniture,' one accepts servitude." In reading the documents submitted by Auphan, de Gaulle found his convictions reinforced, but also felt "an inexpressible sadness." Where had the glorious marshal been led? And what reply could de Gaulle make to this request for a discussion? Pétain had feared civil war, but there had been no insurrection: Not a single district, town, or village, no civil servant, soldier, nor even a private citizen had taken up combat against de Gaulle on behalf of Pétain. And the legitimacy that Pétain claimed to incarnate was rejected by the government of the Republic, for a French government that ceased to be independent could not be legitimate. This legitimacy was now held by de Gaulle, who had roused the nation to war and unity, imposed order, law, and justice, demanding that French rights be respected. "Although I did not fail to recognize the supreme intention which inspired the Marshal's message, and did not doubt that it was significant for the moral future of the nation that in the end Pétain looked toward de Gaulle, I could only reply with silence."[24]

The convoy left in the direction of Mulhouse, moving north after it crossed the Rhine to Friburg in Breisgau for a lunch stop (and where the marshal refused, so Ménétrel's situation report tells us, to receive Laval).[25] Then there were another eighty-six miles to go. The destination was a small town 1,870 feet above sea level called Sigmaringen and its picture postcard of a castle built on a precipice over the Danube; it was a turn-of-the-century reverie. Pétain and his wife were given the top-floor apart-

ments of a prince of Hohenzollern; the marshal possessed, so
Louis-Ferdinand Céline observes in his hallucinating vision of that
place, seven drawing rooms all for himself, in a castle of "stucco,
patchwork in all styles, turrets, chimneys, gargoyles . . . super-
Hollywood! . . ."[26] The marshal kept his distance from his former ministers who also resided in the castle, housed in another
wing.

Apart from his daily promenades, indeed, the marshal lived
the life of a recluse, seeing only his aides. The Germans gave the
Pétains a radio so they could follow the progress of the Allies.[27]
We know from Ménétrel's papers that newspapers were also
reaching them; one was a copy of the August 23, 1944, *France-
Tireur*, a resistance paper now appearing openly in liberated Paris,
which described the posters put up clandestinely in the capital
reproducing the marshal's August 20 farewell message: It was a
"lamentable confession of its own defeat that after having soiled
France with his presence, he comes to beg mutual forgiveness of
insults and asks us to follow those who pursue his work. . . ."[28]

If ever Ménétrel was Pétain's *éminence grise,* it was at this time.
It is at Sigmaringen that Laval was heard to say of him, "I had
foreseen everything, except that France would be run by a doctor."[29] For, of course, this doctor was watching over Pétain's
political health as well as his physical condition, and making the
hard-liners angrier and angrier. In the September 28 entry of
Marcel Déat's diary, reporting the visit of Otto Abetz to the Pétain floor of the castle, Déat heard that Ménétrel was thought to
be setting up an intelligence network via Switzerland. "One wonders why this character has not already been shot," comments Déat,
who confesses two days later: "I attack Ménétrel, threatening to
have him killed if they don't get rid of him. Finally I'm promised
that the decision has been taken, and that everything is in order." At dinner with Abetz, the members of the Brinon "delegation" seemed of one mind with the ambassador: the "permanent
treason" of Pétain's entourage had to be dealt with. (Déat also
provides a description of high mass on Sunday, with Pétain, his
wife, and Ménétrel in the prince's box above the altar. "Ménétrel
plays the choir boy and reads his missal with great attention. The
old lady seems like a fearsome dragon, the Marshal has drawn
features.) . . ."[30]

On September 29, Pétain received Gaston Bruneton, commissioner general of the delegation responsible for the welfare of French laborers in Germany. The marshal made it clear that if he kept the title of chief of state he was no longer exercising his functions: "I remain the moral chief of France and the French, as I always wanted to be." Referring to the work of French officials responsible for the labor force still in Germany, Pétain told Bruneton: "You are like soldiers, you must obey the orders given to you and remain at your posts." But on October 1, speaking at a flag-raising ceremony, Fernand de Brinon toughened up the marshal's language to make it a call to arms: "Tell the French workers in Germany that they are soldiers, that they owe allegiance to me and to no one else, because I remain incontestably and legally the leader of all Frenchmen." Pétain had learned a lesson from that distortion of his message; on October 9 he informed Bruneton that he had suspended all activity and thus could not even confirm Bruneton in his present functions.[31]

XLV
THE PRISONER

The French state was now a French Commission for the Defense of National Interests: It took shape in the castle town of Sigmaringen even as the last of the German occupation forces were being driven from Alsace (the Allies crossed the German border with Belgium September 11). Brinon was its chief, as delegate general of the French government—the title he had been given by Vichy for his Paris mission, and which title he conveniently held on to. The new commission (also known as the delegation) included Déat, responsible for French workers in Germany; Darnand, for law and order; General Bridoux, for war prisoners; Jean Luchaire, one of the best-known collaborationist journalists, for information and propaganda. The Germans granted the commission extraterritoriality, this to be marked by the flag-raising already mentioned. Brinon had invited the marshal to attend, but the invitee did not even reply. In his speech at the ceremony, Brinon thanked the Führer for making it possible for the commission to function in Germany and added: "We are here alongside the Marshal, the only legitimate chief of the French State." He ended:

"Long live France! Long live the Marshal!"[1]

Bernard Ménétrel, who was Pétain's only adviser now, drew up another memorandum for his chief. This one adopted the tone of the subordinate disappointed with his superior's behavior. In essence, Ménétrel asked the marshal to display more courage in making decisions, for otherwise the outside world would assume that he accepted German protection and had joined the Germans against the Allies. Pétain had received Bruneton, although he had been warned not to; he had been urged to break relations with Brinon, but he had not done it. And how could he maintain cordial relations with Renthe-Fink after everything the German envoy had done to him? "One must have the courage for the last time to repeat to the Marshal what he is risking in refusing to face the situation; it's a matter of loyalty."

Pétain could not help France just then, Ménétrel went on. But he had an absolute duty not to do anything that would tarnish his own name. A prisoner could not act without ceasing to be considered a prisoner; anything Pétain did would be taken as pro-German and destroy the effect of the announcement of his captivity. "The Marshal's policy is already difficult to defend," admitted the doctor-adviser; his excuse was German pressure and his desire to avoid the worst. The disabused *éminence grise* concluded that he had done his duty a final time; henceforth, he would avoid political questions, would cease to importune his chief with suggestions, recriminations, criticism.[2]

On October 3, Pétain read Renthe-Fink a formal protest against Brinon's abusive exploitation of him and protested a German news agency report that "the Marshal has decided to leave Belfort for Germany to protect the true interests of the French people."[3] He also drew up a protest to Brinon, making clear that he had given no mission to Brinon or his associates, since he had ceased to exercise his functions on August 20 and thus "deprived myself of any possibility of delegating any authority whatsoever." Henceforth, he would simply turn aside Brinon's communications—which communications continued to treat the marshal as the chief of state whose delegation of powers Brinon enjoyed.[4]

It became something of a game: the last-ditch collaborationists seeking under various pretexts to be received by the marshal; the marshal refusing; the collaborationists pretending to read into the marshal's tolerant and polite refusals an endorsement of their activities; the marshal begging them to stop.[5] A piano recital? It was sponsored by Brinon's commission; the marshal could only decline to attend.[6] Brinon thought that he had an even better pretext to lure the marshal out of his retreat when the news came in of the execution of hard-liner Admiral Charles Platon by the liberated French. On the letterhead of the delegation, Brinon, from his wing of the castle, wrote to Pétain in the other wing to inform him that a religious service would be held for Platon. Brinon took this opportunity for an attack on Ménétrel, whose "diabolical spirit of intrigue" had separated Platon from Laval; those with whom "Mr. Ménétrel seeks to come to terms and to negotiate" had shot Admiral Platon. Pétain replied that in the absence of precise information it was not opportune to render homage to Platon just then, but if Brinon went forward with his plan then he must not speak in Pétain's name "in any way at all." He denied the allegation against Ménétrel and pointed out that he was replying despite Brinon's use of a delegation whose existence Pétain had already refused to accept.[7]

On November 22, Ménétrel was arrested by four burly S.S. troopers, on his return to the Sigmaringen castle from a walk with the marshal. He was placed under house arrest at Scheer, six miles away, and eventually transferred to an S.S. camp in Eisenberg near Komotau (now the Czechoslovak Chomutov) in Bohemia. Pétain protested the removal of his doctor and friend in vain. In his own protest, which took the form of a letter to Renthe-Fink, Ménétrel argued that to be kept away from the marshal was harmful to the old man morally and could become harmful to him medically, adding that professional secrecy prevented him from furnishing further detail.[8]

That winter the Germans counterattacked in the Ardennes, setting U.S. forces off balance; the Germans were able to maintain their pressure until well into January, having driven a wedge between Allied troops which gave the campaign a name: the Battle of the Bulge. When the Allies regained the initiative, they never let go of it again. The last German troops had abandoned France's eastern provinces at the beginning of 1945; by the first day of spring the Allies had won strategic positions on enemy soil. In

France, de Gaulle's provisional government held the nation firmly, and the punishment of citizens accused of collaborating with the enemy was under way. On April 5, from Sigmaringen, Pétain addressed a letter to Hitler. He had learned that the French authorities were going to put him on trial and asked to be allowed to "accomplish my duty." He did not wish it to be thought that he sought refuge outside France. "At my age, one fears only one thing: it is not to have done all one's duty, and I wish to do mine."[9] On April 20 he was informed by the Germans that the military situation required that he leave Sigmaringen in the direction of the southwest. "You know my position," he replied. "I desire only one thing: to return to France, and to return as quickly as possible."[10]

All the same, he had to leave his castle prison immediately. At four the next morning all was ready. Gestapo and S.S. cars accompanied the Pétain party as it drove off in the direction of Wangen, the eastern hook of the Lake of Constance. At Wangen they learned that they were to go to the castle of Zeil some twenty-two miles to the northeast. Pétain protested; it looked as if he was being taken to the redoubt where the Germans planned a last stand. His aide General Debeney describes this journey over roads jammed with retreating troops, interrupted by air raids, a scene reminiscent of the French exodus of 1940. When they reached Zeil later that day, they found that the vast castle was already serving as shelter for German religious communities, an orphanage, a camp for refugees from Berlin and elsewhere.

Next day, April 22, Allied planes began bombing the town, and the German retreat intensified. Pétain, strengthened in his resolve by his military aides, was determined to stay put and await the arrival of Allied troops, as he had wished to do back at Sigmaringen. But that night he was told that he had to move again. He refused, and the tone mounted; it was explained that his escorts had instructions not to let him fall into Allied hands. He argued with the Germans most of the night; finally an exasperated official asked him: "And if I drove you to the Swiss frontier?" "How do I know that you will do that? And that if you do, I'll be allowed to cross it?" He was promised a formal guarantee countersigned by the Swiss; he and his party waited all day for it; that night a Swiss chargé d'affaires arrived to announce that

Pétain and his party were authorized to transit Switzerland.[11]

The Pétain party left Zeil for Bregenz on the Lake of Constance, near the Swiss frontier. They could not cross over that night, so the Pétains were lodged in a small hotel. The morning began with intense bombing of the town. They left Bregenz at 9:30 for the six-mile drive to the Swiss frontier town of Höchts-Sankte Margareten; at 10:00 the barrier was raised. As they entered Switzerland someone greeted him with a "Happy birthday, Marshal," for it was April 24, 1944, and that day he was eighty-nine. He replied: "The nicest gift that I could get for my birthday is this one, my arrival in Switzerland." The formalities took an hour and were accompanied by friendly words, flowers, and chocolate.[12]

The Pétain party, requiring four automobiles, at that moment included General Debeney and nine other officers and aides, including Pétain's personal guards and his valet. The Swiss noted carefully that Pétain possessed one million French francs in cash, which he pledged to take out of the country when he left. From the frontier the party went on to Weesen, on the western tip of the Walensee, to be put up at a hotel; Pétain's confidant Walter Stucki, now in charge of foreign affairs at the political department in Berne, saw him the next day.[13]

When the Swiss had received word of Pétain's desire to transit their country in order to place himself in the hands of the French courts, Pétain was asked to sign an agreement that he would remain in the residence assigned to him in Switzerland until the French were ready to receive him.[14] As for how Charles de Gaulle felt about this development, the previous September, in a dinner conversation with Georges Duhamel, then secretary of the French Academy, he had declared: "Let him go down to the Riviera and be forgotten!"[15] Duhamel was told in February 1945 by General Jean-Marie de Lattre de Tassigny that de Gaulle had ordered that if Pétain appeared at a French frontier he should be sent to Switzerland.[16] But now, in April, Pétain *was* in Switzerland and wished to come back to France. When Carl J. Burckhardt, representing the Swiss government in Paris, called on de Gaulle to inform him of Pétain's arrival on Swiss territory, de Gaulle told him that "the French government was in no hurry to have Pétain extradited."[17] (Later, de Gaulle was to tell an aide, Alain de Boissieu, who married his daughter, that he had offered to furnish Pétain with a staff and all the documentation he would require in Switzerland to justify his attitude in 1940.)[18] Walter Stucki advised Pétain that Paris would not object to his accepting Swiss asylum, to which Pétain replied: "I see the maneuver . . . I want to go to France, and as quickly as possible."[19]

After Stucki's meeting with Pétain at Weesen, the Swiss diplomat gave orders for the transfer of the marshal and his party to the French frontier by the shortest route, so that they would arrive before 8:30 P.M. on April 26; the itinerary was to be kept secret so that reporters would not bother the old man. At 9:00 in the morning of that day Pétain and his wife bid farewell to the hotel owner and staff. Along the way local villagers showed sympathy: There was a crowd to greet the marshal at one town, and flowers, wine for their picnic, at another. By 4:45 P.M. they were in Vallorbe, where Pétain was allowed to rest in the railroad station. The marshal asked his Swiss escorts to find out what was happening on the French side; they reported that there were 150 armed police and soldiers watching the frontier to Hôpitaux-Neufs, where Pétain was to board a train for Paris. There was danger that Pétain might be hooted, or worse: that the FFI might shoot at him.

A French official crossed into Switzerland for a private talk with Eugénie Pétain. She was not under arrest; did she wish to be detained with her husband? She replied affirmatively. The party dined at 6:20 and at 7:00 P.M. proceeded to the frontier. Pétain descended from his car, and the Swiss frontier guards accorded him a military salute. He left their territory, so the precise Swiss report says, at 7:27; on the French side was the village of La Ferrière sous Jougne. The Swiss looked on as Pétain left his car again and offered his hand to General Pierre Koenig, military governor of Paris and, until recently, commander of the FFI; but Koenig remained at attention without giving his own hand or saluting. The Swiss saw no sign of hostility on the part of the local population.[20]

The marshal listened to the notification of his arrest on charges of plotting against the internal security of the state and collusion with the enemy, and signed it. Then the procession of automobiles moved on to the Hôpitaux-Neufs station, where a special train was waiting. The train was given special protection against possible attacks on Pétain (so recalled de Gaulle in his memoirs),[21] but there was a demonstration at Pontarlier when the train stopped there, the crowd shouting "Death to Pétain" and striking and spitting at the window of the Pétain compartment. At the edge of town firecrackers were set off along the tracks; the train was stopped, and another hostile crowd gathered.[22] The train arrived at a small station ten miles south of Paris at 6:30 the next morning—a cold and windy day, the press records. Automobiles stood by to take Pétain, his wife, and the officers of his suite to the Fort de Montrouge.[23]

The French Institute for Public Opinion in October 1944 asked the French: "Should Marshal Pétain be punished?" Only 32 percent of those questioned said yes; 58 percent said no; 10 percent "didn't know." Of all persons interrogated, 22 percent excused the marshal because of mental incapacity; 18 percent wished to respect his age or to respect the man; 5 percent pointed to services rendered in 1940 and during the occupation.[24] In May 1945, after Pétain's arrest, de Gaulle's private secretary Claude Mauriac discovered that his chief was receiving more letters against Pétain than for him, but de Gaulle seemed impressed by the smaller pile. "It needed courage to sign those," he commented (Mauriac hadn't shown him the anonymous letters). "There are still men and women who believe in him; that's a fact," said de Gaulle.[25]

Edgar Faure remembered that just before the liberation of France one of de Gaulle's ministers thought that he had devised suitable punishment for Pétain: He would be stripped of his rank in front of the Arch of Triumph before a line of troops, after which his marshal's stick would be broken solemnly. "We could break it over his head," Faure says he responded, putting an end to the plan.[26]

The old Fort of Montrouge on a desolate stretch of land just south of Paris was then being utilized to execute persons convicted of treason. When the government decided to detain Pétain and his officers there, doors and windows were quickly reinforced and locks installed, and a special detention area was prepared—all this between April 25 and dawn on April 27. Each cell was furnished with a bed, a closet, and a night table.[27] His jailor, Joseph Simon, then fifty-one, who was to follow Pétain from Montrouge to the courtroom in Paris for the trial, then to his prisons at Portalet and the Ile d'Yeu, remembered the first meeting with his prisoner in the early morning of April 27. Pétain said only, "They threw rocks at me while I was in the train." Simon observed that General Koenig offered him his hand when he turned over the prisoners, but refused to shake Pétain's.[28] From the outset it was made clear that Pétain would not be a privileged prisoner, would not be authorized to receive gifts. He was let out of his cell for up to an hour each day for the customary promenade; his diet was watched by a doctor. Most of the prison personnel were veterans of resistance movements.[29]

On April 30, Pierre Bouchardon, chairman of the commission of inquiry of the High Court of Justice, called on Pétain at Montrouge to inform him that he stood accused of plotting against the internal security of the state and collusion with the enemy (repeating the terms of the arrest warrant). The prisoner declared that both charges were false.[30] On May 8, the day of Germany's surrender, Bouchardon arrived with a first list of questions; he asked if Pétain agreed to reply without a lawyer, and Pétain said that he would.[31]

The first question dealt with the vote of the National Assembly on July 10, 1940, which granted constitutional and executive power to Pétain. "I didn't do that alone," Pétain began his reply, "I wasn't a parliamentarian; everybody gave a push." The chief pusher was Laval, he made it clear. The prisoner was asked about his abolition of the Republic, his dismissal of Parliament. "I repeat that I didn't do that alone. I had a total lack of experience. . . ." He denied having known that Vichy's special courts had issued death penalties for prisoners who had already received lesser sentences on the same charges. On Vichy's treatment of Jews: "I always and in the most energetic way defended the Jews, I had Jewish friends. The persecutions were done outside of my presence. . . ."

He blamed Laval for the recruitment of workers for Germany, denied that he had endorsed the Legion of Volunteers against Bolshevism; he justified the orders to French military commanders to resist British and Gaullist attacks but claimed not to recall his telegraphic order of May 15, 1941, to General Dentz in Syria in which he endorsed collaboration with the "new order," and not to recall a letter to Hitler of November 27, 1942, yielding to his decisions. He said he hadn't been able to leave France in November 1942 because he had not wished to abandon the nation to the Germans; he hadn't left in June 1944 after the Normandy landings because he could not find an airplane.[32]

On May 11 he refused to reply to further questions without an attorney; when at last he had defense lawyers, on May 25 he submitted a protest against the first interrogation of May 8. Moved by the sirens of the day's victory celebration, he said, he had not realized that some of the questions he had been asked assumed that offhand remarks he had made in the past were statements of principle. Even his own replies betrayed his thoughts, for, perhaps taking advantage of the fact that he was alone and without a lawyer, he had been asked to review political and military events which he had dealt with over a period of four years.[33]

XLVI
THE TRIAL

How to find an attorney, when all those one used to know had long since died? At the request of his interrogator Bouchardon, the head of the bar association, Jacques Charpentier, came to the Fort of Montrouge to suggest candidates. But in the end Pétain was to be defended by Fernand Payen, who was recommended by a magistrate who had served in Vichy's Riom court. Payen was best known for the practice of civil law, but he had recently published a book calling for national reconciliation; he seemed to Pétain and his friends the best choice after all.[1] On the recommendation of Henry Lémery, Payen asked a younger attorney, Jacques Isorni (then just turning thirty-four), to assist him. Isorni had recently come to public notice with a vigorous defense of Robert Brasillach, the collaborationist journalist, and had succeeded in mobilizing part of the intellectual establishment in his defense; although de Gaulle had rejected the demand for a pardon, and Brasillach was shot for the crime of collusion with the enemy on February 6, 1945, at the Fort of Montrouge.[2]

Although he was the junior member of the team, Isorni offered what seemed a clever tactic, one that might have changed

the course of the trial: He suggested that the defense be reinforced by the addition of a third lawyer, a decorated officer and
resistance fighter, Pierre Véron. Véron himself accepted, with the
reservation that he be free to argue only those issues with which
he could agree, but not such matters as the Special Section with
its retroactive jurisdiction, the delivery of political refugees to the
Germans, the racial laws and persecutions. On June 2, Pétain wrote
to Véron, asking him formally to join the defense, but when Véron called on Payen he found him in ill humor. It was impossible
for a Gaullist like Véron to defend Pétain; there were matters
which Véron refused to deal with yet, argued Payen; as senior
defense attorney it would be up to Payen to decide who would
speak on which points. Véron realized that the atmosphere of the
defense team would be intolerable and withdrew. There would
be a third man all the same, an attorney of appropriately conservative view named Jean Lemaire.[3]

The weeks of interrogation preceding the trial were described not by the senior man on the defense team—he left no
memoirs—but by his articulate number two, Jacques Isorni, in a
series of small books written in the years immediately following
the trial. Thus we have a portrait of Pétain as Isorni first saw him,
in the visiting room of the Fort of Montrouge on May 16, 1945.
"Wearing a gray suit, he was standing, quite straight. What struck
me was his 'youthful' look, his physical equilibrium, the almost
unreal freshness of his pink features, crowned with white hair,
and his expression."[4]

Isorni also notes that the tension between Fernand Payen and
himself came to the surface at once. Payen wished to plead a decline in Pétain's faculties, while invoking the marshal's glorious
record. Isorni, on the contrary, felt that they should unasham-
edly defend Pétain's policies.[5] Soon he was going to Montrouge
to meet Pétain in secret; jailor Simon, who confided that after
each visit of Payen Pétain seemed totally discouraged, helped keep
the secret. But when Payen walked in unexpectedly while Isorni
was working with Pétain and demanded angrily what was going
on, Isorni was saved by Pétain's quick response: "I didn't want to
bother you, so I asked Isorni to come."[6]

The questioning was pursued, relentlessly; Pétain turned to
his attorneys for support, but Payen insisted on silence, for Pétain's helplessness served his theory of defense, i.e., that the mar-

shal was a very old man. Isorni, who tells us that he was revolted by this, went back to the fort the next day to explain the situation to Pétain. "But what must I do?" "What you must do is to remain yourself, to be yourself again. You are Marshal of France, chief of state. You cannot accept any slight to your dignity." When Pétain asked Isorni what they would do to him he says he replied, "Sentence you to death."[7]

Pretrial questioning sought to document the thesis of prewar conspiracy: contacts with the Germans, with Laval, with the Cagoule and other secret movements.[8] Pétain reacted vigorously to the allegations of a prewar conspiracy with extremists. "If they boasted of associating with me they lied." As for the charge that there were former Cagoule men in Vichy: "A chief of state can't know everything that happens around him."[9]

Isorni says that when he showed Pétain the letter from Franklin Roosevelt dated November 8, 1942, announcing the landing in North Africa, Pétain read it with "stupefaction" and said: "If I had known that I would have said, 'Everything is saved.' " Isorni at the time didn't know enough about the history of Vichy to react; later, he realized that this was one of Pétain's lapses of memory. Thus, Isorni noted for May 24: "I see the Marshal at the very end of the day. He is tired. I have some difficulty in making myself understood on some points. Today the Marshal has considerable lapses of memory which prevent reasoning, and you have to repeat the same thing several times." Yet apart from these problems of memory, Pétain was not senile; Isorni claims that he always seemed lucid and had a sharp judgment. A chain of affection grew between the old man and his lawyer. "If I'm saved," Pétain told Isorni one day, "I'll owe it to you."[10]

Pétain gave the interrogators a letter for Admiral Leahy, in which he requested that the former American ambassador testify on his behalf. He told Leahy that "I am now in the position of one who betrayed his country although I did everything I could to defend it. Dear Admiral, you who lived close to me for many months . . . will help convince my accusers that they are making a mistake."[11]

On May 23 the prison doctor reported "growing nervousness" on the part of the prisoner, accompanied by loss of weight. His moral condition varied: Some days he was buried in his papers, turning them over endlessly, and it was impossible to draw a word out of him. At other times he confused dates, recalling distant events but forgetting recent ones. The visits of his attorneys, and the interrogations, were generally followed by prostration. Eugénie Pétain's presence was judged essential.[12]

On May 26 when he arrived at the visiting room, Isorni discovered that all the furniture had been removed save for a table and two chairs. The prisoner was henceforth locked in and had the right to the use of a single room. The prison authorities expected a visit from the Consultative Assembly's Purge Commission and did not wish to appear soft.[13] When Isorni arrived on May 30, Pétain exclaimed, "Ah, here is our messiah." Pétain had frequent lapses as they worked on specific charges and at one point asked, "Am I still chief of state?" On another day, when Reynaud, Daladier, and Blum were mentioned as prosecution witnesses, Pétain asked, "What have they got against me?"[14]

On June 8, Pétain was asked about the alleged secret treaty between Vichy and the British. He said he could not reply because it was against diplomatic usage to speak of such accords without the agreement of the other party (i.e., the British).[15] At another session he denied having opposed resistance activity; he had favored it because it was "the sign of a people's vitality." Laval had been forced on Pétain; it had been a necessary concession, "and in this role of which he was unaware, Laval himself was not without utility to France." The armistice? It had "assured the freedom of a whole population and saved thousands of soldiers. It allowed the creation of a free zone and the protection of the integrity of the empire while waiting for the Allied landings. Finally, it allowed the establishment of an authority that protected the French. In a word, it saved France from becoming a Poland."[16] By this time Pétain was submitting written replies—replies drafted by Isorni.[17]

Just before the trial began, Pétain made a final will, this time giving Eugénie all of his goods and property without exception; Isorni saw in this document the desire of Pétain to exclude surviving members of his family from his succession to the benefit of his wife, who was sharing his captivity.[18]

The trial was to be heard by the High Court, a creation of the liberation government, whose judges were drawn from the top ranks of the judiciary. Twelve jurors were selected from a list of former members of Parliament (among the eighty who had voted against full powers for Pétain in July 1940), another twelve from the ranks of resistance veterans.[19] A courtroom in Paris' Justice Palace was transformed to provide seating for an exceptionally large audience. "It was hard to distinguish the lawyers from the witnesses, the witnesses from the police, the police from the public, the public from the journalists, the journalists from the jurors," reported Joseph Kessel, who was covering the trial for a French newspaper. "There is no perspective in this debate."[20]

At a time when the shortage of paper kept the daily press to a limited number of pages each day, the Pétain trial covered most of the front page of every French daily when it began, and on the following days as well. Opinion ranged from the angry tone of the Communist Party's *L'Humanité*—"In shooting the old traitor, justice will be rendered to France."[21]—to the more conciliatory discourse of François Mauriac in *Le Figaro*. Pétain hadn't conceived a policy; he was its result. "But we should be hypocrites if, before adding our voices to all those who accuse him, each of us failed to ask himself, What did I say, what did I write or think at the time of Munich? How did I feel about the armistice?" One had to consider that "a part of ourselves was perhaps an accomplice, at certain moments, of this crushed old man."[22]

Daily *Combat,* another newspaper born of the resistance, was harsher in an anonymous editorial probably written by Albert Camus: "If he made a gift of his person, it was as a prostitute, but it wasn't to France. Let's hope that the French won't let themselves be seduced or softened again by the tricks of age and vanity."[23]

The trial opened shortly after 1:00 P.M. on July 23, 1945, with a statement by the chief judge Paul Mongibeaux. The trial that was now beginning was one of the greatest in history, he declared; he would make sure that it took place in serenity and dignity. Pétain's senior attorney Payen rose to attack the court's competence; according to the constitution of the Third Republic, only the Senate could judge a president. The public prosecutor André Mornet objected: Pétain had never been elected president legally. After half an hour of deliberation, the magistrates rejected Payen's petition: The High Court, they said, was properly constituted in November 1944 to judge the chief of state of the "government or pseudo-government" that reigned in France after June 1940.

The court clerk read the indictment, which had been written before Pétain's return from Germany, with an addition based on the investigation that had begun after his arrival at the Fort of Montrouge. The essence of the prosecution case was Pétain's having lent his name to anti-Republican causes before the war, his association with conspirators and even with Nazis, which proved his role in a plot against domestic security; his support of Germany's war machine during the occupation proved the charge of collusion with the enemy.[24]

Pétain was given the floor for an opening statement. "He is in uniform," noted a reporter. "His only decoration, the Military Medal. He sits erect, looking at nothing and no one."[25] "As angry as one may be about the role he played, one is relieved to find not a victim at bay but a man who appears twenty years younger than his age," another observer wrote. "No tics, no trembling of hands." Unmoving as the photographers snapped pictures from every possible angle, holding in hand "as if it were his marshal's stick the roll of sheets containing his speech."[26] "It was the French people, through its representatives convened as a National Assembly, who gave me power," began Pétain. "It is to them that I have come to make an accounting." The High Court did not represent the people; he would make no other statement, reply to no questions. He had spent his life in the service of France, had received his power legitimately, had kept France going for four years, laying foundations for the future. If he was to be convicted, then he hoped this would be the last conviction, "that no Frenchman ever be sentenced or detained for having obeyed the orders of his legitimate chief." But, he added, "you will be convicting an innocent man."[27]

Isorni made a series of objections: The case against Pétain had commenced while he was in German captivity; his trial had begun before the principal witnesses had been examined. Crates of documents essential to the defense had not even been opened; specific materials and interrogations had not been given to the defense; some evidence was missing. The prosecutor, and even the chief magistrate, had made pretrial statements showing that they were already convinced of Pétain's guilt. Prosecutor Mornet's denial that he had expressed prejudice led to courtroom protests, not the first or the last; disturbances were to be frequent during the three-week run of the trial. There were rumors that the jurors would be kidnapped; threats circulated, as did a prayer in Pétain's favor.[28] But the number of Frenchmen who favored Pétain's conviction was growing, to over 75 percent at the time of the trial (by that time the number favoring abandoning the prosecution had dropped to 15 percent).[29]

Pétain's decision to remain silent seemed to Charles de Gaulle a wise one, a last bow to military dignity.[30] In fact, Pétain did intervene occasionally, with a comment or a denial. Could he follow what was going on? Apparently he could hear witnesses who testified close to where he sat, but missed much of what the magistrates said.[31] Thus, when the court was considering the telegram to Hitler of August 21, 1942, which bore Pétain's signature and which, after the British-Canadian raid on Dieppe, suggested that France participate in her own defense for the safeguarding of Europe, Pétain refused to defend himself, although during the pretrial interrogation he had denied sending the telegram. But when a juror urged him to respond when his honor was at stake, Pétain finally said, "How can I explain? I don't hear well, I don't even know what the subject is." "Since Marshal Pétain heard my question," the juror replied, "I am going to read him the telegram." "I must tell you that I won't answer." Later, when Judge Mongibeaux commented ironically that "it's his time for not hearing," Isorni snapped: "You know very well that it's not a matter of deafness or no deafness if Marshal Pétain doesn't reply. He told you on the first day that it's a matter of principle for him."[32]

"When he deigns to listen," observed Galtier-Boissière, "he curves his hand like a trumpet around his left ear, then turns back toward the defense bench with a worried look." But Madeline Jacob, a reporter covering the trial, told Galtier-Boissière that Pétain's hearing wasn't as bad as all that. She said that when at one point in the proceedings Payen asked that the session be suspended because Pétain was tired, she had whispered to a neighbor: "The Marshal wants to make peepee," and Pétain turned around to say, "Exactly."[33]

XLVII
THE VERDICT

As the trial proceeded, it became clear that there would be no attempt to deal with the charges against Pétain one by one, no attempt by the defense to reply to them one after the other. Witnesses spoke to all points, without it being known in advance what they would cover. Neither the prosecution nor the defense was familiar with the mountain of material seized in Vichy or in various caches and in the baggage of Pétain and his suite; it would have taken years to go through it methodically (it did). There was considerable reliance on press clippings, on pretrial interrogations.[1] The prosecution directed its fire at the Vichy regime, not at the circumstances surrounding the armistice; for de Gaulle this was a capital error, for all of Vichy's faults began at "that poisoned well."[2]

One after the other, leading personalities of the prewar Republic and of the war of 1939–1940 came to the bar to testify. Reynaud, Daladier, President Lebrun, Jules Jeanneney, Léon Blum, Edouard Herriot, General Weygand, together with some of the chief protagonists of Vichy (many of whom were themselves facing trial). The presentation of key witnesses seemed improvised, and they themselves appeared preoccupied with justifying themselves.[3] For its part, the defense also lacked a strategy; the three lawyers did not consult together (they were barely on speaking terms).[4]

On August 1 the long-awaited reply from Admiral Leahy reached the defense. It was introduced immediately, translated into French by a witness who had just stepped from the stand and who happened to be an ambassador. Leahy expressed the conviction that the marshal's principal concern had been "the welfare and protection of the helpless people of France." Yet "in all honesty" he had to add that "positive refusal to make any concessions to Axis demands, while it might have brought immediately increased hardship to your people, would, in the long view, have been advantageous to France."[5]

That day Claude Mauriac talked to his chief, Charles de Gaulle, about the trial, giving him his impressions of the courtroom as he had seen it in newsreels: on one side the marshal, marmoreal and more imposing than ever; on the other the vain agitation of judges and lawyers whose ridiculous beards, emphatic gestures, laughable appearance showed justice in its least respectable light. And then Mauriac visited the Justice Palace to see for himself; he was struck by the impenetrable silence of the marshal, the stupidity of some of the questions, "sickened" to see a marshal of France "accused by such persons."[6]

Pierre Laval, who had sought in vain to enter Switzerland after his departure from Sigmaringen, had finally managed to obtain permission to enter Spain for three months; at the end of that period he was delivered to the American army in Austria and handed over by the Americans to the French. The announcement in the Pétain courtroom on August 2 that he had arrived in Paris and would be heard as a witness created a sensation. (Claude Mauriac felt pity for the thin little man, hat in hand and briefcase under his arm, "this man hunted and marked for the firing stake"; then he remembered who Laval really was, when Laval referred to the Anglo-American landing in Normandy as an aggression.)[7] Laval's testimony drew a visible reaction from the defendant. Judge Mongibeaux asked Pétain what he thought of Laval's statement endorsing German victory, and Pétain replied: "When I heard it on the radio . . . . I jumped. I thought it had been cut out and I was upset that it had been kept in the speech."[8]

Le Monde published a report on this Pétain-Laval confrontation describing Pétain: "lusterless eyes, bony nose, sunken jaw, " and Laval: "without papers, deteriorated, outcast." "Sad faces of a national calamity." His jailor observes that Pétain was upset by this story, more than by any other he had seen in recent days.[9]

On August 7, Jacques Chevalier told the court what he knew about the attempt to negotiate a secret agreement with the British in 1940, testifying that the accord had been accepted by both parties and had been carried out "for the greater good of France and of Britain."[10] He also brought in the name of the Canadian envoy Pierre Dupuy (provoking much cable traffic between Britain and Canada, and an order to Dupuy not to discuss the matter with the press).[11]

By the end of the trial, sixty-three witnesses had been heard, seventeen for the prosecution, forty-six for the defense—former premiers, parliamentary leaders, party chiefs, generals, admirals, diplomats, a Bourbon prince, a union leader, a mother.[12] Saturday, August 11, was set aside for prosecutor Mornet's charge to the jury. He focused on the crime of the plot against the Republic, not a plot to deliver the country to the enemy but a conspiracy to destroy the regime and install a new one, acts made possible thanks to the occupying forces. Thus, the crimes against the regime and against the external security of the state were joined. Pétain's motives were "the vanity of power for power's sake" and "an authoritarian instinct." Pétain, concluded Mornet, had employed force to maintain himself in power, but it was German force: that was his treason. Mornet demanded the death penalty.

Predictably, defense lawyer Fernand Payen began with an appeal for pity: "Undoubtedly for the first time an old man over whom death watches, an old man of ninety, is dragged before the courts to be sentenced to death. . . ." The defense was a portrait of the aged hero; how could he have begun to conspire at eighty? He presented a rationale for the armistice of 1940; it was Jean Lemaire's task to defuse the charge of a plot against the Republic.[13]

But the speech everyone was waiting for was Jacques Isorni's,

"Never have there been more people in a courtroom," an experienced trial reporter noted.[14] "Mr. Isorni is tall, dark, muscular, with an angel's face." The Isorni defense was that Pétain had sought to obtain material advantages for the French, even at the price of moral concessions. It had been said that a marshal of France should not have done that, but in fact only a marshal could have. Addressing himself to some of the most serious charges, he admitted that the Council of Political Justice, which Pétain had invoked to detain political opponents without trial, was an error, an error "suggested to him by bad advisers." The idea of the Special Section was to save hostages, the hope being that the French judges on these courts would "avoid the worst." The Legion of French Volunteers had been imposed on Vichy. As for the anti-Jewish laws, Pétain should be judged not by what the anti-Semites did, but by his personal action, and here Isorni sought to describe it. He claimed that Pétain's government had protected the Jews—weakly, but protected them all the same.

The summing up was high in drama. Isorni described the scene as it would be at the marshal's execution—and "wherever you are at that instant, even if you are at the other end of the earth, you will all be present. . . . And you will see . . . how this Marshal of France that you have condemned dies. And that great white face will never again leave you. . . ."[15] "We saw people cry," a reporter recorded.[16]

The jurors went out at 9:05 P.M. on August 15. One parliamentary juror later revealed that prosecutor Mornet had told him: "You know, I asked for a death penalty, but *you* don't have to vote it."[17] Indeed, to everyone's surprise, remembered juror Gabriel Delattre, all three judges suggested a sentence of five years' exile. And the arduous discussion began, lasting seven hours. It was noted that the parliamentary jurors seemed more objective, the resistance veterans more passionate. Arguing against death, one of the judges said that Pétain's "delivery" of France was not deliberate treason but involuntary, caused by lack of understanding and weakness.

Death was voted all the same, by fourteen to thirteen, swung by a Communist juror's vote. Immediately thereafter a petition for pardon circulated and seventeen jurors signed it, which, of course, had to include some who had just voted for death.[18] At

4:00 A.M. the bell sounded and the courtroom began filling up again, and in the early hours of August 15 Mongibeaux read the long decision. It presented a Pétain who had "provoked the political crisis which brought him to power," who prevented the government from carrying on the war in North Africa, a Pétain who had done away with free institutions in favor of a regime resembling that of the Axis powers which had made his "internal revolution" possible. Pétain had presided over Vichy's constant surrenders, had assisted the Germans militarily against France's former ally and the Free French, had ordered armed resistance to the Allied landings in Africa—and so on, for the list of charges accepted against Pétain was long. He was sentenced not only to death, but to "national indignity" and the confiscation of his possessions, although the court immediately recommended that in view of his age the death penalty not be carried out.[19]

"At first," a reporter observed, "the Marshal bent his ear forward, trying to hear that emotive, somewhat distant voice. Soon he gave up . . . and remained impassive." Then he turned to Payen to ask what had happened. "His face flushed, he fell back in his chair. . . ."[20]

On the day after the sentence was pronounced, the Communist *L'Humanité* titled its editorial: "The sentence must be executed!" The Socialist *Le Populaire* in an unsigned editorial declared: "France cannot pardon him for having tarnished the glory of Verdun with the shame of Montoire. . . . The treason was possible only with him and by him. It is just that he be punished for it."[21]

On August 17, Charles de Gaulle commuted the death sentence to life imprisonment. In his memoirs de Gaulle explains that he did what he could to protect the old man just then; that is why he had him flown far from Paris at once, and to remote Fort du Portalet. De Gaulle adds that his intention was to let him stay there for two years and then release him to finish his life at Villeneuve-Loubet.[22]

Photographs show the old marshal, peaked cap and gloves in hand, being led by police out of the courtroom, with jailor Simon and lawyer Isorni just behind him.[23] The trial had ended at 4:25 A.M. on that feast of the Assumption; at 5:10 the prisoner was on his way out of the Justice Palace with his guards; at 5:35 had arrived at the Villacoublay military airport, taking off ten minutes later for the southwest. At 10:45 the group entered the cliffside Fort du Portalet. Pétain's cell was damp and cold, his jailor noted (an electric radiator was switched on); the prisoner negotiated the high steps with difficulty. He wrote to Eugénie, but the letter was held up by the prison director pending instructions. "Our installation is lamentable, and if I had known it as I see it now, I should not have sent my worst enemies here."[24] For, of course, he had sent Reynaud and Mandel here, and Léon Blum.

On August 21 a prison official arrived for an inspection; Pétain asked whether he could be transferred to another prison and was told that only the government could make such a decision. When the official left, Pétain broke into tears and tossed on the floor everything that came to hand, so his guards told Simon. But his jailor found Pétain in good physical shape: "Not only is he not senile, but he handles wisecracks and clever remarks with ease." During the long confinement of his prisoner, Simon was to observe both the ordinary and the extraordinary, was to hear, and record, his prisoner's confidences on Vichy, religion, his sex life. (He had already noted, at Montrouge, that during mass a guard heard the marshal let out "a violent fart which caused his scandalized wife to shrug her shoulders.")[25]

At first, hostility dominated on Simon's part. He recorded Pétain's displeasure with his dinner: soup, celery, jam—the same meal served to everyone at the fort—and a guard's reply: "That's what Parisians ate for four years." Pétain: "I don't care about that; I need to eat." Another time Pétain complained that the meat was tough, and jailor Simon pointed out that in Paris the population had been without meat for a month. "He is so selfish that he didn't understand me," recorded Simon. The jailor disliked Eugénie Pétain intensely and enjoyed observing instances when Pétain also seemed to dislike her. But he reported how depressed his prisoner was when Mrs. Pétain had to leave after a long visit. "If there were no bars on the window I'd have jumped off the cliff," Pétain said. Pétain feared that de Gaulle was going to lose the forthcoming elections to the Communists, which could only worsen his situation.[26]

XLVIII
THE ISLAND

In early November 1945 the junior members of Pétain's defense team, Jacques Isorni and Jean Lemaire, traveled down to see him at Fort du Portalet. After examination of their papers they were allowed into the restricted zone patrolled by soldiers, before the climb to the fort (they discovered that the mountain opposite the cliffside fort "was like a wall, so close that one felt one could touch it"). Inside, they found a stairway built into the cliff; to reach Pétain's cell they walked downward. "Poignant impression of sadness, of poverty," noted Isorni. "Tightness of the cell, misery of the furnishings, continual confinement. . . ." "You were right to come now," they quote Pétain; "I wouldn't have survived a third month." He repeated his remark that there were times when he would like to throw himself off the cliff.

The lawyers found the old man reading Émile Laure's biography of himself, admiring the photographs that showed him as a young soldier. He spoke of de Gaulle, said he would have liked the general to profit from his experience; he hoped he would succeed but nevertheless smiled when he considered the difficulties de Gaulle was experiencing. The visitors showed Pétain American newspapers which were calling for his liberation.[1]

Ten days later a Paris daily reported: "Pétain has left the Fort du Portalet for a more lenient climate. . . . Last night, in great secrecy, a convoy of automobiles departed for an unknown destination. . . ."[2]

Below the Brittany peninsula, the Ile d'Yeu is hardly visible on most maps, with its nine square miles; in 1945 it had a population of 1,475, clustered in and around the fishing habor of Port-Joinville. The Fort de la Pierre-Levée, an unused military installation concealed by surrounding trees, was to be Pétain's prison henceforth. He and his jailors arrived from the mainland on an escort vessel of the French navy; for a moment, Joseph Simon noted without pleasure, Pétain thought he had returned to times of splendor, for the naval officers addressed him as Marshal and the boat's captain gave him his own cabin. As the crow flies, the Ile d'Yeu is eleven miles from the "Continent," as islanders call mainland France. From Port-Joinville, a road climbs for about half a mile among the low whitewashed houses typical of the Vendée region, past a cemetery and into the wooded area that conceals the sunken citadel.

The prisoner's situation had indeed improved. Just inside the citadel's entrance a three-story house was made available for Pétain and the prison staff. On the ground floor there was office space for police guards and an engineer corps staff; above were five rooms, two for the prisoner, two for police guards, one for a warden. And above that, in what appeared to be a cottage set on the roof, the residence of prison director Simon. Pétain's bedroom had a hospital bed, a small chest, two chairs, and a wood-burning stove, with a small washroom and toilet. An adjoining room contained another stove, a large table, and an armchair; it was both dining and living room.[3]

Ten days after his arrival Pétain wrote Eugénie: There was room enough, but it was damp, and he had his annual cold. He expressed a desire to read the press so he could follow "the material and moral reconstruction of France"; he also hoped to receive a British or an American political magazine regularly, both to help keep him informed and to improve his English, for he had been studying the language. This letter was transmitted to the prison administration by Simon, who took the opportunity to deny that the fort was damp and added his opinion that the stay of Mrs. Pétain on the island would be taken badly, for all the inhabitants were anti-Pétainist, and many were indignant that the prisoner was still alive.[4]

The large inner courtyard measuring about 110 by 140 yards had been divided in half by barbed wire, and the prisoner had use of one of these halves for his walks. The grounds around the fort were closely guarded, and the watchtower allowed a view of the entire island.[5] But within a month of Pétain's arrival, a reporter from Paris managed to make his way to the prison gate; Simon discovered his ruse and turned him away. Another reporter tried to recruit an inhabitant of the island to inform him when Pétain died but was told: "You'll wait a long time; he's in perfect physical shape."[6]

Pétain's five and a half years on the Ile d'Yeu can be followed from day to day in the notebooks of Joseph Simon; in the impassioned books of his defense lawyer Jacques Isorni; and in the correspondence between the prisoner, his wife, and Isorni.[7] It is a tale of resignation, frequent moments of despair tempered by naïve hope, loss of memory, and the persistent efforts of the faithful to win Pétain's freedom, or at least an improvement in his living conditions. Bad periods were followed by good ones, e.g., one night in February 1946 a guard sat up with the old man for most of the night because he seemed not in possession of his faculties, and when Simon came in the next morning Pétain asked, "What are you doing here? Where am I?" Then when the jailor called in a doctor, Pétain was found physically and mentally fit; he was using two popular language courses to improve his English, and he translated a sentence for the doctor.[8] A month later he was writing a formal note to the prison director notifying him that three issues of Le Monde hadn't arrived, and he needed them to follow the writing of the new French constitution.[9]

In April of the same year, Isorni and Lemaire arrived for their first visit to the island. Isorni discovered a Pétain who had aged a great deal in a few months. It was Pétain's ninetieth birthday, and he had put on his "least tired" suit; Pétain said to his lawyers: "Where will I be for my next birthday? If only I could walk around the island. . . . Prison isn't gay."

What was de Gaulle doing? he wanted to know. When Isorni replied that he had abandoned power when things became dif-

ficult, Pétain said: "That doesn't surprise me. . . . But when things
were still more difficult, I stayed." The lawyers promised that they
would never abandon the prisoner, and when he expressed the
hope that he would be rehabilitated after his death, Isorni said:
"We'll get a hearing while you're alive, Marshal!"[10]

In September, when his lawyers returned, Pétain wrote out a
statement which he signed and turned over to them. "I never accepted my conviction," it began. "I received a pardon which I did
not request." His only recourse was a review of the case, and he
formally requested that his attorneys, when they had assembled
all the necessary documents, introduce a demand for such a review. He added that his lawyers "should carry out this mission
even after my death."[11] Indeed, the lawyers understood that their
only legal remedy was a request for a new trial, since the law setting up the High Court allowed no appeal of its decisions, while
the penal code provided for a rehearing, regardless of the jurisdiction, should there be new evidence. In fact, it would take Isorni
some years to put together documents which he believed represented new evidence, and when he did, as will be seen, he was
informed by a minister of justice that there could be no review
of the case, except by history.[12]

We have Isorni's word that Pétain told his wife, speaking of
French politics in the spring of 1946: "There is one man I have
confidence in, Blum."[13] To Joseph Simon he said: "For me Blum
is the most qualified person in France to run the government.
Besides, he was always very kind to me."[14]

In June 1946, Isorni and Lemaire wrote to the president of
the provisional government, who was now Georges Bidault, to
protest the conditions in which their client was confined. He had
only a military bed which he had to make up himself; he had a
chair, but an armchair had been refused him; there was only occasional electric light. He could walk only twice a day for half an
hour, with a guard and behind barbed wire. He could read only
one newspaper, could talk to his wife and attorneys only in the
presence of guards. In reply, the lawyers were informed that the
prisoner's rights were being scrupulously respected.[15]

Jailor Simon read about this protest in the press and was particularly upset by the criticism of the treatment accorded his prisoner. He noted in his diary that he had given Pétain the best bed

in the fort while he himself slept on a soldier's bunk; that Pétain got fish or meat twice a day, a quarter-liter of wine at each meal; that he was served the food he liked, and milk was carried for over a mile for his Ovaltine, which he was served with tea biscuits. Pétain was able to talk to his guards during his walks, in violation of the rules. He received magazines from his wife, gifts of cake and chocolate, even a spring lobster from local Pétainists. The only thing Simon hadn't allowed was Mrs. Pétain putting flowers everywhere, or seeing her husband without a witness.[16]

At last France got a president of the Republic, in the person of the Socialist Vincent Auriol. Isorni and Lemaire called on him on February 10, 1947. Auriol told them, as Isorni recorded: "I'm going to talk to you frankly. . . . I wasn't moved by what you've just told me. I too was in prison. I'm thinking above all of the sufferings of France. . . ." Auriol did not agree that public opinion would favor charitable treatment of Pétain; on the contrary, he felt that a transfer of Pétain to a rest home would provoke violent reactions.[17]

On March 31, 1947, Bernard Ménétrel was killed in an accident at the wheel of his automobile. He was then forty, released from prison because of his health. Isorni has Pétain commenting: "Dear Bernard, he managed to make himself detested by the Germans and the French."[18] Pétain confided to Joseph Simon that he himself hoped to be freed soon; he was certain that when de Gaulle returned to power, he would be released.[19] A referendum of readers of *L'Aurore* published on April 30, 1947, showed 45,043 favorable to his release, 3,096 for release and rehabilitation, 4,548 for the status quo or probation.[20]

In Paris, many of his former associates had been meeting occasionally and were to participate in a public campaign for his liberation.[21] One result of Isorni's lobbying was a letter sent in April 1947 by the French Academy to Premier Paul Ramadier, appealing for an amelioration of prison conditions, and for the possibility of Mrs. Pétain's living alongside the marshal in the citadel. Ramadier replied negatively.[22]

In June, a parliamentary commission investigating "the events of 1933 to 1945" sailed to the island to interrogate Pétain; they were also hearing such eminent prewar personalities as Blum, Daladier, and Gamelin. "My memory is escaping me," Pétain warned them; he explained that he could talk about the First World War but not about the second one. Concerning his responsibility for the state of military preparedness in the prewar decade, he replied that his advice was no longer being asked for then. He felt that the 1940 armistice had contributed to the rebuilding of the French army in North Africa. Then had he been in agreement with de Gaulle? "I didn't have a chance to agree with him. No one asked for my advice." In a reply suggesting his confusion, he was quoted: "If my trial was stopped before it was over, I'm convinced it's because de Gaulle intervened." It was he who had made use of Laval and not the contrary. Had Admiral Leahy not had to leave France because of the death of his wife, he explained, it was probable that more serious contacts would have been established with the United States. He did not recall having imprisoned Reynaud, Gamelin, Daladier, Blum, or Mandel—certainly not Blum. "You surprise me. . . . How was I able to do that stupid thing?" As the members of the commission prepared to leave he told them: "I've decided to ask for nothing, never to talk about anything. I accepted my punishment. I'll hold on until the end, until death."[23]

Abundant correspondence with his "very dear Annie" (he addressed Eugénie this way) suggests to what extent the lonely prisoner depended on her now. During her stays at Port-Joinville she would walk up the hill from her hotel each day at two for a visit her husband waited for "with impatience," as he wrote during one of her absences.[24] "I have only one desire: to live beside you. It's the only reward I want for the service I may have rendered to France during my career."[25]

In his letter to Eugénie of September 17, 1947, the prisoner welcomed a new member of the family. Eugénie's son Pierre had married his companion Odette. "I'm ready, in advance, to give her my admiration and confidence."[26] In fact, Odette had been to the island several times in attempts to meet him, but she had not been authorized to enter the citadel. On her first visit to his quarters she observed that a keeper sat in the next room, with the door open. Pétain was sad because one of the guards had allowed him to adopt a puppy, but then it was taken away because he couldn't have animals in his cell. But he told her: "I won't ever complain, I ask for nothing."[27]

XLIX
THE YEARS

From 1945 until the final weeks of his life Pétain resided in the island fortress, rarely speaking to anyone save his jailors, his attorneys, his wife. Books had begun to be written, often published privately, in his defense. In 1948 Jacques Isorni and Jean Lemaire published the first of their own books, containing material that they felt justified a reopening of the case.[1] Although they were not made public at the time, opinion polls showed a rise in the percentage of Frenchmen who were prepared to accept the release of the prisoner: 37 percent in May 1948 against 13 percent a year earlier.[2] At a meeting at the home of General Brécard, a number of associates and old friends of the marshal, including four members of the French Academy, decided to found a committee to work in favor of his freedom; resistance veterans opposed the formation of such a committee, and at Isorni's suggestion Pétain wrote a letter to Justice Minister André Marie, declaring that what concerned him was the imprisonment of those who had served him. (As Isorni explained it to Mrs. Pétain, the letter was designed to reply to those who would say that Pétain was thinking only of himself.)[3]

On a visit to the Ile d'Yeu in June 1948, Isorni discerned an acceleration in the aging process; on the second day of the visit he discovered that Pétain had completely forgotten the previous day's conversation.[4] In early September Isorni was back, to observe that the prisoner's lucid intervals had grown shorter. But when he returned in early January 1949, he discovered a vastly improved Pétain: pink complexion, the face filled out, an absence of wrinkles. At 10:00 A.M. he even seemed in good shape mentally, but then at 3:00 he was no longer the same. At the time Isorni was counting on a change in the attitude of the government, now led by Premier Henri Queuille, who if he could have swung it would have transferred Pétain to a military hospital to await death. But the political question was still too hot to handle; after debate, Queuille's cabinet decided only to reinforce medical attention.[5]

In April a doctor assigned to the citadel warned the Justice Ministry that in the event of serious illness it would be impossible to transfer Pétain to a hospital, and equally impossible to care for him on the island. He reported that Pétain had a heart condition and was mentally deficient, but felt that he was being given the best possible care under the circumstances.[6] Isorni wrote that the government considered the problem again at this time but could not agree to a transfer to a mainland hospital, where it would have been easier for Pétainists to stage demonstrations. But in May a contingent of military-hospital attendants arrived to replace the regular staff of guards.[7] In a press conference Charles de Gaulle, then in the opposition, declared that Pétain had had to be convicted because he symbolized capitulation and, perhaps without wishing it entirely, collaboration. "But today we are confronted with an inoffensive old man." He shouldn't be allowed to die without seeing a tree or a lawn. (Isorni felt that the cabinet's decision *not* to do anything about Pétain was a reaction against de Gaulle's statement.)[8]

Pétain was also seeing a prison chaplain regularly. By the time Father André Bailly was introduced to the prisoner at the end of 1949, he was clearly losing his lucidity. Some days he thought that he was still ambassador in Spain and wished the bishop to be present at mass; another time he was at a presidential hunt at Rambouillet Castle. The priest noted that Pétain never partook of the sacrament and confessed only for the Last Sacrament in April 1951.[9]

Isorni even attempted to obtain an audience with Pope Pius XII but was turned down; he guessed that it was because of the Vatican's defensive position after the attacks on its wartime silences.[10] In August 1949, Eugénie Pétain was authorized to spend more time at the citadel and could take meals with her husband, without the presence of guards.[11] A few weeks after that, on September 16, Isorni sailed to the island but found he could no longer get through to his client; this time the absence of lucidity was definitive.[12] Yet in December Eugénie informed Isorni, "The Marshal is in very good form, walking in the courtyard with a vigorous stride. His memory remains the same but his immediate comments are astonishing."[13]

Shortly before his ninety-fifth and last birthday, the venerable prisoner came down with a pulmonary ailment; it was checked but nevertheless represented the final phase of a long decline. Henceforth medical bulletins were issued regularly to keep the outside world informed.[14] Secret codes were worked out to keep the government informed—ahead of the public—of any further serious decline, or of death. Isorni tells us that the government sounded out Eugénie Pétain: If she accepted that her husband receive permanent burial in the Ile d'Yeu cemetery, the government would not insist on temporary burial inside the walls of the citadel. Isorni replied in her name: No. They intended to carry out the marshal's desire to be buried at Douaumont, on the battlefield.[15]

For that ninety-fifth birthday, on April 24, 1951, the lawyers were present, along with nephews and nieces; there was a large cake with the full count of candles.[16] Generalissimo Franco, who had recently issued a statement in support of the marshal, sent fruit from Spain.[17] A nurse who was to be in constant attendance henceforth remembered, for the months beginning in April, a profusion of flowers, flowers that arrived regularly from all over France; she remembered that the prisoner received a hundred letters a day.[18]

In May 1950, in a formal request for a new hearing of the High Court proceedings, lawyers Isorni and Lemaire presented what they claimed to be new evidence based on governmental archives, memoirs, witnesses.[19] But there was now a more urgent matter before the government: Pétain's physical condition. And although the lawyers had never requested any such thing, the government now commuted the original sentence of "life imprisonment in a fortress" to "residence in a hospital or any other place providing appropriate facilities," this residence to allow care of the patient but also his security and the maintenance of order. The decree signed by President Auriol on June 8, 1951, noted that the prisoner continued to refuse a pardon, insisting on complete rehabilitation; the present measure was one of "humanity."[20] So a modest house on one of the lanes leading up from Port-Joinville to the citadel was designated as an annex of the military hospital of Nantes, on the mainland; the prisoner was moved there on a stretcher under conditions of maximum security, and the chief nurse felt that the new environment did wonders for her patient. But there were daily medical bulletins now; they showed steady decline, marked by somnolence, indifference to his surroundings.[21]

Isorni was summoned to the office of Henri Queuille, then serving his last days as premier, to be informed that Pétain was dying, that he could not authorize the transfer of the body to Douaumont, but that Mrs. Pétain could bury her husband in the island's regular cemetery; Queuille added that he had imposed this decision against the wishes of cabinet members who wanted Pétain buried inside the prison fortress.[22] On the morning of July 23, Pétain was found in a coma; a nun recited Ave Marias as the old man faded away. At 9:22 A.M. it was all over, and Eugénie Pétain was called in from the next room; she bent down to kiss the dead man's forehead. "Neither cry nor moan, he always said," she told the nurse, before beginning a prayer.[23] On the island all telephone communications with the mainland were interrupted, and police took up positions in front of the villa. Isorni drew up a list of those who could enter the dead man's room to pay last respects and insisted that the death certificate mention Pétain's title as marshal of France, under a civil code provision that the certificate state the profession of the deceased.[24]

The dead man was dressed in his uniform, with the single decoration he had always worn, the Military Medal; his body was displayed with hands clasping a rosary. A request by Isorni that Verdun veterans be allowed to pay a final tribute in the death chamber was denied, but prayers were said out of doors, notably by islanders in their typical Vendée costumes. A statement by the Assembly of Cardinals and Archbishops of France declared, "Before the tomb of an old man who had known so much glory and so much humiliation, we believe that it is proper to speak only words of peace." Without taking sides—the churchmen left the final judgment to history, "after God"—the assembly noted that "masses would be requested for the repose of his soul." They hoped that these services would not be the pretext for political demonstrations but would be carried out with appropriate dignity.[25]

The funeral was scheduled for the morning of July 25 in the village cemetery above Port-Joinville. The early boat from the mainland brought General Weygand and Admiral Fernet in full uniform, members of Parliament in ceremonial dress, former Vichy ministers. The coffin was carried into the church by veterans of Verdun and former prisoners of war of the Second World War.[26] Monsignor Louis Cazaux, bishop of Luçon on the nearby mainland, delivered the main speech. He admitted that the dead man was a controversial figure but announced that this was the place for a truce. He would not comment on the sentence given to the marshal, but as one of his former soldiers as well as the bishop of the diocese where he came to die, he wished to recall the reasons they were praying for him now. He spoke not only of Verdun but of the second war and Pétain's help to its prisoners; the intentions and sincerity of the man could not be doubted. And if he had not been a practicing Catholic, defeat and detention had in the end revitalized his faith.[27]

Today's visitor will find the cemetery halfway between the prison fortress and the house in which he died. The grave is covered by a horizontal slab of white granite marked by a cross and bearing the inscription:

Philippe Pétain
Maréchal de France

Apparently it is always decorated with wreaths, small vases of flowers, potted plants, plaques marking a visit or a pilgrimage.

L
EPILOGUE

From the moment of his death until the moment of this writing there has never been a diminishing of the angry debate over where the marshal should be buried. At Verdun? At nearby Douaumont, where the remains of thousands of fallen soldiers have been gathered? On May 29, 1966, as president of the Republic Charles de Gaulle presided over the fiftieth anniversary commemoration of the Verdun battle; his speech at Douaumont contained this phrase: "If, by misfortune, in another time, in the extreme winter of his life and at a time of extraordinary events the attrition of age led Marshal Pétain to failures deserving of blame, the glory which he won at Verdun twenty-five years earlier cannot be contested, nor forgotten, by the nation." Taking note of the persistent call for the transfer of the marshal's remains to Douaumont, de Gaulle declared that this monument of national union must not be troubled by controversy and concluded: "Such is the rule of our wise and time-honored tradition which opens our military cemeteries only to those fighters who died on the terrain."[1]

Year after year, Pétainists demand a transfer, resistance veterans condemn the proposal. Once, in 1973, a group of right-wing extremists actually dug up the body and took it to the mainland, intending to find a way to rebury it in Verdun. As soon as the theft was discovered, the police patrolled all roads leading to Verdun; a member of the commando, when arrested, refused to divulge the location of the coffin unless it were placed in the Invalides Church in Paris, but eventually he took police to a garage in a Paris suburb where it had been hidden; it was flown by helicopter back to the island for reburial.[2] Violence continues to be manifested in other ways when the name of Pétain is invoked, against pro-Pétain pilgrimages, against organizations set up to defend "the memory of Marshal Pétain."[3]

In 1980 *Le Figaro* published a poll in which 59 percent of adult men and women sampled accepted the proposition that the marshal "had been sincerely concerned by the national interest, but was overtaken by events," with another 7 percent ready to call him "a hero who sacrificed everything for France and was unjustly convicted." The percentages of respondents who considered him a traitor or ambitious were respectively 8 and 7, while 19 percent expressed no opinion.[4]

Jacques Isorni pursued his campaign to mobilize opinion and the authorities on behalf of rehabilitation, pursued it up to the writing of this book. In 1972 the justice minister of the time, René Pleven, in rejecting an appeal for a rehearing, stressed the exceptional and sovereign nature of the High Court; through it, "the nation passed judgment." As a consequence, normal rules of procedure did not apply. "In this domain, the only rehearing can be that of History."[5] Nine years later, another justice minister declared Isorni's request admissible but made it clear that this did not mean that there were adequate grounds to undertake a rehearing; and indeed, in October 1981 Isorni's eighth request for a revision of the trial was rejected on the grounds that the evidence Isorni wished to use would not justify reopening the case.[6] A year later Isorni announced that he was pursuing his efforts; his "new evidence" this time concerned a letter from King George VI to Pétain in 1940 which, if it had not been destroyed, "would have saved Pétain at the time of his trial," and a comment favorable to Pétain allegedly made by de Gaulle.[7] In still another request in early 1983, Isorni produced as the new evidence testimony alleging that Pétain had helped pass secret information on the French navy from Vichy to the United States.[8]

Eugénie Pétain died in Paris on January 30, 1962. Following the death of her husband, she had returned to her Square de Latour-Maubourg apartment; the marshal's connecting apartment on the same floor had been confiscated and turned over to a leading Free French politician. In 1954, as heir to her husband, she drew up a will to confirm the designation of her son Pierre de Hérain as her own heir; at the same time she declared that if she died before the revision of the Pétain trial and the transfer of her husband's remains to Douaumont, lawyers Isorni and Lemaire were authorized to act for her, in accord with her son—a statement that was designed to ward off claims by other branches of the family to interpret Pétain's last wishes.[9]

The Ermitage at Villeneuve-Loubet, as the property of Philippe Pétain, had also been confiscated after his trial. The house was torn down, the grounds becoming a center of psychotherapeutic treatment run by the social-security administration. In September 1965, the Morcourt family, including Pétain's great-niece Yvonne (née Pomart) and her husband Robert, went to court to contest the validity of Pétain's will of July 21, 1945, which had made Eugénie his heir, on the grounds that the will of a prisoner sentenced to death is invalid; the Morcourts said the purpose of the suit was to prevent Pierre de Hérain from disposing of the marshal's remains and allowing burial in Verdun—when only Douaumont was acceptable.[10] After nearly nine years of litigation, the de Hérains, represented by Isorni, won the case, but before they had succeeded in validating the 1945 will on appeal, Pierre de Hérain had died of cancer.[11]

Pierre's heir was his wife Odette. She in turn named as her heir her son by her previous marriage; as it happened her first husband, like herself, had been Jewish, and so, of course, was their son. There is really no inheritance to speak of, since the state dispossessed convict Philippe Pétain. Had there been a legacy, it would have gone—irony? justice?—to French Jews.[12]

NOTES

Abbreviations:
AN   Archives Nationales (Paris)
DGF   *Documents on German Foreign Policy (1918–1945), Series D*
FRUS   *Foreign Relations of the United States*
PMP   *Le Procès du Maréchal Pétain* (2 vol.), Paris, Albin Michel, 1945
SH   Service Historique de l'Armée de Terre (Vincennes, France)

Chapter I. Young Philippe
1. P.-A. Wimet, "Le Maréchal Pétain et l'Artois," *Bulletin de la Société Académique des Antiquaires de la Morinie* (Saint-Omer) June 1954; Louis-Dominique Girard, *Mazinghem, ou la Vie secrète de Philippe Pétain* (Besançon, 1971); Cf. Jean Ratel, *Notice historique sur le village de Cauchy-à-la-Tour* (Vendin-le-Vieil, 1938).
2. P.-A. Wimet, "Jean-Baptiste Pétain, Paysan d'Artois (1677–1747)," *Bulletin de la Société Académique de la Morinie* (Saint-Omer), June 1952; Girard, *op. cit.*
3. Girard, *op. cit.*
4. Wimet, "Le Maréchal Pétain et l'Artois," *op. cit.*

5. Girard, *op. cit.*

6. Certified copy in AN W-III 277.

7. From André Lavagne.

8. Wimet, "Le Maréchal Pétain et l'Artois," *op. cit.;* E.C., "Deux oncles du Maréchal Pétain," *Bulletin de la Société Académique de la Morinie* (Saint-Omer), December 1952.

9. Girard, *op. cit.;* E.C., "Deux oncles du Maréchal Pétain," *op. cit.*

10. *La Semaine religieuse du diocèse d'Arras,* July 26, 1895, quoted in Girard, *op. cit.*

11. E.C., "Deux oncles du Maréchal Pétain," *op. cit.;* Wimet, "Le Maréchal Pétain et l'Artois," *op. cit.*

12. For information on the Collège Saint-Bertin, the author is indebted to its director Roger Verslype. It was General Émile Laure in his *Pétain* (Paris, 1942) who felt that the school resembled a barracks; alongside it, he adds, there were a military hospital and a recruitment bureau.

13. Chanoine Alexandre Lehembre, "Le College Saint-Bertin," *Le Bertinien* (Saint-Omer), July 1929.

14. *L'Indépendant du Pas-de-Calais* (Saint-Omer), August 7, 1873.

15. From Roger Verslype, Collège Saint-Bertin.

16. Wimet, "Le Maréchal Pétain et l'Artois," *op. cit.;* Dr. Gustave Lancry, "Philippe Pétain au Collège Saint-Bertin, 1870–74," *L'Indépendant du Pas-de-Calais* (Saint-Omer), February 16, 1919.

17. From Roger Verslype.

18. As recalled by history teacher Émile Blin in Chanoine Georges Coolen, "Bibliographie—Le Maréchal Pétain," *Bulletin de la Société Académique de la Morinie* (Saint-Omer), September 1964.

19. AN W-III 277.

20. Wimet, "Le Maréchal Pétain et l'Artois," *op. cit.*

21. The only available account of Pétain's stay at Saint-Bertin by a fellow student contains this information, but it has been ignored: Lancry, *op. cit.*

22. Archives Nationales (where a search was made at the author's request); Collège Saint-Bertin.

23. J. B. Piobetta, *Le Baccalauréat* (Paris, 1937).

24. From Father J. de Metz, archivist, École de Sorèze.

25. Pierre Pradié fils, *Le Massacre des Dominicains d'Arcueil* (Paris, 1879).

26. From Father J. de Metz.

27. Laurent Lecuyer, *La Revanche par l'Education* (Paris, 1871).

28. R. P. Seryillanges, "Le Maréchal chez les Dominicains d'Arcueil," in *Paris au Maréchal* (Paris, 1942).

29. Laure, *op. cit.*

Chapter II. Career Soldier
1. Laure, *op. cit.*
2. Extract of register, SH.
3. Ministère de la Guerre, *Saint-Cyr et la Vie militaire* (Paris, 1929).
4. Eugène Titeux, *Saint-Cyr et l'École Spéciale Militaire en France* (Paris, 1898).
5. Wimet, "Le Maréchal Pétain et l'Artois," *op. cit.*
6. Girard, *op. cit.*
7. Pierre Bourget, *Un certain Philippe Pétain* (Tournai, Belgium, 1966); Guy Raissac, *Un Combat sans merci: L'Affaire Pétain-De Gaulle* (Paris, 1966).
8. Titeux, *op. cit.*
9. *Journal Officiel* (Paris) Sept. 13, 1878.
10. Michel Turpin and Albert Maloire, *Le 24e Bataillon de Chasseurs* (Paris, 1959).
11. Laure, *op. cit.* His reconstituted military record—the original was removed from the War Ministry by Pétain's staff in 1942 and never returned—shows that he ranked eleven out of fifty in the Firing School. Archives SH.
12. AN W-III 277.
13. Bourget, *op. cit.*
14. Joseph Simon, *Pétain, mon prisonnier* (Paris, 1978).
15. From Elisabeth Bourgois (née Salvy).
16. Wimet, "Le Maréchal Pétain et l'Artois," *op. cit.*
17. AN W-III 277.
18. Laure, *op. cit.*
19. Miles (Francis Marre), "Silhouettes de Guerre: le Général Pétain," *Le Correspondant* (Paris), October 10, 1917.
20. *Ibid.*
21. Quoted in Girard, *op. cit.*
22. Lieutenant Colonel Défontaine, *Historique de l'École Supérieure de Guerrex* (Paris, 1913).
23. J. R. Tournoux, *Pétain et de Gaulle* (Paris, 1964).
24. Laure, *op. cit.*
25. AN W-III 277.
26. Reports, École Supérieure de Guerre, Paris.
27. Georges Suarez, *Le Maréchal Pétain* (Paris, 1940). The quote is taken with slight modifications from Lt. Col. H.M., *La Vérité sur la Guerre (1914–1918)* (Paris, 1930).
28. Girard, *op. cit.*
29. Geo-Charles Véran, "Le Maréchal Pétain s'adresse à la population parisienne," *Le Petit Parisien* (Paris), June 4, 1943.

30. Marie-Antoinette Pardee, *Le Maréchal que j'ai connu* (Paris, 1952).
31. *La Semaine religieuse du diocèse d'Arras,* January 20, 1899, in Girard, *op. cit.*
32. AN W-III 277.
33. General Philippe Mathelin, quoted in Laure, *op. cit.*
34. From Mrs. Jacques Rueff, Paul Racine.
35. AN W-III 277.
36. *Ibid.;* Laure, *op. cit.*
37. Archives SH.
38. Laure, *op. cit.*
39. Georges Roux, *L'Affaire Dreyfus* (Paris, 1972).
40. Jacques Kayser, *L'Affaire Dreyfus* (Paris, 1946).
41. Janet Flanner, *Pétain, The Old Man of France* (New York, 1944).
42. Laure, *op. cit.*
43. Pierre Bourget, *Témoignages inédits sur le Maréchal Pétain* (Paris, 1960).
44. Laure, *op. cit.*
45. AN W-III 277.
46. Henri Amouroux, *Pétain avant Vichy* (Paris, 1967).
47. Laure, *op. cit.*
48. État des Services, Archives SH; Ministère de la Guerre, *Annuaire de l'armée française pour 1902* (Paris, 1902); Laure, *op. cit.*
49. Roger de Beauvoir, *Album-Annuaire de l'Armée française* (Paris, 1902).
50. Défontaine, *op. cit.*
51. General Pichot-Duclos, *Réflexions sur ma vie militaire* (Grenoble, 1947).
52. AN W-III 277; Laure, *op. cit.*
53. AN W-III 277.
54. Kayser, *op. cit.*
55. *Journal Officiel, Chambre des Députés* (Paris), October 28, 1904.
56. *Journal Officiel, Chambre des Députés* (Paris), November 4, 1904; Paul-Marie de La Gorce, *La République et son armée* (Paris, 1963).
57. Gen. André, *Cinq ans de ministère* (Paris, 1907). After having agreed to the use of Freemason sources, Percin himself had second thoughts and tried to convince André to put an end to the procedure, but without success. Dossier Percin, Archives SH.
58. For example, see J. Saintoyant, *Une oeuvre maçonnique en France aux XVIIIe et XIXe siècles* (Paris-Limoges, 1941).
59. *Les Documents Maçonniques* (Vichy), January 1944. A post-Vichy memoir by a retired general who had been a student of Pétain at the War College alleged that Pétain's card bore the single word: "Clerical." Pichot-Duclos, *op. cit.*
60. "Procès des Sociétés Secrètes," *Paris-Presse* (Paris) November 27, 1946, quoted in Dominique Rossignol, *Anti-Franc-Maçonnerie, Anti-Sociétés*

Secrètes, Iconographie de la France occupée (1940–1944), Thesis, Académie de Paris, École des Hautes Études en sciences sociales, 1980.

Chapter III. Before the War

1. Military record, AN W-III 277.
2. Laure, *op. cit.*
3. *Ibid.*
4. *Ibid.*
5. AN W-III 277.
6. Laure, *op. cit.*
7. Girard, *op. cit.*
8. Laure, *op. cit.*
9. Défontaine, *op. cit.;* course outline, courtesy of Cours d'histoire, École de Guerre (Paris).
10. Colonel Pétain, *Cours d'Infanterie* (Paris, 1911), courtesy, École de Guerre.
11. Jacques Isorni, *Philippe Pétain*, I (Paris, 1972).
12. Laure, *op. cit.*
13. Miles, *op. cit.*
14. Pichot-Duclos, *op. cit.*
15. AN AG-II 4.
16. Girard, *op. cit.*
17. Private correspondence, AN.
18. Bourget, *Témoignages inédits, op. cit.*
19. Amouroux, *op. cit.*
20. AN 523 Mi-l; cf. Isorni, *op. cit.*
21. AN 523 Mi-l.
22. AN 523 Mi-1.
23. Pétain papers, SH.
24. Laure, *op. cit.*
25. AN W-III 303.
26. Charles de Gaulle, *Mémoires de Guerre*, I, *L'Appel (1940–1942)* (Paris, 1954).
27. Tournoux, *op. cit.*
28. Jean Pouget, *Un certain Capitaine de Gaulle* (Paris, 1973).
29. Laure, *op. cit.;* AN W-III 277.
30. *Le Mémorial Artesien* (Saint-Omer), July 16–17, 1914.
31. Archives of Jacques Isorni.
32. Girard, *op. cit.*
33. Paul Reynaud, *La France a sauvé l'Europe*, I (Paris, 1947).
34. General Paul Azan, *Franchet d'Esperey* (Paris, 1949).
35. Leon Noël, *Un Chef: Le Général Guillaumat* (Paris, 1949).

Chapter IV. The Last Offensive

1. Laure, *op. cit.*
2. Log, courtesy of Carin Rueff.
3. Joseph Chot, *La Furie allemande dans l'Entre-Sambre-et-Meuse* (Charleroi, Belgium, 1919).
4. Laure, *op. cit.*
5. Log, courtesy of Carin Rueff.
6. *Ibid.*
7. Laure, *op. cit.*
8. *Ibid.*
9. *Ibid.*
10. Charles Mangin, *Lettres de guerre (1914–1918)* (Paris, 1950).
11. Laure, *op. cit.*
12. Maréchal Fayolle, *Cahiers secrets de la Grande Guerre* (Paris, 1964).
13. Général Serrigny, *Trente ans avec Pétain* (Paris, 1959). Serrigny's posthumous memoirs have been criticized as exaggerating his own influence on Pétain; Laure, *op. cit.*, says he is occasionally fanciful.
14. Laure, *op. cit.*
15. General Henri Mordacq, *Pourquoi Arras ne fut pas pris (1914)* (Paris, 1934).
16. Alfred Conquet, *Auprès du Maréchal Pétain* (Paris, 1970).
17. Mordacq, *op. cit.*
18. Fayolle, *op. cit.*
19. Major-General Sir Edward Spears, *Two Men Who Saved France: Pétain and de Gaulle* (London, 1966).
20. Laure, *op. cit.*
21. *Discours de réception de M. le Maréchal Pétain à l'Académie Française et Réponse de M. Paul Valéry* (Paris, 1931).
22. Serrigny, *op. cit.*
23. *Ibid.*
24. Fayolle, *op. cit.*
25. *Ibid.;* État des Services, SH.
26. Laure, *op. cit.*
27. Laure, *op. cit.*
28. Conquet, *op. cit.*
29. Fayolle, *op. cit.*
30. Laure, *op. cit.*
31. *Ibid.* Laure notes that Joffre drew the opposite conclusion, writing on August 23 that Arras showed that with powerful means and vigorous attacks in several regions at once, the rupture of enemy lines was possible.
32. Laure, *op. cit.*

33. *Ibid.*
34. *Ibid.*

Chapter V. Verdun

1. Raymond Poincaré, *Au Service de la France*, VIII, *Verdun 1916* (Paris, 1931); Philippe Pétain, *La Bataille de Verdun* (Paris, 1930).
2. Joffre, *Mémoires du Maréchal Joffre (1910–1917)*, II (Paris, 1932).
3. Abel Ferry, *Les Carnets secrets (1914–1918)* (Paris, 1957). Pétain himself later said that Joffre had merely described the situation and told him to report to Castelnau for instructions. Pétain, *La Bataille de Verdun, op. cit.*
4. Laure, *op. cit.*
5. Serrigny, *op. cit.*
6. Laure, *op. cit.*
7. Serrigny, *op. cit.* By the time Pétain moved on to Bar-le-Duc in early May, 40 divisions had served at Verdun; by September, 78 divisions. Laure, *op. cit.* (The French army disposed of 116 infantry divisions in 1916.)
8. Serrigny, *op. cit.*
9. Laure, *op. cit.;* Serrigny, *op. cit.*
10. Serrigny, *op. cit.*
11. *Ibid.*
12. Maurice Barrès, *Chronique de la Grande Guerre*, VIII (Paris, 1935).
13. Girard, *op. cit.*
14. *Ibid.*
15. Serrigny, *op. cit.*
16. Poincaré, *op. cit.*
17. Henry Bordeaux, *Histoire d'une vie*, V, *Douleur et gloire de Verdun* (Paris, 1959).
18. Poincaré, *op. cit.*
19. *Ibid.*
20. Alistair Horne, *The Price of Glory: Verdun 1916* (London, 1962).
21. Joffre, *op. cit.*
22. Jérôme et Jean Tharaud, "Dernière Bataille," in *Philippe Pétain, Maréchal de France* (Paris, 1951).
23. Jean de Pierrefeu, *G.Q.G. Secteur 1*, II (Paris, 1920).
24. Dr. Lucien-Graux, *Les Fausses Nouvelles de la Grande Guerre*, II (Paris, 1918).
25. Fayolle, *op. cit.*
26. Serrigny, *op. cit.*
27. AN 523 Mi-l.
28. AN 523 Mi-l; Serrigny, *op. cit.*

29. Serrigny, *op. cit.*
30. Mangin, *op. cit.*
31. Paul Painlevé, *Comment j'ai nommé Foch et Pétain* (Paris, 1923).
32. Laure, *op. cit.*

Chapter VI. The General in Chief

1. Painlevé, *op. cit.*
2. Raymond Poincaré, *Au Service de la France*, IX, *L'Année terrible 1917* (Paris, 1932).
3. Fayolle, *op. cit.*
4. Laure, *op. cit.*
5. Alexandre Ribot, *Journal et correspondances inédites (1914–1922)* (Paris, 1936).
6. Serrigny, *op. cit.*
7. Poincaré, IX, *op. cit.*
8. Serrigny, *op. cit.*
9. Ribot, *op. cit.*
10. *Ibid.*
11. *Ibid.;* Painlevé, *op. cit.*
12. Serrigny, *op. cit.;* Laure, *op. cit.*
13. *Le Matin* (Paris), July 8, 1917.
14. Laure, *op. cit.*
15. Maréchal Pétain, *Une crise morale de la nation française en guerre (16 avril–23 octobre 1917)* (Paris, 1966). In English: "A Crisis of Morale in the French Nation at War," in Spears, *op. cit.*
16. Guy Pedroncini, *Les mutineries de 1917* (Paris, 1967); Guy Pedroncini, *1917: les mutineries de l'Armée française* (Paris, 1968). Cf. Guy Pedroncini, *Pétain Général en chef (1917–1918)* (Paris, 1974).
17. Serrigny, *op. cit.*
18. Pétain, *Une crise morale, op. cit.*
19. Laure, *op. cit.*
20. *Ibid.* Pedroncini, *Pétain Général en chef, op. cit.*, says that this represents one execution for ten death sentences, or the execution of one mutineer in eight hundred. The fact that the first executions took place on June 10 when the outbreaks were on the decline leads Pedroncini to doubt that they were responsible for ending the crisis. Serrigny, *op. cit.*, says that Pétain's policy of prosecution and execution caused conflict with Painlevé, who objected to the short-circuiting of judicial review and presidential pardon.
21. August 23, 1917 letter in Pétain, *Une crise morale, op. cit.*
22. *Ibid.*
23. Spears, *op. cit.*

24. Douglas Haig, *The Private Papers of Douglas Haig (1914–1919)* (London, 1952).

25. General John J. Pershing, *My Experiences in the World War,* I (New York, 1931).

26. Serrigny, *op. cit.*

27. Pierrefeu, *op. cit.*

28. Serrigny, *op. cit.*

29. For this and other details on Pétain's command: Pedroncini, *Pétain Général en Chef, op. cit.,* containing the essentials of Pedroncini's thesis, *Le Haut Commandement français et la conduite de la guerre (mai 1917–novembre 1918),* Université de Paris I, 1917.

30. Pedroncini, *Pétain Général en chef, op. cit.*

31. *Ibid.*

32. Laure, *op. cit.*

33. Pedroncini, Pétain *Général en chef, op. cit.*

34. *Ibid.*

35. *Ibid.*

Chapter VII. Waiting for the Americans

1. Serrigny, *op. cit.*

2. Haig, *op. cit.*

3. Pershing, I, *op. cit.*

4. Serrigny, *op. cit.*

5. Serrigny papers, SH archives.

6. [John J. Pershing,] *Final Report of Gen. John J. Pershing, Commander-in-Chief, American Expeditionary Forces* (Washington, D.C., 1919).

7. Pershing, *My Experiences,* I, *op. cit.*

8. Poincaré, IX, *op. cit.*

9. *Ibid.*

10. Pershing, *My Experiences,* I, *op. cit.*

11. *Ibid.;* Pershing, *Final Report, op. cit.;* Poincaré, IX, *op. cit.*

12. Pershing, *My Experiences,* I, *op. cit.*

13. John Terraine, *Douglas Haig, The Educated Soldier* (London, 1963).

14. Poincaré, IX, *op. cit.;* Gen.*** [Tournès], *La Crise du Commandement unique* (Paris, 1931).

15. Serrigny, *op. cit.*

16. AN 523 Mi-l.

17. AN AG-II 1.

18. Archives of Jacques Isorni.

19. *Ibid.*

20. Serrigny, *op. cit.*

21. Pedroncini, *Pétain Général en chef, op. cit.*

22. *Ibid.*
23. Poincaré, IX, *op. cit.*
24. Pedroncini, *Pétain Général en chef, op. cit.*
25. General Mordacq, *Le Ministère Clemenceau: Journal d'un témoin,* I (Paris, 1930).
26. Laure, *op. cit.*
27. Pedroncini, *Pétain Général en chef, op. cit.*
28. Pershing, *My Experiences,* I, *op. cit.*
29. Laure, *op. cit.*
30. Pershing, *My Experiences,* I, *op. cit.*
31. Haig, *op. cit.;* [Tournès], *La Crise, op. cit.*
32. Ferry, *op. cit.*
33. Poincaré, *Au Service de la France,* X, *Victoire et Armistice 1918* (Paris, 1933).
34. Laure, *op. cit.;* Pedroncini, *Pétain Général en chef, op. cit.*
35. Terraine, *op. cit.*
36. Laure, *op. cit.;* Pedroncini, *Pétain Général en chef, op. cit.*
37. Haig, *op. cit.* For Pétain's summary of the situation: *Discours de réception, op. cit.*
38. Poincaré, X, *op. cit.*
39. Memorandum by Lord Milner for the British cabinet, in Georges Clemenceau, *Grandeurs et misères d'une victoire* (Paris, 1930); Maréchal Foch, *Mémoires pour servir à l'histoire de la guerre de 1914–1918,* I (Paris, 1931).
40. Mordacq, *Le Ministère Clemenceau,* I, *op. cit.;* Clemenceau, *op. cit.*
41. Poincaré, X, *op. cit.*
42. Clemenceau, *op. cit.*
43. *Ibid.*
44. Haig, *op. cit.*

Chapter VIII. Victory

1. [Tournès], *La Crise, op. cit.*
2. *Ibid.*
3. Fayolle, *op. cit.*
4. Henry Bordeaux, *Histoire d'une vie,* VII, *La Victoire et la traité de Versailles* (Paris, 1960).
5. Poincaré, X, *op. cit.*
6. Pedroncini, *Pétain Général en chef, op. cit.*
7. Pierrefeu, II, *op. cit.*
8. Laure, *op. cit.*
9. Fayolle, *op. cit.*
10. Bordeaux, VII, *op. cit.*

11. Laure, *op. cit.;* Pedroncini, *Pétain Général en chef, op. cit.*
12. *Journal Officiel, Chambre des Députés,* June 5, 1918.
13. General Mordacq, *Le Ministère Clemenceau: Journal d'un témoin,* II (Paris, 1930); Clemenceau, *op. cit.*
14. Pedroncini, *Pétain Général en chef, op. cit.*
15. Poincaré, X, *op. cit.*
16. Fayolle, *op. cit.*
17. Poincaré, X, *op. cit.*
18. Louis Loucheur, *Carnets secrets (1908–1932)* (Brussels, 1962).
19. Amouroux, *op. cit.*
20. Pedroncini, *Pétain Général en chef, op. cit.*
21. Mordacq, *Le Ministère Clemenceau,* II, *op. cit.*
22. Maxime Weygand, *Foch* (Paris, 1947).
23. *Ibid.*
24. *Ibid.*
25. General J.-H. Jauneaud, *J'accuse le Maréchal Pétain . . .* (Paris, 1977).
26. Weygand, *op. cit.*
27. Foch, II, *op. cit.*
28. Pierrefeu, II, *op. cit.*
29. Fayolle, *op. cit.*
30. Pershing, *Final Report, op. cit.;* Pedroncini, *Pétain Général en chef, op. cit.*
31. Mordacq, *Le Ministère Clemenceau,* II, *op. cit.*
32. Bordeaux, *Histoire d'une vie,* VII, *op. cit.*
33. Laure, *op. cit.*
34. Pierrefeu, II, *op. cit.*
35. Mordacq, *Le Ministère Clemenceau,* II, *op. cit.*
36. *Ibid.*
37. *Ibid.*
38. Pierre Renouvin, *L'Armistice de Rethondes* (Paris, 1968).
39. Jules Sauerwein, *30 ans à la une* (Paris, 1962).
40. Diary of Captain Molinier, archives of Jacques Isorni.
41. Pedroncini points out that Pétain was already on record advocating that the war be terminated on German territory. Pedroncini, *Pétain Général en chef, op. cit.*
42. *Discours de récéption, op. cit.*
43. Pardee, *op. cit.*
44. Laure, *op. cit.;* Pierrefeu, II, *op. cit.* (for a photographic reproduction of the victory statement).
45. AN 523 Mi-l; Amouroux, *op. cit.*
46. Colonel Herbillon, *Souvenirs d'un officier de liaison pendant la guerre mondiale,* II, *Du général en chef au gouvernement* (Paris, 1930).

47. AN 523 Mi-l.
48. General Mordacq, *Le Ministère Clemenceau, Journal d'un témoin,* III (Paris, 1931).
49. *L'Illustration* (Paris) November 30, 1918.
50. AN 523 Mi-l.
51. There is an oft-told story that Foch whispered during the ceremony: "To think that we got him there by kicks in the seat of his pants." Colonel Roger Gasser, Weygand's aide de camp, told the author that he does not believe that Foch or any of his entourage made the remark.
52. Bordeaux, *Histoire d'une vie,* VII, *op. cit.*

Chapter IX. Commander in Peacetime

1. *L'Illustration* (Paris) December 18, 1920.
2. *L'Indépendant du Pas-de-Calais* (Saint-Omer), October 1, 1919.
3. AN W-III 277. Or nearly 2.7 million of today's francs.
4. Jacques Nobécourt, *Une Histoire politique de l'armée,* I, *De Pétain à Pétain (1919–1942)* (Paris, 1967).
5. *Ibid.*
6. Letter from Germaine Lubin in Girard, *op. cit.*
7. AN 523 Mi-2.
8. AN 523 Mi-2.
9. Laure, *op. cit.*
10. *Ibid.*
11. *Ibid.*
12. Minutes, Conseil Supérieure de la Guerre, archives SH.
13. Laure, *op. cit.;* General Paul-Émile Tournoux, *Haut Commandement, Gouvernement et Défense des Frontières du Nord et de l'Est (1919–1939)* (Paris, 1960).
14. Résumé succinct des séances du Conseil Supérieure de la Guerre (1920–1928), archives SH. Session of December 15, 1926.
15. Laure, *op. cit.*
16. Girard, *op. cit.*
17. AN 523 Mi-2; Amouroux, *op. cit.*
18. AN 523 Mi-2; Isorni, *Philippe Pétain,* I, *op. cit.*
19. AN 523 Mi-2.
20. Archives of Jacques Isorni.
21. *Ibid.*
22. Girard, *op. cit.*
23. AN AG-II 1.
24. AN AG-II 2.
25. AN W-III 277.

26. Quoted in Bourget, *Un certain Philippe Pétain, op. cit.*
27. Deed, courtesy of Mrs. Odette de Hérain. Pétain added parcels of land in 1921, 1923, 1924, 1931, 1932, and 1941, on this last date paying 250,000 francs, or about 210,000 of today's francs, for two parcels. AN W-III 278.
28. AN AG-II 1.
29. Report by Paul Caujolle, June 16, 1945, AN W-III 277.
30. Girard, *op. cit.*
31. *Ibid.*
32. AN 523 Mi-3.
33. Girard, *op. cit.*
34. AN W-III 278.
35. Paul Reynaud, *La France a sauvé l'Europe,* II (Paris, 1947).
36. *L'Illustration* (Paris), February 11, March 10, May 5, June 2, 1928, February 2, 1929.
37. In a postcard from London on June 17, 1922, to the daughter of Jacqueline de Castex: "Banquet tonight . . . I've got to give them Verdun again." Courtesy of Renée de Séguin (née Castex).
38. Wladimir d'Ormesson, *Présence du Général de Gaulle* (Paris, 1971).
39. AN AG-II 1; Laure, *op. cit.*
40. Simon, *op. cit.*
41. Isorni, *Philippe Pétain,* I, *op. cit.*
42. From Jacques Isorni.
43. From Renée de Séguin.
44. AN AG-II 3.
45. Archives of Jacques Isorni.
46. From Renée de Séguin.

Chapter X. War in the Rif

1. AN, Painlevé papers, 313 AP 247.
2. *Ibid.*
3. Pierre Sement, "Un maréchal républicain: Philippe Pétain," *Histoire de notre temps* (Paris), Spring 1967. Sement previously published this anecdote in 1959 and 1961; there seems to be no corroborating evidence.
4. Letter to Eugénie Pétain, AN 523 Mi-3. On Lyautey's achievement as a "poem," see Capitaine G. Loustaunau-Lacau and Capitaine P. Montjean, *Au Maroc Français en 1925: Le Rétablissement de la situation militaire* (Paris, 1928).
5. Georges Loustaunau-Lacau, *Mémoires d'un Français rebelle* (Paris, 1948).
6. Laure, *op. cit.*
7. Georges Bonnet, *Vingt ans de vie politique (1918–1938)* (Paris, 1969).

8. *L'Illustration* (Paris), July 25, 1925.
9. AN 523 Mi-3.
10. Bonnet, *op. cit.*
11. Laure, *op. cit.*
12. "Observations," July 22, 1925. Archives SH 2 N 19.
13. AN 523 Mi-3.
14. Transcription of coded telegram, AN Painlevé papers, 313 AP 244.
15. Émile Laure, *La Victoire franco-espagnole dans le Rif* (Paris, 1927).
16. Laure, *Pétain, op. cit.*
17. *Ibid.*
18. AN AG-II 3.
19. August 26, 1925 letter to Painlevé, AN AG-II 3.
20. Laure, *Pétain, op. cit.*
21. André Le Révérend, *Un Lyautey inconnu: Correspondance et journal inédits (1874–1934)* (Paris, 1980).
22. General Catroux, *Lyautey le Marocain* (Paris, 1952).
23. Letter from General Bernard, November 12, 1925, in Fournier-Foch papers, archives SH.
24. Laure, *La Victoire franco-espagnole, op. cit.*
25. Laure, *Pétain, op. cit.*
26. Girard, *op. cit.*
27. Laure, *Pétain, op. cit.; L'Illustration* (Paris), February 13, 1926.
28. Laure, *Pétain, op. cit.*
29. *Ibid.*
30. Le Révérend, *op. cit.*

Chapter XI. Among Soldiers

1. Samples in AN AG-II 4.
2. AN AG-II 9.
3. Military records, archives SH; General [Émile] Laure, "Notes militaires et politiques (Avril 1939–Juillet 1948)," unpublished manuscript; from General René Laure.
4. Letters to Pétain to Laure, December 4, 1928, February 27, 1929, in archives of Jacques Isorni; *L'Illustration* (Paris), November 24, December 8, December 15, 1928.
5. Tournoux, *Pétain et de Gaulle, op. cit.*
6. Raissac, *op. cit.*
7. *Ibid.*
8. *Paris-Match* (Paris), January 29, 1972. See Raissac, *op. cit.;* Charles de Gaulle, *Lettres, Notes et Carnets (1919–Juin 1940)* (Paris, 1980).
9. Isorni, *Philippe Pétain, I, op. cit.;* Pouget, *op. cit.* De Gaulle's draft chapter "The French of 1914" is reproduced with Pétain's comments

in Philippe Pétain, *Actes et Ecrits* (Paris, 1974); Isorni, *Philippe Pétain,* I, *op. cit.* reproduces an outline by Laure and some of de Gaulle's work corrected by Pétain.

10. Charles de Gaulle, *Lettres, Notes et Carnets (Juin 1940–Juillet 1941)* (Paris, 1981).
11. Pouget, *op. cit.*
12. De Gaulle, *Lettres (1919–Juin 1940), op. cit.*
13. *Ibid.*
14. *Paris-Match* (Paris), January 29, 1972.
15. Tournoux, *Pétain et de Gaulle, op. cit.*
16. Pétain, *Actes et Ecrits, op. cit.*
17. Laure, *Pétain, op. cit.*
18. Reynaud, *La France a sauvé l'Europe,* I, *op. cit.*
19. Tournoux, *Haut Commandement, op. cit.*
20. Archives SH.
21. Jean Wilmès, "Déclarations du maréchal Pétain à *Candide,*" in *Candide* (Paris), March 8, 1939.
22. Laure, *Pétain, op. cit.* Vauthier's book was *Le Danger aérien et l'avenir du Pays.*
23. Minutes of Supreme Council of National Defense, July 30, 1931, archives SH.
24. Letter from Pétain to minister of national defense, April 18, 1932, archives SH.
25. Reynaud, *La France a sauvé l'Europe,* I, *op. cit.*
26. Laure, *Pétain, op. cit.*
27. Note, February 25, 1932, archives SH.
28. Minutes, archives SH.
29. October 12, 1932, archives SH.
30. Preface by Pétain, Major General E. B. Ashmore, *Défense Antiaérienne* (Paris, 1933).
31. Maurice Vaisse, *Sécurité d'abord* (Paris, 1981).
32. Michel Soulié, *La Vie politique d'Edouard Herriot* (Paris, 1962).
33. October 24, 1932, note, Pétain papers, archives SH.
34. February 24, 1933, note, archives SH.
35. La Gorce, II, *op. cit.*

Chapter XII. The Dignitary

1. Letter of May 14, 1929, archives of Jacques Isorni.
2. Maurice Martin du Gard, *La Chronique de Vichy (1940–1944)* (Paris, 1975).
3. Jérôme Carcopino, *Souvenirs de sept ans (1937–1944)* (Paris, 1953).
4. Louis Gillet, "Récéption de M. le Maréchal Pétain à l'Académie

Française," *Revue des Deux Mondes* (Paris), February 1, 1931.

5. Léon Blum, "La Guerre à l'Académie," *Le Populaire* (Paris), January 25, 1931.

6. Laure, *Pétain, op. cit.*

7. Pétain papers, archives SH.

8. *New York Times* (New York), August 26, 1931.

9. *New York Times* (New York), August 30, 1931.

10. *L'Illustration* (Paris), October 31, 1931.

11. *New York Times*, October 16, 1931.

12. *New York Times*, October 17, 1931.

13. *New York Times*, October 18, 1931.

14. René de Chambrun, *Général comte de Chambrun sorti du rang* (Paris, 1980).

15. *New York Times*, October 19 and 21, 1931.

16. *New York Times*, October 24 and 25, 1931; Pétain, *Actes et Ecrits, op. cit.*

17. *New York Times*, October 26, 1931.

18. *New York Times*, October 27, 1931.

19. *New York Times*, October 29, 1931.

20. Chambrun, *op. cit.*

21. Flanner, *op. cit.*

22. *New York Times*, November 6, 1931.

23. AN AG-II 4.

24. René Remond, *La Droite en France* (Paris, 1963); Richard F. Kuisel, *Ernest Mercier, French Technocrat* (Berkeley and Los Angeles, 1967).

25. *Les Cahiers du Redressement Français* (Paris), 1st series, no. 2, 1927; 2nd series, no. 9, 1933.

26. *Les Cahiers du Redressement Français*, 2nd series, *Politique Extérieure: Rapports des Commissions et Journées d'Etudes*, 1932.

27. Quoted in Philippe Machefer, *Ligues et fascismes en France (1919–1939)* (Paris, 1974).

28. *Les Cahiers du Redressement Français*, 2nd series, *Politique Extérieure, op. cit.*

29. Minutes, January 22, 1934 session. Grandclément papers, archives SH.

30. Letter of November 26, 1935 to André Grandclément, AN AG-II 5.

31. Kuisel, *op. cit.*

32. August 23, 1945, report of Police Judiciaire, AN W-III 46.

33. Kuisel, *op. cit.*

34. Alibert memorandums, October 1, 1944, and September 8, 1952, courtesy of Henri Amouroux.

35. Statement to High Court, AN W-III 47.

36. Pétain and Brécard statements, AN W-III 46.

Chapter XIII. The Minister

1. Tournoux, *Pétain et de Gaulle, op. cit.*

2. From Mrs. Bernard Ménétrel; Dr. Louis Ménétrel, *Histoire, Theories, Technique, Application Clinique de la Méthode Aérothermique* (Paris, 1904); "Dr. Louis Ménétrel," in *La Presse Médicale* (Paris, March 25, 1936).

3. From Mrs. Bernard Ménétrel. From Bernard Ménétrel's diary, December 16, 1934: "I give [Pétain] a bleeding because he asks for it, saying it always makes him feel better." Courtesy of Mrs. Ménétrel. In a letter to his wife Pétain speaks of being treated for a cough and cold by Bernard Ménétrel with "blue rays." AN 523 Mi-3.

4. 1934 and 1936 diaries of Bernard Ménétrel, courtesy of Mrs. Ménétrel.

5. Simon, *op. cit.*

6. Caujolle report, *op. cit.;* April 25, 1945, report on apartment, AN W-III 277.

7. Conquet, *op. cit.*

8. AN 523 Mi-3.

9. Photographs in AN AG-II 4. See also Pardee, *op. cit.*

10. For example, letter to Pétain, October 22, 1938, AN W-III 277.

11. AN 523 Mi-3.

12. AN AG-II 1.

13. Girard, *op. cit.*

14. Laure, *Pétain, op. cit.*

15. Letter from Mrs. Gaston Doumergue to Jacques Isorni, October 1, 1952, quoted in Isorni, *Philippe Pétain, op. cit.*

16. *Le Temps* (Paris), February 11, 1934.

17. Letter to Patrick Heidsieck, February 11, 1934, in Le Révérend, *op. cit.*

18. *Le Populaire* (Paris), February 10, 1934.

19. Laure, *Pétain, op. cit.*

20. Nobécourt, I, *op. cit.;* P.-E. Tournoux, *op. cit.;* testimony of General Weygand, March 31, 1949, in *Rapport fait au nom de la Commission chargée d'enquêter sur les événements survenus en France de 1933 à 1945,* Appendices, VI (Paris, 1949).

21. Laure, *Pétain, op. cit.;* Commission de l'Armée (Sénat), session of March 7, 1934, in AN W-II 3.

22. Commission de l'Armée, March 7, 1934.

23. Conquet, *op. cit.*

24. Charles de Gaulle, *Vers l'Armée de métier* (Paris, 1934).

25. Tournoux, *Pétain et de Gaulle, op. cit.*
26. Archives SH, quoted in Lieutenant Colonel Henry Dutailly, *Les Problèmes de l'armée de terre française (1935–1939)* (Paris, 1980).
27. Conquet, *op. cit.*
28. March 26, 1934, archives SH 5 N 577.
29. Laure, *Pétain, op. cit.*
30. Conquet, *op. cit.*
31. Colonel P. Vauthier, *La Doctrine de guerre du Général Douhet* (Paris, 1935).
32. Minutes, July 3, 1934, archives of Assemblée Nationale.

Chapter XIV. Politics All the Same
1. Laure, *Pétain, op. cit.*
2. *Le Populaire* (Paris), October 13, 1934.
3. *L'Illustration* (Paris), October 27, 1934.
4. Le Progrès (Lyons), December 3, 1934.
5. Fernand de Brinon, *Mémoires* (Paris, 1949).
6. Pétain, *Actes et Ecrits, op. cit.*
7. *Le Populaire* (Paris), October 30, 1934. This paper added that it found it hard to take the report seriously.
8. Henry Lémery, *D'une république à l'autre* (Paris, 1964).
9. Amouroux, *op. cit.;* Isorni, *Philippe Pétain,* I, *op. cit.*
10. *Le Populaire* (Paris), November 9, 1934.
11. General Gamelin, *Servir,* II, *Le Prologue du drame (1930–Août 1939)* (Paris, 1946).
12. Testimony of Daladier, PMP; Pierre Cot, *Le Procès de la Républicque,* II (New York, 1944).
13. *Le Petit Journal* (Paris), January 10, 1935.
14. *Le Petit Journal,* January 11, 1935.
15. *Ibid.* (interview by Philippe Boegner).
16. AN W-III 278. Cf. Gustave Hervé, *C'est Pétain qu'il nous faut!* (Paris, 1935).
17. *Vu* (Paris) Hors série. November 30, 1935.
18. *Le Figaro* (Paris), March 16, 1936: Wladimir d'Ormesson, *Présence du Général de Gaulle* (Paris, 1971).
19. Diary and memorandum of June 20, 1936, courtesy of Mrs. B. Ménétrel.
20. Statement by François Valentin, in Raymond Tournoux, *Pétain et la France* (Paris, 1980).
21. DGF, III 1951.
22. Hubert Cole, *Laval* (London, 1963).
23. Alfred Mallet, *Pierre Laval,* I (Paris, 1954); Cole, *op. cit.* René de Chambrun was in regular contact with Pétain from 1935 to the be-

ginning of the war but denied serving as intermediary between him and Laval: Geoffrey Warner, *Pierre Laval and the Eclipse of France* (London, 1968).

Chapter XV. Friends
1. Laure, *Pétain, op. cit.*
2. Conquet, *op. cit.*
3. *Le Temps* (Paris), June 1 and 2, 1935.
4. *L'Action Française* (Paris), June 2, 1935.
5. *Journal Officiel, Chambre des Députés,* June 5, 1935.
6. Lounstaunau-Lacau, *Mémoires, op. cit.*
7. *Le Journal* (Paris), April 30, 1936. Conquet says it was he who wrote the "interview": Conquet, *op. cit.*
8. Paul Creyssel, *La Rocque contre Tardieu* (Paris, 1938); *L'Action Française* (Paris), May 1, 1936.
9. Parti Social Français, *Une Mystique, un programme* (Paris, n.d.).
10. Conquet, *op. cit.*
11. Aide-mémoire of Loustaunau-Lacau, May 1945, High Court, AN W-III 278.

Chapter XVI. The Next War
1. Minutes, archives SH 2 N 19.
2. Minutes, January 23, 1935, archives SH.
3. Cot, II, *op. cit.*
4. Paris, 1939.
5. November–December correspondence, archives of Jacques Isorni.
6. Testimony of Gamelin, December 16, 1947, *Rapport . . . sur les événements survenus, op. cit.,* appendices, II.
7. Marcel Croze, *Tableaux démographiques et sociaux* (Paris, 1976).
8. Tax declaration for 1937 income: AN AG-II 4.
9. Caujolle report, *op. cit.;* memorandum of Finance Ministry, May 4, 1945, AN W-III 277.
10. AN 523 Mi-3.
11. Loustaunau-Lacau, *Mémoires, op. cit.*

Chapter XVII. Munich
1. Lémery, *op. cit.*
2. Tournoux, *Pétain et la France, op. cit.*
3. Pardee, *op. cit.*
4. Girard, *op. cit.*
5. AN 523 Mi-3.
6. Tournoux, *Pétain et de Gaulle, op. cit.*
7. De Gaulle, *Lettres (1919–Juin 1940), op. cit*

8. *Paris-Match* (Paris), January 29, 1972.
9. De Gaulle, *Lettres (1919–Juin 1940), op. cit.*
10. *Ibid.*
11. Letter of October 6, 1938, in Tournoux, *Pétain et de Gaulle, op. cit.*
12. De Gaulle, *Lettres (1919–Juin 1940), op cit.*
13. For example, Pouget, *op. cit.;* Conquet, *op. cit.*
14. Charles de Gaulle, *La France et son armée* (Paris, 1938).
15. Pétain, *Actes et Ecrits, op. cit.*
16. *Ibid.*
17. Pardee, *op. cit.*
18. Statement by Bonnet in Bourget, *Un certain Philippe Pétain, op. cit.*
19. Georges Bonnet, *Dans la tourmente (1938–1948)* (Paris, 1971).
20. *L'Excelsior* (Paris), March 3, 1939.
21. *Candide* (Paris), March 8, 1939.
22. *Le Populaire* (Paris), March 3, 1939.
23. *L'Humanité* (Paris), March 24, 1939.
24. AN AG-II 11. See testimony of General Vauthier, August 1, 1945, PMP.
25. Jacques Isorni, *Le Condamné de la Citadelle* (Paris, 1982); memorandum of February 14, 1939, archives of Jacques Isorni.
26. Laure, *Pétain, op. cit.;* Bourget, *Témoignages inédits, op. cit.*
27. AN W-III 279. The previous year Pétain declared 206,000 francs as total income. AN AG-II 4.
28. AN 523 Mi-3

Chapter XVIII. Spain

1. March 17, 1939, Pétain report, archives of Edouard Daladier, Fondation Nationale des Sciences Politiques (Paris); AN W-III 279.
2. March 28, 1939. AN W-III 279.
3. Testimony of Armand Gazel, July 26, 1945, PMP.
4. Simon, *op. cit.*
5. Bourget, *Témoignages inédits, op. cit.*
6. AN W-III 279: archives of Edouard Daladier, Fondation Nationale des Sciences Politiques.
7. Pétain to Bonnet, April 22, 1939. *Documents diplomatiques français*, 2e série (1936–1939), Paris, 1981.
8. AN 523 Mi-3; Isorni, *Philippe Pétain*, I, *op. cit.*
9. Lémery, *op. cit.*
10. Testimony of Gazel, PMP.
11. Elie J. Bois, *Le Malheur de la France* (London, 1941).
12. Laure, *Pétain, op. cit.*

13. Jules Jeanneney, *Journal politique (Septembre 1939–Juillet 1942)* (Paris, 1972).
14. *Ibid.;* Bois, *op. cit.*
15. AN W-III 279.
16. Tournoux, *Pétain et de Gaulle, op. cit.*
17. AN W-III 279.
18. Testimony of Daladier, July 24, 1945, PMP.

Chapter XIX. May 1940
1. Archives of Édouard Daladier, Fondation Nationale des Sciences Politiques.
2. Laure, *Pétain, op. cit.*
3. *Le Temps* (Paris), January 2–3, 1940.
4. AN W-III 279.
5. Louis Gillet, "Février 1916–Février 1940," in *Paris-Soir* (Paris), February 17, 1940.
6. Pardee, *op. cit.*
7. March, 12, 1940. Courtesy of Mrs. B. Ménétrel.
8. AN W-III 279.
9. Henri Amouroux, *Le Peuple de désastre* (Paris, 1976).
10. AN AG-II 3.
11. AN 523 Mi-3.
12. AN W-III 287.
13. Agenda 1940 of Commandant Léon Bonhomme, AN W-III 279.
14. Dominique Leca, *La Rupture de 1940* (Paris, 1978).
15. Henri Béraud, "L'Amiral m'a dit," in *Gringoire* (Marseille), May 30, 1941.
16. Interview with Franco in *Le Figaro* (Paris), June 12, 1958, quoted in Isorni, *Philippe Pétain*, I, *op. cit.*
17. Agenda 1940 of Commandant Bonhomme, *op. cit.;* Laure, *Pétain, op. cit.*
18. Leca, *op. cit.*
19. *Ibid.*
20. Jacques Benoist-Méchin, *Soixante jours qui ébranlèrent l'occident (10 mai–10 juillet 1940)*, I (Paris, 1956).
21. Reynaud, *La France a sauvé l'Europe*, II, *op. cit.*
22. *L'Action Française* (Paris), May 19, 1940.
23. Paul Baudouin, *Neuf mois au gouvernement* (Paris, 1948).
24. *Ibid.*
25. Anatole de Monzie, *Ci-devant* (Paris, 1941).
26. Agenda 1940 of Commandant Bonhomme, *op. cit.;* May 22, 1940, letter to Eugénie Pétain, AN 523 Mi-3.

27. From Mrs. B. Ménétrel.
28. AN AG-II 3.
29. Agenda 1940 of Commandant Bonhomme, *op. cit.*
30. Memorandum of Alibert to High Court, 1947, courtesy of H. Amouroux.
31. Statement by Georges Wormser, June 12, 1945, AN W-III 278.
32. Reynaud, *La France a sauvé l'Europe,* II, *op. cit.*
33. Jeanneney, *op. cit.* Daladier left the cabinet on June 6.
34. *I Documenti Diplomatici Italiani, Nona Serie (1939–1943),* IV (Rome, 1960).

Chapter XX. The Fall of Paris
1. Baudouin, *op. cit.*
2. Edward L. Spears, *Assignment to Catastrophe,* I, *Prelude to Dunkirk (July 1939–May 1940)* (London, 1955).
3. AN W-II 10; Maxime Weygand, *Mémoires, II, Rappelé au service* (Paris, 1950).
4. Spears, *Assignment,* I, *op. cit.*
5. Baudouin, *op. cit.*
6. Louis Noguères, *La Véritable Procès du Maréchal Pétain* (Paris, 1955).
7. Reynaud, *La France a sauvé l'Europe,* II, *op. cit.*
8. Weygand, *Mémoires,* III, *op. cit.*
9. Weygand presentation at Riom trial, August 26, 1940, in AN W-III 280; W-II 30.
10. Baudouin, *op. cit.*
11. DGF.
12. AN 523 Mi-3.
13. Edward L. Spears, *Assignment to Catastrophe,* II, *The Fall of France (June 1940)* (London, 1954).
14. Baudouin, *op. cit.*
15. *Ibid.*
16. Albert Lebrun, *Témoignage* (Paris, 1945).
17. Agenda 1940 of Commandant Bonhomme, *op. cit.*
18. Laure, *Pétain, op. cit.;* Noguères, *op. cit.*
19. Testimony of Maxime Weygand, July 31, 1945, PMP.
20. De Gaulle, *Mémoires,* I, *op. cit.*
21. Minutes by Captain Roland de Margerie, in Reynaud, *La France a sauvé l'Europe,* II, *op. cit.;* testimony of Weygand, PMP; Winston Churchill, *The Second World War,* II, *Their Finest Hour* (Boston, 1949).
22. The Earl of Avon (Anthony Eden), *The Eden Memoirs: The Reckoning* (London, 1965).
23. Churchill, *op. cit.*

24. Avon/Eden, *op. cit.*
25. Churchill, *op. cit.*
26. Spears, *Assignment to Catastrophe*, II, *op. cit.*
27. Churchill, *op. cit.*
28. Reynaud, *La France a sauvé l'Europe*, II, *op. cit.*
29. Yves Bouthillier, *Le Drame de Vichy*, I, *Face à l'ennemi, face à l'allié* (Paris, 1950).
30. *Ibid.*
31. Baudouin, *op. cit.*
32. Bouthillier, *op. cit.;* testimony of Louis Marin, July 26, 1945, PMP.
33. Bouthillier, *op. cit.*
34. Laure, *Pétain, op. cit.*
35. *Ibid.*
36. Bouthillier, *op. cit.*
37. Agenda 1940 of Commandant Bonhomme, *op. cit.*
38. Baudouin, *op. cit.*

Chapter XXI. A Pétain Cabinet

1. Agenda 1940 of Commandant Bonhomme, *op. cit.;* Laure, *Pétain, op. cit.*
2. De Gaulle, *Mémoires*, I, *op. cit.*
3. *Ibid.*
4. Reynaud, *La France a sauvé l'Europe*, II, *op. cit.;* testimony of Reynaud, July 24, 1945, PMP; Baudouin, *op. cit.*
5. Churchill, *op. cit.*
6. Weygand, *Mémoires*, III, *op. cit.*
7. Memorandum by Alibert, October 1, 1944, courtesy of H. Amouroux.
8. Paul de Villelume, *Journal d'une défaite (Août 1939–Juin 1940)* (Paris, 1976).
9. Baudouin, *op. cit.;* June 16, 1940, Pétain letter, AN W-III 280.
10. Bouthillier, *op. cit;* Churchill, *op. cit.*
11. Testimony of Reynaud, July 24, 1945, PMP; Lebrun, *op. cit.;* Bouthillier, *op. cit.*
12. Bouthillier, *op. cit.;* Baudouin, *op. cit.*
13. Edouard Herriot, *Épisodes (1940–1944)* (Paris, 1950); Jeanneney, *op. cit.*
14. Reynaud, *La France a sauvé l'Europe*, II', *op. cit.*
15. Lebrun, *op. cit.*
16. Lebrun, *op. cit.;* Lémery, *op. cit.;* Baudouin, *op. cit.;* Weygand, *Mémoires*, III, *op. cit.*
17. Charles Pomaret, *Le Dernier témoin* (Paris, 1960).

18. Le Maréchal Pétain, *Paroles aux Français: Messages et Ecrits (1934–1941)* (Lyon, 1941).
19. Baudouin, *op. cit.*
20. Churchill, *op. cit.*
21. Jeanneney, *op. cit.*
22. Original order for Buhrer arrest in Bibliothèque Nationale, Manuscripts (June 17, 1940).
23. Jeanneney, *op. cit.*
24. Pomaret, *op. cit.;* Jeanneney, *op. cit.;* testimony of Louis Rollin, January 20, 1949, *Rapport . . . sur les événements survenus, op. cit.;* draft of Pétain letter courtesy of Mrs. B. Ménétrel.
25. Pomaret, *op. cit.*
26. Testimony of A. Lebrun, July 25, 1945, PMP.
27. Lebrun, *op. cit.*
28. Testimony of Jeanneney, July 26, 1945, PMP; testimony of Lebrun, July 25, 1945, PMP; Reynaud, *La France a sauvé l'Europe,* II, *op. cit.;* Herriot, *op. cit.*
29. Andreas Hillgruber, *Les Entretiens secrets de Hitler (Septembre 1939–Décembre 1941)* (Paris, 1969).
30. Statement of Field Marshal Wilhelm Keitel and General Alfred Jodl at Nuremberg trial; Hitler's direction no. 18, also from Nuremberg, quoted in A. Goutard, "Pourquoi et comment l'armistice a-t-il été 'accordé' par Hitler?" *La Revue de Paris* (Paris), October 1960.
31. *I Documenti Diplomatici Italiani,* V (Rome, 1965).
32. Baudouin, *op. cit.*
33. Philippe Pétain, *Quatre années au pouvoir* (Paris, 1949).
34. Baudouin, *op. cit.*
35. *Ibid.*
36. Camille Fernand-Laurent, *Un peuple ressuscité* (New York, 1943); affidavits of Fernand-Laurent and Pierre de Font-Reaulx, AN W-III 46; Jean Montigny, *Toute la vérité sur un mois dramatique de notre histoire* (Clermont-Ferrand, 1940).
37. Montigny, *op. cit.;* Herriot, *op. cit.*
38. Baudouin, *op. cit.*
39. *Ibid.*
40. Charles-Roux, *Cinq mois tragiques aux Affaires étrangères* (Paris, 1949).
41. Jacques Bardoux, *Journal d'un témoin de la Troisième* (Paris, 1957).
42. Reynaud, *La France a sauvé l'Europe,* II, *op. cit.*
43. Baudouin, *op. cit.*
44. *Ibid.*
45. Pétain, *Quatre années au pouvoir, op. cit.*
46. Montigny, *op. cit.*

47. Memorandum by Alibert, October 1, 1944, *op. cit.*
48. Jeanneney, *op. cit.*
49. Emmanuel Berl, *Interrogatoire par Patrick Modiano* (Paris, 1976).
50. Pétain, *Quatre années au pouvoir, op. cit.*
51. Baudouin, *op. cit.*
52. *Ibid.*
53. *Ibid.*
54. *Ibid.*

Chapter XXII. Chief of State
1. Baudouin, *op. cit.*
2. Lebrun, *op. cit.*
3. FRUS. The American embassy had moved from Bordeaux to La Bourboule before suitable quarters were found in Vichy. Ambassador Bullitt returned temporarily to Paris, the Vichy mission becoming an embassy only when the Paris embassy was shut down. From Woodruff Wallner.
4. Bardoux, *op. cit.*
5. Baudouin, *op. cit.*
6. Robert Aron, *Histoire de Vichy (1940–1944)* (Paris, 1954).
7. Bouthillier, I, *op. cit.*
8. FRUS.
9. Baudouin, *op. cit.*
10. Hillgruber, *op. cit.*
11. Montigny, *op. cit.*
12. *Journal Officiel, Chambre des Députés,* July 9, 1940.
13. Jeanneney, *op. cit.*
14. Testimony of Pierre Laval, *Le Procès Laval* (Paris, 1946).
15. Minutes, in *Rapport . . . sur les événements survenus, op. cit.*
16. *Ibid.*
17. Testimony of Jules Jeanneney, July 26, 1945, PMP; Jean Thouvenin, *La France Nouvelle,* I, *Les Premiers Actes du Maréchal Pétain* (Paris, 1940).
18. Interrogation of Laval, October 5, 1945, AN W-III 46.
19. Baudouin, *op. cit.*
20. Testimony of Pierre Berdelle de Lapommeraye, August 3, 1945, PMP.
21. Testimony of Laval, *Le Procès Laval, op. cit.*
22. Affidavit of General Brécard, May 22, 1945, AN W-III 301.
23. Philippe Pétain, *Appels aux Français (1940)* (Paris, 1941).
24. Baudouin, *op. cit.*

25. Weygand, *Mémoires*, III, *op. cit.*

26. Lucien Rebatet, *Les Décombres* (Paris, 1942).

27. AN AG-II 459.

28. Dossier on Repartition des chambres, AN AG-II 459; Charles-Roux, *op. cit.*

29. Charles-Roux, *op. cit.*

30. René Gillouin, *J'étais l'ami du Maréchal Pétain* (Paris, 1966).

31. Caujolle report, *op. cit.* For an estimate of the value of 1940 francs in 1981, multiply by .97; for 1941, by .81; for 1942, .68; 1944, .49.

Chapter XXIII. Pétain's Men

1. Weygand, *Mémoires*, III, *op. cit.*

2. Gillouin, *op. cit.*

3. Henri Du Moulin de Labarthète, *Le Temps des illusions* (Geneva, 1946); Gillouin, *op. cit.*

4. Memorandum by Alibert, *op. cit.*

5. Affidavit of Maurice Fabry, April 7, 1945, AN W-III 46.

6. Affidavit of B. Ménétrel, Nov. 10, 1945, AN W-III 47.

7. Pierre Nicolle, *Cinquante mois d'Armistice*, I (Paris, 1947).

8. Military records, archives SH.

9. Inventory, AN AG-II.

10. From Elisabeth Bourgois.

11. Joseph Barthélemy, *Mémoires d'un ministre du Maréchal*, I (Auch, 1948).

12. Du Moulin de Labarthète, *op. cit.*

13. Gillouin, *op. cit.;* Martin du Gard, *op. cit.*

14. Du Moulin de Labarthète, *op. cit.;* Vice-Admiral Fernet, *Aux Côtés du Maréchal Pétain (1940–1944)* (Paris, 1953).

15. Dominique Rossignol, *Vichy et les francs-maçons* (Paris, 1981).

16. Yves Bouthillier, *Le Drame de Vichy*, II, *Finances sous la contrainte* (Paris, 1951).

17. Nicolle, *op. cit.;* Bouthillier, II, *op. cit.*

18. Bouthillier, II, *op. cit.*

19. Du Moulin de Labarthète, *op. cit.*

20. See chapter XLIV.

21. From Pierre Bourgois; Gillouin, *op. cit.*

22. From Mrs. B. Ménétrel.

23. For example, see Marcel Peyrouton, *Du service public à la prison commune* (Paris, 1950).

24. Gillouin, *op. cit.*

25. From Odette de Hérain.

26. Breakdown of responsibilities, January 5, 1941: AN W-III 292.

27. From Mrs. B. Ménétrel and Paul Racine.
28. From Paul Racine.
29. Martin du Gard, *op. cit.*
30. From Paul Racine; Marcel Haedrich, *Le Maréchal et la dactylo* (Paris, 1977).
31. Martin du Gard, *op. cit.*
32. Aron, *op. cit.*
33. *Ibid.*
34. Gillouin, *op. cit.*
35. AN AG-II 82.
36. AN AG-II 77. Michael R. Marrus and Robert O. Paxton, *Vichy et les Juifs* (Paris, 1981) quotes a German police report to the effect that Ménétrel said in June 1943 that while Pétain insisted on a humane solution to the Jewish question, he himself admired the Germans' "final eradication."
37. AN W-III 291.
38. Du Moulin de Labarthète, *op. cit.*
39. From Elisabeth Bourgois (to whom Ménétrel told this story).
40. Simon, *op. cit.*

Chapter XXIV. The Shaping of the State

1. Baudouin, *op. cit.*
2. *Ibid.;* Du Moulin de Labarthète, *op. cit.*
3. Bouthillier, I, *op. cit.*
4. Serrigny, *op. cit.*
5. Jeanneney, *op. cit.*
6. Thouvenin, I, *op. cit.*
7. Marrus and Paxton, *op. cit.*
8. Thouvenin, I, *op. cit.*
9. Henri Michel, *Le Procès de Riom* (Paris, 1979).
10. Du Moulin de Labarthète, *op. cit.*
11. Xavier Vallat, *Le Nez de Cléopatre: Souvenirs d'un Homme de droite (1919–1944)* (Paris, 1957); Du Moulin de Labarthète, *op. cit.*
12. *La Légion* (fortnightly, Vichy), June 15 and December 15, 1941, October 15, 1943.
13. *La Légion* (monthly, Vichy), April 1942.
14. Du Moulin de Labarthète, *op. cit.*
15. Pétain message quoted in Pierre Lucius, *La Doctrine Corporative du Maréchal* (Vichy, 1943).
16. Philippe Pétain, *La France Nouvelle: Principes de la Communauté—Appels et messages (17 Juin 1940–17 Juin 1941)* (Paris, 1941).
17. Du Moulin de Labarthète, *op. cit.*

18. Fernet, *op. cit.*
19. AN AG-II 30.
20. AN AG-II 30.

Chapter XXV. Feelers
1. Amiral Auphan, *Histoire élémentaire de Vichy* (Paris, 1979).
2. Pétain, *Appels aux Français, op. cit.*
3. *Ibid.*
4. Winston Churchill, *War Speeches (1940–1945)* (London, 1946).
5. Baudouin, *op. cit.*
6. Jean Thouvenin, *La France Nouvelle*, II, *D'Ordre du Maréchal Pétain* (Paris, n.d. [1940]).
7. Louis-Dominique Girard, *Montoire, Verdun diplomatique* (Paris, 1976).
8. Du Moulin de Labarthète, *op. cit.*
9. Quoted in Pierre Chevallier, *Histoire de la Franc-Maçonnerie française,* III (1877–1944) (Paris, 1975).
10. Rossignol, *Anti-Franc-Maçonnerie, op. cit.;* Carcopino, *op. cit.;* Du Moulin de Labarthète, *op. cit.*
11. Du Moulin de Labarthète, *op. cit.*
12. Aron, *op. cit.*
13. Rossignol, *Anti-Franc-Maçonnerie, op. cit.*
14. Bernard Faÿ, "Responsabilité Maçonnique," *Les Documents Maçonniques* (Vichy), January 1943.
15. Du Moulin de Labarthète, *op. cit.*
16. Letter from Weygand in Tournoux, *Pétain et la France, op. cit.*
17. Baudouin, *op. cit.;* Charles-Roux, *op. cit.*
18. Foreign Office, *Despatch to His Majesty's Ambassador in Paris regarding relations between His Majesty's Government in the United Kingdom and the Vichy Government in the Autumn of 1940* (London, 1945). See also AN 72 AJ 250 and Rt. Hon. Sir Samuel Hoare, *Ambassador on Special Mission* (London, 1946).
19. Baudouin, *op. cit.*
20. Louis Rougier, *Mission secrète à Londres: Les accords Pétain-Churchill* (Geneva, 1946).
21. *Ibid.*
22. Foreign Office, *Despatch to His Majesty's Ambassador in Paris, op. cit.* The contested document is reproduced in Rougier, *op. cit.* Cf. Sir Llewelyn Woodward, *British Foreign Policy in the Second World War,* I (London, 1970).
23. Du Moulin de Labarthète, *op. cit.*
24. Girard, *Montoire, op. cit.*
25. Churchill, *Second World War,* II, *op. cit.*

26. War Cabinet, Contacts with the Vichy Government, memorandum by the secretary of state for foreign affairs (Lord Halifax), December 19, 1940. Public Records Office (UK), FO 371/24361.

Chapter XXVI. Montoire

1. Pétain, *Quatre années au pouvoir, op. cit.*
2. FRUS.
3. Fernet, *op. cit.*
4. AN W-III 303.
5. Testimony of Laval, August 3, 1945, PMP.
6. DGF.
7. *Ibid.*
8. Henry Bordeaux, *Images du Maréchal Pétain* (Paris, 1941); Du Moulin de Labarthète, *op. cit.*
9. Du Moulin de Labarthète, *op. cit.*
10. Paul Schmidt, *Sur la scène internationale: Ma figuration auprès de Hitler (1933–1945)* (Paris, 1950).
11. *Ibid.*
12. DGF; Hillgruber, *op. cit.*
13. DGF.
14. DGF. William L Shirer in *The Rise and Fall of the Third Reich* (London, 1960) wrote that Pétain did sign this agreement.
15. Du Moulin de Labarthète, *op. cit.;* testimony of Fernand de Brinon, August 9, 1945, PMP.
16. Du Moulin de Labarthète, *op. cit.*
17. *Le Petit Parisien* (Paris), November 2, 1940.
18. Pétain, *Quatre années au pouvoir, op. cit.*
19. Gillouin, *op. cit.*
20. From a memorandum by von Ribbentrop's secretariat, DGF.
21. Henry Bordeaux, *Histoire d'une vie*, XII, *Lumière au bout de la nuit* (Paris, 1970).
22. Baudouin, *op. cit.*
23. November 9, 1940. Weygand, *Mémoires*, III, *op. cit.*
24. *Ibid.*
25. Churchill, *Second World War*, II, *op. cit.*

Chapter XXVII. The Reasons Why

1. Du Moulin de Labarthète, *op. cit.*
2. Brinon, *op. cit.*
3. Peyrouton, *op. cit.*
4. Baudouin, *op. cit.*
5. Richard Griffiths, *Marshal Pétain* (London, 1970).

6. Preface by Marc Boegner to Gillouin, *op. cit.*
7. Testimony of André Lavagne, August 10, 1945, PMP.
8. Testimony of René Norguet, August 9, 1945, PMP.
9. Vallat, *op. cit.*
10. Marrus and Paxton, *op. cit.*
11. Du Moulin de Labarthète, *op. cit.*
12. November 12, 1940. Institut d'Histoire du Temps Présent (Paris).
13. Jeanneney, *op. cit.*
14. Carcopino, *op. cit.*
15. Tournoux, *Pétain et al France, op. cit.*
16. *Le Travail du Maréchal (1940–Juillet 1942)* (Vichy, n.d.).
17. Peyrouton, *op. cit.*
18. Robert Vaucher, *Quand le Maréchal Pétain prend son baton de pélerin* (Marseille, 1941).
19. AN AG-II 20.
20. Laure, "Notes militaires et politiques," *op. cit.*
21. FRUS.

Chapter XXVIII. Crisis in Collaboration

1. Jacques Isorni, *Pétain a sauvé la France* (Paris, 1964); "Les accords franco-anglais: un document capital révèle la vérité sur l'accord secret Pétain-George VI," *Le Monde et la Vie* (Paris), Hors série *(Pétain vingt ans après serait acquitté)*, 1965.
2. Testimony of Chevalier, August 7, 1945, PMP. Cf. Haute Cour de Justice, *Procès du Maréchal Pétain*, published by the *Journal Officiel*, 1945.
3. War Cabinet, Contacts with the Vichy Government, December 19, 1940, *op. cit.*
4. Report on M. Pierre Dupuy's Visit to Vichy, November–December 1940. Historical Division, Department of External Affairs, Canada.
5. Appendix to Dupuy report, November–December 1940, *op. cit.*
6. Jacques Chevalier memorandum reproduced in Raissac, *op. cit.*
7. FRUS.
8. Churchill, *Second World War*, II, *op. cit.*
9. *Documents on Canadian External Relations (1939–1941)*, II, 8 (Ottawa, 1976).
10. August 8, 1945, report, Visits of M. Pierre Dupuy to Vichy, Historical Division, Department of External Affairs, Canada.
11. Report on Dupuy visit, November–December 1940, *op. cit.*
12. *Documents on Canadian External Relations, op. cit.*
13. Bouthillier, I, *op. cit.*
14. Baudouin, *op. cit.*
15. Report of mission of General de La Laurencie, August 19–December 19, 1940, AN 72 AG 249.

16. Saint Paulien, *Histoire de la Collaboration* (Paris, 1964).
17. Testimony of General de La Laurencie, in Otto Abetz, *D'une prison* (Paris, 1949).
18. Du Moulin de Labarthète, *op. cit.*
19. Haedrich, *op. cit.*
20. Brinon, *op. cit.*
21. Bouthillier, I, *op. cit.*
22. *Ibid.;* Peyrouton, *op. cit.;* memorandum of Alibert to High Court.
23. Brinon, *op. cit.*
24. Nobécourt, I, *op. cit.;* report of Sûreté Nationale, May 5, 1945, in AN W-III 278; Georges A. Groussard, *Service secret (1940–1945)* (Paris, 1964).
25. Groussard, *op. cit.*
26. Baudouin, *op. cit.*
27. *Ibid.;* Bouthillier, I, *op. cit.;* Peyrouton, *op. cit.;* testimony of Jean Berthelot, August 8, 1945, PMP.
28. Baudouin, *op. cit.*
29. Bouthillier, I, *op. cit.*
30. Du Moulin de Labarthète, *op. cit.;* Groussard, *op. cit.*
31. La Laurencie, *op. cit.*

Chapter XXIX. The Morning After

1. AN AG-II 450.
2. DGF.
3. Jean Thouvenin, *La France Nouvelle,* IV, *Pétain tient la barre* (Paris, 1941).
4. La Laurencie, *op. cit.*
5. Otto Abetz, *Histoire d'une politique franco-allemande (1930–1950)* (Paris, 1953).
6. Bouthillier, I, *op. cit.*
7. La Laurencie, *op. cit.*
8. Abetz telegram to Berlin, December 18, 1940, DGF. Du Moulin de Labarthète, *op. cit.,* says that Pétain was aware Laval had been arrested.
9. DGF.
10. Du Moulin de Labarthète, *op. cit.*
11. Abetz telegram to Berlin, December 18, 1940, DGF.
12. Baudouin, *op. cit.*
13. Fernet, *op. cit.*
14. DGF.
15. DGF.
16. Abetz telegram to Berlin, December 18, 1940, DGF.
17. Abetz telegram to Berlin, December 21, 1940, DGF.

18. DGF.
19. Affidavit of Charles Maurras, July 15, 1945, AN W-III 301.
20. Du Moulin de Labarthète, *op. cit.*
21. Charles Maurras, *De la colère à la justice: Réflexions sur un désastre* (Geneva, 1942).
22. AN W-III 281.
23. Du Moulin de Labarthète, *op. cit,* who says that Pétain objected to the excesses of pro-Pétain propaganda: "The French aren't that stupid."
24. Bouthillier, I, *op. cit.*
25. Du Moulin de Labarthète, *op. cit.*
26. *Ibid.*
27. Peyrouton, *op. cit.*
28. Du Moulin de Labarthète, *op. cit.*
29. Jacques Duquesne, *Les Catholiques français sous l'occupation* (Paris, 1966); Auphan, *op. cit.*
30. Du Moulin de Labarthète, *op. cit.*
31. *Ibid.*
32. From André Lavagne.
33. Statements by Henry Corvisy and Maurice Gabolde, Institut Hoover, *La Vie de la France sous l'occupation,* II, Paris, 1958.
34. AN W-III 290.
35. Barthélemy, I, *op. cit.*

Chapter XXX. Admirals
1. Du Moulin de Labarthète, *op. cit.;* FRUS.
2. FRUS; William D. Leahy, *I Was There* (London, 1950).
3. William L. Langer, *Our Vichy Gamble* (New York, 1947).
4. Leahy, *op. cit.*
5. *Ibid.*
6. FRUS.
7. *Ibid.*
8. *Ibid.*
9. Leahy, *op. cit.*
10. *Ibid.*
11. FRUS.
12. *Ibid.*
13. January 15, 1941, letter, Historical Division, Department of External Affairs, Canada.
14. Report by Dupuy on January–March 1941, visit; March 14, 1941, Dupuy telegram to Mackenzie King; April 3, 1941, Dupuy letter to Mackenzie King, Historical Division, Department of External Affairs, Canada.

15. DGF.
16. DGF.
17. Serrigny, *op. cit.*
18. *L'Oeuvre* (Paris), February 4, 1941.
19. *L'Oeuvre* (Paris), February 5, 1941.
20. Du Moulin de Labarthète, *op. cit.*
21. Minutes, AN W-III 287; Du Moulin de Labarthète, *op. cit.;* January 19, 1941, telegram, DGF.
22. DGF.
23. Hillgruber, *op. cit.*
24. Jean Thouvenin, *La France Nouvelle,* V, *Un Seul Chef* (Paris, 1941).
25. *Ibid.*
26. March 17, 1941, AN AG-II 52.
27. AN AG-II 447.
28. Jean Galtier-Boissière, *Mon journal pendant l'occupation* (Garas, 1944).
29. Serrigny, *op. cit.*

Chapter XXXI. Military Collaboration
1. Certificate, archives of Jacques Isorni.
2. In 1929. Isorni, *Philippe Pétain,* I, *op. cit.*
3. *Ibid.*
4. Thouvenin, V, *op. cit.*
5. Pétain, *Actes et Ecrits, op. cit.*
6. Pétain, *Quatre années au pouvoir, op. cit.*
7. Pétain, *Actes et Ecrits, op. cit.*
8. AN AG-II 135.
9. Pardee, *op. cit.*
10. Barthélemy, I, *op. cit.*
11. *Ibid.*
12. Du Moulin de Labarthète, *op. cit.*
13. Pétain, *Actes et Ecrits, op. cit.;* Barthélemy papers, AN.
14. DGF.
15. DGF.
16. Marrus and Paxton, *op. cit.*
17. *Ibid.*
18. Michel, *op. cit.*
19. Jeanneney, *op. cit.*
20. For example, statement by Alfred Conquet in Institut Hoover, *op. cit.*
21. Langer, *op. cit.*
22. DGF.
23. Text of May 6, 1941, telegram in PMP.
24. AN AG-II 656.

25. FRUS.
26. Pétain, *Actes et Ecrits, op. cit.*
27. Noguères, *op. cit.*
28. AN AG-II 656.
29. See for example testimony of Berthelot, August 8, 1945, PMP.
30. Du Moulin de Labarthète, *op. cit.*
31. Weygand, *Mémoires,* III, *op. cit.*
32. Du Moulin de Labarthète, *op. cit.*
33. Pétain, *Actes et Ecrits, op. cit.*

Chapter XXXII. The Person of the Marshal

1. Gillouin, *op. cit.*
2. Rémy, in *Carrefour* (Paris), April 11, 1950, quoted in Isorni, *Le Condamné, op. cit.*
3. De Gaulle, *Mémoires,* I, *op. cit.*
4. Colonel Passy, *Souvenirs,* I, *2e Bureau-Londres* (Monte Carlo, 1947).
5. Jean Tracou, *Le Maréchal aux liens* (Paris, 1945).
6. Pierre Laval, *Laval parle* (Geneva, 1947).
7. René Benjamin, *Les Septs étoiles de la France* (Paris, 1942).
8. Affidavit of Louis Croutzet, May 16, 1945, AN W-III 281.
9. Affidavit of Robert Ehret, May 16, 1945, AN W-III 281.
10. Du Moulin de Labarthéte, *op. cit.*
11. Institut d'Histoire du Temps Présent.
12. AN AG-II 27.
13. AN AG-II 136.
14. Noël d'Ornans, *Les Jeudis du Maréchal* (Paris, n.d.).
15. AN AG-II 143.
16. Du Moulin de Labarthéte, *op. cit.*
17. AN AG-II 27.
18. Archives of Institut d'Histoire du Temps Présent.

Chapter XXXIII. Reassuring Hitler

1. Dupuy report on Third Mission to Vichy, Historical Division, Department of External Affairs, Canada.
2. Leahy, *op. cit.*
3. Paul Paillole, *Services Spéciaux (1935–1945)* (Paris, 1975).
4. FRUS.
5. *Actes et Documents du Saint Siège relatifs à la Seconde guerre mondiale,* V, *Le Saint Siège et la Guerre Mondiale (Juillet 1941–Octobre 1942)* (Vatican City, 1969).
6. *Ibid.*
7. AN W-III 297; *Le Procès d'Xavier Vallat* (Paris, 1948)

8. *Ibid.*
9. *Actes et Documents du Saint Siège relatifs à la Seconde guerre mondiale,* VIII, *Le Saint Siège et les victimes de la guerre (Janvier 1941–Décembre 1942)* (Vatican City, 1969).
10. Pétain, *Quatre années au pouvoir, op. cit.*
11. Langer, *op. cit.*
12. Pétain, *Paroles aux Français, op. cit.*
13. *La Légion* (monthly, Vichy), September 1941.
14. Noguères, *op. cit.*
15. *Le Petit Parisien* (Paris), November 6, 1941.
16. Du Moulin de Labarthète, *op. cit.*
17. Aron, *op. cit.;* Noguères, *op. cit.;* Hervé Villeré, *L'Affaire de la Section Spéciale* (Paris, 1973).
18. AN W-III 283; Pétain, *Actes et Ecrits, op. cit.;* DGF.
19. Pétain, *Actes et Ecrits, op. cit.*
20. Du Moulin de Labarthète, *op. cit.*
21. DGF; AN W-III 303.
22. DGF.
23. Laure, Notes militaires et politiques, *op. cit.*
24. DGF.
25. *Le Petit Parisien* (Paris), November 17, 1941.

Chapter XXXIV. The Double Game

1. AN W-III 295.
2. Du Moulin de Labarthète, *op. cit.*
3. Pétain, *Actes et Ecrits, op. cit.*
4. From General René Laure.
5. Weygand, *Mémoires,* III, *op. cit.*
6. *Ibid.*
7. Laure, Notes militaires et politiques, *op. cit.*
8. Weygand, *Mémoires,* III, *op. cit.*
9. Georges Riond, *Chroniques d'un autre monde* (Paris, 1979).
10. Du Moulin de Labarthète, *op. cit.*
11. FRUS.
12. Leahy, *op. cit.*
13. To Adolf Galland. Roger Manvell and Heinrich Frankel, *Hermann Göring* (London, 1962).
14. DGF.
15. AN AG-II 656.
16. Du Moulin de Labarthète, *op. cit.*
17. FRUS.
18. FRUS.

19. Leahy, *op. cit.*
20. FRUS.
21. Pétain, *Quatre années au pouvoir, op. cit.*
22. Du Moulin de Labarthète, *op. cit.*
23. *Ibid.*
24. AN AG-II 439.
25. Ministère de l'Intérieur, Synthèse des rapports des Préfets, January 1942. AN.
26. *Pétain et les allemands: Memorandum d'Abetz sur les rapports franco-allemands* (Paris, 1948).
27. Laure, Notes militaires et politiques, *op. cit.*
28. FRUS.

Chapter XXXV. The Return of Laval
1. Raymond Tournoux, *Le Royaume d'Otto* (Paris, 1982).
2. Rassemblement Nationel Populaire, *Vichy contre le Maréchal* (Paris, 1942).
3. Fernand-Laurent, *op. cit.*
4. Serrigny, *op. cit.*
5. FRUS.
6. *La Légion* (fortnightly, Vichy), February 15, 1942.
7. *La Légion* (fortnightly, Vichy), March 15, 1942.
8. *La Légion* (fortnightly, Vichy), June 15, 1942.
9. Du Moulin de Labarthète, *op. cit.*
10. AN W-III 282.
11. Du Moulin de Labarthète, *op. cit.*
12. Barthélemy, I, *op. cit.*
13. Michel, *op. cit.*
14. *Léon Blum devant la Cour de Riom* (Paris, 1944).
15. Michel, *op. cit.*
16. Du Moulin de Labarthète, *op. cit.*
17. Abetz telegram to von Ribbentrop, March 21, 1942, in Carcopino, *op. cit.*
18. Laure, Notes militaires et politiques, *op. cit.*
19. Du Moulin de Labarthète, *op. cit.;* Laure, Notes militaires et politiques, *op. cit.*
20. Du Moulin de Labarthète, *op. cit.*
21. *Ibid.*
22. Statement by Georges Féat in Institut Hoover, *La Vie de la France sous l'occupation,* III (Paris, 1958).
23. FRUS.
24. Pierre Pucheu, *Ma Vie* (Paris, 1948); Brinon, *op. cit.* Cf. Langer, *op. cit.*

25. April 10, 1942, telegram from Italian embassy, Paris, to Rome. Ministry of Foreign Affairs, Rome, Archivio Storico Diplomatico.
26. Carcopino, *op. cit.*
27. *Laval Parle, op. cit.*
28. Serrigny, *op. cit.*
29. Laure, Notes militaires et politiques, *op. cit.*
30. FRUS.
31. Walter Stucki, *La Fin du régime de Vichy* (Neuchâtel, Switzerland, 1947).

Chapter XXXVI. Figurehead
1. Synthèse des rapports mensuels, April 1942. AN.
2. Adolf Hitler, *Libres propos sur la guerre et la paix, recueillis sur l'ordre de Martin Bormann,* II (Paris, 1954).
3. *La Légion* (fortnightly, Vichy), June 15, 1942.
4. Carcopino, *op. cit.*
5. Serrigny, *op. cit.*
6. *Pétain et les allemands, op. cit.*
7. Testimony of Jean Jardel, August 10, 1945, PMP.
8. Serrigny, *op. cit.*
9. Marc Boegner, *L'Exigence oecuménique* (Paris, 1968).
10. Centre de Documentation Juive Contemporaine. Cf. Marrus and Paxton, *op. cit.*, who indicate that Pétain had a few friends he wished to have exempted, while other Vichy leaders had their own lists of candidates for exemption. Vichy did not require that Jews wear yellow stars but in December 1942 ordered that ration cards of Jews carry a stamp identifying them as Jews.
11. Minutes, AN. During most of the Vichy years, as under the Third Republic, there were no minutes of cabinet meetings, but such minutes were made in 1942 and were found in Pétain's baggage at the Liberation. See PMP.
12. Marrus and Paxton, *op. cit.*
13. Minutes, AN W-III 281.
14. *Actes et Documents du Saint Siège,* VIII, *op. cit.*
15. Lourie letter of June 18, 1945, to High Court, AN.
16. Aron, *op. cit.*
17. Session of August 11, 1945, PMP. Cf. session of August 4.
18. Jean Berthelot, *Sur les rails du pouvoir* (Paris, 1968).
19. Synthèse des rapports mensuels, July 1942. AN.
20. Lémery, *op. cit.*
21. Abetz telegram to Berlin, August 16, 1942. AN W-III 303.
22. Abetz telegram to Berlin, August 22, 1942, AN W-III 303.
23. *Le Cri du Peuple* (Paris), August 24, 1942.

24. Report by Walter Stucki in Tournoux, *Pétain et la France, op. cit.*
25. Sessions of July 25 and 26, 1945, PMP. But Noguères, *op. cit.*, feels proof still lacks that Pétain knew of the telegram before it was sent.
26. *La Légion* (fortnightly, Vichy), September 15, 1942.
27. Georges Villiers, *Témoignages* (Paris, 1978).

Chapter XXXVII. November 1942

1. AN W-III 277.
2. Testimony of Michel Clemenceau, July 28, 1945, PMP. Clemenceau said he was unable to elicit a response from Pétain on Mandel or Reynaud.
3. Serrigny, *op. cit.*
4. Winston S. Churchill, *The Second World War*, IV, *The Hinge of Fate* (Boston, 1950).
5. Session of August 11, 1945, PMP.
6. *Ibid.* Cf. FRUS for Tuck's translation of Pétain's message.
7. Anonymous memorandum, AN W-III 284.
8. FRUS.
9. From Woodruff Wallner (then a member of the American embassy staff in Vichy).
10. AN W-III 281.
11. AN W-III 303.
12. Churchill, *The Second World War*, IV, *op. cit.*
13. Alain Darlan, *L'Amiral Darlan parle* (Paris, 1952); Amiral Auphan, *L'Honneur de servir* (Paris, 1978); Auphan, *Histoire élémentaire, op. cit.;* testimony of Captain Archambaud, August 9, 1945, PMP; testimony of General Juin, August 10, 1945, PMP; testimony of Bergeret, August 8, 1945, PMP; Pétain, *Actes et Ecrits, op. cit.* See also affidavit of B. Ménétrel, August 1, 1945, AN W-III 297. Concerning doubts: Charles de Gaulle, *Mémoires de Guerre*, II, *L'Unité (1942–1944)* (Paris, 1956); General G. Schmitt, *Les Accords secrets franco-brittaniques de novembre–décembre 1940* (Paris, 1957). Churchill, *Second World War*, IV, *op. cit.*, accepts the story of the secret code.
14. Auphan, *L'Honneur de servir, op. cit.*
15. *Ibid.*
16. Noguères, *op. cit.*
17. Ménétrel notes in *ibid.*
18. Weygand, *Mémoires*, III, *op. cit.*
19. AN W-III 285; Jeanneney, *op. cit.*
20. AN W-III 285.
21. Auphan, *L'honneur de servir, op. cit.*
22. Lémery, *op. cit.*

23. General Chambe, "Le Maréchal Pétain à l'heure d'Alger," *La Revue de Paris* (Paris), December 1966.
24. Noguères, *op. cit.*
25. Auphan, *L'Honneur de servir, op. cit.*
26. *Ibid.;* Auphan, *Histoire élémentaire, op. cit.;* testimony of Captain Archambaud, PMP.
27. Noguères, *op. cit.*
28. Abetz telegram to Berlin, November 16, 1942, AN W-III 303.
29. Noguères, *op. cit.*
30. *Ibid.; Le Petit Parisien* (Paris) November 17, 1942.
31. Barthélemy, I, *op. cit.*
32. Pétain, *Actes et Ecrits, op. cit.*
33. Barthélemy, I, *op. cit.*
34. AN W-III 284.
35. Auphan, *L'Honneur de servir, op. cit.*
36. From Jardel trial, quoted in Raissac, *op. cit.*
37. AN W-III 282.
38. Churchill, *Second World War*, IV, *op. cit.*
39. *Le Monde* (Paris), December 15, 1979, January 18, February 1 and 20, 1980.
40. AN W-III 282.
41. Pétain, *Actes et Ecrits, op. cit.*
42. Told by Mrs. B. Ménétrel to Tournoux, *Pétain et la France, op. cit.*
43. Synthèse des Rapports mensuels, December 1942. Institut d'Histoire du Temps Présent.

Chapter XXXVIII. Private Life

1. From Elisabeth Bourgois.
2. Auphan, *L'Honneur de servir, op. cit.*
3. Tournoux, *Le Royaume d'Otto, op. cit.*
4. From Woodruff Wallner.
5. Jacques Isorni, *Correspondance de l'Ile d'Yeu* (Paris, 1966).
6. From Henri Amouroux, Paul Racine; Jacques Isorni, *Philippe Pétain*, II (Paris, 1973).
7. Affidavit by Jean Jardel, May 1, 1945, AN W-III 301.
8. AN W-III 289.
9. Interview with Alart in Bourget, *Témoignages inédits, op. cit.*
10. Villiers, *op. cit.*
11. The *Times* (London), November 12, December 10, 1941.
12. Pardee, *op. cit.*
13. From Renée de Séguin; Isorni, *Philippe Pétain*, II, *op. cit.*
14. From Elisabeth Bourgois.

15. Du Moulin de Labarthète, *op. cit.*
16. Simon, *op. cit.*
17. September 16, 1970, letter from Jacques Isorni to Bousquet, archives of Jacques Isorni.

Chapter XXXIX. Another Crisis in Collaboration

1. January 4, 1943. Archives of Jacques Isorni.
2. Serrigny, *op. cit.*
3. Comte Galeazzo Ciano, *Journal politique (1939–1943),* II (Neuchâtel, Switzerland, 1948).
4. March 9, 1943, telegram from Ambassador Gino Buti (Paris) to Rome. Ministry of Foreign Affairs, Rome, Archivio Storico Diplomatico.
5. Telegram from German embassy (Paris) to Berlin, AN W-III 303.
6. German telegrams in AN W-III 287.
7. Report from Italian embassy in Berlin to Rome, cited in Rome telegram to Paris, March 31, 1943, Ministry of Foreign Affairs, Rome, Archivio Storico Diplomatico.
8. Testimony of Darnand, PMP.
9. *La Légion* (fortnightly, Vichy), January 15, 1943.
10. Pétain, *Quatre années au pouvoir, op. cit.*
11. Serrigny, *op. cit.*
12. Rudolf Schleier telegram to Berlin, April 24, 1943, quoted in Tournoux, *Le Royaume d'Otto, op. cit.;* Italian Foreign Ministry telegram to Berlin, April 27, 1943, Italian Ministry of Foreign Affairs, Rome, Archivio Storico Diplomatico.
13. AN AG-II 616; W-III 283; Auphan, *Histoire élémentaire, op. cit.*
14. Martin du Gard, *Chronique, op. cit.*
15. Jean Calvet, *Visages d'un demi-siècle* (Paris, 1959).
16. Noguères, *op. cit.*
17. July 19, 1943. AN AG-II 488.
18. AN W-III 294; Centre de Documentation Juive Contemporaine; Marrus and Paxton, *op. cit.*
19. Marrus and Paxton, *op. cit.*
20. Gabriel Jeantet, *Pétain contre Hitler* (Paris, 1966).
21. September 8, 1943, telegram to Berlin, AN W-III 303.
22. Tournoux, *Pétain et de Gaulle, op. cit.;* Tournoux *Pétain et la France, op. cit.* The former publishes a letter from Colonel Solborg confirming Gorostarzu's story but adding that the Americans would not negotiate with Pétain while he remained in German control.
23. Bordeaux, *Histoire d'une vie,* XII, *op. cit.*
24. Brinon, *op. cit.*
25. August 28, 1943, telegram to Berlin, AN W-III 303

Chapter XL. Constitutional Crisis

1. Fernet, *op. cit.*
2. Auphan, *L'Honneur de servir, op. cit.;* Auphan, *Histoire élémentaire, op. cit.*
3. AN W-III 281.
4. Brinon, *op. cit.*
5. Jacques Isorni and Jean Lemaire, *Requête en révision pour Philippe Pétain* (Paris, 1950); Auphan, *L'Honneur de servir, op. cit.*
6. Auphan, *L'Honneur de servir, op. cit.;* Stucki, *op. cit.*
7. AN W-III 283.
8. Auphan, *L'Honneur de servir, op. cit.;* Jacques Bardoux, *La Délivrance de Paris* (Paris, 1958).
9. Notes by Ménétrel in Jeantet, *op. cit.*
10. René Belin, *Du Secretariat de la CGT au Gouvernement de Vichy* (Paris, 1978).
11. Martin du Gard, *Chronique, op. cit.*
12. Serrigny, *op. cit.*
13. Stucki, *op. cit.*
14. Brinon, *op. cit.*
15. Auphan, *L'Honneur de servir, op. cit.*
16. AN W-III 283.
17. Brinon, *op. cit.*
18. Stucki, *op. cit.*
19. Von Ribbentrop letter to Pétain, December 23, 1943, AN W-III 287; Auphan, *L'Honneur de servir, op. cit.*
20. Aron, *op. cit.;* Auphan, *L'Honneur de servir, op. cit.*
21. Auphan, *L'Honneur de servir, op. cit.*
22. January 1, 1944, telegram to Berlin, AN W-III 303; Bardoux, *Délivrance, op. cit.*
23. January 1, 1944, telegram to Berlin, AN W-III 303.
24. Tracou, *op. cit.*
25. Pardee, *op. cit.*
26. January 4, 1944, telegram to Berlin, January 9, 1944, Abetz memorandum, AN W-III 303; Tracou, *op. cit.*
27. Noguères, *op. cit.*
28. Tracou, *op. cit.*
29. *Procès des Grands Criminels de Guerre devant le Tribunal Militaire International,* Nuremberg, V, 1947 (session of January 19, 1946).
30. AN W-III 303.

Chapter XLI. The Spring of 1944

1. Tracou, *op. cit.*

2. *Ibid.*
3. Galtier-Boissière, *op. cit.*
4. From Louis-Dominique Girard.
5. Tracou, *op. cit.*
6. From Louis-Dominique Girard.
7. Tracou, *op. cit.*
8. Jeantet, *op. cit.*
9. Tracou, *op. cit.*
10. AN W-III 287.
11. Aron, *op. cit.*
12. Tracou, *op. cit.*
13. *Ibid.*
14. *Aujourd'hui* (Paris), March 15, 1944.
15. AN AG-II 450.
16. Tracou, *op. cit.*
17. Quoted in Tournoux, *Pétain et la France, op. cit.*
18. Tracou, *op. cit.*
19. General Jean Perré, in *Le Monde et la Vie* (Paris), Hors série: *Pétain vingt ans après serait acquitté,* 1965.
20. Martin du Gard, *Chronique, op. cit.*
21. Tracou, *op. cit.*
22. Letter from Tessier in *La Voix du Maréchal* (Royat), Christmas 1975–January 1976; letter from Tessier, December 6, 1975, in archives of Jacques Isorni; AN W-III 282.
23. AN W-III 282.
24. Tracou, *op. cit.*
25. *Ibid.*
26. *Le Petit Parisien* (Paris), April 27, 1942.

Chapter XLII. Normandy
1. Tracou, *op. cit.*
2. AN W-III 282.
3. Tracou, *op. cit.* Testimony of Tracou, August 9, 1945, PMP.
4. Auphan, *Histoire élémentaire, op. cit.*
5. Tracou, *op. cit.*
6. Stucki, *op. cit.*
7. AN W-III 287; Tracou, *op. cit.*
8. *L'Echo de la France* (Paris), May 10, 1944.
9. AN W-III 287.
10. Serrigny, *op. cit.*
11. Tracou, *op. cit.*
12. Isorni, *Philippe Pétain,* II, *op. cit.;* from Renée de Séguin.

13. Berlin to Paris, April 16, 1944; Abetz to Berlin, May 9, 1944; AN W-III 303.
14. Tracou, *op. cit.*
15. *Ibid.;* Auphan, *Histoire élémentaire, op. cit.*
16. Tracou, *op. cit.*
17. Fernet, *op. cit.*
18. Tracou, *op. cit.*
19. *Ibid.;* AN W-III 289.
20. Tracou, *op. cit.;* Jeantet, *op. cit.;* AN W-III 294.
21. Tracou, *op. cit.*
22. Tracou, *op. cit.* Dated July 9, the letter is published in Pétain, *Actes et Ecrits, op. cit.* Signed original: AN W-III 283.
23. Martin du Gard, *Chronique, op. cit.*

Chapter XLIII. Last Weeks of Vichy
1. Tracou, *op. cit.*
2. *Ibid.*
3. Stucki, *op. cit.;* Tracou, *op. cit.*
4. AN W-III 283.
5. Tracou, *op. cit.*
6. Auphan, *L'Honneur de servir, op. cit.*
7. *Ibid.*
8. Testimony of General Henri Lacaille, August 6, 1945, with statement by Pierre Bloch, PMP.
9. AN W-III 303.
10. Testimony of Darnand, *Les Procès de Collaboration* (Paris, 1948).
11. Stucki, *op. cit.*
12. Affidavit, Direction Générale de la Police Nationale (Sûreté), Vichy, September 5, 1944. AN W-III 300.
13. AN W-III 287.
14. Notes of General Eugène Bridoux, in Institut Hoover, III, *op. cit.*
15. Stucki, *op. cit.*
16. Henry Ingrand, *Libération de l'Auvergne* (Paris, 1974); de Gaulle, *Mémoires*, II, *op. cit.*
17. Ingrand, *op. cit.;* Jeantet, *op. cit.*
18. Ingrand papers, AN 72 AG 521–524.
19. Emmanuel d'Astier de la Vigerie papers, AN 72 AG 408–410.
20. Statement by Perré, Institut Hoover, III, *op. cit.*

Chapter XLIV. Departure
1. Stucki, *op. cit.*
2. *Ibid.*

3. Testimony of Laval, August 4, 1945, PMP.
4. Stucki, *op. cit.;* Fernet, *op. cit.;* AN W-III 288.
5. Stucki, *op. cit.* Photographs of the broken doors have been published, e.g., in Pétain, *Quatre années au pouvoir, op. cit.*
6. Stucki, *op. cit.*
7. *Ibid.*
8. Auphan, *L'Honneur de servir, op. cit.*
9. Henri Massis, *Maurras et son temps* (Paris, 1961).
10. Stucki, *op. cit.;* Pétain, *Quatre années au pouvoir, op. cit.*
11. Stucki, *op. cit.;* Ingrand papers; Perré, in Institut Hoover, III, *op. cit.*
12. Robert Aron, *Histoire de la Libération de la France* (Paris, 1959).
13. AN W-III 303.
14. La Situation du Maréchal Pétain, August 20–October 7, 1944, found in Pétain's baggage at Fort de Montrouge, 1945, AN W-III 288; narrative by Colonel de Longueau Saint Michel, courtesy of Mrs. B. Ménétrel.
15. Ménétrel papers, Fort de Montrouge, AN W-III 288.
16. La Situation du Maréchal Pétain, *op. cit.*
17. AN W-III 288; statement by Mrs. Viellard, 1945, courtesy of Mrs. B. Ménétrel; narrative by Colonel de Longueau.
18. Louis Noguères, *La Dernière étape: Sigmaringen* (Paris, 1956).
19. Documents found in baggage of General Victor Debeney, Fort de Montrouge, AN W-III 288.
20. Noguères, *La Dernière étape, op. cit.*
21. *Ibid.*
22. La Situation du Maréchal Pétain, *op. cit.;* Noguères, *La Dernière étape, op. cit.;* testimony of Laval, August 4, 1945, PMP.
23. Tournoux, *Pétain et de Gaulle, op. cit.*
24. De Gaulle, *Mémoires,* II, *op. cit.*
25. La Situation du Maréchal Pétain, *op. cit.*
26. Louis Ferdinand Céline, *D'un château l'autre* (Paris, 1957).
27. Bourget, *Témoignages inédits, op. cit.*
28. AN W-III 283.
29. Direction Générale de la Sûreté Nationale, "Activité des Emigrés Français à Sigmaringen," Paris, September 14, 1945, Institut d'Histoire du Temps Présent.
30. Tournoux, *Le Royaume d'Otto, op. cit.*
31. Noguères, *La Dernière étape, op. cit.*

Chapter XLV. The Prisoner
1. Noguères, *La Dernière étape, op. cit.*

2. Note sur la situation de M. le Maréchal, Sigmaringen, October 3, 1944, found in Pétain's baggage, Fort de Montrouge, AN W-III 288.
3. AN W-III 287.
4. Noguères, *La Dernière étape, op. cit.*
5. Tournoux, *Le Royaume d'Otto, op. cit.* (Déat diary).
6. Noguères, *La Dernière étape, op. cit.*
7. AN W-III 288.
8. AN W-III 288; notes prepared by Ménétrel in his defense, 1945, courtesy of Mrs. Ménétrel.
9. AN W-III 288.
10. Testimony of General Victor Debeney, August 8, 1945, PMP. Actually, as Pétain's Note Verbale of April 20 shows, the Germans said they were moving him eastward. AN W-III 288.
11. Testimony of Debeney, August 8, 1945, PMP. Cf. Mrs. Pétain's account of this trip (from Sigmaringen through Switzerland) in Noguères, *La Dernière étape, op. cit.*
12. *Ibid.*
13. Official Swiss report on Pétain's transit, archives of Jacques Isorni.
14. Dispatch from Henri Hoppenot, French ambassador in Switzerland, to French Foreign Ministry, April 24, 1945, AN W-III 300.
15. Georges Duhamel, "Ombres et Lumières sur une figure historique," *France-Illustration* (Paris), July 28, 1951.
16. *Ibid.*
17. Charles de Gaulle, *Mémoires de Guerre*, III, *Le Salut (1944–1946)* (Paris, 1959).
18. General Alain de Boissieu, *Pour combattre avec de Gaulle (1940–1946)* (Paris, 1981).
19. Report of Stucki to Berne, April 28, 1945, in Tournoux, *Pétain et la France, op. cit.*
20. Official Swiss report, archives of Jacques Isorni.
21. De Gaulle, *Mémoires*, III, *op. cit.*
22. Bourget, *Témoignages inédits, op. cit.;* report of Swiss police in Tournoux, *Pétain et de Gaulle, op. cit.*
23. Report of arrest, AN W-III 300; *Le Monde* (Paris), April 28, 1945; *New York Herald Tribune* (Paris), April 28, 1945.
24. Archives of Jacques Isorni.
25. Claude Mauriac, *Le Temps Immobile: Un autre de Gaulle, Journal (1944–1954)* (Paris, 1970).
26. Edgar Faure, *Mémoires*, I, *Avoir toujours raison . . . c'est un grand tort* (Paris, 1982), quoted in *Le Monde* (Paris), November 24, 1982.
27. Ministère de la Justice, *Bulletin hebdomadaire d'informations judiciaires* (Paris), June 2, 1945.

28. Simon, *op. cit.*
29. *Bulletin hebdomadaire d'informations judiciaires,* June 2, 1945.
30. Affidavit, AN W-III 300.
31. AN W-III 300.
32. Isorni, *Le Condamné, op. cit.*
33. Jacques Isorni, *Souffrance et mort du Maréchal* (Paris, 1951).

Chapter XLVI. The Trial
1. Isorni, *Souffrance et mort, op. cit.*
2. Jacques Isorni, *Le Procès de Robert Brasillach* (Paris, 1946).
3. From Pierre Véron; Isorni, *Le Condamné, op. cit.;* Isorni, *Souffrance et mort, op. cit.*
4. Isorni, *Souffrance et mort, op. cit.*
5. *Ibid.*
6. Isorni, *Le Condamné, op. cit.*
7. *Ibid.*
8. AN W-III 300.
9. Isorni, *Souffrance et mort, op. cit.;* Simon, *op. cit.*
10. Isorni, *Souffrance et mort, op. cit.*
11. *France-Libre* (Paris), May 26, 1945; Jacques Isorni, *C'est un péché de la France* (Paris, 1962).
12. AN W-III 304.
13. Isorni, *Souffrance et mort, op. cit.*
14. *Ibid.*
15. *Le Monde* (Paris), June 9, 1945; *Combat* (Paris), June 9, 1945.
16. *Le Monde* (Paris), June 12, 1945.
17. Isorni, *Le Condamné, op. cit.*
18. Isorni, *Souffrance et mort, op. cit.*
19. Haute Cour de Justice, *Procès du Maréchal Pétain,* Paris, 1945; cf. PMP.
20. Joseph Kessel, "Un vieil homme dans un fauteuil," *La Nouvelle République* (Bordeaux), July 24, 1945.
21. *L'Humanité* (Paris), July 24, 1945.
22. François Mauriac, "Le Procès d'un seul homme," *Le Figaro* (Paris), July 26, 1945.
23. *Combat* (Paris), July 25, 1945.
24. PMP.
25. Kessel, *op. cit.*
26. Jean Schlumberger in *Le Figaro,* reprinted in Jean Schlumberger, *Le Procès Pétain* (Paris, 1945).
27. PMP.
28. Gabriel Delattre, "J'étais premier juré au procès Pétain," *L'Histoire*

pour tous (Paris), April 1964; Fred Kupferman, *Le Procès de Vichy: Pucheu, Pétain, Laval* (Brussels, 1980).
29. Jean-Pierre Roux, "L'épuration en France: 1944–1945," *L'Histoire* (Paris), October 1978.
30. De Gaulle, *Mémoires*, III, *op. cit.*
31. Isorni, *Le Condamné*, *op. cit.*
32. PMP.
33. Jean Galtier-Boissière, *Mon journal depuis la libération* (Paris, 1945).

Chapter XLVII. The Verdict
1. From Jacques Isorni.
2. De Gaulle, *Mémoires*, III, *op. cit.*
3. Schlumberger, *op. cit.*
4. From Jacques Isorni; Isorni, *Le Condamné*, *op. cit.*
5. *New York Times* (New York), August 2, 1945, in Langer, *op. cit.*
6. Claude Mauriac, *op. cit.*
7. *Ibid.*
8. PMP.
9. Simon, *op. cit.*
10. PMP.
11. Historical Division, Department of External Affairs, Canada.
12. *Le Figaro* (Paris), August 15, 1945.
13. PMP.
14. Frédéric Pottecher, *Le Procès Pétain* (Paris, 1980).
15. PMP.
16. Pottecher, *op. cit.*
17. Petrus Faure, *Un Témoin raconte* (Saint-Etienne, 1962).
18. *Ibid.;* Delattre, *op. cit.*
19. PMP.
20. *Le Monde* (Paris), August 16, 1945.
21. *L'Humanité* (Paris) and *Le Populaire* (Paris), August 16, 1945.
22. De Gaulle, *Mémoires*, III, *op. cit.*
23. Bourget, *Témoignages inédits*, *op. cit.*
24. AN W-III 304; Simon, *op. cit.*
25. Simon, *op. cit.*
26. *Ibid.*

Chapter XLVIII. The Island
1. Isorni, *Souffrance et mort*, *op. cit.* The reference may be to the formation of an American Committee to Free Pétain, which took a half-page advertisement in the *New York Sun* on October 20. *New York Herald Tribune* (Paris), October 22, 1945.

2. *Paris-Press l'Intransigeant* (Paris), November 16, 1945.
3. AN W-III 305; Simon, *op. cit.*
4. AN W-III 304.
5. Simon, *op. cit.*
6. AN W-III 305.
7. Simon, *op. cit.;* Isorni, *Correspondance, Souffrance et mort, Le Condamné, op. cit.*
8. AN W-III 305.
9. Simon, *op. cit.*
10. Isorni, *Souffrance et mort, op. cit.*
11. Archives of Jacques Isorni. Cf. Isorni, *Philippe Pétain,* II, *op. cit.*
12. From Jacques Isorni. Jacques Isorni, *Lettre anxieuse au Président de la République au sujet de Philippe Pétain* (Paris, 1975).
13. Isorni, *Le Condamné, op. cit.*
14. Simon, *op. cit.*
15. Isorni, *Correspondance, op. cit.*
16. Simon, *op. cit.*
17. Isorni, *Correspondance, op. cit.*
18. Isorni, *Souffrance et mort, op. cit.*
19. Simon, *op. cit.*
20. Isorni, *Le Condamné, op. cit.*
21. From Jacques Isorni; Simon, *op. cit.*
22. Isorni, *Correspondance, op. cit.*
23. *Rapport . . . sur les événements survenus,* Annexes, I, *op. cit.*
24. February 16, 1947. *Le Monde et la Vie: Pétain vingt ans après, op. cit.*
25. September 17, 1947. Isorni, *Le Condamné, op. cit.*
26. *Ibid.*
27. From Odette de Hérain.

Chapter XLIX. The Years

1. *Documents pour la Révision* (Paris, 1948).
2. Simon, *op. cit.* In May 1948, 47 percent of readers of *L'Aurore* (Paris), 44 percent of *Le Figaro* readers (vs. 5 percent of *Le Populaire* readers, 3 percent of *L'Humanité* readers) favored release. *Ibid.*
3. Isorni, *Correspondance, op. cit.;* Isorni, *Le Condamné, op. cit.*
4. Isorni, *Souffrance et mort, op. cit.*
5. Isorni, *Le Condamné, op. cit.*
6. AN W-III 304.
7. Isorni, *Le Condamné, op. cit.*
8. Isorni, *Correspondance, op. cit.*
9. Bourget, *Témoignages inédits, op. cit.*
10. Isorni, *Le Condamné, op. cit.*

11. Isorni, *Correspondance, op. cit.*
12. Isorni, *Souffrance et mort, op. cit.*
13. Isorni, *Correspondance, op. cit.*
14. Report of Renseignements Généraux, La Roche sur Yon, August 1951, archives of Jacques Isorni.
15. Isorni, *Le Condamné, op. cit.*
16. M.-A. Combaluzier, *J'ai vu mourir Philippe Pétain* (Paris, 1966).
17. Isorni, *Correspondance, op. cit.*
18. Combaluzier, *op. cit.*
19. Isorni and Lemaire, *Requête en révision, op. cit.*
20. Isorni, *Souffrance et mort, op. cit.*
21. Isorni, *Le Condamné, op. cit.*; Combaluzier, *op. cit.*
22. Isorni, *Le Condamné, op. cit.*
23. Combaluzier, *op. cit.*
24. Isorni, *Le Condamné, op. cit.*; *Paris-Presse l'Intransigeant* (Paris), July 24, 1951.
25. Isorni, *Le Condamné, op. cit.*
26. *Ibid.*
27. Combaluzier, *op. cit.*

Chapter L. Epilogue

1. Charles de Gaulle, *Discours et Messages*, V, *Vers le terme* (Paris, 1970).
2. Archives of Jacques Isorni.
3. *Le Monde* (Paris), November 15 and November 25, 1980.
4. *Le Figaro Magazine* (Paris), May 17, 1980.
5. October 18, 1972. Isorni, *Lettre anxieuse,. op. cit.*
6. *Le Monde* (Paris), October 17, 1981.
7. *Le Monde* (Paris), November 12, 1982.
8. *Le Monde* (Paris), March 11, 1983.
9. Isorni, *Correspondance, op. cit.*
10. Girard, *Mazinghem, op. cit.*
11. Isorni, *Le Condamné, op. cit.*
12. From Jacques Isorni, Odette de Hérain. Mrs. de Hérain told the author that her son wanted to have nothing to do with the legacy. He married a Catholic, and his children were baptized.

11. Ibrahim, C. Interview, op. cit.
12. Loutfi, 50 D. Interview, op. cit.
13. Ibrahim, C. Interview, op. cit.
14. Report of Reinsertion into Germany. La Roche sur Yon, August, 1961, archives of Jacques Bloch.
15. Ibrahim, C. Interview, op. cit.
16. M. A. Combaluzier, Tel que nous l'avons, Rahden, Vera Okott, 1961.
17. Ibrahim, Correspondence, op. cit.
18. Combaluzier, op. cit.
19. Ibrahim and Lemaitre, Report of the child, op. cit.
20. Ibrahim, Interview, op. cit.
21. Ibrahim, Le Combat, op. cit., Combaluzier, p. 240.
22. Ibrahim, Le Combat, op. cit.
23. Combaluzier, p. 47.
24. Ibrahim, Le Combat, op. cit., Paris-Match, Ghimonti, Paris, July 24, 1961.
25. Ibrahim, Le Combat, op. cit.
26. Ibid.
27. Combaluzier, op. cit.

Chapter 1. Entering

1. Orphans de l'aide sociale, Pédiatrie, Nestlé, Paris, 1970.
2. Archives of Jacques Loren.
3. La Monde (Paris), November 4 and November 25, 1950.
4. Le Figaro Magazine (Paris), May 17, 1980.
5. October 15, 19, 2, Ibrahim, Correspondance, op. cit.
6. La Presse (Paris), October 19, 1951.
7. Le Monde (Paris), November 19, 1952.
8. L'Aurore (Paris), April 14, 1953.
9. Ibrahim, Correspondance, op. cit.
10. Ibrahim, Interview, op. cit.
11. Ibrahim, Interview, op. cit.
12. Froid Jacques Jacqui, Orion.   Henri Ahasfe, He said that the author, if other son who wanted to have nothing to do with the legacy, the inheritance in solution, and his children or 5 bajonen.

INDEX